The Morality of War

The
Morality of War

A Reader

edited by
David Kinsella
Craig L. Carr

LYNNE
RIENNER
PUBLISHERS

BOULDER
LONDON

Published in the United States of America in 2007 by
Lynne Rienner Publishers, Inc.
1800 30th Street, Boulder, Colorado 80301
www.rienner.com

and in the United Kingdom by
Lynne Rienner Publishers, Inc.
3 Henrietta Street, Covent Garden, London WC2E 8LU

Library of Congress Cataloging-in-Publication Data
The morality of war : a reader / editors, David Kinsella and Craig L. Carr.
    p. cm.
  Includes index.
  ISBN-13: 978-1-58826-377-3 (hardcover : alk. paper)
  ISBN-13: 978-1-58826-353-7 (pbk. : alk. paper)
  1. Military ethics. 2. War—Moral and ethical aspects. I. Kinsella,
David Todd. II. Carr, Craig L., 1948–
  U22.M595 2007
  172'.42—dc22

                                      2006024725

British Cataloguing in Publication Data
A Cataloguing in Publication record for this book
is available from the British Library.

Printed and bound in the United States of America

5 4 3 2 1

Contents

Acknowledgments

T he idea for this anthology emerged as we were assembling the reading list for an undergraduate course we teach called "War and Morality." Therefore, we want first to thank our students at Portland State University who have read and reacted to the selections included here, and from whom we have learned how best to present and introduce the material. Our thanks also to the graduate students and staff who have helped with various tasks, including tracking down original sources, scanning and transcribing, and securing permissions to reprint previously published material: Christopher Cooney, Alan Ely, Michael Harter, Reilly Hirst, and Timothy Stoddard.

Marilyn Grobschmidt at Lynne Rienner Publishers has our gratitude for the guidance she provided throughout this project, one that turned out to be far more complicated than we ever imagined. Finally, and perhaps most important, we want to thank Ronald Tammen, director of the Hatfield School of Government at Portland State, without whose support and assistance this work would not have been possible.

1 Introduction

Warfare is one of the most paradoxical of all human activities. Even though warfare is almost universally condemned as one of the most horrible of human events, it is also a tragically commonplace feature of human life. It may not be a great exaggeration to say that the story of humankind could plausibly be told in terms of the history of warfare. If so, it would not be much of a story, for very little that is good comes out of warfare. Few, if any, other human activities can begin to parallel warfare for brutality, cruelty, and the horrible destruction of life and property. Yet, ironically, warfare also elicits much that is noble and honorable in human beings. For it is also true that few, if any, other human activities can parallel warfare for displays of courage, character, and heroism from those brave warriors whose lot it is to fight. Despite the apparent paradox, there is good reason for the citizens of many if not most states to honor and praise their warriors, past and present, even while they condemn warfare itself.

This paradoxical view of warfare has not always existed, and does not necessarily exist in all places in today's world. In the ancient world, war was simply a fact of life and hardly objectionable from a moral point of view. The philosopher Aristotle, for example, describes warfare—the art of war—as an aspect in the art of acquisition; it was a part of the way that human beings cared for themselves by acquiring the things they needed to live. Its legitimacy was thus linked to its necessity for the survival of the community. Seen in this fashion, warfare becomes a noble and heroic enterprise precisely because the fate of the community is tied to the art of war. If warfare is considered necessary for the survival of the community, it will likely also be regarded as a natural aspect of life, for it is natural to do what is necessary to survive. Viewing warfare in this way is prelude to valuing warfare and cultivating a heroic morality in which the art of war—the ability to fight wars well—is pursued and the warrior is praised for his courage, valor, and skill. The result is a vicious circle of sorts: The more warfare is seen as a necessary and natural feature of human life, the more the art of war is cultivated; and the more the art of war is cultivated, the more it is viewed as a necessary and natural feature of human life. Thus warfare became a rather commonplace feature of the ancient world and conquest remained the primary way for communities to expand their wealth and secure their environment.

This somewhat glorified view of warfare might have continued to typify thinking about war in the western world but for the occurrence of two important events. First, as states grew in size and state sovereignty began to solidify in the wake of the chaos that followed the collapse of Rome, regions became more self-sufficient and the need for acquisition through warfare began to diminish. Second, Christianity emerged as the dominant religious belief and brought with it a valuation of human life that made killing in war morally suspect. Of these two events, the second is arguably the most important for thinking about the emergence of what can plausibly be called the morality of warfare. For it is difficult if not impossible to hold that killing one's fellow human beings is terribly wrong from a theological and moral point of view and still regard war as something that is natural to human beings.

Yet the emergence of a Christian ethic that condemns taking human life in principle did not obviate the apparent need to do so at certain times and under certain circumstances. Killing and warfare continued throughout Europe, as well as other parts of the world touched by the Christian faith, despite the Christian insistence that people should love one another and not do violence to each other. Nor was this simply an indication of bad moral faith or a blatant disregard for Christian teaching, for the Christian belief in the sanctity of life proved hard to live by in practice. As the states of Europe slowly emerged and the state system that we know today began to take shape, states still found it necessary to rely upon warfare as their last line of self-defense and the final method for sustaining their interests in an often hostile environment.

Consequently, a paradoxical attitude about war began to emerge. While war seemed to remain a necessary feature of the human condition, even if it was no longer accepted as an altogether natural one, it became increasingly difficult to reconcile recourse to war with the simple demands of morality. If war involves killing, and if killing is wrong on its face, then warfare should be rejected as wrong. But if it turns out to be necessary at times to resort to war, perhaps in the name of national self-defense, how could warfare be considered immoral on its face? This problem is simply an aspect of a larger moral problem introduced by the principled moral prohibition against killing. Sometimes it seems people must resort to deadly force in order to deal with threats to their lives. If killing is wrong, what are we to do about those individuals who elect to disregard their moral obligations and kill anyway? Does morality require the potential victims of the use of deadly force to abandon any effort to protect and defend themselves from an unwarranted attack? This view has never gained much, if any, moral support, and a right of self-defense that permits the use of deadly force to repel an attacker emerged as a necessary, even natural, response to the problems raised by the threat of impending violence. But if individuals are morally permitted to defend themselves in this manner, it would seem that communities and states should be permitted to do so as well. This conclusion is merely a logical extension of the right of self-defense.

If a right of communal or national self-defense legitimates warfare from a moral point of view, however, it does not necessarily justify all warfare; nor does it entitle defenders to do anything to their attackers in the name of collective self-defense. Instead, it raises troubling ethical questions about when and why states are justified in going to war as well as how wars ought to be fought in ways consistent with the right of national self-defense. The efforts of theologians, philosophers, statesmen, and lawyers to put answers to these questions have produced a variety of rules and principles that inform and control thinking about the morally justifiable nature and limits of warfare. Taken together, these rules and principles form what can be called the morality of warfare.

The most important initial step in the emergence of this morality was taken by St. Augustine, who identified several reasons why a state could justifiably go to war. He argued first that war could only be waged by the appropriate legal authority and claimed further that a legitimate war required a just cause and should also be fought with just or rightful intentions. Wars that had as their end the securing of peace or punishing the wrongful actions of others were held to be justified by Augustine provided the war was fought to achieve these legitimate ends. But wars fought for reasons of aggrandizement or for seizing that which was not one's own were considered illegitimate and hence unjust.

The Augustinian view received further articulation and support in the writings of St. Thomas Aquinas, whose work helped shape the just war doctrine adopted by the Roman Catholic Church. However, a more comprehensive development of the morality of warfare had to wait until the seventeenth and eighteenth centuries when just war theory was systematically explored by philosophers working within the natural law tradition. Two events during this period served to underscore the development of just war thinking. First, the state system as we know it today began to take shape following the Peace of Westphalia (1648). The discrete states that emerged in the wake of the Thirty Years' War began to recognize one another as independent sovereign units with significant interstate relations. Warfare soon came to be regarded as a means of last resort for protecting and defending a state's interests in an environment where states had reason to be wary of the actions and intentions of other states.

This international situation was infused with a distinctive set of moral concerns that began to formalize as philosophical inquiry into moral matters separated from theological dogma. Philosophical inquiry retained from its theological basis the view that the relations of all persons were governed by a set of natural laws. Reason contained the key to identifying and understanding these laws, and by means of rational inquiry it was possible for human beings to discern which actions were right or just and which were not. It was but a small step to move from the view that natural law defined the proper moral relations of persons to the concurrent view that it also defined the proper moral relations of states. In this regard, the works of Francisco de Vitoria, Hugo Grotius, and Samuel Pufendorf were of special importance. The title of Pufendorf's first major work in political theory, *The Elements of Universal Jurisprudence,* published initially in 1660, is illustrative of the thinking of the times. As the title implies, Pufendorf held (typically for his age) that all human relations are governed by certain basic natural (and hence universal) laws, including the relations of individuals acting under the authority of secular sovereignty. But it was Grotius (especially in his *The Law of War and Peace*) who was most prominent in developing natural law doctrine and applying it to the relations of states, an effort that gained him—justifiably—the reputation of being the father of modern international law.

Philosophical efforts to develop a morality of warfare in the form of just war doctrine turned out to be of considerable political value. In a Europe convinced that natural law controlled the proper relations of human beings, philosophical insight into the morality of warfare did much to permit states to justify their actions in the international environment and claim that right was on their side. Thus the development of international relations during this period was inspired as much by theoretical argument as it was by national interest. States gained in the pursuit of their national interests if they could demonstrate that these interests were supported by the principles of natural law. Consequently, the development of a morality of warfare was driven both by the intellectual commitment to fathom the proper relations of human beings and by the desire of states to enlist the law of nature in defense of their own political interests.

The emergence through time of a morality of warfare makes the fact of war an even more paradoxical feature of the international environment. With the evolution of international law, statesmen and international lawyers have been inclined to formalize and systematize these rules into an international law of warfare. Yet there is hardly anything approaching moral consensus on the nature, legitimacy, or exact meaning of many, if not most, of these rules. They are and will likely remain a subject of dispute and disagreement that will continue to engage theologians, philosophers, statesmen, and international lawyers. Moreover, while the dispute matters from a moral point of view, it is hard to be confident that any fruits it might bear will qualify as anything but academic in the worst possible sense. The old saw that says, "All is fair (i.e., anything goes) in love and war," gets to the point. Leaving aside the issue of love, the morality of war indicates that not all *is* fair in war. But when states actually find themselves at war, it seems unlikely that they will adhere to something like an internationalized Marquis of Queensbury set of rules if doing so risks losing the war or winning by means of a strategically unnecessary sacrifice. The principle of necessity that legitimates warfare in the first place will also likely undermine, when push comes to shove, a state's commitment to fighting according to legally stipulated standards, and unfortunately in warfare push is altogether likely to come to shove.

It might also be argued that the emergence of a morality of warfare is deeply objectionable because it legitimizes and institutionalizes an international activity so morally obnoxious that it should be condemned in principle and eliminated altogether from the face of the planet. This argument could be pressed in a different direction by contending that the morality of warfare is in fact little more than a code of conduct invented and supported by powerful states and imposed upon the less powerful. The morality of warfare may not fit well with the conditions and/or cultures of all the states of the world, and will not fit well if some of these states adhere to moral viewpoints quite dissimilar from the ones that inspired the formation of the morality of war. If this morality is formalized in international law, the more powerful states with an interest in enforcing the standards of the international law of war will succeed only in making international criminals out of the leaders of those states who happen to reject some or all of the elements of the morality of war.

The blade associated with this latter argument also cuts in the other direction. If powerful states take it upon themselves not only to control the enforcement of an international law of war but also to manage the development of its content, questions naturally arise about the product that emerges. How can all states of the world be confident that the morality of war does little more than serve the political interests of the powerful states responsible for its development? Additionally, when powerful states go to war, presumably under color of justifiable action, how might the international community be confident that their leaders will be held legally accountable for their own war efforts? The United States, for example, was quick to try numerous Axis leaders for various crimes associated with their activities in World War II, but no one was inclined to question the potential criminality of US activities during the war, even though the dropping of the atomic bomb on Nagasaki, to take what is perhaps the most morally questionable US action during the war, may have warranted prosecution of a war crime under the morality of war. (This gives US military decisionmakers the benefit of the doubt by assuming that use of the first atomic bomb against Hiroshima had a legitimate moral justification, perhaps a large assumption.) It is difficult to see, in short, how the morality of war can be established in international law in a way that makes it anything but conquerors justice. There is, then, reason for states and the citizens of all states to be somewhat cynical about the morality of war and about its formulation into an international law of war.

These are difficult issues to be sure, but they matter greatly to the development of a viable morality of war that can support a serviceable law of war. And it probably does little to mollify the concerns they raise to note that these difficulties also trouble the development and enforcement of domestic legal systems. The ideal of the rule of law presumes that it is possible to articulate a system of rules that all those who are subject to it can recognize as fair and impartial. The great difficulty here is that what is taken to be fair and impartial to some, given perhaps their moral point of view, may be considered oppressive to others given their distinctive moral viewpoint. If law is to work as a viable system of justice, all those subject to its authority must acknowledge its authoritative nature, and this is not easily accomplished in a world where disparate normative viewpoints exist and where individuals, as well as states, may be inclined to read their own particular interests into their moral visions.

But the rule of law remains a noble ideal both on the domestic and international stage. It is arguably the best chance humankind has for learning to live together amicably and abandoning the resort to force and violence to resolve disputes. It has, in any event, had salutary consequences on the domestic side in those states that have managed to approximate the ideal of fairness and impartiality, and this is reason to think that it might be of a similar service in the international environment as well. Perhaps ironically, it may be that the best way to press in the direction of a viable international law of warfare is to engage the debate over the morality of war and involve all states of the world in the process. Doing so may have the positive effect of generating a degree of consensus over the requirements of this morality and exposing those issues over which consensus might prove to be too much to ask. This, in any event, is reason to take the dispute seriously in spite of the difficulties that surround it. If we are to take the morality of war seriously, however, and explore its possibilities for introducing a more just order in the relations of states, it is necessary to understand and appreciate its present standing and the moral problems that drive the disputes that surround it. At the very least, this involves understanding how and why the rules constitutive of the morality of war emerged, the nature of the form they presently take, and the problems and controversies that continue to surround the various components of this morality.

This reader surveys the basic elements and fundamental themes of the just war tradition. Its purpose is to acquaint students and interested readers with historical and contemporary thinking about when and why war is justified *(jus ad bellum)* and about how wars ought, morally speaking, to be fought *(jus in bello)*. Following the events of 9/11, government officials in the United States were quick to declare a "war on terrorism," a war presumably to be fought against those individuals identified by the US government as terrorists. While this "war" is exceptional in the sense that Congress has not issued a declaration of war, the commitment of US forces in Afghanistan and Iraq naturally raises significant questions about the justification of US military action, both with regard to the use of force itself and with regard to the way the US military and government officials prosecute the war. As we have suggested, these questions are hardly exceptional; they arise in the western intellectual tradition whenever states commit, or contemplate committing, to warfare. This reader is intended to inform and guide efforts to address these questions by introducing readers to the notion of a just war as this notion has evolved in the arguments of those philosophers, jurists, and warriors whose work has shaped the just war tradition. While the events of 9/11 signal the contemporary pertinence of such a reader, the selections we have chosen are intended to inform thinking on the justice of warfare itself.

The volume is divided into four parts. Part 1 introduces readers to the just war tradition by comparing it with alternative views on the legitimacy of warfare and by presenting excerpts from the primary historical thinkers whose work has generated and configured the tradition. Chapter 2 considers the so-called realist school of thought, which tends to dismiss moral concerns about the justification of state policies, including warfare, and focus instead on the promotion of a state's interests. Like the just war tradition, realism has a long history, and just war theory may be viewed as a moral response to realist views. Chapter 3 explores the pacifist tradition, which finds little or no moral justification for warfare. While pacifism has not enjoyed the theoretical popularity of either realism or the just war tradition, the arguments associated with this position are not inconsequential, and the selections in this chapter help to expand moral thinking about the justification of warfare and raise issues that need to be considered and addressed by just war theorists. Chapter 4 presents the historical development of the just war tradition; here the views on warfare of such seminal thinkers as Augustine, Aquinas, Vitoria, Grotius, and Pufendorf are presented. These readings present the historical pedigree of the just war tradition and detail themes that comprise the tradition.

The remainder of the volume explores topics from three different dimensions, each of which entails a unique form of moral judgment: the resort to war, the conduct of war, and the criminality of war. Statesmen usually feel compelled to justify their resort to armed conflict and the readings in Part 2 are addressed to those sorts of rationales—*jus ad bellum,* in the parlance of just war theory. There is a consensus among just war theorists that states may resort to wars for reasons of self-defense; the principle is also codified in international law. Thus, the first set of readings in this part take up the question of aggression (Chapter 5), how it has been defined by the international community, and what responses are allowed.

Self-defense in the face of overt armed aggression is perhaps the most straightforward case to make from a moral and legal point of view, but states have often engaged in the first-use of military force while justifying their acts as something other than aggression. Preemption is one such exception (Chapter 6), and the Bush administration's forthright defense of its policy of not waiting for dangers to gather has sparked a renewed debate about the legitimacy of preemptive and preventive war. This debate is connected to US (and other) efforts to fashion an appropriate military response to the scourge of transnational terrorism (Chapter 7), a phenomenon not easily analyzed from within the just war tradition—though the current war on terrorism has occasioned many efforts to apply just war concepts. Readings in Part 2 also examine the moral arguments for and against armed intervention in the domestic affairs of other states (Chapter 8), especially in response to humanitarian crises.

In regard to the conduct of war, the just war tradition has had a profound impact on the international law of war. The readings in Part 3 examine what constitutes proper methods of warfare and the restraints to be observed in their use—*jus in bello*. During wartime, soldiers are, literally, licensed to kill. A large portion of the law of war is devoted to the rights to be afforded to lawful combatants (Chapter 9): when and how they may be killed by opposing forces; how they should be treated if captured; and when they must be released. The abuse of prisoners in Afghanistan and Iraq by US military and intelligence personnel, as well as the debates surrounding the rights of enemy combatants and the definition of inhumane treatment, amply demonstrate the continued relevance of these established moral limits and the temptation to transgress them for reasons of "military necessity."

Probably the best-known principle, but one that has often been violated, is the immunity of civilians from targeted attacks (Chapter 10). The somber experience of World War II prompted a renewed effort to clarify and reinforce the rights of noncombatants, culminating in the 1949 Geneva Conventions. The imposition of economic sanctions is often defended as less destructive than overt warfare as a means of redressing grievances; indeed, the UN Charter calls on the Security Council to employ such methods before resorting to military force. Yet the morality of blockades and sanctions (Chapter 11) raises difficult questions, given the hardships inflicted on civilian populations, hardships that are often avoided by the political and military leaders whose policies brought them on. The very technologies of war (Chapter 12) both challenge and reinforce moral limits established by *jus in bello*. Weapons of mass destruction, of course, obliterate the distinction between combatants and noncombatants, while "smart weapons" allow ever more precise targeting, presumably with benefits for civilian populations who might otherwise be caught in the crossfire of modern war.

The just war tradition identifies what is just and unjust in the resort to war and the conduct of war; international law identifies what is legal and illegal. Part 4 of this collection turns to the subject of criminality and the judgment of guilt in the aftermath of war—*jus post bellum.* At the end of World War II, the victors of that war sought to clarify precisely who bears responsibility for crimes of war and therefore who should be punished (Chapter 13). The exercise has been repeated with subsequent wars, but with the international community, as represented by the United Nations, playing an increasingly prominent role, first in helping to establish ad hoc war crimes tribunals and then in creating a permanent International Criminal Court (ICC).

Although states go to war, war crimes are committed by individuals, and the question of justiciability is a difficult one in an international legal system in which rights and obligations generally attach to states, not individual human beings. States have their own legal systems for prosecuting criminals, including war criminals, which raises the question of jurisdiction as well. The Rome Statute creating the ICC did not resolve the potential for politically motivated prosecutions to the satisfaction of the United States, prompting the Bush administration to effectively "unsign" the treaty. The prosecution of war crimes and crimes against humanity has long been hampered by the absence of an authoritative enforcement mechanism in the international legal system (Chapter 14). The arrival of the ICC does not change that, but some war-ravaged states have opted for more conciliatory approaches for dealing with widespread criminality in an effort to ease the transition to stability and peace.

We introduce each chapter of readings with a brief commentary intended to highlight some of the main issues and debates surrounding the topic. We point out how contemporary developments illustrate the continuing significance of moral argument about war, and argue that scholars, policymakers, and concerned citizens can and do draw on the moral insights of just war theory. However, we also emphasize the many ways modern war, including the war on terrorism, puts pressure on these same moral principles, and ask whether some of them have indeed been pushed to the breaking point.

■ About the Editing

The readings collected for this volume have been edited so that readers can focus on the material we find most pertinent. If readers find ellipses (. . .) where they would have preferred further discussion, they may consult the original source. In fact, it is our hope that the excerpted material appearing in this volume will generate sufficient interest that readers will want to spend more time with at least some of these great works.

■ A Note on the Text

Authors' footnotes have been retained only when they provide the source for direct quotations (although notes referencing quotes from religious texts, like the Christian Bible, are dropped). All the footnotes that remain have been reformatted using a consistent citation style. The paragraph numbering, which is used in several of the classic texts excerpted below, has not been retained. However, paragraph numbering in the material excerpted from international treaties and conventions has been reproduced.

Part 1

Historical and Philosophical Approaches to the Morality of War

2 Realism

Power = military economic

2.1 _____

Introduction
The Editors

The notion of realism as it is used here refers to a tradition of thought within the area of international relations theory. Credit for developing the idea of realism in international relations is generally given to the contemporary international relations theorist Hans Morgenthau. In its most simple terms, realism holds that the states of the world exist in an anarchical and rather hostile international environment. In order to survive and prosper in such an environment, it is in a state's best interest to develop and expand its power as best it can.

The notion of power at home in realist thought is both somewhat complex and rather ambiguous. In its most brute form, power involves military might. States that are militarily strong are relatively immune from attack and can use their might to secure their interests if and when they wish. But military might is not the only form power can take. Power is also enhanced by economic strength, for example, by strategic location, natural resources, population, and international prestige among other things. These things, including military might, are resources states can use to expand and solidify their power, and power can be measured in term of the kinds of resources available to states. But power is also a relational term. To say that state A is powerful is to say that it has more power resources at its disposal than other states against which its power resources are measured. Thus states can expand and develop their power by cultivating the resources that translate into power, and this is what realists think states do and, given the anarchical nature of the international setting, what they should do.

Realism is somewhat ambiguous when it comes to the morality of warfare. If states are considered agents dedicated to the pursuit of their interests, it makes little sense to think that they would be constrained by standards of morality in the event these standards work against their ability to realize these interests. This is indicative of the hard-headed thinking from which realism draws its name. It is simply unrealistic to suppose that states will adhere to moral rules when and if they would be better off ignoring them. But it might also be in a state's interest to appear law abiding and willing to adhere to the morality of warfare under certain circumstances. States recognized as law abiding, for example, may seem trustworthy to the remainder of the international community and this might make them both good trade partners and reliable military allies. Thus law abidingness may qualify as a power resource that states can exploit. But to appear law abiding, states must actually be law abiding in their dealings with other states at least some of the time, and this is reason for states to accept and follow standards of international law at least up to a point.

Realism also advocates an independent normative posture in the international relations of states. On the one hand, realism is inspired by what might be called a scientific commitment to objectivity. Realists may insist that they are not moralists who worry about what states ought to do morally speaking. They are, once again, more realistic than this; they want first to understand how states do behave because this is a necessary first step in getting clear on the nature of interstate relations. Once we understand how states do behave, it becomes possible to develop a picture of how states will respond to new or changing developments in the international environment. But these social scientific ruminations are usually followed by additional normative claims. States not only do seek power, in the realist view, but they *ought* to do so as well. It is possible to interpret this normative claim as something of a moral imperative if we suppose that the "ought" in this normative proposition functions to express a moral requirement. It may make more sense, however, to interpret the "ought" claim asserted by realists as a prudential requirement. States are better able to promote and protect their interests by developing their power resources. Given the nature of the international arena, this is simply the most prudent thing for them to do.

It would be a mistake, however, to suppose that realists are proponents or advocates of warfare, for they are not. War is an extreme measure, and the costs of war are likely to be great. So it seems best, in general, for states to avoid war, and this is one reason why realists think states should cultivate power. The more powerful a state, the less inclined other states will be to go to war with it. States that properly understand how states behave in the international arena are better positioned to avoid war. For example, states may articulate their interests to other states in a fashion that indicates what interests matter to them to such an extent that they are willing to fight for them and what interests are more negotiable. During the Cuban Missile Crisis, for example, the United States needed to make clear to the Soviet Union that intermediate-range ballistic missiles in Cuba intruded upon primary US interests to such an extent that the United States would willingly go to war if they were not removed) Once this message became clear, it was up to the Soviet Union to decide if having these missiles in Cuba was of such great interest to them that they would fight to keep them there. From a realist perspective, the clear articulation of interests in conjunction with the cultivation of power becomes an effective way to avoid the scourge of war.

The pursuit of interests and the clear articulation of interests that matter are thus identified as the basic common denominator against which states can measure and anticipate the behavior of other states. And this, realists suppose, is the logic states should adopt and follow in their international relations. It is simply imprudent for states to think that other states will not go to war, or will fight by something like the Marquis of Queensbury rules if they do, in the absence of a morally justifiable reason. It is imprudent to suppose that the morality of war will restrain states from aggressive action if their leaders think important interests will be sacrificed as a result. The renaissance political thinker Machiavelli, who is sometimes—albeit rather erroneously—identified as the father of realism, instructed his prince to follow prudence rather than morality because in a world where so many forsake moral action in favor of self-interest, he would surely be brought to ruin if he did not. This is advice that realists tend to read into the international relations of states.

If realism as a theory of international relations is a relative newcomer on the intellectual stage, the prudential and self-interested behavior of states is hardly news. Yet rarely has it been stated and advocated with the clarity and power found in the section of Thucydides' *Peloponnesian War,* entitled "The Talks at Melos." Thucydides, a former Athenian commander, chronicled the events of the Athenian war against Sparta in an effort to explain how and why Athens managed to grasp defeat from the jaws of victory. The talks at Melos involved the efforts of the Athenians to enlist Melian support for their war effort. If the Melians refused to support the Athenian effort, the Athenians threatened to destroy Melos. The Athenians were vastly more powerful than the Melians and supposing their threat to be credible thought that the Melians had no alternative but to acquiesce to their demands. The Melian response, however, contended (among other things) that Athens had no right to implicate her in the Athenian fight with Sparta. Claims of right, however, carried no weight whatsoever with the Athenians, who saw the issue in decidedly realist terms. Might is not presumed to make right from the Athenian view, but it does permit the mighty to get what they want—or else. And in the end, this is all that mattered to them. Questions of right were simply beside the point, and when the Melians refused to succumb to Athenian pressure, the Athenians had no qualms in bringing about the destruction of Melos.

What has all this to do with the morality of war? The most straightforward answer to this question is to note that realists are not strong advocates of just war theory. They do not think states will necessarily adhere to the morality of war, and thus they do not think this morality should be used as a guide to a state's foreign policy unless appearing to do so can advance a state's power in the international setting. But realism might be overly cynical about the motives of state authorities and about the anarchical character of the international setting. It is in a state's best interest to get along with others, particularly in an era when the military capacity of the more powerful states enables them to devastate their foes so completely. And getting along is enhanced by endorsing and accepting clear rules that define permissible and impermissible behavior in the relations of states.

The morality of warfare and the development of an international law of war works in this direction, and this is reason for all states of the world to take it seriously. It is perhaps unnecessary to think that the rules and principles constitutive of the morality of war have some objective or immutable truth about them. What matters is that they work to promote and safeguard a peaceful coexistence among the states of the world, and thus to transform an otherwise anarchical environment into a more orderly and domesticated one.

2.2 ———

The Talks at Melos
Thucydides

The following summer, Alcibiades sailed to Argos with twenty ships, seized three hundred Argives still suspected of having Spartan sympathies, and then imprisoned them on nearby islands under Athenian control. The Athenians also sent a fleet against the island of Melos. Thirty of the ships were their own, six were from Chios, and two were from Lesbos. Their own troops numbered twelve hundred hoplites, three hundred archers, and twenty mounted archers. There were also about fifteen hundred hoplites from their allies on the islands. The Melians are colonists from Sparta and would not submit to Athenian control like the other islanders. At first, they were neutral and lived peaceably, but they became openly hostile after Athens once tried to compel their obedience by ravaging their land. The generals Cleomedes, son of Lycomedes, and Tisias, son of Tisimachus, bivouacked on Melian territory with their troops, but before doing any injury to the land, they sent ambassadors to hold talks with the Melians. The Melian leadership, however, did not bring these men before the popular assembly. Instead, they asked them to discuss their mission with the council and the privileged voters. The Athenian ambassadors spoke as follows.

"We know that what you are thinking in bringing us before a few voters, and not before the popular assembly, is that now the people won't be deceived after listening to a single long, seductive, and unrefuted speech from us. Well, those of you who are sitting here can make things even safer for yourselves. When we say something that seems wrong, interrupt immediately, and answer, not in a set speech, but one point at a time. But say first whether this proposal is to your liking."

The Melian councilors said, "There can be no objection to the reasonableness of quiet, instructive talks among ourselves. But this military force, which is here, now, and not off in the future, looks different from instruction. We see that you have come as judges in a debate, and the likely prize

From *Peloponnesian War* by Thucydides, ed. Jennifer Tolbert Roberts and Walter Blanco, trans. Walter Blanco. Copyright © 1998 by W. W. Norton & Company. Used by permission of W. W. Norton & Company. Excerpt from book 5: chaps. 84–116 ("The Talks at Melos").

will be war if we win the debate with arguments based on right and refuse to capitulate, or servitude if we concede to you."

ATHENIANS

Excuse us, but if you're having this meeting to make guesses about the future or to do anything but look at your situation and see how to save your city, we'll leave. But if that's the topic, we'll keep talking.

MELIANS

It's natural and understandable that in a situation like this, people would want to express their thoughts at length. But so be it. This meeting is about saving our city, and the format of the discussion will be as you have said.

ATHENIANS

Very well.

We Athenians are not going to use false pretenses and go on at length about how we have a right to rule because we destroyed the Persian empire, or about how we are seeking retribution because you did us wrong. You would not believe us anyway. And please do not suppose that you will persuade *us* when you say that you did not campaign with the Spartans although you were their colonists, or that you never did us wrong. No, each of us must exercise what power he really thinks he can, and we know and you know that in the human realm, justice is enforced only among those who can be equally constrained by it, and that those who have power use it, while the weak make compromises.

MELIANS

Since you have ruled out a discussion of justice and forced us to speak of expediency, it would be inexpedient, at least as we see it, for you to eradicate common decency. There has always been a fair and right way to treat people who are in danger, if only to give them some benefit for making persuasive arguments by holding off from the full exercise of power. This applies to you, above all, since you would set an example for others of how to take the greatest vengeance if you fall.

ATHENIANS

We're not worried about the end of our empire, if it ever does end. People who rule over others, like the Spartans, are not so bad to their defeated enemies. Anyway, we're not fighting the Spartans just now. What is really horrendous is when subjects are able to attack and defeat their masters. But you let us worry about all that. We are here to talk about benefiting our empire and saving your city, and we will tell you how we are going to do that, because we want to take control here without any trouble and we want you to be spared for both our sakes.

MELIANS

And just how would it be as much to our advantage to be enslaved, as for you to rule over us?

ATHENIANS

You would benefit by surrendering before you experience the worst of consequences, and we would benefit by not having you dead.

MELIANS

So you would not accept our living in peace, being friends instead of enemies, and allies of neither side?

ATHENIANS

Your hatred doesn't hurt us as much as your friendship. That would show us as weak to our other subjects, whereas your hatred would be a proof of our power.

MELIANS

Would your subjects consider you reasonable if you lumped together colonists who had no connection to you, colonists from Athens, and rebellious colonists who had been subdued?

ATHENIANS

They think there's justice all around. They also think the independent islands are strong, and that we are afraid to attack them. So aside from adding to our empire, your subjugation will also enhance our safety, especially since you are islanders and we are a naval power. Besides, you're weaker than the others—unless, that is, you show that you too can be independent.

MELIANS

Don't you think there's safety in our neutrality? You turned us away from a discussion of justice and persuaded us to attend to what was in your interest. Now it's up to us to tell you about what is to our advantage and to try to persuade you that it is also to yours. How will you avoid making enemies of states that are now neutral, but that look at what you do here and decide that you will go after them one day? How will you achieve anything but to make your present enemies seem more attractive, and to force those who had no intention of opposing you into unwilling hostility?

ATHENIANS

We do not think the threat to us is so much from mainlanders who, in their freedom from fear, will be continually putting off their preparations against us, as from independent islanders, like you, and from those who are already chafing under the restraints of rule. These are the ones who are most likely to commit themselves to ill-considered action and create foreseeable dangers for themselves and for us.

MELIANS

Well then, in the face of this desperate effort you and your slaves are making, you to keep your empire and they to get rid of it, wouldn't we, who are still free, be the lowest of cowards if we didn't try everything before submitting to slavery?

ATHENIANS

No, not if you think about it prudently. This isn't a contest about manly virtue between equals, or about bringing disgrace on yourself. You are deliberating about your very existence, about standing up against a power far greater than yours.

MELIANS

But we know that there are times when the odds in warfare don't depend on the numbers. If we give up, our situation becomes hopeless right away, but if we fight, we can still hope to stand tall.

ATHENIANS

In times of danger, hope is a comfort that can hurt you, but it won't destroy you if you back it up with plenty of other resources. People who gamble everything on it (hope is extravagant by nature, you see) know it for what it really is only after they have lost everything. Then, of course, when you can recognize it and take precautions, it's left you flat. You don't want to experience that. You Melians are weak, and you only have one chance. So don't be like all those people who could have saved themselves by their own efforts, but who abandoned their realistic hopes and turned in their hour of need to invisible powers—to prophecies and oracles and all the other nonsense that conspires with hope to ruin you.

MELIANS

As you well know, we too think it will be hard to fight both your power and the fortunes of war, especially with uneven odds. Still, we believe that our fortune comes from god, and that we will not be defeated because we take our stand as righteous men against men who are in the wrong. And what we lack in power will be made up for by the Spartan League. They will have to help us, if only because of our kinship with them and the disgrace they would feel if they didn't. So it's not totally irrational for us to feel hopeful.

ATHENIANS

Well, when it comes to divine good will, we don't think we'll be left out. We're not claiming anything or doing anything outside man's thinking about the gods or about the way the gods themselves behave. Given what we believe about the gods and know about men, we think that both are always forced by the law of nature to dominate everyone they can. We didn't lay down this law, it was there—and we weren't the first to make use of it. We took it as it was and acted on it, and we will bequeath it as a living thing to future generations, knowing full well that if you or anyone else had the same power as we, you would do the same thing. So we probably don't have to fear any disadvantage when it comes to the gods. And as to this opinion of yours about the Spartans, that you can trust them to help you because of their fear of disgrace—well, our blessings on your innocence, but we don't envy your foolishness. The Spartans do the right thing among themselves, according to their local customs. One could say a great deal about their treatment of others, but to put it briefly, they are more conspicuous than anyone else we know in thinking that pleasure is good and expediency is just. Their mindset really bears no relation to your irrational belief that there is any safety for you now.

MELIANS

But it's exactly because of this expediency that we trust them. They won't want to betray the Melians, their colonists, and prove themselves helpful to their enemies and unreliable to their well-wishers in Greece.

ATHENIANS

But don't you see that expediency is safe, and that doing the right and honorable thing is dangerous? On the whole, the Spartans are the last people to take big risks.

MELIANS

We think they'll take on dangers for us that they wouldn't for others and regard those dangers as less risky, because we are close to the Peloponnese from an operational point of view. Also, they can trust our loyalty because we are kin and we think alike.

ATHENIANS

Men who ask others to come to fight on their side don't offer security in good will but in real fighting power. The Spartans take this kind of thing more into consideration than others, because they have so little faith in their own resources that they even attack their neighbors with plenty of allies. So it's not likely that they'll try to make their way over to an island when we control the sea.

MELIANS

Then maybe they'll send their allies. The sea of Crete is large, and it is harder for those who control the sea to catch a ship than it is for the ship to get through to safety without being noticed. And if that doesn't work, they might turn against your territory or attack the rest of your allies, the ones Brasidas didn't get to. And then the fight would shift from a place where you have no interest to your own land and that of your allies.

ATHENIANS

It's been tried and might even be tried for you—though surely you are aware that we Athenians have never abandoned a siege out of fear of anyone.

But it occurs to us that after saying you were going to talk about saving yourselves, you haven't in any of this lengthy discussion mentioned anything that most people would rely on for their salvation. Your strongest arguments are in the future and depend on hope. What you've actually got is too meager to give you a chance of surviving the forces lined up against you now. You've shown a very irrational attitude—unless, of course, you intend to reach some more prudent conclusion than this after you send us away and begin your deliberations. For surely you don't mean to commit yourselves to that "honor" which has been so destructive to men in clear and present dangers involving "dishonor." Many men who could still see where it was leading them have been drawn on by the allure of this so-called "honor," this word with its seductive power, and fallen with open eyes into irremediable catastrophe, vanquished in their struggle with a fine word, only to achieve a kind of dishonorable honor because they weren't just unlucky, they were fools. You can avoid this, if you think things over carefully, and decide that there is nothing so disgraceful in being defeated by the greatest city in the world, which invites you to become its ally on fair terms—paying us tribute, to be sure, but keeping your land for yourselves. You have been given the choice between war and security. Don't be stubborn and make the wrong choice. The people who are most likely to succeed stand up to their equals, have the right attitude towards their superiors, and are fair to those beneath them.

We will leave now. Think it over, and always remember that you are making a decision about your country. You only have one, and its existence depends on this one chance to make a decision, right or wrong.

Then the Athenians withdrew from the discussion. The Melians, left to themselves, came to the conclusion that had been implied by their responses in the talks. They answered the Athenians as follows: "Men of Athens, our decision is no different from what it was at first. We will not in this brief moment strip the city we have lived in for seven hundred years of its freedom. We will try to save it, trusting in the divine good fortune that has preserved us so far and in the help we expect from the Spartans and from others. We invite you to be our friends, to let us remain neutral, and to leave our territory after making a treaty agreeable to us both."

That was the Melian response. The talks were already breaking up when the Athenians said, "Well, judging from this decision, you seem to us to be the only men who can make out the future more clearly than what you can see, and who gaze upon the invisible with your mind's eye as if it were an accomplished fact. You have cast yourselves on luck, hope, and the Spartans, and the more you trust in them, the harder will be your fall."

Then the Athenian envoys returned to the camp. Since the Melians would not submit, the Athenian generals immediately took offensive action and, after dividing their men according to the cities they came from, began to build a wall around Melos. Later the Athenians left a garrison of their own and allied men to guard the land and sea routes and then withdrew with most of their army. The men who were left behind remained there and carried on the siege.

At about this same time, the Argives invaded the territory of Phlius, where they fell into an ambush set by the Phliasians and the Argive exiles, who killed about eighty of them. The Athenian raiders on Pylos took a great deal of booty from Spartan territory, but despite even this, the Spartans did not renounce the treaty and declare war. They did, however, announce that if any of their people wished to raid Athenian territory, they could do so. The Corinthians made war on the Athenians over some private quarrels, but the rest of the Peloponnesians held their peace. The Melians staged a night attack on the part of the Athenian wall opposite their market and captured it. They killed some men and withdrew into the city carrying grain and as many other useful provisions as they could, taking no further action. The Athenians kept a better watch from then on. And so the summer came to an end.

The following winter, the Spartans were about to march into Argive territory, but the omens from sacrifices made before crossing the border were unfavorable and they turned back. This balked expedition led the Argives to suspect some of their citizens. They arrested some, but others managed to escape. At about the same time, the Melians again captured yet another part of the Athenian wall when only a few men were on guard duty. Because of this, another contingent later came from Athens, under the command of Philocrates, son of Demeas. By now, the Melians were completely cut off, and there were traitors within the city itself. So, on their own initiative, they agreed to terms whereby the Athenians could do with them as they liked. The Athenians thereupon killed all the males of fighting age they could capture and sold the women and children into slavery. The Athenians then occupied the place themselves and later sent out five hundred colonists.

2.3 _____

Political Power and International Morality

Hans J. Morgenthau

▨ What Is Political Power?

As Means to the Nation's Ends

International politics, like all politics, is a struggle for power. Whatever the ultimate aims of international politics, power is always the immediate aim. Statesmen and peoples may ultimately seek freedom, security, prosperity, or power itself. They may define their goals in terms of a religious, philosophic, economic, or social ideal. They may hope that this ideal will materialize through its own inner force, through divine intervention, or through the natural development of human affairs. They may also try to further its realization through nonpolitical means, such as technical co-operation with other nations or international organizations. But whenever they strive to realize their goal by means of international politics, they do so by striving for power. The Crusaders wanted to free the holy places from domination by the Infidels; Woodrow Wilson wanted to make the world safe for democracy; the Nazis wanted to open Eastern Europe to German colonization, to dominate Europe, and to conquer the world. Since they all chose power to achieve these ends, they were actors on the scene of international politics.

Two conclusions follow from this concept of international politics. First, not every action that a nation performs with respect to another nation is of a political nature. Many such activities are normally undertaken without any consideration of power, nor do they normally affect the power of the nation undertaking them. Many legal, economic, humanitarian, and cultural activities are of this kind. Thus a nation is not normally engaged in international politics when it concludes an extradition treaty with another nation, when it exchanges goods and services with other nations, when it co-operates with other nations in providing relief from natural catastrophes, and when it promotes the distribution of cultural achievements throughout the world. In other words, the involvement of a nation in international politics is but one among many types of activities in which a nation can participate on the international scene.

Second, not all nations are at all times to the same extent involved in international politics. The degree of their involvement may run all the way from the maximum at present attained by the United States and the Soviet Union, through the minimum involvement of such countries as Switzerland, Luxembourg, or Venezuela, to the complete noninvolvement of Liechtenstein and Monaco. Similar extremes can be noticed in the history of particular countries. Spain in the sixteenth and seventeenth centuries was one of the main active participants in the struggle for power on the international scene, but plays today only a marginal role in it. The same is true of such countries as Austria, Sweden, and Switzerland. On the other hand, nations like the United States, the Soviet Union, and China are today much more deeply involved in international politics than they were fifty or even twenty years ago. In short, the relation of nations to international politics has a dynamic quality. It changes with the vicissitudes of power, which may push a nation into the forefront of the power struggle, or may deprive a nation of the ability to participate actively in it. It may also change under the impact of cultural transformations, which may make a nation prefer other pursuits, for instance commerce, to those of power. The tendency of countries to be involved to a greater or lesser extent in the struggle for power prompted Arnold Wolfers to observe that they occupied positions at opposite extremes of a spectrum extending from what he called the pole of power to the pole of indifference. . . .

■ The Depreciation of Political Power

The aspiration for power being the distinguishing element of international politics, as of all politics, international politics is of necessity power politics. While this fact is generally recognized in the practice of international affairs, it is frequently denied in the pronouncements of scholars, publicists, and even statesmen. Since the end of the Napoleonic Wars, ever larger groups in the Western world have been persuaded that the struggle for power on the international scene is a temporary phenomenon, a historical accident that is bound to disappear once the peculiar historic conditions that have given rise to it have been eliminated. . . . Adherents of free trade, such as Cobden and Proudhon were convinced that the removal of trade barriers was the only condition for the establishment of permanent harmony among nations, and might even lead to the disappearance of international politics altogether. . . . For Marx and his followers, capitalism is at the root of international discord and war. They maintain that international socialism will do away with the struggle for power on the international scene and will bring about permanent peace. During the nineteenth century, liberals everywhere shared the conviction that power politics and war were residues of an obsolete system of government, and that the victory of democracy and constitutional government over absolutism and autocracy would assure the victory of international harmony and permanent peace over power politics and war. . . .

[T]he struggle for power is universal in time and space and is an undeniable fact of experience. It cannot be denied that throughout historic time, regardless of social, economic, and political conditions, states have met each other in contests for power. Even though anthropologists have shown that certain primitive peoples seem to be free from the desire for power, nobody has yet shown how their state of mind and the conditions under which they live can be recreated on a worldwide scale so as to eliminate the struggle for power from the international scene. It would be useless and even self-destructive to free one or the other of the peoples of the earth from the desire for power while leaving it extant in others. If the desire for power cannot be abolished everywhere in the world, those who might be cured would simply fall victims to the power of others.

The position taken here might be criticized on the ground that conclusions drawn from the past are unconvincing, and that to draw such conclusions has always been the main stock in trade of the enemies of progress and reform. Though it is true that certain social arrangements and institutions have always existed in the past, it does not necessarily follow that they must always exist in the future. The situation is, however, different when we deal not with social arrangements and institutions created by man, but with those elemental bio-psychological drives by which in turn society is created. The drives to live, to propagate, and to dominate are common to all men. Their relative strength is dependent upon social conditions that may favor one drive and tend to repress another, or that may withhold social approval from certain manifestations of these drives while they encourage others. Thus, to take examples only from the sphere of power, most societies condemn killing as a means of attaining power within society, but all societies encourage the killing of enemies in that struggle for power which is called war. Dictators look askance at the aspirations for political power among their fellow citizens, but democracies consider active participation in the competition for political power a civic duty. Where a monopolistic organization of economic activities exists, competition for economic power is absent, and in competitive economic systems certain manifestations of the struggle for economic power are outlawed, while others are encouraged. Ostrogorsky, invoking the authority of Tocqueville, states that "the passions of the American people are not of a political, but of a commercial, nature. In that world awaiting cultivation, the love of power aims less at men than at things."[1]

Regardless of particular social conditions, the decisive argument against the opinion that the struggle for power on the international scene is a mere historic accident must be derived from the nature of domestic politics. The essence of international politics is identical with its domestic counterpart. Both domestic and international politics are a struggle for power, modified only by the different conditions under which this struggle takes place in the domestic and in the international spheres.

The tendency to dominate, in particular, is an element of all human associations, from the family through fraternal and professional associations and local political organizations, to the state. On the family level, the typical conflict between the mother-in-law and her child's spouse is in its essence a struggle for power, the defense of an established power position against the attempt to establish a new one. As such it foreshadows the conflict on the international scene between the policies of the status quo and the policies of imperialism. Social clubs, fraternities, faculties, and business organizations are scenes of continuous struggles for power between groups that either want to keep what power they already have or seek to attain greater power. Competitive contests between business enterprises as well as labor disputes between employers and employees are frequently fought not only, and sometimes not even primarily, for economic advantages, but for control over each other and over others; that is, for power. Finally, the whole political life of a nation, particularly of a democratic nation, from the local to the national level, is a continuous struggle for power. In periodic elections, in voting in legislative assemblies, in lawsuits before courts, in administrative decisions and executive measures—in all these activities men try to maintain or to establish their power over other men. The processes by which legislative, judicial, executive, and administrative decisions are reached are subject to pressures and counterpressures by "pressure groups" trying to defend and expand their positions of power. . . .

In view of this ubiquity of the struggle for power in all social relations and on all levels of social organization, is it surprising that international politics is of necessity power politics? And would it not be rather surprising if the struggle for power were but an accidental and ephemeral attribute of international politics when it is a permanent and necessary element of all branches of domestic politics? . . .

▩ International Morality

. . . [T]here is the misconception, usually associated with the general depreciation and moral condemnation of power politics . . . that international politics is so thoroughly evil that it is no use looking for moral limitations of the aspirations for power on the international scene. Yet, if we ask ourselves what statesmen and diplomats are capable of doing to further the power objectives of their respective nations and what they actually do, we realize that they do less than they probably could and less than they actually did in other periods of history. They refuse to consider certain ends and to use certain means, either altogether or under certain conditions, not because in the light of expediency they appear impractical or unwise but because certain moral rules interpose an absolute barrier. Moral rules do not permit certain policies to be considered at all from the point of view of expediency. Certain things are not being done on moral grounds, even though it would be expedient to do them. Such ethical inhibitions operate in our time on different levels with different effectiveness. Their restraining function is most obvious and most effective in affirming the sacredness of human life in times of peace.

■ The Protection of Human Life

Protection of Human Life in Peace
International politics can be defined . . . as a continuing effort to maintain and to increase the power of one's own nation and to keep in check or reduce the power of other nations. The relative power of nations depends, however, . . . upon the quantity and quality of human beings in terms of size and quality of population, size and quality of military establishment, quality of government, and, more particularly, of diplomacy. Viewed as a series of technical tasks into which moral considerations do not enter, international politics would have to consider as one of its legitimate purposes the drastic reduction or even the elimination of the population of a rival nation, of its most prominent military and political leaders, and of its ablest diplomats. And when international politics was considered exclusively as a technique, without moral significance, for the purpose of maintaining and gaining power, such methods were used without moral scruples and as a matter of course. . . .

Such methods to attain political ends are no longer widely practiced today. Yet the political motives for employing them exist today as they did when practices of this kind actually prevailed. It is not a matter of indifference for the nations engaged in the competition for power whether or not their competitor can avail itself of the services of outstanding military and political leaders. Thus they may hope that an outstanding leader or governing group will be compelled to give up the reins of power, either through a political upheaval or through infirmity and death. We know now that during the Second World War speculations as to how long Hitler and Mussolini would stay alive, or at least in power, formed an important part of the power calculations of the antifascist alliance, and that the news of President Roosevelt's death revived Hitler's hopes of victory. During the Cold War one factor in American policy toward the Soviet Union had been the expectation that the Soviet regime might disintegrate from within because of the inability of its rulers to keep themselves in power. The technical difficulties of engineering such removals from power by violent means are not greater today than they were in previous periods of history. Such removals are still as desirable and feasible as they always were. What has changed is the influence of civilization, which makes some desirable and feasible policies morally reprehensible and, hence, normally impossible of execution. . . .

A foreign policy that does not permit mass extermination as a means to its end does not impose this limitation upon itself because of considerations of political expediency. On the contrary, expediency would counsel such a thorough and effective operation. The limitation derives from an absolute moral principle, which must be obeyed regardless of considerations of national advantage. A foreign policy of this kind, therefore, actually sacrifices the national interest where its consistent pursuit would necessitate the violation of a moral principle, such as the prohibition of mass killings in times of peace. This point cannot be too strongly made; for frequently the opinion is advanced that this respect for human life is the outgrowth of "the obligation not to inflict *unnecessary* death or suffering on other human beings, i.e., death or suffering not necessary for the attainment of some higher purpose which is held, rightly or wrongly, to justify a derogation from the general obligation."[2] On the contrary, the fact of the matter is that nations recognize a moral obligation to refrain from the infliction of death and suffering under certain conditions despite the possibility of justifying such conduct in the light of a "higher purpose," such as the national interest. . . .

Protection of Human Life in War

Similar moral limitations are placed upon international policies in times of war. They concern civilians and combatants unable or unwilling to fight. From the beginning of history through the better part of the Middle Ages, belligerents were held to be free, according to ethics as well as law, to kill all enemies whether or not they were members of the armed forces, or else to treat them in any way they saw fit. Men, women, and children were often put to the sword or sold into slavery by the victor without any adverse moral reactions taking place. Hugo Grotius presents an impressive catalogue of acts of violence committed in ancient history against enemy persons without discrimination. Grotius himself, writing in the third decade of the seventeenth century, still regarded most of them as justified in law and ethics, provided the war was waged for a just cause.

This absence of moral restraints upon killing in war resulted from the nature of war itself. In those times war was considered a contest between all the inhabitants of the territories of the belligerent states. The enemy to be fought was the total number of individuals owing allegiance to a certain lord or living within a certain territory rather than the armed forces of the legal abstraction called a state in the modern sense. Thus every individual citizen of the enemy state became an enemy of every individual citizen of the other side. . . .

International Morality and Total War

Thus, in contrast to antiquity and the better part of the Middle Ages, the modern age places moral limitations upon the conduct of foreign affairs in so far as they might affect the lives of individuals or groups of individuals. However, certain important factors in the present condition of mankind point toward a definite weakening of those moral limitations. Let us remember that the absence of moral limitations with regard to the destruction of life was concomitant with the total character of warfare in which whole populations faced each other as personal enemies. Let us remember, too, that the gradual limitation of killing in war, and its subjection to certain conditions, coincided with the gradual development of limited war in which only armies faced each other as active opponents. With war taking on in recent times, to an ever greater degree and in different respects, a total character, the moral limitations upon killing are observed to an ever lessening degree. Indeed, their very existence in the consciences of political and military leaders as well as of the common people becomes ever more precarious and is threatened with extinction.

War in our time has become total in four different respects: (1) with regard to the fraction of the population engaged in activities essential for the conduct of the war, (2) with regard to the fraction of the population affected by the conduct of the war, (3) with respect to the fraction of the population completely identified in its convictions and emotions with the conduct of the war, and (4) with respect to the objective of the war.

Mass armies supported by the productive effort of the majority of the civilian population have replaced the relatively small armies of previous centuries, which consumed only a small portion of the national product. The success of the civilian population in keeping the armed forces supplied may be as important for the outcome of the war as the military effort itself. Therefore, the defeat of the civilian population (the breaking of its ability and will to produce) may be as important as the defeat of the armed forces (the breaking of their ability and will to resist). Thus the character of modern war, drawing its weapons from a vast industrial machine, blurs the distinction between soldier and civilian. The worker, the engineer, the scientist are not innocent bystanders cheering on the armed forces from the side lines. They are as intrinsic and indispensable a part of the military organization as are the soldiers, sailors, and airmen. Thus a modern nation at war must seek to disrupt and destroy the productive processes of its enemy, and the modern technology of war provides the means for the realization of that aim. The importance of civilian production for modern war and the interest in injuring enemy production were already generally recognized in the First World War. Then, however, the technological means of affecting the civilian productive processes directly were but in their infancy. The belligerents had to resort to indirect means, such as blockades and submarine warfare. They attempted to interfere directly with civilian life through air attacks and long-range bombardment only sporadically and with indifferent results. . . .

Modern war is in large measure push-button war, anonymously fought by people who have never seen their enemy alive or dead and who will never know whom they have killed. Nor will the victims ever see the face of the enemy. The only connection between the enemies is the machinery with which they try to kill each other. Such a technologically dehumanized war is bound to be morally dehumanized as well. For the operator of the machinery, the experience of target practice is hardly different from that of a real attack, and an attack upon a military installation is for him indistinguishable from that upon a civilian target. As a pilot who flew bombing missions in Vietnam put it: "It's like being trained to fix TV's, like being a technician." Thus the technology of modern war drastically weakens, if it does not destroy altogether, the ability to make those factual distinctions without which it is impossible to discriminate between moral and immoral acts of war.

Under the impact of this fundamental change in the conception of warfare, not only were the moral limitations upon killing in war . . . extensively violated during the Second World War, but belligerents have tended to justify on moral grounds the refusal to take prisoners, the killing of prisoners, and the indiscriminate killing of members of the armed forces and of civilians, and thus to assuage their moral scruples, if not to shake them off altogether. Thus, while the moral limitations upon killing in times of peace remain intact, the moral limitations upon killing in war have proved to be largely ineffective. What is by and large more important for the purposes of this discussion, they have shown a tendency under the impact of a fundamentally altered conception of war to weaken and disappear altogether as rules of conduct. . . .

▓ Notes

1. M. Ostrogorsky, *Democracy and the Organization of Political Parties* (New York: Macmillan, 1902), vol. II, p. 592.

2. E. H. Carr, *The Twenty Years' Crisis, 1919–1939* (London: Macmillan and Company, 1939), p. 196.

3 Pacifism

3.1 ———

Introduction
The Editors

In its purest and perhaps most coherent form, the doctrine of pacifism holds that war is never justified from a moral point of view. The philosophical origins of the doctrine are often said to lie in the works of Desiderius Erasmus of Rotterdam (1466–1536), but it is not clear that Erasmus was absolutely opposed to all war. Writing at the dawn of the sixteenth century, Erasmus was strongly opposed to warfare among Christians, and in his most powerful denunciation of war, *The Complaint of Peace,* argued that Christians ought never make war on one another. He also suggested in *The Complaint of Peace* that Christians ought not war against infidels either but should follow the teachings of Christ and embrace them as their brothers. However, in his *Instructions to a Christian Prince,* Erasmus conceded that there may be occasions when warfare against infidels is justified.

Erasmus condemned warfare on the grounds that there was never a justifiable reason for Christians to kill one another. Focusing almost exclusively on the initial cause of war, he contended that wars are invariably initiated by princes for vain, selfish, or ambitious reasons, none of which justify undertaking hostilities against fellow Christians or anyone else. In this he was followed by Leo Tolstoy, who also opposed war on the grounds that the motive to fight was invariably base and self-aggrandizing. But Tolstoy's opposition to war is arguably somewhat stronger than Erasmus's. Tolstoy condemns all war as little more than the most extreme example of human folly, ambition, and arrogance, while Erasmus held out the possibility that warfare against the infidels may be justified under certain circumstances. Tolstoy stands with Erasmus, however, in his belief that war is deeply objectionable from a moral point of view because princes or sovereign leaders require innocents to fight and die for their own interests and self-aggrandizement.

Pacifism is generally distinguished from the just war tradition on the grounds that war is never justifiable for the pacifist but is justified under specific identifiable circumstances under just war theory. The absolute opposition to war does not follow from the Erasmian view that war is invariably caused by the base motives of the prince who initiates hostilities. As we shall see, wars generated by such base motives are opposed by just war theorists as well as pacifists. Unlike pacifists, however, just war theorists hold that war is justified if it is fought for a morally worthwhile end and if it is fought in order to achieve this end. For pacifism to be coherent, the pacifist must claim that such reasons to fight simply cannot exist and, for this to make sense, pacifists must have strong reasons to hold that war, by its very nature, is the greatest of moral evils.

Because pacifism involves the strong *moral* opposition to war (unlike realism, which rejects the pertinence of any such opposition to war), the coherence of the doctrine of pacifism depends upon the pacifist's ability to advance moral reasons that justify the conclusion that under no circumstances should wars be fought. At this point, two strategies of argument are open to the pacifist. First, the pacifist could argue that war is immoral because it involves killing or violence, or both, and these are terrible moral wrongs. Moral philosophers sometimes refer to this as a deontological form of argument because it is premised upon certain principles that are presumed to obligate persons regardless of any concern for the greater good that might or might not be realized by setting them aside.

Erasmus seems to argue in this fashion. Christians ought not fight wars because war involves killing, and Christ's teaching tells us that it is wrong to kill fellow human beings. This puts an end to the matter for Erasmus (in spite of his attitude toward infidels) because Christ's command against killing is absolute and Christ spoke with the authority of God, whose word is law for all human beings. The argument is both simple and compelling, but it hits the rocks when we ask if one might not use violence, perhaps even deadly violence, in order to prevent some third party from taking another's life. This question does not challenge the moral imperative against killing, but it does call into question its absoluteness. Should a pacifist stand idly by while someone kills others even if the pacifist could prevent these deaths by intervening? To take Christ's admonition against killing in this absolute way may mean that the pacifist must allow great moral wrong to happen even though it is preventable. So there is room to wonder if faithfulness to the prohibition against killing might be interpreted in a way that permits a person to intervene, perhaps even with deadly force if necessary, to prevent a great loss of innocent life. Put more generally, it seems important to ask if the prohibition against killing works only as a negative restraint upon action or whether it requires good Christians to adopt an affirmative responsibility to help safeguard life when it is threatened by unscrupulous individuals.

In more secular times, pacifists may make much of Lockean claims about a natural right to life and liberty, and contend that killing in war is wrong absolutely because it violates one's right to life. But a similar problem, perhaps in even more pronounced form, arises here as well. If individuals have rights, ought not those with the ability to protect and preserve them assume an obligation to do so? Under just war theory, forceful intervention in the internal affairs of a state may be justifiable in order to defend the rights of innocents whose lives are threatened by more powerful groups in the state. Pacifists must reject this conclusion if they are to sustain their absolute prohibition against war, but it is not clear that they can manage to do this in a fashion consistent with their own belief in the natural rights of all persons.

It may be possible for pacifists to deflect some of these criticisms by adopting a theory of qualified pacifism. From the deontological perspective, war is wrong because it involves killing and/or violence and these things are wrong. Pacifists may qualify their argument, however, by saying that killing and violence are only prima facie wrong (i.e., wrong on the face of it) but not absolutely wrong. Cases of self-defense, necessity, and the protection of innocents may require the justifiable use of violence even up to the use of deadly force. But if pacifists qualify their argument in this way, it seems they must give up their strong stand on the absolute immorality of warfare. From the moral claim that killing is only prima facie wrong, it is not logically possible to conclude that war is absolutely wrong. The argument goes through only if it is also claimed (and justifiably) that killing in war never involves those things that count as legitimate exceptions to the prima facie claim that killing is wrong. But if violence, including deadly violence, is justifiable in situations of personal self-defense, it would seem that it must also be justifiable in the collective self-defense of the community and the individuals who comprise it. If, however, pacifists concede this and adjust their view to hold only that war is prima facie wrong, their argument has begun to slide toward just war theory.

The second way pacifists might support their absolute rejection of warfare as immoral is to advance a consequentialist argument. Consequentialism holds an action to be morally wrong if doing it would make people worse off than not doing it. But consequentialist reasoning cannot support the absolute rejection of warfare that characterizes pacifism. At most it can provide reasons for opposing particular wars, and then only if the outcome of fighting the war is projected to be worse than the outcome that will be realized if the war is not fought. For consequentialism to support the view that war is always immoral, it must be claimed that fighting a war will always and invariably produce a worse outcome than not fighting the war. But although pacifists might naturally think this to be true, it is simply not possible to know this in advance.

Nonetheless, Bertrand Russell's impassioned opposition to British involvement in World War I offers a powerful example of consequentialist pacifism. Russell supposes that passive resistance to Germany would be less costly to British life than involvement in the war. He imagines (and with little apparent evidence) that fewer British lives would be lost through passive resistance than from open hostilities. The carnage would be less, the cost of human life would be less, and eventually life in Britain would go on about as it did in the past.

There are, however, several problems with this argument. For one thing, given the stakes at issue, it seems terribly difficult to accomplish the cost-benefit analysis required by consequentialist argument. Russell merely imagines the likely outcome of passive resistance, but his imaginings may tragically underestimate the evil that might be done to Britain under German occupation. Further, even if Russell's musings about the likely outcome of passive resistance were generally accurate, the British might still have powerful principled reasons to engage in war. Imagine that German occupation brought with it a policy to enslave a portion of the British population and that even here this outcome was still better than the loss of life that would plausibly result from engaging in warfare. There is still something objectionable about thinking that the citizens of Britain should stand idly by while the Germans systematically enslave some of their fellow citizens. Here it is tempting to think that consequentialist thinking simply breaks down, and citizens have an obligation to protect and defend the lives of their neighbors regardless of the potential cost. Pacifism, at the very least, is a controversial and troubled doctrine.

Pacifists are certainly right to find war morally abhorrent, but there are other morally abhorrent aspects of humankind's inhumanity that may rival and even surpass warfare. If so, there may be times when war seems a morally justifiable response to desperately inhuman conduct. If this possibility is granted, pacifism becomes a difficult doctrine to sustain.

3.2 ⸻

The Complaint of Peace

Desiderius Erasmus

Now, if I, whose name is Peace, am a personage glorified by the united praise of God and man, as the fountain, the parent, the nurse, the patroness, the guardian of every blessing which either heaven or earth can bestow; if without me nothing is flourishing, nothing safe, nothing pure or holy, nothing pleasant to mortals, or grateful to the Supreme Being; if, on the contrary, war is one vast ocean, rushing on mankind, of all the united plagues and pestilences in nature; if, at its deadly approach, every blossom of happiness is instantly blasted, every thing that was improving gradually degenerates and dwindles away to nothing, every thing that was firmly supported totters on its foundation, every thing that was formed for long duration comes to a speedy end, and every thing that was sweet by nature is turned into bitterness; if war is so unhallowed that it becomes the deadliest bane of piety and religion; if there is nothing more calamitous to mortals, and more detestable to heaven, I ask, how in the name of God, can I believe those beings to be rational creatures; how can I believe them to be otherwise than stark mad; who, with such a waste of treasure, with so ardent a zeal, with so great an effort, with so many arts, so much anxiety, and so much danger, endeavour to drive me away from them, and purchase endless misery and mischief at a price so high?

If they were wild beasts who thus despised and rejected me, I could bear it more patiently; because I should impute the affront to nature, who had implanted in them so savage a disposition. If I were an object of hatred to dumb creatures, I could overlook their ignorance, because the powers of mind necessary to perceive my excellence have been denied to them. But it is a circumstance equally shameful and marvelous, that though nature has formed one animal, and one alone, with powers of reason, and a mind participating of divinity; one animal, and one alone, capable of sentimental affection and social union; I can find admission among the wildest of wild beasts, and the most brutal of brutes, sooner than with this one animal; the rational, immortal animal called man. . . .

By such and so many plain indications of her meaning has Nature

From *The Complaint of Peace* by Desiderius Erasmus, translated from the *Querela Pacis* (A.D. 1521) of Erasmus. Chicago: Open Court, 1917.

taught mankind to seek peace, and ensure it. She invites them to it by various allurements, she draws them to it by gentle violence, she compels them to it by the strong arm of necessity. After all, then, what infernal being, all-powerful in mischief, bursting every bond of nature asunder, fills the human bosom with an insatiable rage for war? If familiarity with the sight had not first destroyed all surprise at it, and custom, soon afterwards, blunted the sense of its evil, who could be prevailed upon to believe that those wretched beings are possessed of rational souls, the intellects and feelings of human creatures, who contend, with all the rage of furies, in everlasting feuds, and litigations, ending in murder! Robbery, blood, butchery, desolation, confound, without distinction, every thing sacred and profane. The most hallowed treaties, mutually confirmed by the strongest sanctions, cannot stop the enraged parties from rushing on to mutual destruction, whenever passion or mistaken interest urges them to the irrational decision of the battle.

Though there were no other motive to preserve peace, one would imagine that the common name of man might be sufficient to secure concord between all who claim it. But be it granted that Nature has no effect on men as men (though we have seen that Nature rules as she ought to do in the brute creation), yet, must not Christ therefore avail with Christians? Be it granted that the suggestions of nature have no effect with a rational being (though we see them have great weight even on inanimate things without sense), yet, as the suggestions of the Christian religion are far more excellent than those of nature, why does not the Christian religion persuade those who profess it, of a truth which it recommends above all others, that is, the expediency and necessity of peace on earth, and good-will towards men; or at least, why does it fail of effectually dissuading from the unnatural, and more than brutal, madness of waging war?

When I, whose name is Peace, do but hear the word Man pronounced, I eagerly run to him as to a being created purposely for me, and confidently promising myself, that with him I may live for ever in uninterrupted tranquility; but when I also hear the title of Christian added to the name of Man, I fly with additional speed, hoping that with Christians I may build an adamantine throne, and establish an everlasting empire. . . .

At the nativity of Christ did the angels sound the clarion of war? The horrid din might have been addressed to the ears of Jews, for they were allowed to wage war. Such auspices were well enough adapted to those who thought it lawful to hate their enemies; but to the pacific race of future Christians, the angels of peace sounded a far different note. Did they blow the shrill trumpet? Did they promise triumphs and trophies of victory? Far from it. What then did they announce? Peace and good will, in conformity with the predictions of the prophets; and they announced them not to those who breathe war and bloodshed, who delight in the instruments of destruction, but to those whose hearts are inclined to concord.

Let me cover their malice with what cloke they please; it is certain, that if they did not delight in war, they would not be constantly engaged in its conflicts.

But as for Christ, what else did he teach and inculcate, but peace? He addressed those whom he loved, with the auspicious words of peace: Peace be with you, he repeatedly says; and prescribes this form of salutation, as alone worthy of the Christian character. And the apostles, duly mindful of his precept and example, preface their epistles with a wish for peace to those whom they love. He who wishes health to his friend, wishes a most desirable blessing; but he who wishes him peace, wishes him the summit of human felicity.

As Christ had recommended peace during the whole of his life, mark with what anxiety he enforces it at the approach of his dissolution. Love one another, says he; as I have loved you, so love one another; and again, my peace I give unto you, my peace I leave you. Do you observe the legacy he leaves to those whom he loves? Is it a pompous retinue, a large estate, or empire? Nothing of this kind. What is it then? Peace he giveth, his peace he leaveth; peace, not only with our near connexions, but with enemies and strangers! . . .

When Christ calls himself the vine, and his disciples the branches, what else did he mean to express, but the most perfect union between him and them, and between themselves? It would be a prodigy, indeed, if a branch were to contend with a branch of the same tree; and, is it less a prodigy, that a Christian fights with a Christian?

If there be anything sacred to Christians, surely that ought to be deemed singularly sacred, and to sink deeply into their hearts, which Christ delivered to them in his last dying commands; when he was, as it were, making his will and testament, and recommending to his sons those things which he wished might never fall into oblivion. And what is it which, on this solemn occasion, he teaches, commands, prescribes, entreats; but that they should preserve inviolate, mutual good-will, or charity? And what means the communion of the holy bread and wine, but a renewed sanction of indissoluble amity? As Christ knew that Peace could not be preserved, where men were struggling for office, for glory, for riches, for revenge, he roots out from the hearts of his disciples all passions which lead to these things; he forbids them absolutely and without exception, to resist evil; he commands them to do good to those who use them ill, and to pray for those who curse them. And, after this, shall kings presume to think themselves Christians, who, on the slightest injury embroil the world in war? . . .

God made man unarmed. But anger and revenge have mended the work of God, and furnished his hands with weapons invented in hell. Christians attack Christians with engines of destruction, fabricated by the devil. A cannon! a mortar! no human being could have devised them originally; they must have been suggested by the evil one. Nature, indeed, has armed lions with teeth and claws, and bulls with horns; but who ever saw them go in bodies to use their arms for mutual destruction? What man ever saw so small a number as even ten lions congregated to fight ten bulls, and drawn up in battle array? But how often have twenty thousand Christians met an equal number on the same plain, all prepared to shoot each other, through the heart, or to plunge the sword or bayonet through each other's bowels. So little account do they make of hurting their brethren, that they have not the smallest scruple to spill every drop of blood in their bodies. Beasts of the forest; your contests are at least excusable, and sometimes amiable; ye fight only when driven to madness by hunger, or to defend your young ones; but as for those who call themselves your lords (men and Christians) the faintest shadow of an affront is sufficient to involve them in all the horrors of premeditated war. . . .

But I am well aware of the excuse which men, ever ingenious in devising mischief to themselves as well as others, offer in extenuation of their conduct in going to war. They allege, that they are compelled to it; that they are dragged against their will to war. I answer them, deal fairly; pull off the mask; throw away all false colours; consult your own heart, and you will find that anger, ambition, and folly are the compulsory force that has dragged you to war, and not any necessity; unless indeed you call the insatiable cravings of a covetous mind, necessity.

Reserve your outside pretences to deceive the thoughtless vulgar. God is not mocked with paint and varnish. Solemn days and forms of fasting, prayer, and thanksgiving, are appointed. Loud petitions are offered up to heaven for peace. The priests and the people roar out as vociferously as they can "give peace in our time, O Lord! We beseech thee to hear us, O Lord." Might not the Lord very justly answer and say, "why mock ye me, ye hypocrites? You fast and pray that I would avert a calamity which you have brought upon your own heads. You are deprecating an evil, of which yourselves are the authors." . . .

There is scarcely any peace so unjust, but it is preferable, upon the whole, to the justest war. Sit down, before you draw the sword, weigh every article, omit none, and compute the expence of blood as well as treasure which war requires, and the evils which it of necessity brings with it; and then see at the bottom of the account whether, after the greatest success, there is likely to be a balance in your favour. . . .

Let kings then grow wise; wise for the people, not for themselves only; and let them be truly wise, in the proper sense of the word, not merely cunning, but really wise; so as to place their majesty, their felicity, their wealth, and their splendor in such things, and such only, as render them personally great, personally superior to those whom the fortune of birth has ranked, in a civil sense, below them. Let them acquire those amiable dispositions towards the commonwealth, the great body of the people, which a father feels for his family. Let a king think himself great in proportion as his people are good; let him estimate his own happiness by the happiness of those whom he governs; let him deem himself glorious in proportion as his subjects are free; rich, if the public are rich; and flourishing, if he can but keep the community flourishing, in consequence of uninterrupted peace.

Such should be our king, if we wish to establish a firm and lasting peace; and let the noblemen and magistrates imitate the king, rendered by these means worthy of imitation. Let the public good be the rule of their conduct; and so will they ultimately promote most effectually even their own private advantage. . . .

There are occasions when, if peace can be had in no other way, it must be purchased. It can scarcely be purchased too dearly, if you take into the account how much treasure you must inevitably expend in war; and what is of infinitely greater consequence than treasure, how many of the people's lives you save by peace. Though the cost be great, yet war would certainly cost you more; besides (what is above all price) the blood of men, the blood of your own fellow-citizens and subjects, whose lives you are bound, by every tie of duty, to preserve, instead of lavishing away in prosecuting schemes of false policy, and cruel, selfish, villainous ambition. Only form a fair estimate of the quantity of mischief and misery of every kind and degree which you escape, and the sum of happiness you preserve in all the walks of private life, among all the tender relations of parents, husbands, children, among those whose poverty alone makes them soldiers, the wretched instruments of involuntary bloodshed; form but this estimate, and you will never repent the highest price you can pay for peace. . . .

But if there is a fatal propensity in the human heart to war, if the dreadful disease is interwoven with the constitution of man, so that it cannot abstain from war, why is not vent given to the virulence in exertions against the common enemy of Christianity, the unbelieving Turk? Yet—even here let me pause—is not the Turk a man—a brother? Then it were far better to allure him by gentle, kind, and friendly treatment, by exhibiting the beauty of our Christian religion in the innocence of our lives, than by attacking him with the drawn sword, as if he were a savage brute, without a heart to feel, or a reasoning faculty to be persuaded. Nevertheless, if we must of necessity go to war, as I said before, it is certainly a less evil to contend with an infidel, than that Christians should mutually harass and destroy their own fraternity. If charity will not cement their hearts, certainly one common enemy may unite their hands, and though this may not be a cordial unity, yet it will be better than a real rupture.

Upon the whole it must be said, that the first and most important step towards peace, is sincerely to desire it. They who once love peace in their hearts, will eagerly seize every opportunity of establishing or recovering it.

All obstacles to it they will despise or remove, all hardships and difficulties they will bear with patience, so long as they keep this one great blessing (including as it does so many others) whole and entire. On the contrary, men, in our times, go out of their way to seek occasions of war; and whatever makes for peace, they run down in their sophistical speeches, or even basely conceal from the public; but whatever tends to promote their favourite war system, they industriously exaggerate and inflame, not scrupling to propagate lies of the most mischievous kind, false or garbled intelligence, and the grossest misrepresentation of the enemy. I am ashamed to relate what real and dreadful tragedies in real life, they found on these vile despicable trifles, from how small an ember they blow up a flame and set the world on fire. Then they summon before them the whole catalogue of supposed injuries received, and each party views its own grievance with a glass that magnifies beyond all bounds; but as for benefits received, they all fall into the profoundest oblivion as soon as received; so that upon the whole, an impartial observer would swear that great men love war for its own sake, with their hearts and souls, provided their own persons are safe.

After all the pretences thrown out, and the artifices used, to irritate the vulgar, there often lurks (as the true cause of wars) in the bosom of kings, some private, mean, and selfish motive, which is to force their subjects to take up weapons to kill one another, at the word of command, and as they wish to evince their loyalty. But, instead of a private and selfish object, there ought to be an object, in which not only the public, that is, not only one single community, but in which man, human nature, is deeply interested to justify the voluntary commencement of a war.

But when kings can find no cause of this kind, as indeed they seldom can, then they set their wits to work to invent some fictitious but plausible occasion for a rupture. They will make use of the names of foreign countries, artfully rendered odious to the people, in order to feed the popular odium, till it becomes ripe for war, and thirsts for the blood of the outlandish nation, whose very name is rendered a cause of hostility. This weakness and folly of the very lowest classes of the people, the grandees increase by artful insinuations, watchwords, and nicknames, cunningly thrown out in debates, pamphlets, and journals. Certain of the clergy, whose interest it is to cooperate with the grandees in any unchristian work, join, with great effect, aided by religion, in a pious imposition on the poor. . . .

I appeal to all who call themselves Christians! I urge them, as they would manifest their sincerity, and preserve their consistency, to unite with one heart and one soul, in the abolition of war, and the establishment of perpetual and universal peace. . . .

3.3 _____

Last Message to Mankind
Leo Tolstoy

Dear Brothers,

We have met here to fight against war. War, the thing for the sake of which all the nations of the earth—millions and millions of people—place at the uncontrolled disposal of a few men or sometimes only one man, not merely milliards of rubles, talers, francs or yen (representing a very large share of their labor), but also their very lives.

And now we, a score of private people gathered from the various ends of the earth, possessed of no special privileges and above all having no power over anyone, intend to fight—and as we wish to fight we also wish to conquer—this immense power not only of one government but of all governments, which have at their disposal these milliards of money and millions of soldiers and who are well aware that the exceptional position of those who for the governments rests on the army alone: the army which has a meaning and a purpose against which we wish to fight and which we wish to abolish.

For us to struggle, the forces being so unequal, must appear insane. But if we consider our opponent's means of strife and our own, it is not our intention to fight that will seem absurd, but that the thing we mean to fight will still exist. They have millions of money and millions of obedient soldiers; we have only one thing, but that is the most powerful thing in the world—Truth. . . .

The truth in its full meaning lies in what was said thousands of years ago (in the law accepted among us as the Law of God) in four words: "Thou shalt not kill." The truth is that man may not and should not in any circumstances or under any pretext kill his fellow man.

The truth is so evident, so binding, and so generally acknowledged, that it is only necessary to put it clearly before men for the evil called war to become quite impossible.

And so I think that if we who are assembled here at this Peace Congress should, instead of clearly and definitely voicing this truth, address ourselves to the governments with various proposals for lessening the evils of war or

---

From "Last Message to Mankind" by Leo Tolstoy. Written for the 18th International Peace Congress held at Stockholm in 1909.

gradually diminishing its frequency, we should be like men who having in their hand the key to a door, should try to break through walls they know to be too strong for them.

Before us are millions of armed men, ever more and more efficiently armed and trained for more and more rapid slaughter. We know that these millions of people have no wish to kill their fellows and for the most part do not even know why they are forced to do that repulsive work, and that they are weary of their position of subjection and compulsion; we know that the murders committed from time to time by these men are committed by order of the governments; and we know that the existence of the governments depends on the armies.

Can we then who desire the abolition of war, find nothing more conducive to our aim than to propose to the governments which exist only by the aid of armies and consequently by war—measures which would destroy war? Are we to propose to the governments that they should destroy themselves?

The governments will listen willingly to any speeches of that kind, knowing that such discussions will neither destroy war nor undermine their own power, but will only conceal yet more effectively what must be concealed if wars and armies and themselves in control of armies are to continue to exist.

"But," I shall be told, "this is anarchism; people never have lived without governments and States, and therefore governments and States and military forces defending them are necessary for the existence of nations."

But leaving aside the question of whether the life of Christian and other nations is possible without armies and wars to defend their governments and States, or even supposing it to be necessary for their welfare that they should slavishly submit to institutions called governments (consisting of people they do not personally know), and that it is necessary to yield up the produce of their labor to these institutions and fulfill all their demands—including the murder of their neighbors—granting them all that, there yet remains in our world an unsolved difficulty.

This difficulty lies in the impossibility of making the Christian faith (which those who form the governments profess with particular emphasis) accord with armies composed of Christians trained to slay. However much you may pervert the Christian teaching, however much you may hide its main principles, its fundamental teaching is the love of God and one's neighbor; of God—that is the highest perfection of virtue, and of one's neighbor—that is all men without distinction. And therefore it would seem inevitable that we must repudiate one of the two, either Christianity is love of God and one's neighbor, or the State with its armies and wars.

Perhaps Christianity may be obsolete, and when choosing between the two—Christianity and love of the State and murder—the people of our time will conclude that the existence of the State and murder is more important than Christianity, we must forgo Christianity and retain only what is important: the State and murder.

That may be so—at least people may think and feel so. But in that case they should say so! They should openly admit that people in our time have ceased to believe in what the collective wisdom of mankind has said, and what is said by the Law of God they profess: have ceased to believe in what is written indelibly on the heart of each man, and must now believe only in what is ordered by various people who by accident or birth have happened to become emperors and kings, or by various intrigues and elections have become presidents or members of senates and parliaments—even if those orders include murder. That is what they ought to say!

But it is impossible to say it; and yet one of these two things has to be said. If it is admitted that Christianity forbids murder, both armies and governments become impossible. And if it is admitted that government acknowledges the lawfulness of murder and denies Christianity, no one will wish to obey a government that exists merely by its power to kill. And besides, if murder is allowed in war it must be still more allowable when a people seek its rights in a revolution. And therefore the governments, being unable to say either one thing or the other, are anxious to hide from their subjects the necessity of solving the dilemma.

And for us who are assembled here to counteract the evil of war, if we really desire to attain our end, only one thing is necessary: namely to put that dilemma quite clearly and definitely both to those who form governments and to the masses of the people who compose the army.

To do that we must not only clearly and openly repeat the truth we all know and cannot help knowing—that man should not slay his fellow man—but we must also make it clear that no considerations can destroy the demand made by the truth on people in the Christian world.

Therefore I propose that our Meeting draw up and publish an appeal to all men, and especially to the Christian nations, in which we clearly and definitely express what everybody knows, but hardly anyone says: namely war is not—as most people assume—a good and laudable affair, but that like all murder, it is a vile and criminal business not only for those who voluntarily choose a military career but for those who submit to it from avarice, or fear of punishment.

With regard to those who voluntarily choose a military career, I would propose to state clearly and definitely that notwithstanding all the pomp, glitter, and general approval with which it is surrounded, it is a criminal and shameful activity; and that the higher the position a man holds in the military profession the more criminal and shameful his occupation.

In the same way with regard to men of the people who are drawn into military service by bribes or by threats of punishments, I propose to speak clearly about the gross mistake they make—contrary to their faith, morality and common sense—when they consent to enter the army; contrary to their faith because when they enter the ranks of murderers contrary to the Law of God which they acknowledge; contrary to morality, because for pay or from fear of punishment they agreed to what in their souls they know to be wrong; and contrary to common sense, because if they enter the army and war breaks out they risk having to suffer any consequences, bad or worse than those they are threatened with if they refuse. Above all they act contrary to common sense in that they join that caste of people which deprives them of freedom and compels them to be soldiers.

With reference to both classes I propose in this appeal to express clearly the thought that for men of true enlightenment, who are therefore free from the superstition of military glory (and their number is growing every day), the military profession and calling notwithstanding all the efforts to hide its real meaning, is as shameful a business as the executioner's and even more so. For the executioner only holds himself in readiness to kill those who have been adjudged to be harmful and criminal, while a soldier promises to kill all who he is told to kill, even though they may be the dearest to him or the best of men.

Humanity in general, and our Christian humanity in particular, has reached a stage of such acute contradiction between its moral demands and the existing social order, that a change has become inevitable, and a change not in society's moral demand which are immutable, but in the social order which can be altered. The demand for a different social order, evoked by that inner contradiction which is so clearly illustrated by our preparations for murder, becomes more and more insistent every year and every day. . . .

What form of life men will take after they repudiate murder we do not and cannot know; but one thing is certain: that it is more natural for men to be guided by reason and conscience with which they are endowed, than to submit slavishly to people who arrange wholesale murders; and that therefrom the form of social order assumed by the lives of those who are guided in their actions not by violence based on threats of murder, but by reason and conscience, will in any case be no worse than that under which they now live.

That is all I want to say. I shall be sorry if it offends or grieves anyone or evokes any ill feeling. But for me, a man eighty years old, expecting to die at any moment, it would be shameful and criminal not to speak out the whole truth as I understand it—the truth which, as I firmly believe, is alone capable of relieving mankind from the incalculable ills produced by war.

3.4 _____

War and Non-Resistance

Bertrand Russell

The principle that it is always wrong to employ force against another human being has been held in its extreme form by Quakers and by Tolstoy, but has always been rejected by the great majority of mankind as inconsistent with the existence of civilized society. In this, no doubt, the majority of mankind are in the right. But I think that the occasions where forcible resistance is the best course are much fewer than is generally believed, and that some very great and important advances in civilization might be made if this were more widely recognized. The so-called "right of self-defence," in particular, seems to have only a very to limited sphere of application, and to be often supported by arguments involving both mistakes as to political questions and a wrong conception of the best type of character.

No one who holds that human conduct ought to be such as to promote certain ends—no matter what ends may be selected—will expect any absolute hard-and-fast rules of conduct to which no possible exception can be found. Not to lie, not to steal, not to murder, are very good precepts for ordinary cases: it may be, in view of the likelihood of biased judgments, that most men will act better if they always follow these precepts unquestioningly than if they consider each case on its merits. Nevertheless, it is obvious that there are cases where lying and stealing are justifiable, and the same must be said of murder by those who hold that some wars are righteous. Tolstoy does not judge conduct by its consequences: he considers actions inherently right or wrong. This makes it possible for him to say that no use of force is ever right. But if we judge conduct, as I think we ought, by its power of promoting what we consider a good life or a good society, we cannot expect such simplicity in our moral precepts, and we must expect all of them to be subject to exceptions. Whatever we may have to say must be regarded as in the nature of practical maxims, to be applied with common sense, not as logically universal rules to be tested by extreme cases.

Broadly speaking, I think the use of force is justifiable when it is ordered in accordance with law by a neutral authority, in the general interest

From *Prophecy and Dissent, 1914–16* (The Collected Papers of Bertrand Russell, Volume 13), ed. Richard A Rempel et al. London: Unwin Hyman, 1988. Excerpt from chap. 28 ("War and Non-Resistance").

and not primarily in the interest of one of the parties to the quarrel. On this ground, the use of force by the police is justifiable, provided (as is no doubt sometimes the case) the authorities are employing the police in the general interest and not merely in the interest of the holders of power. In international affairs, if there were a Council of the Powers, strong enough to restrain any aggressive nation without great difficulty, any army or navy employed in obedience to its orders might be regarded as a police force, and justified on the same grounds on which the police are justified. I think there is more hope of ultimately achieving universal peace by this method than by the adoption of non-resistance. But this has no bearing upon the question whether non-resistance would be a good policy, if any nation could be induced to adopt it. So long as no Council of the Powers exists there is no neutral authority to order resistance, and we have to consider the justification of repelling an attack when the nation attacked is the judge in its own cause.

The justification of non-resistance is more easily seen in the case of quarrels between individuals. If I encountered the traditional highwayman, and he demanded my money or my life, I should unhesitatingly give him my money, even if it were in my power to shoot him before he shot me. I should do this, not from cowardice or lack of spirit, but because I would rather part with money than have a man's blood on my conscience. And for the same reason, if I were compelled to engage in a duel, I would rather let my adversary shoot me than shoot him. In this I believe all humane people would agree. At the same time, if he were a worthless fellow, and I had just made an important mathematical discovery which I had not yet had time to record, it might be right to preserve my life at his expense. Arguments of this sort would justify civilized communities in defending themselves against savages. But conflicts between civilized nations are more like conflicts between rival metaphysicians, each of whom considers his own system admirable and the other man's abominable, while to outsiders it is obvious that both are equally fantastic.

In private life, most situations can be met by the double principle of neither employing force nor obeying it. It is a familiar Platonic thesis that the man who inflicts injustice is more to be pitied than the man who suffers it. But such statements are read with a smile, as charming literary paradoxes, and are not taken as practical wisdom for the guidance of life. Yet the use of force to coerce another man's will, even in those rare cases in which it is justifiable, produces a brutal and tyrannous state of mind, and is more destructive of inward peace than any misfortune that can be inflicted from without. The greatest good that can be achieved in this life is to have will and desire directed to universal ends, purged of the self-assertion which belongs to instinctive will. A man who has once known this good will not consider any private end important enough to be fought for: he may be willing to enter upon a contest of force, but if so, it will be for some end outside his own life, since what is best in his own life cannot be taken from him by another. But although he will not dictate to others for his own ends, he will also not be turned aside from universal ends by others: he will be no more willing to obey than to command. He will preserve his own liberty as scrupulously as he respects the liberty of others.

Exactly similar considerations apply to the conduct of nations, but they are obscured by traditional phrases about "honour," "patriotism," "sacred traditions," or "the protection of women and children." It is assumed that a nation which does not oppose force with force must be actuated by cowardice, and must lose whatever is valuable in its civilization. Both these are illusions. To oppose force by passive non-obedience would require more courage, and would be far more likely to preserve the best elements of the national life. It would also do far more to discourage the use of force. This would be the way of practical wisdom, if men could be brought to believe it. But I fear men are too much wedded to the belief that patriotism is a virtue, and too fond of proving their superiority to others in a contest of force. People who object to the doctrine that might is right always contend that it will be disproved by showing that might is on their own side. Yet that would only be a disproof if their side were in the wrong, and their argument shows that they really believe the doctrine they are pretending to combat. Those who genuinely disbelieve the doctrine will not attempt to disprove it by getting might on their side.

Let us imagine that England were to disband its army and navy, after a generation of instruction in the principles of passive resistance as a better defence than war. Let us suppose that England at the same time publicly announced that no armed opposition would be offered to an invader, that all might come freely, but that no obedience would be yielded to any commands that a foreign authority might issue. What would happen in this case?

Suppose, to continue the argument, that the German Government wished to take advantage of England's defenceless condition. It would be faced, at the outset, by the opposition of whatever was not utterly brutal in Germany, since no possible cloak could be found to hide the nakedness of aggression. All civilized countries, when they engage in war, find some decent excuse: they fight, almost always, either in self-defence or in defence of the weak. No such excuse could be found in this case. It could no longer be said, as the Germans now say, that England's naval preponderance keeps other nations in bondage, and threatens the very existence of any nation which depends upon imported food. It could no longer be said that we were oppressing India, since India would be able to separate from the British Empire whenever it wished to do so. All the usual pretexts by which aggression is justified would be lacking. . . .

If England had no army and no navy, the Germans would be hard put to find a pretext for invasion. All the Liberal elements in Germany would oppose any such enterprise; so would all other nations, unless Germany offered them a share of the plunder. But let us suppose all home opposition overcome, and a force dispatched to England to take possession of the country. Such a force, since it would meet with no military opposition, would not need to be large, and would not be in the state of mingled fear and ferocity which characterizes an invading army among a hostile population. There would be no difficulty in preserving military discipline, and no opportunity for the rape and rapine which have always been displayed by troops after victory in battle. There would be no glory to be won, not even enough to earn one iron cross. The Germans could not congratulate themselves upon their military prowess, or imagine that they were displaying the stern self-abnegation believed to be shown by willingness to die in the fight. To the soldierly mind, the whole expedition would be ridiculous, causing a feeling of disgust instead of pride. Perhaps a few impudent street-boys might have to have their ears boxed, but otherwise there would be nothing to lend dignity to the expedition.

However, we will suppose the invading army arrived in London, where they would evict the King from Buckingham Palace and the Members from the House of Commons. A few able bureaucrats would be brought over from Berlin to consult with the Civil Servants in Whitehall as to the new laws by which the reign of Kultur was to be inaugurated. No difficulty would be expected in managing so tame a nation, and at first almost all the existing officials would be confirmed in their offices. For the government of a large modern State is a complicated matter, and it would be thought well to facilitate the transition by the help of men familiar with the existing machinery.

But at this point, if the nation showed as much courage as it has always shown in fighting, difficulties would begin. All the existing officials would refuse to cooperate with the Germans. Some of the more prominent would be imprisoned, perhaps even shot, in order to encourage the others. But if the others held firm, if they refused to recognize or transmit any order given by Germans, if they continued to carry out the decrees previously made by the English Parliament and the English Government, the Germans would have to dismiss them all, even to the humblest postman, and call in German talent to fill the breach.

The dismissed officials could not all be imprisoned or shot: since no fighting would have occurred, such wholesale brutality would be out of the question. And it would be very difficult for the Germans suddenly, out of nothing, to create an administrative machine. Whatever edicts they might issue would be quietly ignored by the population. If they ordered that German should be the language taught in schools, the schoolmasters would go on as if no such order had been issued; if the schoolmasters were dismissed, the parents would no longer send the children to school. If they ordered that English young men should undergo military service, the young men would simply refuse; after shooting a few, the Germans would have to give up the attempt in despair. If they tried to raise revenue by customs duties at the ports, they would have to have German customs officers; this would lead to a strike of all the dock labourers, so that this way of raising revenue would become impossible. If they tried to take over the railways, there would be a strike of the railway servants. Whatever they touched would instantly become paralyzed, and it would soon be evident, even to them, that nothing was to be made out of England unless the population could be conciliated.

Such a method of dealing with invasion would, of course, require fortitude and discipline. But fortitude and discipline are required in war. For ages past, education has been largely directed to producing these qualities for the sake of war. They now exist so widely that in every civilized country almost every man is willing to die on the battlefield whenever his Government thinks the moment suitable. The same courage and idealism which are now put into war could quite easily be directed by education into the channel of passive resistance. I do not know what losses England may suffer before the present war is ended, but if they amount to a million no one will be surprised. An immensely smaller number of losses, incurred in passive resistance, would prove to any invading army that the task of subjecting England to alien domination was an impossible one. And this proof would be made once for all, without dependence upon the doubtful accidents of war. . . .

But it may be said that, even if the Germans could not actually take over the government of England, or rob us of internal self-government, they could do two things which would injure us vitally: they could take away our Empire, and they could lévy a tribute by the threat of depriving us of food supplies.

The Germans could not take away the self-governing parts of our Empire, since they would encounter there the same difficulties as would prevent them from governing England. They could take away those parts of our Empire which we hold by force, and this would be a blow to our pride: the oppression of subject races is one of the chief sources of patriotic satisfaction, and one of the chief things for which Germany envies us. But it is not a source of pride to any rational or humane man. European rule over uncivilized races is, in fact, a very sordid affair. The best of the men whom it employs are those engaged in the attempt at government, who live in exile and usually die of fever; the rest grow rich selling rum to natives or making them work in mines. Meanwhile the natives degenerate: some die of drink, some of diseases caught from white men, some of consumption in the mines; those who survive contract the vices of civilization without losing the vices of barbarism. It can only be a blessing to any nation to be deprived of this source of pride, which is a canker of corruption and immorality in the life of democratic communities.

That the Germans could levy a tribute on England by threatening our food supplies is obviously true. The ethics of such a demand would be exactly the same as that of the highwayman who demands "your money or your life." The same reasons which would lead a reasonable man to give his money rather than shoot or be shot would also lead a reasonable nation to give a tribute rather than resist by force of arms. The greatest sum that foreigners could theoretically exact would be the total economic rent of the land and natural resources of England. In fact, economic rent may be defined as what can be, and historically has been, extorted by such means. . . .

It is very doubtful, indeed, whether the Germans would exact from us a larger tribute than we exact from ourselves in resisting them. There is no knowing what this war will have cost England when it ends, but we shall probably not exaggerate if we place the cost at a thousand million pounds. This represents an annual payment of forty million pounds. All this, together with the annual expenditure on our Army and Navy, we might have paid to the Germans without being any poorer than we shall be when the war ends. This represents an incredibly larger tribute than we derive from India; yet the Germans assure us that we are full of commercial cunning, and that we govern India solely for our own profit. If they believe this, it is hardly to be supposed that the receipt of such a tribute would fail to satisfy them. Meanwhile we should have avoided the death of our young men, the moral degradation of almost our whole population, and the lowering of the standard of civilization slowly achieved through centuries which were peaceful in comparison with our present condition.

But, of course, all that I have been saying is fantastic, degrading, and out of touch with reality. I have been assuming that men are to some extent guided by reason, that their actions are directed to ends such as "life, liberty, and the pursuit of happiness." This is not the case. Death, slavery, and unhappiness (for others) are the chief ends pursued by States in their external relations. It is the preference of such ends to one's own happiness that constitutes patriotism, that shows a man to be free from materialism, and that raises him above the commercial, money-grubbing level of the mere shopkeeper. The Prussian feels himself noble because he is willing to be killed provided men of other nations are killed at the same time. His nobility and his freedom from commercialism consists in the fact that he desires the misery of others more than his own happiness. And there is a Prussian lurking in each of us, ready to make us reject any national advantage which is not purchased by injury to some other nation. It is this lurking Prussian in our instincts who assures us that a policy of non-resistance would be tame and cowardly, unworthy of a great and proud nation, a failure to perform our duty of chastizing an exactly similar pride in other nations.

Pride has its place among virtues, in the lives of individuals as well as in the lives of nations. Pride, in so far as it is a virtue, is a determination not to be turned aside from the ends which a man thinks good, no matter what outside pressure may be brought to bear upon him. . . . Such pride is the noblest form of courage: it shows that self-determination of the will which is the essence of spiritual freedom. But such pride should have as its complement a just conception of what constitutes human welfare, and as its correlative a respect for the freedom of others as absolute as the determination to preserve freedom for ourselves. Exactly the same kind of pride is good in the life of a nation. If we think ill of war, while some other nation thinks well of it, let us show our national pride by living without war, whatever temptations the other nation may put in our way to live according to their ideals rather than according to our own. . . .

But this kind of pride is not the kind which patriots exhort us to display. The pride that they admire is the kind which aims at thwarting others; it is the pride of power. . . . This kind of pride consists merely in love of dominion. Dominion and power can only be conclusively shown by compelling others to forego what they desire. By a natural consequence, those in whom the love of power is strong are led to inflict pain and to use force against the perfectly legitimate desires of those whom they wish to subdue. In nations, this attitude is commended. Generally the heroes of a nation's history are not those who have benefited mankind, but those who have injured other nations. If we prided ourselves upon the good and not the harm that we have done, we should have put Shakespeare on the Nelson Monument, and given Apsley House to Darwin. But the citizens whom every nation honours most are those who have killed the greatest number of foreigners.

It is this pride of power which makes us unwilling to yield to others in matters of no intrinsic importance. The Germans cherish a desire to own African swamps, of which we have a superfluity. No one in England benefits by the possession of them, except a few financial magnates, mostly of foreign origin. If we were reasonable, we should regard the German desire as a curious whim, which we might gratify without any real national loss. Instead of that, we regard the German desire as a crime, and our resistance to it as a virtue. We teach school children to rejoice because so much of the map is painted red. In order that as much as possible may be painted red, we are willing to sacrifice those ideals of freedom in which we have led mankind, and, if necessary, to adopt all the worst features of the Prussian spirit. This is because we fear the external enemy, who kills the body, more than the internal enemy, who kills the soul. The soul of a nation, if it is a free soul, without slavishness and without tyranny, cannot be killed by any outward enemy. And if men would realize this, the panic fear which the nations feel one toward another would be expelled by a better pride than that of diplomatists and war-lords. . . .

4 Just War Theory

Introduction
The Editors

Just war theory is the theoretical foundation for the morality of war. It holds that war can sometimes be morally justified, but even when it is justified the means or methods used to fight a war are still limited by moral considerations. It is sometimes suggested that just war theory occupies a middle ground between the extremes of realism, under which moral concerns are simply irrelevant to the propriety of war, and pacifism, which holds in its strongest form that war is never morally justified. But this is something of a misconception because there is no clear middle ground between these competing views on the morality of warfare. Realists are not necessarily more inclined to support or condone war than just war theorists; they simply use prudential rather than moral considerations when evaluating the legitimacy of warfare. Realism, in other words, is incommensurable with both pacifism and just war theory. The difference between just war theory and pacifism, on the other hand, is fundamentally moral in nature. Natural law theorists can concede that war is prima facie wrong from a moral point of view, but they also think it possible to identify overriding moral considerations that under specific circumstances can legitimate warfare.

The origins of just war theory can be traced back to St. Ambrose and his student St. Augustine. Augustine (354–430) argued that war was morally justified if it was declared by the appropriate secular authority, if it had a just cause, and if it was fought with rightful intentions. A cause was just, according to Augustine, if it involved fighting to bring about a condition of peace or to punish wrongdoers and promote the good. Correspondingly, intentions were rightful if the prince who waged the war did so with the intent of realizing one or more of these justifying causes. These conditions of just war were later endorsed by St. Thomas Aquinas (1225–1275), who revived Augustine's view and built it into his monumental inquiry into the law of nature, which he understood to govern the relations of all human beings. Like Augustine, Aquinas was chiefly concerned with the just cause of war *(jus ad bellum)* and claimed that if a war qualified as just, all means could be used to bring it to a desirable conclusion. Presumably, the just intentions of those who waged war permitted them to use all means necessary to a victorious outcome, and there was no further reason to be concerned with moral limitations on how a just war was to be fought *(jus in bello)*.

Just war theory received further development in the work of Francisco de Vitoria (1485–1546), one of the leading Catholic theologians of the sixteenth century. Vitoria was inspired to consider the morality of warfare as a result of the Spanish efforts to defeat the Indian nations they encountered in America. He also endorsed the Augustinian view that war was justified if it had a just cause and if it was fought with rightful intentions. Vitoria applied this reasoning to both defensive and offensive wars. States were justified, according to Vitoria, not only in defending themselves and reclaiming property taken from them in warfare, but also in avenging previous injustice, punishing wrongdoers, and protecting themselves against tyrants who might otherwise threaten them with impunity.

Vitoria pressed his analysis of just war further than his predecessors had taken the subject. He insisted that the only legitimate cause for a just offensive war was to avenge a harm done and punish the wrongdoer, but not all wrongs justified war in his view. The circumstances of war were so horrible that not all offenses justified warfare as a response. Moreover, Vitoria pushed his inquiry beyond the issue of *jus ad bellum* and into the subject of *jus in bello*. His claim that a prince could do anything in warfare to secure a positive outcome and secure peace—the primary end of war in his view—establishes the grounds for what would become the principle of military necessity. Yet Vitoria also argued that even in warfare it was never permissible to kill innocent individuals, unless they are the unintended victims of an otherwise legitimate military operation. And his insistence that the evil done in war should not outweigh the good gained from it points in the direction of what would become the principle of proportionality in international law.

In spite of the thoroughness of Vitoria's analysis, his chief contribution to the development of the morality of war may be found in the fact that his discussion reveals the difficulty and subtlety of the moral problems posed by warfare. His contention that offensive wars may be waged to deter tyrants sits awkwardly beside his belief that just war requires a just cause and this is limited to avenging previous harms. His defense of offensive war appears to justify preventive wars—initiating hostilities to prevent being attacked. But if states must wait until they have actually been harmed before waging war, such offensive wars would seem to be out of the question. Similarly, his defense of military necessity seems to contradict his strong insistence that innocents should not be killed as well as his belief in proportionality. These tensions are perhaps inevitable, for Vitoria was keenly sensitive to the paradoxical nature of something like a morality of warfare. On the one hand, war is a horrible event in which the stakes run high and violence is the standard. If it is right to wage war, it should also be right to do what is necessary to win the war. But on the other hand, even in warfare the requirements of morality would seem to have their place, and this would suggest that in spite of the terrible violence and exceptional stakes one encounters in war, states should still fight them in a manner that retains a sense of moral propriety—whatever this might happen to be.

The question about what this might happen to be received considerable attention from the political philosophers who helped shape the tradition of modern natural law. Of these, perhaps the most notable contribution to just war theory was made by the Dutch jurist Hugo Grotius (1583–1645). Grotius's importance as a political thinker extends well beyond just war theory. He reconfigured natural law in a manner that moved a concern for individual rights onto center stage, and much of his political thought can be understood in terms of his effort to develop the way rights are transformed by means of individual expressions of consent and the legal mechanism of the contract. He argued that peace was the natural condition for humankind and one that human beings ought therefore work to cultivate and promote. Disputes over rights, on the other hand, are the chief cause of war. States not only have the right, in Grotius's view, to defend their rights by means of war, but also to prosecute war in order to punish states that have violated their rights.

Grotius developed arguments on both *jus ad bellum* and *jus in bello* with his customary detail and precision, and his work both standardized the discussion of these two issues and established a target for future thinkers to attack. His concern for peace and human sociality was taken up by his successor, the Saxon philosopher Samuel Pufendorf (1632–1694), who built a comprehensive theory of the state around them. Although Pufendorf's often modest disagreements with the Grotian view of just war suggest something of the moral parameters of dispute within the just war tradition, his greatest contribution to just war theory may lie with his success in popularizing this theory and modern natural law more generally. Pufendorf summarized his theory of the state, which he developed in his major work on political theory, *The Law of Nature and Nations,* in a short epitome published under the title, *On the Duty of Man and Citizen* (1673). This work served as a basic text throughout Europe for the next one hundred years, but when the work was finally abandoned, Pufendorf's name (but not his influence) faded from the landscape of political thought.

As an element of the natural law tradition, just war theory belongs to a larger theoretical tradition in which states are viewed as sovereign units possessing rights that should be respected throughout the international arena. As these rights are formalized and acknowledged, they gain a status and importance that is easily distinguished from their initial moral foundation in natural law. And as they gained standing in the international community, they became the foundation for the development of international law. But emergent international law was also influenced by the rejection of natural law reasoning, and as legal theory moved toward positivism, so too did theoretical views of international law. Legal positivism differs from natural law chiefly in terms of the conditions for recognizing how law is known. Under the natural law tradition, law is known by the moral character of its content, while positivists recognize law by virtue of its source. Positivists find two sources of international law: customary practice and treaty formation. Philosophical insistence that war was justified only under certain conditions does not establish customary practice, however, and thus just war theory fell out of favor with international lawyers working within a positivist framework.

The primary positivist objection to just war theory is that there is no common international judge, recognized as such, that can adjudicate questions about whether a state has in fact been wronged by another in a manner that justifies warfare. While war might be morally justified from the point of view of a given state, this has no bearing on the legality of the war from the standpoint of international positive law. The justness of a war could be determined, in the absence of an authoritative voice, only if the states that were a party to the war agreed on this normative judgment, and this seems highly unlikely. Consequently, just war theory seemed to have little place in emergent international law.

In spite of this, there is still reason to take seriously the morality of war. While it is of importance to think about how a system of international law can develop in ways that resemble the development of domestic legal systems, and to see this question in structural terms in the manner that concerns legal positivists, there is still room to think about what the content of this law *ought* to be. Insofar as warfare remains a scourge for human beings, defining its legitimate parameters should continue to matter, for it is difficult to know how else a reasonable international law of warfare can emerge. And to the extent that states, and the citizens of states, must sacrifice in order to fight wars, it is important to know that the cause is just and the means used to prosecute the war legitimate within the moral parameters human beings employ to judge these matters.

4.2 _____

The City of God

St. Augustine

▪ The Fruits of the Romans' Wars Both to Themselves and to Those with Whom They Warred

For what doth it matter in respect of this short and transitory life, under whose dominion a mortal man doth live, as long as he be not compelled to acts of impiety or injustice? But did the Romans ever hurt any of the nations whom they conquered and gave laws unto, but in the very fury and war of the conquest? If they could have given those laws by agreement, it had been better (but then there had been no place for triumph), for the Romans lived under the same laws themselves that they gave to others. This had been sufficient for the State, but that Mars, Bellona, and Victory should then have been displeased, and displaced also, if they had had no wars and no victories. Would not then the state of Rome and other nations have been all one, especially if that had been done which was most gravely and worthily performed afterwards, every man that belonged to the Roman Empire receiving the freedom of the city, as though they were now all citizens of Rome, whereas before there were but a very few, so that such as had no lands had to live at the public expense? This sustenance would have been supplied more readily unto good governors by men who were sharers in the commonwealth than it would have been had it been extorted from them as a conquered people. For how does the fact that some conquer and others are conquered promote men's safety, manners, or dignities either? I see no good it does, but only that it adds unto their intolerable vainglory, who aim at such matters, and war for them, and lastly receive them as their labour's reward. Does not their land pay tribute to the State as well as others? Yes. May they learn anything that others may not? No. And are there not many senators that never saw Rome? True. Take away vainglory and what are men but men? And if the perverseness of the age would permit the very best men to bear away the greatest honours, even then should not this human honour be so prizeworthy, being but a breath and a light smoke. But let us

From *The City of God (De Civitate Dei)* by St. Augustine, ed. R. V. G. Tasker, trans. John Healey. London: J. M. Dent, 1945. Excerpt from book 5: chaps. 17, 22; book 19: chaps. 5–7, 12.

use these things, to do ourselves good towards God. Let us consider what obstacles these men have scorned, what pains they have taken, what desires they have suppressed, and only for this human glory which afterwards they received as the reward of their virtues; and let this serve to suppress our pride also, that seeing the city wherein we are promised habitation and kingdom is as far different from this in excellence as heaven from earth, life eternal from mirth temporal, firm glory from fuming vainglory, angels' company from men's, and His light that made the sun and moon from the light of the sun and moon; we may feel that the citizens of this heavenly region have done just nothing for attaining this celestial dwelling, seeing that the others have taken such pains in that habitation of earth which they had already attained. Especially does the remission of sins call us as citizens to that eternal dwelling; and this has a kind of resemblance to Romulus' sanctuary, by which he gathered a multitude of people into his city through hope of impunity. . . .

■ That the Origins and Conclusions of Wars Are All at God's Disposal

So likewise does He with the times and ends of war, be it His pleasure justly to correct or mercifully to pity mankind, ending them sooner or later as He wills. Pompey's pirate war, and Scipio's third African war, were ended with incredible celerity. The slaves' war also, though it cost Rome two consuls and many captains, making all Italy feel the smart of it, yet in the third year after it was begun, it was finished. The Picenes, Marsians, Pelignians (Italians all) sought to pluck their necks from their long and strict servitude unto Rome, though it now had subdued huge dominions, and razed Carthage. In this war the Romans were sorely foiled, two consuls killed, and many a tall soldier and worthy senator left dead: yet this war had continuance but unto the fifth year. But the second African war lasted a great while, eighteen years, to the great weakening of the commonwealth, and almost the utter ruin thereof, seventy thousand soldiers falling in two battles. The first African war held three-and-twenty years; Mithridates' war forty years. And lest any one should think that in the ancient laudable times the Romans had any better rules to dispatch war sooner than the rest, the Samnites' war lasted almost fifty years, wherein the Romans were conquered even unto slavery. But because they loved not glory for justice, but justice for glory, they broke the peace and league which they had made. These things I write, because some being ignorant of antiquities, and some others being dissemblers of what they know, might otherwise upon discovery of a long war since the time of Christianity, fly in the face of our religion, and say if it were not for that, and if the old adorations were restored, that war would have been ended by the Romans' virtues and the assistance of Mars and Bellona, as soon as the rest were. Let them that read of their wars but recollect what uncertain fortune the ancient Romans had in the wars with the whole world, being tossed like a tempestuous sea with a thousand storms of invasions and arms: and then let them needs confess, what so fain they would conceal, and cease in this opposition against God's power, to possess others with errors, and be the butchers of their own souls. . . .

■ Of Living Sociably with Our Neighbour: How Fit It Is, and yet How Subject to Crosses

We do worthily approve their enjoining a wise man to live in mutual society; for how should our celestial city (the nineteenth book whereof we now have in hand) have ever come to its origin, development, or perfection, unless the saints live all in sociable union? But yet who is he that can recount all the miseries incident unto the societies of mortals? . . . And those inconveniences that Terence pins on the back of love, as injuries, enmities, war, and peace again, do not all these wait upon our mortality continually? Do not these invade sometimes the friendliest affections? And does not all the world regard as certain evils injuries, enmities, and wars? And our peace is as uncertain, as we are ignorant of their hearts on whom it depends; and though we know to-day what they would do, to-morrow we may not. Who should be greater friends than those of one family? Yet how many secret plots of malice lie even amongst such, to expel security; their firmer peace becoming fouler malice; and being reputed most loyal, whereas it was only most craftily feigned? . . . Wherefore that which the holy scripture says, "A man's foes are those of his own household," this we hear with great grief: for though a man have fortitude to endure it, or prevention to avoid it, yet if he be a good man, he must needs feel great grief at the badness of those so near him; be it that they have been accustomed unto this viperous dissimulation of old, or have learnt it but of late. So, then, if a man's own private house afford him no shelter from these incursions, what shall the city do, which, as it is larger, so is it fuller of squabbles, and suits, and quarrels, and accusations, even if we grant the absence of seditions and civil contentions, which are too often present, and whereof the cities are in continual danger, when they are in their safest estate?

■ The Error of Human Judgments in Cases Where Truth Is Not Known

And how lamentable and miserable are those men's judgments whom the cities must perforce use as magistrates, even in their most settled peace, concerning other men! They judge them whose consciences they cannot see, and therefore are often driven to wring forth the truth by tormenting of innocent witnesses. And what say you when a man is tortured in his own case, and tormented, even when it is a question whether he be guilty or no? And though he be innocent, yet suffers he assured pains when they are not assured he is faulty. In most of these cases the judge's ignorance turns to the prisoner's misery. Nay (which is more lamentable, and deserves a sea of tears to wash it away), the judge in torturing the accused, lest he should put him to death being innocent, oftentimes through his wretched ignorance kills that party though innocent with torture, whom he had tortured to avoid the killing of an innocent. For if (according unto their doctrine) he had rather leave this life than endure those miseries, then he says that he did the thing whereof he is clear indeed. And being thereupon condemned and executed, still the judge cannot tell whether he were guilty or no. He tortured him lest he should execute him guiltless, and by that means killed him ere he knew that he was guilty. Now, in these mists of mortal society, ought the judge to sit or no? Yes, he must sit. He is bound to it by his place, which he holds it wickedness not to discharge, and by the State's command, which he must obey. But he never holds it wickedness to torture guiltless witnesses in other men's causes; and when the tortures have overcome the patience of the innocent, and made them their own accusers, to put them to death as guilty (whom they tortured but to try), being guiltless: nor to let many of them die even upon the very rack itself, or by that means, if they do escape the hangman. Again, what do you say to this, that some bringing a just accusation against this man or that for the good of the State, the accused endures all the tortures without confession, and so the innocent plaintiffs, not being able to prove their plea, are by the judge's ignorance cast and condemned? These now, and many more than these, the judge holds no sins, because his will is not assenting unto them, but his service to the State compels him, and his ignorance of hurt it is that makes him do it, not any will to hurt. This, now, is misery in a man, if it be not malice in a wise man. Is it the troubles of his place and of ignorance that cause those effects, and does he think that it is not enough for him to be held free from accusation, but he must needs sit in beatitude? How much more wisdom and discretion would he show in acknowledging his mortality in those troubles, and in detesting this misery in himself, crying out unto God (if he be wise) with the psalmist: "Lord, take me out of all my troubles."

▓ Difference of Language an Impediment to Human Society. The Miseries of the Justest Wars

After the city follows the whole world, wherein the third kind of human society is resident, the first being in the house, and the second in the city.

Now the world is as a flood of waters, the greater, the more dangerous: and first of all, difference of language divides man from man. For if two meet, who perchance are compelled by some accident to abide together and confer, if neither of them can understand the other, you may sooner make two brute beasts of two different kinds sociable to one another than these two men. For when they would commune together, their tongues do not agree; which being so, all the other helps of nature are nothing; so that a man had rather be with his own dog than with another man of a strange language. But the great western Babylon endeavours to communicate her language to all the lands she has subdued, to procure a fuller society, and a greater abundance of interpreters on both sides. It is true, but how many lives has this vanity cost! And suppose that done, the worst is not past: for although she never wanted stranger nations against whom to lead her forces, yet this large extension of her empire procured greater wars than those named civil and confederate wars; and these were they that troubled the souls of mankind both while they were being waged, with desire to see them extinct, and when they had died down, with fear to see them renewed. If I should stop to recite the massacres, and the extreme effects thereof, as I might (though I cannot do it as I should), the discourse would be infinite. Yea, but a wise man, say they, will wage none but just war. He will not! As if the very remembrance that himself is man ought not to procure his greater sorrow in that he has cause of just wars, and must needs wage them, which if they were not just, it were not for him to deal in, so that a wise man should never have war. For it is the other men's wickedness that makes his cause just that he ought to deplore, whether it produce wars or not. Wherefore he that does but consider with compassion all those extremes of sorrow and bloodshed, must needs say that this is a mystery; but he that endures them without a sorrowful emotion or thought thereof, is far more wretched to imagine he has the bliss of a god, when he has lost the natural feeling of a man. . . .

◼ That the Bloodiest War's Chief Aim Is Peace; The Desire of Which Is Natural in Man

Who will not confess this with me, who marks man's affairs and the general form of nature? For joy and peace are desired alike of all men. The warrior would but conquer, and war's aim is nothing but glorious peace. For what is victory but a suppression of resistance, which being done, peace follows? And so peace is war's purpose, the scope of all military discipline, and the limit at which all just contentions aim. All men seek peace by war, but none seek war by peace. For they that perturb the peace they live in, do it not for hate of it, but to show their power in alteration of it. They would not disan-

nul it, but they would have it as they like; and though they break into seditions against the rest, yet must they hold a peaceful show with their fellows
that are engaged with them, or else they shall never effect what they intend.
Even the thieves themselves that molest all the world besides them, are at
peace amongst themselves. Admit one be so strong or subtle that he will
have no fellow, but plays all his parts of roguery alone, yet with such as he
can neither kill, and to whom he does not care to make known his deeds, he
must needs maintain a kind of peace. And at home, with his wife and family, must he needs observe quietness; and without question he delights in
their obedience unto him, which if they fail in, he chases and chides and
strikes, setting all in order by force if need be, or by cruelty: which he sees
he cannot do, unless all the rest be subjected under one head, which is himself. And might he have the sway of a city or province in such sort as he has
that of his house, he would put off his thievish nature, and put on a king's,
albeit his covetousness and malice would remain unchanged. Thus then you
see that all men desire to have peace with such as they would have lived
according to their liking. For those against whom they wage war, they
would make their own if they could; and if they conquer them they give
them such laws as they like.

But let us imagine some such unsociable fellow as the poet's fable
records, calling him "half-man," for his inhuman barbarism.

Now although his kingdom lay in a lightless cave, and his villainies
were so singular that they gave him that name of Cacus, which is, evil;
though his wife never had good word for him, and he never played with his
children, nor ruled them in their manlier age, and though he never spoke
with friend, not so much as with his father Vulcan (than whom he was far
more happy in that he begat no such monster as Vulcan had in begetting
him); though he never gave to any, but robbed and spoiled all that he could
grip from all manner of persons, yea and the persons themselves, yet in that
horrid dungeon of his, whose floor and walls were always dank with the
blood of new slaughters, he desired nothing but to rest in peace therein,
without molestation. He desired also to be at peace with himself; and what
he had, he enjoyed; he ruled over his own body, and to satisfy his own hun-
gry nature that menaced the separation of soul and body, he fell to his rob-
beries with celerity; and though he were barbarous and bloody, yet in all
that, he had a care to provide for his life and safety. And therefore if he
would have had that peace with others, which he had in the cave with himself alone, he would neither have been called half-man nor monster. But if it
were his horrible shape and breathing of fire that made men avoid him, then
was it not will, but necessity that made him live in that cave and play the
thief for his living. But there was no such man, or if there were, he was not
such as the poets feign him. For unless they had mightily belied Cacus, they
could not sufficiently have commended Hercules. But, as I said, it is likely
that there was no such man, any more than there is truth in many other of

their fictions. For the very wild beasts (part of whose brutishness they place in him) do preserve a peace each with other in their kind, begetting, breeding, and living together amongst themselves, being in other respects the unsociable births of the deserts. I speak not here of sheep, deer, pigeons, starlings, or bees, but of lions, foxes, eagles, and owls. For what tiger is there that does not purr over her young ones, and fawn upon them in their tenderness? What kite is there, though he fly solitarily about for his prey, but will seek his female, build his nest, sit his eggs, feed his young, and assist his mate in her motherly duty, all that in him lies? Far stronger are the bands that bind man unto society and peace with all that are peaceable. The worst men of all do fight for their fellows' quietness, and would (if it lay in their power) reduce all into a distinct form of state, drawn by themselves, whereof they would be the heads, which could never be, but by a coherence either through fear or love. For herein is perverse pride an imitator of the goodness of God, hating equality of others with itself under Him, and laying a yoke of obedience upon its fellows, under itself instead of Him. Thus hates it the just peace of God, and builds an unjust one for itself. Yet can it not but love peace, for no vice, however unnatural, can pull nature up by the roots.

But he that can discern between good and bad, and between order and confusion, may soon distinguish the godly peace from the wicked. Yet even that perverse confusion must of necessity be in, or in dependence upon, or in connection with some part of the order of things, for otherwise it would not exist at all. Let us take an example. Hang a man up with his head downwards, and all his posture is confounded; that which should be lowest having the highest place, and vice versa. This confusion disturbs the flesh, and is troublesome to it. But it is the soul's peace with the body that causes the feeling of that disturbance. Now if the soul leave the body by the means of those troubles, yet as long as the body's form remains it has a certain peace with itself; and the very fact that it remains suspended shows that it desires to be placed in the peace of nature, the very weight seeming to demand a place for rest; and though life be gone, yet very nature sways it unto that order wherein she placed it. For if the dead body be preserved from putrefaction by unguents and embalmings, yet the peace of nature is kept, for the body's weight is applied thereby to a suitable earthly site, and convenient place for it to rest in. But if it be not embalmed, but left to nature's dissolving, it is so long altered by ill-tasting vapours, until each part be wholly reduced to the particular natures of the elements, yet is not a little of the Creator's all-disposing law withdrawn. For if there grow out of this carcass many more living creatures, each body of these serves the quantity of life that is in it, according to the same law of creation. And if that be devoured up by other ravenous beasts or birds, it shall follow the ordinance of the same law, disposing all things congruently, into what form of nature soever it be changed.

4.3 _____

War and Killing

St. Thomas Aquinas

■ *Summa Theologiae:* **On War**

Whether It Is Always a Sin to Wage War

If a war is to be just, three things are required. First, the authority of the prince by whose command war is to be waged. For it does not pertain to a private person to declare war, because he can prosecute his rights at the tribunal of his superior; similarly, it does not pertain to a private person to summon the people together, which must be done in time of war. Rather, since the care of the commonwealth is entrusted to princes, it pertains to them to protect the commonwealth of the city or kingdom or province subject to them. And just as it is lawful for them to use the material sword in defence of the commonwealth against those who trouble it from within, when they punish evildoers, according to the Apostle, "He beareth not the sword in vain: for he is the minister of God, a revenger to execute wrath upon him that doeth evil"; so too, it pertains to them to use the sword of war to protect the commonwealth against enemies from without. . . .

Second, a just cause is required: that is, those against whom war is to be waged must deserve to have war waged against them because of some wrongdoing. Hence Augustine says in the book *Quaestiones in heptateuchum:* "A just war is customarily defined as one which avenges injuries, as when a nation or state deserves to be punished because it has neglected either to put right the wrongs done by its people or to restore what it has unjustly seized."

Third, it is required that those who wage war should have a righteous intent: that is, they should intend either to promote a good cause or avert an evil. Hence Augustine says: "Among true worshippers of God, those wars which are waged not out of greed or cruelty, but with the object of securing peace by coercing the wicked and helping the good, are regarded as peaceful." For it can happen that even if war is declared by a legitimate authority and for a just cause, that war may be rendered unlawful by a wicked intent. For Augustine says in the book *Contra Faustum:* "The desire to do harm,

---

the cruelty of vengeance, an unpeaceable and implacable spirit, the fever of rebellion, the lust to dominate, and similar things: these are rightly condemned in war." . . .

Whether It Is Lawful to Make Use of Ambushes in War

The purpose of ambushes is to deceive enemies. But there are two ways in which someone may be deceived by what someone else does or says. In one way, by being told something false or by not having a promise kept; and this is always unlawful. No one ought to deceive an enemy in this way, for there are certain rights of war and covenants which should be observed even among enemies, as Ambrose says in the book *De officiis*. In another way, someone may be deceived by what we say or do because we do not reveal our thoughts or intentions to him. But we are not always bound to do this, for even in sacred doctrine many things are to be kept hidden, especially from unbelievers, lest they mock them, according to Matthew: "Give not that which is holy unto the dogs." So much more, then, ought our preparations against the enemy to be kept hidden. One of the most important parts of a military education, therefore, as is clear from Frontinus's book *Strategemata,* is the art of concealing one's plans lest they come to the enemy's knowledge. And the planning of ambushes, which may lawfully be used in a just war, belongs to this art of concealment; nor can such ambushes properly be called deceptions; nor are they repugnant to justice or to a rightly-ordered will, for a man would have a disordered will if he were unwilling that anything should be hidden from him by others. . . .

■ Summa Theologiae: On Homicide

Whether It Is Unlawful to Kill Any Living Thing

There is no sin in using something for its proper purpose. Now in the natural order of things, imperfect things exist for the sake of perfect, just as, in the process of generation, nature proceeds from the imperfect to the perfect. Hence, just as in the generation of man there was first a living thing, then an animal, and finally a man, so too such things as plants, which merely have life, all exist for the sake of animals, and all animals exist for the sake of man. And so it is not unlawful if man makes use of plants for the benefit of animals, and animals for the benefit of men, as the Philosopher [Aristotle] shows at *Politics* I. But among the possible uses, the most necessary seems to be that animals use plants, and men animals, as food; and this cannot be done without killing them. And so it is lawful both to kill plants for the use of animals, and animals for the use of men; and this, indeed, is by Divine ordinance, for it is said at Genesis: "Behold I have given you every herb and all trees to be your meat, and to all beasts of the earth." Again, it is said at Genesis: "Everything that moveth and liveth shall be meat for you." . . .

Whether It Is Lawful to Kill Sinners

As stated above, it is lawful to kill brute beasts insofar as they are naturally ordained to man's use as imperfect is ordained to perfect. Now every part is directed to the whole as imperfect to perfect; and so every part naturally exists for the sake of the whole. For this reason we see that if the health of the whole body requires the removal of some member, perhaps because it is diseased or causing the corruption of other members, it will be both praiseworthy and wholesome for it to be cut away. Now every individual person stands in relation to the whole community as part to whole. And so if some man is dangerous to the community, causing its corruption because of some sin, it is praiseworthy and wholesome that he be slain in order to preserve the common good; for "a little leaven corrupteth the whole lump." . . .

Whether It Is Lawful for a Private Person to Kill a Man Who Has Sinned

As stated above, it is lawful to kill a malefactor insofar as doing so is directed to the health of the whole community; but so to do pertains only to him to whom the task of preserving the community's health has been entrusted, just as it pertains to the physician to cut off a decayed member when he has been entrusted with the care of the health of the whole body. Now the care of the common good is entrusted to <u>princes having public authority; and so they alone, and not private individuals, can lawfully kill malefactors</u>. . . .

Whether It Is Lawful for Someone to Slay Himself

It is altogether unlawful to slay oneself, for three reasons. First, because everything naturally loves itself, and to this belongs the fact that everything naturally preserves itself in being and resists corruption as far as it can. And so for anyone to slay himself is contrary to the inclination of nature, and contrary also to charity, whereby every man should love himself. To slay oneself is therefore always a mortal sin, as being contrary to the natural law and to charity. Second, because every part, as such, belongs to the whole. Now every man is part of a community, and so, as such, belongs to that community. Hence one who slays himself does injury to the community, as the Philosopher [Aristotle] shows at *Ethics* V, because life is as it were a divine gift bestowed upon man, and is subject to the power of Him who kills and makes alive. Hence he who deprives himself of life sins against God, just as he who slays another's slave sins against the master of that slave, and just as he sins who usurps judgment to himself in a matter not entrusted to him. For it pertains to God alone to pronounce sentence of death and life, according to Deuteronomy: "I kill and I make alive." . . .

Whether It Is Lawful to Kill the Innocent

A man can be considered in two ways. In one way, in himself; in another way, in relation to something else. If a man be considered in himself, it is unlawful to kill anyone, since in everyone, even the sinner, we ought to love the nature which God has made, and which is destroyed by slaying him. On the other hand, as stated above, the slaying of a sinner becomes lawful in relation to the common good, which is corrupted by sin, whereas the common good is conserved and promoted by the life of righteous men, for they are the foremost part of the community. Therefore it is in no way lawful to slay the innocent. . . .

proportionality

Whether It Is Lawful to Kill Someone in Self-Defence

Nothing prevents a single act from having two effects, only one of which is intended while the other is beside the intention. Now moral acts take their species from what is intended, not from what is beside the intention, since this is accidental, as explained above. Accordingly, an act of self-defence may have two effects, one of which is the saving of one's own life while the other is the slaying of an attacker. If one's intention is to save one's own life, the act is not unlawful, because it is natural for everything to keep itself in being as far as possible. Yet an act may be rendered unlawful even though proceeding from a good intention if it is out of proportion to the end. Hence if a man uses more violence in self-defence than is necessary, this will be unlawful, whereas if he repels force with force in moderation, his defence will be lawful. . . . Nor is it necessary to salvation that a man refrain from an act of moderate self-defence in order to avoid killing another man, since one is bound to take more care of one's own life than of another's. But since it is unlawful for anyone to take a man's life except a public authority acting for the common good, as stated above, it is not lawful for one man to intend to kill another in self-defence, except in the case of those who have public authority, who, though intending to kill a man in self-defence, refer this to the public good: for instance, a soldier fighting against the enemy and a minister of the judge fighting with robbers; although even these sin if they are motivated by private animosity. . . .

4.4

On the Law of War

Francisco de Vitoria

I will deal with four principal questions. First, Whether Christians may make war at all; secondly, Where does the authority to declare or wage war repose; thirdly, What may and ought to furnish causes of just war; fourthly, What and how extensive measures may be taken in a just war against the enemy? . . .

Christians may serve in war and make war. This is the conclusion of St. Augustine in the many passages where he thoroughly considers the question. . . . And, as St. Augustine shows, this is proved by the words of John the Baptist to the soldiers, "Do violence to no man, neither accuse any falsely." . . .

Secondly, there is proof in the reason of the thing. To draw the sword and use arms against internal wrongdoers and seditious citizens is lawful according to Romans, "He beareth not the sword in vain, for he is the minister of God, a revenger of wrath upon him that doeth evil." Therefore it is lawful also to use the sword and arms against external enemies. . . .

Thirdly, this was also allowable by the law of nature, as appears from the case of Abraham, who fought against four kings, and also by the written law, as appears from the cases of David and the Maccabees. But the Gospel law forbids nothing which is allowed by natural law . . . , and that is why it is called the law of liberty. Therefore, what was lawful under natural law and in the written law is no less lawful under the Gospel law.

Fourthly, since there can be no doubt that in a defensive war force may be employed to repel force, this is also proved with regard to an offensive war, that is, a war where we are not only defending ourselves or seeking to repossess ourselves of property, but also where we are trying to avenge ourselves for some wrong done to us. This, I say, is proved by the authority of St. Augustine . . . , "Those wars are described as just wars which are waged in order to avenge a wrong done, as where punishment has to be meted out to a city or state because it has itself neglected to exact punishment for an offense committed by its citizens or subjects or to return what has been wrongfully taken away."

From *De Indis et de Ivre Belli Relectiones* by Francisco de Vitoria, ed. Ernest Nys. Washington, D.C.: Carnegie Institution, 1917. Excerpt from "The Second Relectio: On the Indians, or on the Law of War Made by the Spaniards on the Barbarians."

A fifth proof with regard to an offensive war is that even a defensive war could not be waged satisfactorily, were no vengeance taken on enemies who have done or tried to do a wrong. For they would only be emboldened to make a second attack, if the fear of retribution did not keep them from wrongdoing.

A sixth proof is that, as St. Augustine says, the end and aim of war is the peace and security of the State. But there can be no security in the State unless enemies are made to desist from wrong by the fear of war, for the situation with regard to war would be glaringly unfair, if all that a State could do when enemies attack it unjustly was to ward off the attack and if they could not follow this up by further steps.

A seventh proof comes from the end and aim and good of the whole world. For there would be no condition of happiness for the world, nay, its condition would be one of utter misery, if oppressors and robbers and plunderers could with impunity commit their crimes and oppress the good and innocent, and these latter could not in turn retaliate on them.

My eighth and last proof is one which in morals carries the utmost weight, namely, the authority and example of good and holy men. Such men have not only defended their country and their own property in defensive wars, but have also in offensive wars sought reparation for wrongs done or attempted by their enemies. . . .

Second question: In whose hands lies the authority to declare and to make war?

Herein let my first proposition be: Any one, even a private person, can accept and wage a defensive war. This is shown by the fact that force may be repelled by force. Hence any one can make this kind of war, without authority from any one else, for the defense not only of his person, but also of his property and goods.

A doubt, however, arises in connection with this proposition, namely, whether one who is attacked by a robber or enemy can strike his assailant back if escape by flight is possible. . . . If, then, armed resistance is permissible in defense of property . . . , much more is it permissible in order to protect the body from hurt, such hurt being more serious than wrong to property. This opinion can be safely held and with possibility of demonstration, especially as the civil law admits as much. Now, no one sins who acts under warrant of the law, inasmuch as the law affords justification in the forum of conscience. Accordingly, even if natural law does not allow killing in defense of property, this is rendered lawful by the civil law and is available, so long as no scandal is caused, not only to laymen, but to clerics and professed persons.

Second proposition: Every State has authority to declare and to make war. In course of proof of this be it noted that the difference herein between a private person and a State is that a private person is entitled, as said above, to defend himself and what belongs to him, but has no right to avenge a wrong done to him, nay, not even to recapture property that has been seized from him if time has been allowed to go by since the seizure. But defense can only be resorted to at the very moment of the danger, or, as the jurists say, *in continenti,* and so when the necessity of defense has passed there is an end to the lawfulness of war. In my view, however, one who has been contumeliously assaulted can immediately strike back, even if the assaulter was not proposing to make a further attack. . . . But a State is within its rights not only in defending itself, but also in avenging itself and its subjects and in redressing wrongs. . . . But it can not adequately protect the public weal and the position of the State if it can not avenge a wrong and take measures against its enemies, for wrongdoers would become readier and bolder for wrongdoing, if they could do wrong with impunity. . . .

Third question: What may be a reason and cause of just war? . . . Here my first proposition is: Difference of religion is not a cause of just war. . . . And it is the opinion of St. Thomas and the common opinion of the doctors—indeed, I know of no one of the opposite way of thinking.

Second proposition: Extension of empire is not a just cause of war. This is too well known to need proof, for otherwise each of the two belligerents might have an equally just cause and so both would be innocent. This in its turn would involve the consequence that it would not be lawful to kill them and so imply a contradiction, because it would be a just war.

Third proposition: Neither the personal glory of the prince nor any other advantage to him is a just cause of war. This, too, is notorious. For a prince ought to subordinate both peace and war to the common weal of his State and not spend public revenues in quest of his own glory or gain, much less expose his subjects to danger on that account. . . .

Fourth proposition: There is a single and only just cause for commencing a war, namely, a wrong received. The proof of this rests in the first place on the authority of St. Augustine . . . , and it is the conclusion arrived at by St. Thomas and the opinion of all the doctors. Also, an offensive war is for the purpose of avenging a wrong and of taking measures against an enemy, as said above. But there can be no vengeance where there is no preceding fault and wrong. . . . Also, a prince has no greater authority over foreigners than over his own subjects. But he may not draw his sword against his own subjects, unless they have done some wrong. Therefore not against foreigners either. . . .

Fifth proposition: Not every kind and degree of wrong can suffice for commencing a war. The proof of this is that not even upon one's own fellow-countrymen is it lawful for every offense to exact atrocious punishments, such as death or banishment or confiscation of property. As, then, the evils inflicted in war are all of a severe and atrocious character, such as slaughter and fire and devastation, it is not lawful for slight wrongs to pursue the authors of the wrongs with war, seeing that the degree of the punishment ought to correspond to the measure of the offence.

The fourth question is about the law of war, namely, what kind and degree of stress is lawful in a just war. Here let my first proposition be: In war everything is lawful which the defense of the common weal requires. This is notorious, for the end and aim of war is the defense and the preservation of the State. . . .

Second proposition: It is permissible to recapture everything that has been lost and any part of the same. This is too notorious to need proof. For war is begun or undertaken with this object.

Third proposition: It is lawful to make good out of enemy property the expenses of the war and all damages wrongfully caused by the enemy. This is clear, for the enemy who has done the wrong is bound to give all this redress. Therefore the prince can claim it all and exact it all by war. . . . Also, if there were any competent judge over the two belligerents, he would have to condemn the unjust aggressors and authors of wrong, not only to make restitution of what they have carried off, but also to make good the expenses of the war to the other side, and also all damages. But a prince who is carrying on a just war is as it were his own judge in matters touching the war, as we shall forthwith show. Therefore he can enforce all these claims upon his enemy.

Fourth proposition: Not only are the things just named allowable, but a prince may go even further in a just war and do whatever is necessary in order to obtain peace and security from the enemy; for example, destroy an enemy's fortress and even build one on enemy soil, if this be necessary in order to avert a dangerous attack of the enemy. This is proved by the fact that, as said above, the end and aim of war is peace and security. . . .

Fifth proposition: Not only is all this permissible, but even after victory has been won and redress obtained and peace and safety been secured, it is lawful to avenge the wrong received from the enemy and to take measures against him and exact punishment from him for the wrongs he has done. In proof of this be it observed that princes have authority not only over their own subjects, but also over foreigners, so far as to prevent them from committing wrongs, and this is by the law of nations and by the authority of the whole world. . . .

Many doubts are suggested by what has just been said. In the first place, there is a doubtful point in connection with the justice of a war, whether it be enough for a just war that the prince believes himself to have a just cause. On this point let my first proposition be: This belief is not always enough. And for proof I rely, first, on the fact that in some matters of less moment it is not enough either for a prince or for private persons to believe that they are acting justly. This is notorious, for their error may be vincible and deliberate, and the opinion of the individual is not enough to render an act good, but it must come up to the standard of a wise man's judgment. . . .

Second proposition: It is essential for a just war that an exceedingly careful examination be made of the justice and causes of the war and that the reasons of those who on grounds of equity oppose it be listened to. For (as the comic poet says) "A wise man must make trial of everything by words before resorting to force," and he ought to consult the good and wise and those who speak with freedom and without anger or bitterness or greed. . . . This is self-evident.

Second doubt: Whether subjects are bound to examine the cause of a war or whether they may serve in the war without any careful scrutiny thereof, just as the lictors had to enforce the praetor's decree without questioning. On this doubt let my first proposition be: If a subject is convinced of the injustice of a war, he ought not to serve in it, even on the command of his prince. This is clear, for no one can authorize the killing of an innocent person. But in the case before us the enemy are innocent. Therefore they may not be killed. . . . Therefore soldiers also are not excused when they fight in bad faith. . . .

Hence flows the corollary that subjects whose conscience is against the justice of a war may not engage in it whether they be right or wrong. This is clear, for "whatever is not of faith is sin."

Second proposition: Senators and petty rulers and in general all who are admitted on summons or voluntarily to the public council or the prince's council ought, and are bound, to examine into the cause of an unjust war. This is clear; for whoever can save his neighbor from danger and harm is bound to do so, especially when the danger is that of death and greater ills, as is the case in war. . . .

Third proposition: Other lesser folk who have no place or audience in the prince's council or in the public council are under no obligation to examine the causes of a war, but may serve in it in reliance on their betters. This is proved, first, by the fact that it is impossible and inexpedient to give reasons for all acts of state to every member of the commonalty. Also by the fact that men of the lower orders, even if they perceived the injustice of a war, could not stop it, and their voice would not be heeded. . . .

Fourth proposition: Nevertheless the proofs and tokens of the injustice of the war may be such that ignorance would be no excuse even to subjects of this sort who serve in it. This is clear, because such ignorance might be deliberate and adopted with evil intent towards the enemy. . . .

Third doubt: What should be done when the justice of the war is doubtful, that is, when there are apparent and probable reasons on both sides. First proposition: As regards the princes themselves, it seems that if one be in lawful possession, the other may not try to turn him out by war and armed force, so long as the doubt remains. . . . Therefore it is not lawful to dispossess the possessor in favor of a doubtful cause. . . .

Second proposition: If the city or province in regard of which the doubt arises has no lawful possessor . . . , it seems that, if one party wants to settle and make a division or compromise as to part of the claim, the other is bound to accept his proposal, even if that other be the stronger and able to seize the whole by armed force; nor would he have a just cause of war. . . .

Third proposition: He who is in doubt about his own title is bound, even though he be in peaceable possession, to examine carefully into the cause and give a quiet hearing to the arguments of the other side, so he may thus attain certitude either in favor of himself or the other. This is proved by the fact that a man who is in doubt and neglects to ascertain the truth is not in possession in good faith. . . .

Fourth proposition: After examination of the case the lawful possessor is not bound to quit possession so long as the doubt reasonably persists, but may lawfully retain it. . . .

But let this be my fifth proposition: In the first place, there is no doubt that in a defensive war subjects may, even though the matter be doubtful, follow their prince to the war; nay, that they are bound to follow him, and also in an offensive war. The first proof is in the fact that, as has been said, a prince is not able, and ought not, always to render reasons for the war to his subjects, and if subjects can not serve in war except they are first satisfied of its justice, the State would fall into grave peril and the door would be opened to wrongdoing. . . . Nor does it avail to say that such a person ought to get rid of his doubt and make his conscience acquiesce in the justice of the war, for it remains that, morally speaking, this is impossible, as in other cases of doubt. . . . [I]f I am in doubt whether this war is just for my prince or whether there be a just cause for this war, it immediately follows that I am in doubt whether or not I ought to go to this war. I admit that I am no wise justified in doing what my conscience doubts about and that, if I am doubtful about the lawfulness of doing any given thing, I sin if I do it. But any doubt of mine about the justice of this war does not necessarily involve a doubt whether I ought to fight or serve in this war. Nay, it is quite the other way about. For although I may doubt whether the war is just, yet the next point is that I may lawfully serve in the field at my prince's command. It is precisely the same as with a lictor who has his doubts whether the judge's decree is just, it does not follow therefrom that he doubts whether or not he ought to carry it into execution. . . .

The fourth doubt is: Whether a war can be just on both sides. The following is my answer: First proposition: Apart from ignorance the case clearly can not occur, for if the right and justice of each side be certain, it is unlawful to fight against it, either in offense or in defense. Second proposition: Assuming a demonstrable ignorance either of fact or of law, it may be that on the side where true justice is the war is just of itself, while on the other side the war is just in the sense of being excused from sin by reason of good faith, because invincible ignorance is a complete excuse. . . .

With regard to another question, namely, what degree of stress is lawful in a just war, there are also many doubts. The first is: Whether it is lawful in war to kill the innocent. . . .

With regard to this doubt, let my first proposition be: The deliberate slaughter of the innocent is never lawful in itself. This is proved, firstly, by *Exodus,* "The innocent and righteous slay thou not." Secondly, the basis of a just war is a wrong done, as has been shown above. But wrong is not done by an innocent person. Therefore war may not be employed against him. Thirdly, it is not lawful within a State to punish the innocent for the wrong-doing of the guilty. Therefore this is not lawful among enemies. . . .

Second proposition: Sometimes it is right, in virtue of collateral circumstances, to slay the innocent even knowingly, as when a fortress or city is stormed in a just war, although it is known that there are a number of innocent people in it and although cannon and other engines of war can not be discharged or fire applied to buildings without destroying innocent together with guilty. The proof is that war could not otherwise be waged against even the guilty and the justice of belligerents would be balked. . . .

Great attention, however, must be paid to the point already taken, namely, the obligation to see that greater evils do not arise out of the war than the war would avert. For if little effect upon the ultimate issue of the war is to be expected from the storming of a fortress or fortified town wherein are many innocent folk, it would not be right, for the purpose of assailing a few guilty, to slay the many innocent by use of fire or engines of war or other means likely to overwhelm indifferently both innocent and guilty. In sum, it is never right to slay the guiltless, even as an indirect and unintended result, except when there is no other means of carrying on the operations of a just war. . . .

Here a doubt may arise whether the killing of guiltless persons is lawful when they may be expected to cause danger in the future; thus, for example, the children of Saracens are guiltless, but there is good reason to fear that when grown up they will fight against Christians and bring on them all the hazards of war. Moreover, although the adult male civilians of the enemy who are not soldiers are presumed to be innocent, yet they will hereafter carry a soldier's arms and cause the hazard named. Now, is it lawful to slay these youths? It seems so, on the same principle which justifies the incidental killing of other guiltless persons. . . .

My answer is that although this killing may possibly be defended, yet I believe that it is in no wise right, seeing that evil is not to be done even in order to avoid greater evil still, and it is intolerable that any one should be killed for a future fault. . . .

The second doubtful point is whether in a just war it is lawful to despoil innocent enemy-subjects. Let my first proposition be: It is certainly lawful to despoil the innocent of goods and things which the enemy would use against us, such as arms, ships, and engines of war. This is clear, because otherwise we could not gain the victory, which is the aim of war. . . . Hence follows the corollary that if the war goes on for an indefinitely long time it is lawful utterly to despoil all enemy subjects, guilty and guiltless alike, for it is from their resources that the enemy is feeding an unjust war, and, on the other hand, his strength is sapped by this spoliation of his citizens.

Second proposition: If a war can be carried on effectively enough without the spoliation of the agricultural population and other innocent folk, they ought not to be despoiled. . . . But the spoliation of foreigners and travelers on enemy soil, unless they are obviously at fault, is in no wise lawful, they not being enemies.

Third proposition: If the enemy refuse to restore things wrongfully seized by them and the injured party can not otherwise properly recoup himself, he may do so wherever satisfaction is obtainable, whether from guilty or from innocent. . . .

The third doubtful point is: Assuming the unlawfulness of the slaughter of children and other innocent parties, is it permissible, at any rate, to carry them off into captivity and slavery? This can be cleared up in a single proposition, namely: It is in precisely the same way permissible to carry the innocent off into captivity as to despoil them, liberty and slavery being included among the good things of Fortune. And so when a war is at that pass that the indiscriminate spoliation of all enemy-subjects alike and the seizure of all their goods are justifiable, then it is also justifiable to carry all enemy-subjects off into captivity, whether they be guilty. . . . But inasmuch as, by the law of nations, it is a received rule of Christendom that Christians do not become slaves in right of war, this enslaving is not lawful in a war between Christians; but if it is necessary having regard to the end and aim of war, it would be lawful to carry away even innocent captives, such as children and women, not indeed into slavery, but so that we may receive a money-ransom for them. . . .

The fourth doubtful point is: Whether it is lawful at any rate to kill hostages who have been taken from the enemy, either in time of truce or on the conclusion of a war. . . . If the hostages are in other respects among the guilty, as, for instance, because they have borne arms, they may rightfully be killed in that case; if, however, they are innocent, as, for instance, if they be children or women or other innocent folk, it is obvious from what has been said above that they can not be killed.

The fifth doubt is: Whether in a just war it is lawful to kill, at any rate, all the guilty. Prefatory to an answer be it noted that, as is shown by what has been said above, war is waged: Firstly, in defense of ourselves and what belongs to us; secondly, to recover things taken from us; thirdly, to avenge a wrong suffered by us; fourthly, to secure peace and security.

This premised, let my first proposition be: In the actual heat of battle, either in the storming or in the defense of a city, all who resist may be killed indiscriminately; and, briefly, this is so as long as affairs are in peril. This is manifest, because combatants could not properly effect their purpose save by removing all who hinder and resist them. All the doubt and difficulty, however, is to know whether, when we have won our victory and the enemy is no longer any danger to us, we may kill all who have borne arms against us. Manifestly, yes. For, as shown above, one of the military precepts given by the Lord was that when a city of the enemy had been taken all dwellers in it were to be killed. The words of the passage are: "When thou comest nigh unto a place to fight against it, then proclaim peace unto it. And it shall be if it make thee answer of peace, and open unto thee, that all the people that is found therein shall be saved and shall be tributaries unto thee and shall serve thee. But if it will make no peace with thee, but will make war against thee, then thou shalt besiege it. And when the Lord thy God hath delivered it into thine hands, thou shalt smite every male thereof with the edge of the sword, but not the women and the little ones."

Second proposition: Even when victory has been won and no danger remains, it is lawful to kill the guilty. The proof is that, as said above, war is ordained not only for the recovery of property, but also for the avenging of wrongs. Therefore the authors of a past wrong may be killed. . . .

Third proposition: Merely by way of avenging a wrong it is not always lawful to kill all the guilty. The proof is that even among citizens it would not be lawful, not even where the wrong was done by the whole city or district, to kill all the delinquents; nor in a common rebellion would it be permissible to slay and destroy the whole population. Accordingly, for such a deed, St. Ambrose interdicted Theodosius from the church. For such conduct would not be for the public good, which is nevertheless the end and aim of both war and peace. Therefore, it is not right to kill all the guilty among the enemy. We ought, then, to take into account the nature of the wrong done by the enemy and of the damage they have caused and of their other offenses, and from that standpoint to move to our revenge and punishment, without any cruelty and inhumanity. . . .

Fourth proposition: Sometimes it is lawful and expedient to kill all the guilty. The proof is that war is waged in order to get peace and security. But there are times when security can not be got save by destroying all one's enemies: and this is especially the case against unbelievers, from whom it is useless ever to hope for a just peace on any terms. And as the only remedy is to destroy all of them who can bear arms against us, provided they have already been in fault. . . . Otherwise, however, in a war with Christians, where I do not think this would be allowable. For, as it needs must be that scandals come and also wars between princes, it would involve the ruin of mankind and of Christianity if the victor always slew all his enemies, and the world would soon be reduced to solitude, and wars would not be waged for the public good, but to the utter ruin of the public. The measure of the punishment, then, must be proportionate to the offense, and vengeance ought to go no further, and herein account must be taken of the consideration that, as said above, subjects are not bound, and ought not, to scrutinize the causes of a war. . . .

Sixth doubt: Whether it is lawful to slay those who have surrendered or been captured, supposing them also to have been guilty. My answer is that, speaking absolutely, there is nothing to prevent the killing of those who have surrendered or been captured in a just war so long as abstract equity is observed. Many of the rules of war have, however, been fashioned by the law of nations, and it seems to be received in the use and custom of war that captives, after victory has been won . . . and all danger is over, are not to be killed, and the law of nations must be respected, as is the wont among good people. . . .

All this can be summarized in a few canons or rules of warfare. First canon: Assuming that a prince has authority to make war, he should first of all not go seeking occasions and causes of war, but should, if possible, live in peace with all men. . . . Moreover, he should reflect that others are his neighbors, whom we are bound to love as ourselves, and that we all have one common Lord, before whose tribunal we shall have to render our account. . . .

Second canon: When war for a just cause has broken out, it must not be waged so as to ruin the people against whom it is directed, but only so as to obtain one's rights and the defense of one's country and in order that from that war peace and security may in time result.

Third canon: When victory has been won and the war is over, the victory should be utilized with moderation and Christian humility, and the victor ought to deem that he is sitting as judge between two States, the one which has been wronged and the one which has done the wrong, so that it will be as judge and not as accuser that he will deliver the judgment whereby the injured state can obtain satisfaction, and this, so far as possible should involve the offending state in the least degree of calamity and misfortune, the offending individuals being chastised within lawful limits. . . .

4.5 ⎯⎯⎯⎯

The Rights of War and Peace

Hugo Grotius

■ Book I

The disputes arising among those who are held together by no common
bond of civil laws to decide their dissensions, like the ancient Patriarchs,
who formed no national community, or the numerous, unconnected communities, whether under the direction of individuals, or kings, or persons
invested with Sovereign power, as the leading men in an aristocracy, and the
body of the people in a republican government; the disputes, arising among
any of these, all bear a relation to the circumstances of war or peace. But
because war is undertaken for the sake of peace, and there is no dispute,
which may not give rise to war, it will be proper to treat all such quarrels, as
commonly happen, between nations, as an article in the rights of war: and
then war itself will lead us to peace, as to its proper end.

In treating of the rights of war, the first point, that we have to consider,
is, what is war, which is the subject of our inquiry, and what is the right,
which we seek to establish. Cicero styled war a contention by force. But the
practice has prevailed to indicate by that name, not an immediate action, but
a state of affairs; so that war is the state of contending parties, considered as
such. This definition, by its general extent, comprises those wars of every
description, that will form the subject of the present treatise. . . . Justice is
not included in the definition of war, because the very point to be decided
is, whether any war be just, and what war may be so called. Therefore we
must make a distinction between war itself, and the justice of it.

As the Rights of War is the title, by which this treatise is distinguished,
the first inquiry, as it has been already observed, is, whether any war be just,
and, in the next place, what constitutes the justice of that war. For, in this
place, right signifies nothing more than what is just, and that, more in a negative than a positive sense; so that *right* is that, which is not unjust. Now
any thing is unjust, which is repugnant to the nature of society, established
among rational creatures. Thus for instance, to deprive another of what

From *The Rights of War and Peace* by Hugo Grotius, ed. A. C. Campbell. New
York: M. Walter Dunne, 1901. Excerpt from book 1: chap. 1; book 2: chaps. 1,
22–25.

belongs to him, merely for one's own advantage, is repugnant to the law of nature. . . .

There is another signification of the word *right,* different from this, but yet arising from it, which relates directly to the person. In which sense, *right* is a moral quality annexed to the person, justly entitling him to possess some particular privilege, or to perform some particular act. This right is annexed to the person, although it sometimes follows the things, as the services of lands, which are called *real rights,* in opposition to those merely *personal.* . . .

Civilians call a faculty that Right, which every man has to his own; but we shall hereafter, taking it in its true and proper sense, call it a right. This right comprehends the power, that we have over ourselves, which is called liberty, and the power, that we have over others, as that of a father over his children, and of a master his slaves. It likewise comprehends property, which is either complete or imperfect; of the latter kind is the use or possession of any thing without the property, or power of alienating it, or pledges detained by the creditors till payment be made. There is a third signification, which implies the power of demanding what is due, to which the obligation upon the party indebted, to discharge what is owing, corresponds.

Right, strictly taken, is again twofold, the one, *private,* established for the advantage of each individual, the other, *superior,* as involving the claims, which the state has upon individuals, and their property, for the public good. Thus the Regal authority is above that of a father and a master, and the Sovereign has a greater right over the property of his subjects, where the public good is concerned, than the owners themselves have. . . .

Natural right is the dictate of right reason, shewing the moral turpitude, or moral necessity, of any act from its agreement or disagreement with a rational nature, and consequently that such an act is either forbidden or commanded by God, the author of nature. The actions, upon which such a dictate is given, are either binding or unlawful in themselves, and therefore necessarily understood to be commanded or forbidden by God. This mark distinguishes natural right, not only from human law, but from the law, which God himself has been pleased to reveal, called, by some, the voluntary divine right, which does not command or forbid things in themselves either binding or unlawful, but makes them unlawful by its prohibition, and binding by its command. But, to understand natural right, we must observe that some things are said to belong to that right, not properly, but, as the schoolmen say, by way of accommodation. These are not repugnant to natural right, as we have already observed that those things are called *just,* in which there is no injustice. . . .

We must farther remark, that natural right relates not only to those things that exist independent of the human will, but to many things, which necessarily follow the exercise of that will. Thus property, as now in use,

[handwritten margin note: Natural Law vs. Law. Human vs. God's Law]

was first a creature of the human will. But, after it was established, one man was prohibited by the law of nature from seizing the property of another against his will. . . .

◼ Book II

Defence of Person and Property

The causes of war by which are meant the justifiable causes, are now to be considered. For in some cases motives of interest operate distinctly from motives of justice. . . . But though there is an actual distinction between the justifiable causes, the pretexts, and the beginning of war; yet the terms used to express them are often confounded. . . .

The justifiable causes generally assigned for war are three, defence, indemnity, and punishment, all which are comprised in the declaration of Camillus against the Gauls, enumerating all things, which it is right to defend, to recover, and the encroachment on which it is right to punish. . . .

St. Augustine, in defining those to be just wars, which are made to avenge injuries, has taken the word avenge in a general sense of removing and preventing, as well as punishing aggressions. This appears to be his meaning from the following sentence of the passage, in which he does not enumerate the particular acts, which amount to injury, but adds, by way of illustration, that "the state or nation, which has neglected to punish the aggressions of its own subjects, or to make reparation for the losses occasioned by those aggressions, is a proper object of hostility and attack." Prompted by this natural knowledge of right and wrong, the Indian King, as we are informed by Diodorus, accused Semiramis of having commenced war against him without having received any injury. Thus the Romans expostulated with the Senones, that they ought not to attack a people who had given them no provocation. Aristotle in the second book and second chapter of his Analytics, says, war generally is made upon those who have first done an injury. . . .✱A just cause then of war is an injury, which though not actually committed, threatens our persons or property with danger. . . .

Some writers have advanced a doctrine which can never be admitted, maintaining that the law of nations authorises one power to commence hostilities against another, whose increasing greatness awakens her alarms. As a matter of expediency such a measure may be adopted, but the principles of justice can never be advanced in its favour. The causes which entitle a war to the denomination of just are somewhat different from those of expediency alone. But to maintain that the bare probability of some remote, or

✱

future annoyance from a neighbouring state affords a just ground of hostile aggression, is a doctrine repugnant to every principle of equity.)Such however is the condition of human life, that no full security can be enjoyed. The only protection against uncertain fears must be sought, not from violence, but from the divine providence, and defensive precaution.

There is another opinion, not more admissible, maintaining that the hostile acts of an aggressor may be considered in the light of defensive measures, because, say the advocates of this opinion, few people are content to proportion their revenge to the injuries they have received; bounds which in all probability the party aggrieved has exceeded, and therefore in return becomes himself the aggressor. Now the excess of retaliation cannot, any more than the fear of uncertain danger, give a colour of right to the first aggression, which may be illustrated by the case of a malefactor, who can have no right to wound or kill the officers of justice in their attempts to take him, urging as a plea that he feared the punishment would exceed the offense. The first step, which an aggressor ought to take, should be an offer of indemnity to the injured party, by the arbitration of some independent and disinterested state. And if this mediation be rejected, then his war assumes the character of a just war. . . .

On the Unjust Causes of War

. . . By having before examined and established the principles of just and necessary war, we may form a better idea of what goes to constitute the injustice of the same. As the nature of things is best seen by contrast, and we judge of what is crooked by comparing it with what is straight. But for the sake of perspicuity, it will be necessary to treat upon the leading points.

It was shewn above that (apprehensions from a neighbouring power are not a sufficient ground for war.) For to authorize hostilities as a defensive measure, they must arise from the necessity, which just apprehensions create; apprehensions not only of the power, but of the intentions of a formidable state, and such apprehensions as amount to a moral certainty. For which reason the opinion of those is by no means to be approved of, who lay down as a just ground of war, the construction of fortifications in a neighbouring country, with whom there is no existing treaty to prohibit such constructions, or the securing of a stronghold, which may at some future period prove a means of annoyance. For as a guard against such apprehensions, every power may construct, in its own territory, strong works, and other military securities of the same kind, without having recourse to actual war. . . .

Nor can the advantage to be gained by a war be ever pleaded as a motive of equal weight and justice with necessity.

Neither can the desire of emigrating to a more favourable soil and climate justify an attack upon a neighbouring power. . . .

There is no less injustice in setting up claims, under the pretence of newly discovered titles, to what belongs to another.

Neither can the wickedness, and impiety, nor any other incapacity of the original owner justify such a claim. For the title and right by discovery can apply only to countries and places, that have no owner. . . .

[N]either the independence of individuals, nor that of states, is a motive that can at all times justify recourse to arms, as if all persons *indiscriminately* had a natural right to do so. For where liberty is said to be a natural right belonging to all men and states, by that expression is understood a right of nature, antecedent to every human obligation or contract. But in that case, liberty is spoken of in a negative sense, and not by way of contrast to independence, the meaning of which is, that no one is by the law of nature doomed to servitude, though he is not forbidden by that law to enter into such a condition. For in this sense no one can be called free, if nature leaves him not the privilege of chusing his own condition. . . .

And there is equal injustice in the desire of reducing, by force of arms, any people to a state of servitude, under the pretext of its being the condition for which they are best qualified by nature. It does not follow that, because anyone is fitted for a particular condition, another has a right to impose it upon him. For every reasonable creature ought to be left free in the choice of what may be deemed useful or prejudicial to him, provided another has no just right to a controul over him. . . .

As the imperfect obligations of charity, and other virtues of the same kind are not cognizable in a court of justice, so neither can the performance of them be compelled by force of arms. For it is not the moral nature of a duty that can enforce its fulfillment, but there must be some legal right in one of the parties to exact the obligation. For the moral obligation receives an additional weight from such a right. This obligation therefore must be united to the former to give a war the character of a just war. Thus a person who has conferred a favour, has not, strictly speaking, a *right* to demand a return, for that would be converting an act of kindness into a contract.

It is necessary to observe that a war may be just in its origin, and yet the intentions of its authors may become unjust in the course of its prosecution. For some other motive, not unlawful *in itself,* may actuate them more powerfully than the original right, for the attainment of which the war was begun. It is laudable, for instance, to maintain national honour; it is laudable to pursue a public or a private interest, and yet those objects may not form the justifiable grounds of the war in question.

A war may gradually change its nature and its object from the prosecution of a right to the desire of seconding or supporting the aggrandizement of some other power. But such motives, though blamable, when even connected with a just war, do not render the war *itself* unjust, nor invalidate its conquests.

On Doubtful Causes

... [I]t must be laid down as a necessary principle, that although an action may in reality be just, yet if the party doing it, after weighing every circumstance, cannot reconcile the act to his conscience, he incurs some degree of guilt. ... For God has given conscience a judicial power to be the sovereign guide of human actions by despising whose admonitions the mind is stupefied into brutal hardness. For it often happens that judgment can point out nothing certain, but hesitates; and when such doubts and hesitations cannot satisfactorily be cleared up, the rule of Cicero is a safe one to follow, who says, that it is an excellent injunction, which forbids us to do a thing of the rectitude or impropriety of which we entertain a doubt.

But this rule cannot be applied, where of two things, in the choice of which there is equal doubt, the one must be done, in which case that must be selected, which seems to be the least unjust. For on all occasions, where a choice cannot be avoided, the less of two evils assumes the appearance of a virtue. ...

["lesser of two evils"]

It may happen in many disputed points, that the intrinsic merits of the case, or the opinions of the learned, are equal on both sides. When that happens, if the matters in discussion are of no great importance, there is nothing to blame in the person, that makes his choice either way. But in matters of moment, where the lives of men are at stake, the decision should incline to the safer side, according to the proverbial maxim, which pronounces it better to acquit the guilty than to condemn the innocent.

[proportionality? — costs? — benefits?]

War then being an object of such weighty magnitude, in which the innocent must often be involved in the sufferings of the guilty, between wavering opinions the balance should incline in favour of peace. ...

Although in doubtful cases, both sides are bound to devise every means of avoiding hostilities, yet it is a duty more incumbent upon the claimant than upon the immediate possessor of whatever may be the subject of dispute. For it is a rule not only of civil, but of natural law, that, where the pretensions are equal, those of the possessor are to be preferred.

To the foregoing remarks an additional observation may be made, that if any one, knowing his pretensions to be just, cannot produce sufficient proofs to convict the intruder of injustice, he cannot lawfully have recourse to arms, because he has no *ostensible right,* by which he can compel the intruder to relinquish the possession.

But where the right is ambiguous, and neither party has possession, the pretender, who refuses to divide the claims, may reasonably be charged with injustice.

From what has been said it will not be difficult to settle a much agitated question, whether, with respect to those, who are the principal movers of a war, there can be justice on both sides. For there are distinctions proper to be made in the various acceptations of the word *just.*

A thing is said to be just, either as to its causes, or its effects. The causes too may be confined either to justice in a *particular* acceptation, or they may be extended so as to include under that name every kind of rectitude. Again, a particular acceptation may be divided into two kinds, one relating to the *action,* and the other to the agent. An agent may be said to act justly, when, in what he does, he commits no breach of *strict law,* though his conduct may not be conformable to equity.

In a *particular* acceptation of the word justice, with regard to a matter in dispute, it cannot in war, any more than in legal proceedings, apply to both sides. For there can be no moral principle, commanding us, under the same circumstances, both to *do,* and to *abstain* from a particular action. It may happen indeed that neither of two belligerent powers may act unjustly. For no one can be charged with acting unjustly unless he knows that he is doing so; but there are many, who are not aware of the nature, extent, and consequences of their measures. . . .

In a *general* acceptation, an action may be called just, where the agent is free from every kind of blame. Yet in many cases an agent may deviate from the strict rules of legal justice, and be liable to no blame, when that deviation is owing to unavoidable ignorance, there having been neither time nor opportunity sufficient for him to know the substance, or perhaps existence of the law. . . .

If we denominate a thing to be just, from its effect in conferring certain rights, in this sense it is plain that in war there may be justice on both sides. In the same manner, a sentence not strictly legal, or a possession not perfectly just may nevertheless confer certain rights. . . .

The Causes of Undertaking War for Others

In speaking of belligerent powers, it was shewn that the law of nature authorises the assertion not only of our own rights, but of those also belonging to others. The causes therefore, which justify the principals engaged in war, will justify those also, who afford assistance to others. But whether any one presides over a household, or a state, the first and most necessary care is the support of his dependents or subjects. . . .

Yet the cause of any subject, although it may be a just cause, does not always bind sovereigns or rulers to take arms: but only when it can be done without inconvenience to all, or the greater part of their subjects. For the interests of the whole community, rather than those of particular parts, are the principal objects of a sovereign's care; and the greater any part is, the nearer its claims and pretensions approximate to those of the whole. . . .

Next to subjects, and even upon an equal footing with them, as to claims of protection, are allies, a name including, in its consequences and effects, both those, who have formed a subordinate connection with another power, and those who have entered into engagements of mutual assistance.

Yet no such compacts can bind either of the parties to the support or prosecution of unjust wars. . . . To which an additional observation may be made, that no ally is bound to assist in the prosecution of schemes, which afford no possible prospect of a happy termination. For this would be defeating the very end of alliances, which are contracted from motives of public advantage, and not for a participation in ruin. But any power is obliged to defend an ally even against those, with whom it is already connected by subsisting treaties, provided those treaties contain no express condition prohibiting such defence. . . .

A third case is that, where assistance has not been expressly promised to a friendly power, and yet is due on the score of friendship, if it can be given without inconvenience. . . .

The last and most extensive motive is the common tie of one *common nature*, which alone is sufficient to oblige men to assist each other.

It is a question, whether one man is bound to protect another, or one people another people from injury and aggression. . . .

But . . . it is certain that no one is bound to give assistance or protection, when it will be attended with evident danger. For a man's own life and property, and a state's own existence and preservation are either to the individual, or the state, objects of greater value and prior consideration than the welfare and security of other individuals or states. . . .

"Defend my your rights in the same way I would do my rights"

4.6 _____

On the Law of War

Samuel Pufendorf

Since individuals who live in natural liberty have no less power accorded them than states to defend themselves against an unjust threat of violence, and to have recourse to force in maintaining their rights, when they have been infringed upon or denied by others, I feel that it would be fitting to examine first, what the wars of individuals and states have in common, and secondly, what belongs in a special way to the latter by their nature, or by the customs of nations.

Now it is one of the first principles of natural law that no one unjustly do another hurt or damage, as well as that men should perform for each other the duties of humanity, and show especial zeal to fulfil the matters upon which they have entered into particular agreements. When men observe these duties in their relations one with another, it is called peace, which is a state most highly agreeable to human nature and fitted to preserve it, the creation and preservation of which constitutes one of the chief reasons for the law of nature being placed in the hearts of men. . . . Nay, peace is a state especially reserved to human nature as such, since it springs from a principle which belongs to man, as distinct from animals, while war arises from a principle common to them both. Of course, even animals depend upon a natural instinct to defend and preserve themselves by force, but man alone understands the genius of peace. For it is characteristic of him voluntarily to do something for another, and to refrain from injury, by reason of a certain obligation residing in one, and of a certain right residing in another person, all of which is unintelligible without the use of reason. . . .

Despite all this war is lawful and sometimes even necessary for man, when another with evil intent threatens me with injury, or withholds what is my due. For under such circumstances my care for my own safety gives me the power to maintain and defend myself and mine by any means at my disposal, even to the injury of my assailant. . . . And yet nature permits war, on the condition that he who wages it shall have as his end the establishment of peace. . . . Furthermore, although he who has injured me gives me by that

From *De Jure Naturae et Gentium Libri Octo* by Samuel Pufendorf, trans. C. H. Oldfather and W. A. Oldfather. Oxford: Clarendon Press, 1934. Excerpt from book 8: chap. 6.

act the fullest power to find recourse against him in war, yet I should consider how much good or evil such a course will probably contain for me, or for others who have not injured me. For I need not fly to arms to avenge such injuries as do not mean my utter ruin, if that will mean greater disadvantages than advantages to me and mine, or if others with whom I am still at peace will by reason of my war suffer great losses, which I should, by the law of humanity, have warded off from them by allowing such an injury as was done me to go unpunished. Therefore, if a man feels that the avenging of an injury done him will mean more evil than good, he acts in a just and praiseworthy manner in refusing to punish it by recourse to war.

The causes of just wars may be reduced to the following heads: To preserve and protect ourselves and our possessions against others who attempt to injure us, or take from us or destroy what we have; to assert our claim to whatever others may owe us by a perfect right, when they refuse to perform it for us of their own accord; and, finally, to obtain reparation for losses which we have suffered by injuries, and to extort from him who did the injury guarantees that he will not so offend in the future. As a result of these causes we have the division of just wars into offensive and defensive, of which we consider the latter to be those in which we defend and strive to retain what is ours, the former those by which we extort debts which are denied us, or undertake to recover what has been unjustly taken from us, and to seek guarantees for the future. . . .

But in general the causes of wars, and of offensive wars in particular, should be clear and leave no chance for doubt. For time and again doubts arise on this point, either from ignorance of fact, when it is not clearly established whether a thing was done or not, or what was the purpose of the doing, or from an obscure comparison of strict right with the law of charity, or from an uncertain balancing of the advantages which are likely to follow upon the declaration or avoidance of war. Therefore, in the matter before us, neither should we rashly advance any vague claim, nor, on the other hand, fly at once to arms; but we should by all means try one of three courses in order to prevent the affair from breaking out into open war, to wit, either a conference between the parties concerned or their representatives; or an appeal to arbitrators; or, finally, the use of the lot. . . .

The unjust causes for wars are reviewed by Grotius, . . . of which some have no grounds at all, while some have a slight foundation, though weak at the best. To the first belong avarice and the lust for superfluous possessions, ambition and a craving to lord it over others, and a burning desire to gather fame from the oppression of their fellows. . . .

To the second class belongs fear of the strength and power of a neighbour. . . . Yet fear alone does not suffice as a just cause for war, unless it is established with moral and evident certitude that there is an intent to injure us. For an uncertain suspicion of peril can, of course, persuade you to sur-

round yourself in advance with defences, but it cannot give you a right to be
the first to force the other by violence to give a real guarantee, as it is
called, not to offend. . . . For so long as a man has not injured me, and is not
caught in open preparation to do so (for sometimes an incompleted injury
can be avenged by a war no less than a completed one), it should be presumed that he will perform his duty in the future, especially when he con-
firms it by protestations and his pledged word. But it would be unjust to
extort a real guarantee from such a one through force, since by such a procedure his condition would be worse than ours, in that he is required to
abide by our mere given word. But supposing there exists a just cause for
war, in that case an unusual increase in a neighbour's power comes in for
serious consideration in the debates upon war, since experience well shows
that most men, as their strength increases, grow more eager to lord it over
others. . . .

But if we are correctly to understand how far we may proceed with
violence against an enemy and his possessions, we should observe that the
licence to be used against an enemy is one thing, as it arises from a simple
state of hostility, and another, as the mercifulness of natural law orders
control and temperance in its indulgence. That is, since according to the
law of nature there should be a mutual performance of the duties of peace,
whoever takes the first step in violating them against me, has, so far as he
is able, freed me from my performance of the duties of peace, and therefore, in confessing that he is my enemy, he allows me a licence to use
force against him to any degree, or so far as I may think desirable. This is
especially true because the end of war, whether offensive or defensive,
could not be gained without this licence, if it were necessary to hold the
use of force against an enemy within a certain limit, and never to proceed
to extremities. For this reason even open wars partake somewhat of the
nature of a contract like this: "Try whatever you can, I will likewise use
every means at my disposal." And this holds good not merely if an enemy
has undertaken to use every extremity against me, but also if he simply
wishes to injure me within certain limits, for he has no greater right to do
me a slight injury than a severe one. Therefore, not only may I use force
against an enemy until I have warded off the peril with which he threatened me, or have received or extorted from him what he had unjustly
robbed me of, or refused to furnish, but I can also proceed so far as to
secure guarantees for the future. And if he allows that to be forced from
him, he shows clearly enough that he still intends to injure me again in the
future. Nor is it in fact always unjust to return a greater evil for a less, for
the objection made by some that retribution should be rendered in proportion to the injury, is true only of civil tribunals, where punishments are
meted out by superiors. But the evils inflicted by right of war have properly no relation to punishments, since they neither proceed from a superior
as such, nor have as their direct object the reform of the guilty party or

others, but the defence and assertion of my safety, my property, and my rights. To secure such ends it is permissible to use whatever means I think will best prevail against such a person, who, by the injury done me, has made it impossible for me to do him an injury, however I may treat him, until we have come to a new agreement to refrain from injuries for the future.

But now the law of humanity would not only have one consider how much an enemy can suffer without injury, but also what should be the deeds of a humane and, above all, a generous victor. Therefore, we should take care that, so far as it is possible, and as our defence and future security allow, we suit the evils inflicted upon an enemy to the process usually observed by a civil court in meting out justice in offences and other quarrels. . . .

It is everywhere recognized that men wage wars not merely on their own behalf but also frequently on behalf of others. For this to be lawful, there is required in him to whom aid is brought, a just cause for war, and on him who undertakes to bring it to another there should lie a special obligation, whereby he is bound to the principal belligerent, and which is of such a nature, that, in order to favour one man, I can treat another man as though he were my enemy. . . .

Now among those whom we not only rightly can but should defend, are our subjects; and this is not only because they are a part, as it were, of the government, but also because it was to enjoy such defence that free men of their own accord set up governments or submitted to them. . . . Yet it is only proper for the heads of states to go to war for individual citizens, if it can be done without entailing a greater hardship upon all or a majority of the other citizens, since their duty is more concerned with the whole body of citizens than with a part, and the greater the part the more closely it approximates the whole.

The next persons after subjects for whom we are obligated to take up arms, are allies, who have made this an article of their treaty with us. But they yield under every circumstance to our subjects, provided aid cannot be furnished both of them at once, and no despite is done to the treaty, for no state is obligated to any one more than to its own citizens. Therefore, when a government promises aid to others, it is understood to do so on the condition that such aid can be given without impairing its obligation towards its own citizens. And so he is even a fool who puts any trust in a treaty when its observance is of no importance to the other party. And just as no man should undertake unjust or rash wars, so no man is obligated to give aid to an ally who engages in such wars. And although this statement applies primarily to offensive wars, yet it applies in a way to defensive ones as well, for if any ally of mine sees that he is not the equal of an enemy, even with my aid, and yet persists in courting certain ruin when he could close with him on tolerable terms, it would be insane of me to join myself to his folly. . . .

After allies come friends, or such as we are joined to by reason of some kindness or favour. Although no certain and definite aid is promised these by an express treaty, yet the striking up of mutual friendship is understood to imply a promise that the safety of the one will be the other's care, so far as more binding obligations permit, and will in fact weigh more heavily with him than the ties of human brotherhood ordinarily demand. And this alone can be sufficient to make a man undertake another's defence against the manifest injuries of his enemies, especially since it can very easily be our highest interest, and in fact redound to the general good of mankind, to prevent a man from injuring and insulting others with impunity. . . . Yet there ought to be some restraint in this, so that not every man, even though he live in natural liberty, should have the right to coerce and punish by war any person who has done any other person an injury, on the sole excuse that the public good demands that injuries to the innocent should not go unpunished, and that what concerns one should concern all. For since he who is attacked in this fashion is not deprived of his right to meet with equal violence the violence of him whom he himself has never injured, the result would be that for one war to distress and embroil mankind there would be two. Nay, for a person to thrust himself forward as a kind of arbitrator of human affairs, is opposed even to the equality granted by nature, not to mention the fact that such a thing could easily lead to great abuse, since there is scarcely a man living against whom this could not serve as an excuse for war. Therefore, an injury done another can only give us cause for war when the injured party calls upon us for aid, so that whatever we do in such a case is done not in our name but in that of the person wronged. . . .

A man can acquire, in a just war, by the law of nature, and with a clear conscience, from the possession of enemies, whatever is owed him, or its equivalent, and such things as caused him to take up arms, because his enemies refused to pay them, including all expenses he was put to in vindicating the violation of his right, and whatever else he may have felt was necessary in order that he might secure guarantees from his enemy. Therefore, if a man was led to injure others by confidence in his wealth, it is lawful to take from him, when defeated, his superfluous possessions, so that he may be less over-bearing in the future. But by the customs of nations a man becomes owner in a formal war of such things as he took from the enemy, although they be beyond all bounds and reason, and far exceed the claim for which the war was begun. . . . But we should observe, in this connexion, that seizure in war acquires only a right which prevails against some third party, and that for the captor to acquire a dominion which will prevail also against him from whom the things were taken, the latter must have concluded peace with the other, and made a legal transfer. For without this a right to such things is understood to remain with the former owner, whenever he regains enough strength to recover them from his enemy.

Part 2

Resort to War
(Jus ad Bellum)

5 Aggression and Self-Defense

5.1 ___

Introduction
The Editors

Nation-states are members of a community of states, and therefore are understood to have rights. Foremost among them are the rights to territorial integrity and political independence. In domestic society, the violation of an individual's rights is a crime. In general, the violation of a state's rights, according to international law, is also considered a crime—the crime of aggression. The difficulty for both just war theorists and international legal scholars, not to mention policymakers, is how to determine when a state's territorial integrity and/or political independence have been violated by the actions of another state. When those rights have in fact been violated, the victim may use military force to secure those rights; self-defense is a just cause for war. This principle of *jus ad bellum* dates to the earliest formulations of just war theory.

In contemporary international law, self-defense is the *only* legitimate purpose for which a state may resort to war. The position of just war theorists in the Middle Ages was more permissive, however. Thomas Aquinas lists two just causes for war in addition to self-defense: to retake something that was unjustly seized and to punish those responsible. Although we get the sense from canonical thought that just war was seen as an instrument by which good would prevail over evil—an expansive notion that was worrisome to Grotius—we ought not make too much of the modern view that war is just only when undertaken for reasons of self-defense narrowly conceived. Defensive wars today often involve the reacquisition of territory taken by an aggressor, and postwar reparations sometimes appear rather punitive. The 1992 war triggered by Iraq's invasion and occupation of Kuwait is a case in point.

As Yoram Dinstein discusses, in the late nineteenth and early twentieth centuries, states signed various treaties placing legal limits on their use of war as a means to redress grievances with each other. This is not to say that such mechanisms had the desired effect of banishing war as an instrument of world politics, but they did reflect the increasingly widespread moral position that states' liberty to resort to force ought to be constrained and that international law could serve that purpose. The Covenant of the League of Nations obliged member states to respect each other's territorial integrity and political independence, a pledge that is repeated in Article 2 of the United Nations Charter. The founders of both organizations were not so idealistic that they believed states would no longer have need to defend themselves. The charter, in Article 51, asserts that none of its provisions are intended to impair "the inherent right of individual or collective self-defense."

While recognizing that states would never consent to being stripped of their right of self-defense, the UN's founders still hoped to fashion a more effective means of dealing with the problem of aggression. Chapter VII of the charter describes the role of the organization's fifteen-member Security Council in maintaining international peace and security. The council, having been given the authority to assemble armed forces from UN member states, was charged with responding not only to acts of aggression, but also to any "breach of the peace" or "threat to the peace." The exact meaning of these terms was deliberately left unstated so that the council would have maximum flexibility in fulfilling its role as guarantor of international peace and security. As it turned out, the council was very nearly immobilized by the Cold War and even today does not function as the framers of the UN Charter had imagined.

It is nevertheless interesting to note how the experience of World War II led the would-be architects of the postwar international order to attempt to restrict states' rights to employ armed force. The Security Council would decide (subject to its voting rules) how to respond to aggression not only against one or more of its fifteen members, but to aggression against any UN member state. An individual state's right of self-defense is limited in two ways by Article 51. First, whereas the council may act in response to mere breaches and threats, a state acting without Security Council sanction may resort to self-defense "if an armed attack occurs." Second, states acting in self-defense are permitted to do so "until the Security Council has taken measures necessary to maintain international peace and security." Those measures may involve, and in practice always have involved, continued participation of the state acting in self-defense, but the charter does seem to envision the council as the ultimate authority.

The flipside of the debate over self-defense is the question of what constitutes aggression. What counts as a violation of another state's territorial integrity or political independence? As Myres McDougal and Florentino

Feliciano explain, legal efforts to define aggression have generally taken one of two forms. One approach is to identify the sorts of acts that, on their face, are aggressive acts; the aggressor is the state that first commits one of those acts. A different approach is to construct a general formula for illuminating the inherent aggressiveness of any and all aggressive acts.

Both approaches are evident in the definition of aggression provided by the UN General Assembly in Resolution 3314. (The resolution does not have the force of international law, but nearly identical language has been incorporated into the 1947 Rio Treaty, signed by most states in the western hemisphere, making these provisions binding on them.) Article 2 of the resolution suggests a default formula for identifying an aggressive act, one that appeals to common sense: "the first use of armed force." But first use of armed force constitutes only prima facie evidence of aggression; the Security Council may determine that the aggressor is not in fact the state that first resorted to force. Article 3 then lists the first uses of force that are typically understood as aggressive: invasion and occupation, bombardment, blockade, and so on. In most cases, acts like these are fairly plain to see, but others are more open to dispute. For example, a state that sends, or is "substantially involved" in sending, irregular military forces to carry out aggressive acts against another state may also qualify as an aggressor. Many states have been involved in such activities, and many victims have invoked self-defense to justify the resort to war. The US invasion of Afghanistan in 2001 following the September 11 attacks by Al-Qaida was justified as an act of self-defense primarily on these grounds.

The General Assembly's definition of aggression includes a controversial exception. According to Article 7, the prohibition of acts listed in Article 3 is not intended to prejudice a people's right to self-determination, "particularly peoples under colonial and racist regimes or other forms of alien domination." The exception is not so much a license for peoples to resort to aggressive acts against their oppressors—this not being a matter of inter*state* relations—but rather seems to allow a state to support a people's struggle for liberation without thereby being guilty of aggression toward the state against which that people is fighting.

McDougal and Feliciano, writing nearly fifty years ago, also touch on an issue that has become a topic of intense debate today: under what conditions may a state invoke self-defense in order to justify the preemptive use of military force against another state? The readings in Chapter 5 address the issue more thoroughly, but for now it is worth mentioning what McDougal and Feliciano refer to as "necessity" as a requirement for anticipatory self-defense. The least permissive interpretation of necessity has become known as the *Caroline* standard. In 1837, Canadian insurgents fighting the British were taking refuge on the US side of the Niagara River. The US steamship *Caroline* had been involved in supporting the insurgency, mainly by ferrying Canadian rebels and new recruits to various points along the river, and was subsequently boarded by British colonial troops, set afire, and sent over Niagara Falls. US secretary of state Daniel Webster would later reject Britain's justification for the attack, which invoked the right of self-defense, because Britain failed to show a "necessity of self-defense, instant, overwhelming, leaving no choice of means and no moment for deliberation." McDougal and Feliciano maintain that the *Caroline* standard seems to impose paralysis until the aggressor is at the doorstep. The standard has certainly come under much criticism as overly restrictive today, an age in which global terrorism and the proliferation of weapons of mass destruction have increased immeasurably the costs of unanticipated attacks.

It may not be an exaggeration to say that the international community is now no closer to a consensus on what constitutes aggression than it was a century ago. At the Nuremberg Trials following World War II, certain Nazi officials were convicted of waging wars of aggression—"crimes against peace," they were called—despite their argument that aggression was not then recognized as a crime under international law and was not defined by the London Charter that created the Nuremberg Tribunal. Despite the absence of an agreed-upon definition of aggression, in planning Germany's wars, these leaders had clearly conspired to violate treaties to which Germany was party, including the nonaggression pact with the Soviet Union, and that was sufficient, in the Tribunal's view, for their conviction of crimes against peace.

Like the London Charter, the 1998 Rome Statute establishing the International Criminal Court provides no definition of aggression, even though "the crime of aggression" is one of four types to be prosecuted at the ICC (see Chapter 13). But in contrast to the Nuremberg Tribunal, until such time that aggression is defined, the ICC has no jurisdiction to hear cases brought against those accused of that crime.

5.2

The Legal Status of War

Yoram Dinstein

■ The Extra-legality of War

War occurs in human history so repetitively that there is a tendency to take it for granted. For many centuries, war was discerned with resignation as a perennial fact of life. The popular outlook was that war is tantamount to a "providential visitation to be compared with plague or flood or fire."[1] In similarity to these and other natural disasters (such as earthquakes and volcanic eruptions), war was expected to inflict itself on mankind in cyclical frequency. Like the plague, war would appear every once in a while, leave death and devastation in its wake, and temporarily pass away to return at a later date.

The analogy between war and catastrophes ordained by nature influenced lawyers, who have occasionally suggested that war falls into the same "category of events, considered incapable of legal control but entailing legal consequences."[2] Just as no legal system can forbid thunderbolts or droughts, it has been assumed that international law cannot possibly interdict war. War has been deemed beyond the reach of international law and, therefore, "neither legal nor illegal."[3] . . .

The phraseology typical of those who represent war as an extra-legal phenomenon is that international law only "finds" or "accepts" war as a *fait accompli*. It is universally acknowledged that, once war begins, international law can and does regulate the relations between belligerents (as well as between them and neutrals). However, the exponents of the extra-legality of war believe that, while there is plenty of room for a *jus in bello* (governing conduct in warfare), there can be no real *jus ad bellum* (imposing normative limitations on the unleashing of hostilities). "Law cannot say *when,* but only *how* war is to be waged."[4]

The proposition that war is a metajuridical occurrence may be tempting, but it is devoid of foundation. The assimilation of war to events taking place in nature is artificial and delusive. Unlike earthquakes and epidemics, war is caused by human beings. Every form of human behaviour is susceptible of regulation by law. No category of human behaviour is excluded *a priori* from the range of application of legal norms (actual or potential). At bottom, the undisputed ability of international law to control the conduct of combatants in the course of war *(jus in bello)* proves that it can also restrict the freedom of action of belligerents in the generation of war *(jus ad bellum)*. When an epidemic is raging, law is utterly unable to dictate to the virus not only when (and if) to mount an assault upon the human body, but also how to go about it. From a jurisprudential standpoint, there is no real difference between governing the "when" and the "how" of war.

Certainly, international law does not "establish" war. For that matter, domestic law does not "establish" murder or robbery. War, as a form of human conduct, resembles murder or robbery more than flood or drought. In the same way that murder and robbery are prohibited by domestic law, war can be forbidden by international law.

For a long time international law did refrain from obtruding upon the liberty of States to go to war. Yet, this forbearance did not mean that international law had a built-in impediment depriving it of the power to ban war. In reality, by not prohibiting recourse to war, international law indicated that war was tolerated and, therefore, permitted. War can be legal or illegal, but it is misleading to suggest that it is extra-legal.

Upon analysis, the theory of the extra-legality of war is of far greater potential moment than the concept of its legality. Moving from the latter to the former is a transition from bad to worse. If war is lawful in a given era, it can still be proscribed afterwards. But if war is extra-legal, it can never be made unlawful. Consequently, the prohibition of aggressive war in the twentieth century implies (i) a denial of the doctrine of its extra-legality; as well as (ii) a confirmation of the hypothesis that, prior to the interdiction, war used to be legal.

▇ The Legality of War

Subsequent to the virtual demise of the just war doctrine, the predominant conviction in the nineteenth (and early twentieth) century was that every State had a right—namely, an interest protected by international law—to embark upon war whenever it pleased. The discretion of States in this matter was portrayed as unfettered. States could "resort to war for a good reason, a bad reason or no reason at all."[5] Among the legitimate reasons for war would figure the desire to use it as a sanction against non-compliance with international law. . . . Equally, war could be employed as a means to challenge and upset the international legal status quo. At one and the same time, war "had a static as well as a dynamic function": to enforce existing rights and to defy them.[6]

War came to be characterized as "a right inherent in sovereignty itself."[7] Moreover, the war-making right was thought of as the paramount attribute of sovereignty. When the statehood of a specific political entity was in doubt, the best litmus test was comprised of checking whether the prerogative of launching war at will was vested in it. The international legal freedom to wage war for whatever reason even impacted upon the constitutions and organic laws of quite a few countries. Some of these instruments, when spelling out to which branch of Government the war-making power was entrusted, overtly applied different procedures to the initiation of offensive and defensive wars.

When observed through the lens of legal theory, the freedom to indulge in war without thereby violating international law seemed to create an egregious anomaly. It did not make much sense for the international legal system to be based on respect for the sovereignty of States, while each State had a sovereign right to destroy the sovereignty of others. On the one hand, it was incumbent on every State to defer to a plethora of rights accorded to other States under both customary and conventional international law. On the other hand, each State was at liberty to attack any other State whenever it pleased. . . .

The apparent incongruity may be examined from a somewhat different point of departure. In the final analysis, every legal system has to protect the vital interests of its subjects. States are the primary subjects of international law. Hence, it is arguable that "[a] system of international law must premise the right of states to exist."[8] When international law recognized the privilege of States to engage in war at their discretion, the net result was that the right of the target State to exist could be repudiated at any moment. What emerged was a deep-rooted inconsistency in the international legal order, which "both asserts and denies the right of states to exist."[9] Some scholars even reasoned that the inconsistency was calamitous to international law. To their minds, by not restraining war and thus failing to protect the fundamental interests of its principal subjects (the States), international law was not true law.

This was by no means the prevalent opinion. Many writers totally disavowed the notion that the freedom of war was not in harmony with the existence of a genuine international legal system. Others simply sidestepped the issue. In any event, irrespective of any scholarly bafflement, States and statesmen in the nineteenth (and early twentieth) century did not consider the freedom of war to be a fatal flaw in the structure of international law. Nor did they find it inconceivable that, in the name of sovereignty, each State was empowered to challenge the sovereignty of other States. The practice of States in that period was "dominated by an unrestricted right of war,"[10] and conceptual criticisms were largely ignored.

▉ Exceptions to the General Liberty to Go to War

Special Arrangements

Precisely because the liberty to go to war was regarded by States as the general rule, there is no dearth of bilateral treaties in the nineteenth (and early twentieth) century, in which the contracting parties assumed an obligation not to resort to war in their particular relations. Concomitantly, the parties consented to seek an amicable settlement (e.g. mediation or arbitration) whenever a dispute might arise between them. Such a treaty was applicable, however, only *inter partes,* without detracting from the freedom of action of signatories *vis-à-vis* third States. In addition, the treaty was usually limited to a fixed time, although it could be subject to extension. When the prescribed period expired, every contracting party had the right to terminate the treaty on notice. Once the treaty was no longer in force, all States concerned regained the option to commence hostilities against one another.

As an illustration, we may take a treaty concluded between Honduras and Nicaragua in 1878, in which these two countries agreed that "there shall in no case be war" between them and, in the event of a dispute, undertook to turn to arbitration by a friendly nation. Each party was entitled to give notice after four years, so as to terminate the treaty.

The trend of concluding bilateral treaties of this kind continued well into the post–World War I era. But in the 1920s and 1930s, States preferred to couch their obligations in terms of "non-aggression pacts" (thereby clearly retaining the right to wage wars of self-defence). A good example is a 1926 treaty between Persia (present-day Iran) and Turkey, wherein the parties committed themselves "not to engage in any aggression against the other" and "not to participate in any hostile action whatsoever directed by one or more third Powers against the other Party."

Occasionally, a non-aggression pact had more than two contracting parties. The most important non-aggression instrument of the period was the 1925 Locarno Treaty of Mutual Guarantee, in which Germany and France, and also Germany and Belgium, were mutually bound not to "resort to war against each other."

A different approach was reflected in a series of bilateral agreements, known as the Bryan treaties (after the American Secretary of State who originated them), concluded between the United States and dozens of other countries on the eve of World War I. In these treaties, the contracting parties agreed to submit all disputes to investigation by an International Commission, and the Commission was instructed to complete its report within one year. Pending the investigation and report, the parties pledged "not to declare war or begin hostilities."

The Bryan treaties did not negate the right of any State to start war eventually. What the treaties sought to accomplish was the introduction of a "cooling-off period" of one year to enable passions to subside. The underlying assumption was that delay as such (or the gaining of time) would be advantageous, since the parties were expected to become progressively more amenable to reason. As a matter of fact, reliance on lapse of time as a factor allaying suspicions and fears is not empirically corroborated in all instances. Some international disputes are easier to tackle, and to settle, at an earlier stage. Passage of time, far from cooling off hot tempers, may only exacerbate incipient tensions.

The Hague Conventions

The first steps, designed to curtail somewhat the freedom of war in general international law (through multilateral treaties), were taken in the two Hague Peace Conferences of 1899 and 1907. Under Article 2 of Hague Convention (I) of both 1899 and 1907 for the Pacific Settlement of International Disputes, contracting parties agreed that in case of a serious dispute, before making "an appeal to arms," they would resort ("as far as circumstances allow") to good offices or mediation of friendly States. The liberty to go to war was circumscribed here in an exceedingly cautious way, leaving to the discretion of the parties the determination whether to employ force or to search for amicable means of settling the dispute.

Article 1 of Hague Convention (II) of 1907 Respecting the Limitation of the Employment of Force for the Recovery of Contract Debts—often called the Porter Convention (after the American delegate who had proposed it)—obligated contracting parties "not to have recourse to armed force" for the recovery of contract debts (claimed from one Government by another as being due to its nationals), unless the debtor State refused an offer of arbitration, prevented agreement on a compromise or rejected an arbitral award. Hague Convention (II) echoed the Drago Doctrine (named after an Argentinian Foreign Minister), which had denied the justification of war as a mode of compelling payment of a public debt. The scope of the limitation on the freedom of war, as formulated in the Convention, was quite narrow. First, war was still permissible if the debtor State refused to go through the process of arbitration or abide by its results. Secondly, the Convention did not apply to direct inter-governmental loans and was confined to contractual debts to foreign nationals (whose claims were espoused by their respective Governments). Still, it is arguable that, from this modest beginning, "a shift in the notion of the *jus ad bellum*" started to take place.[11]

The Covenant of the League of Nations

The Covenant of the League of Nations qualified the right to go to war in a more comprehensive way. In Article 10, Members of the League pledged "to respect and preserve as against external aggression the territorial integrity and existing political independence of all Members of the League." This was an abstract provision, which lent itself to more than one interpretation. Hence, Article 10 had to be read in conjunction with, and subject to, the more specific stipulations following it.

Article 11 enunciated that any war or threat of war was a matter of concern to the entire League. Pursuant to Article 12, if any dispute likely to lead to rupture arose between Members of the League, they were required to submit it to arbitration, judicial settlement or inquiry by the League's Council. Members were bound "in no case to resort to war until three months after the award by the arbitrators or the judicial decision, or the report of the Council." The award of the arbitrators or the judicial decision had to be rendered "within reasonable time." The Council's report had to be arrived at no later than six months after the submission of the dispute.

Article 13 specified which subject-matters were "generally suitable" for submission to either arbitration or judicial settlement. Members were obligated to carry out in good faith any arbitral award or judicial decision. They agreed that they "will not resort to war" against another Member complying with the award or decision.

In accordance with Article 15, disputes between Members, when not submitted to arbitration or judicial settlement, had to be brought before the Council. The Council's role was restricted to issuing recommendations, as distinct from binding decisions. However, under paragraph 6 of the Article, if the Council's report was carried unanimously (excluding the parties to the dispute), Members consented "not to go to war with any party to the dispute which complies with the recommendations of the report." If the Council failed to reach a unanimous report (apart from the parties to the dispute), paragraph 7 reserved the right of Members to take any action that they considered necessary for the maintenance of right and justice. Paragraph 8 precluded the Council from making any recommendation, if it thought that the dispute had arisen out of a matter "which by international law is solely within the domestic jurisdiction of that party." Article 15 also enabled referral of the dispute from the Council to the Assembly of the League, in which case it was the Assembly that was empowered to make recommendations. An Assembly report, if adopted by the votes of all the Members of the Council and a majority of the other Members (again not counting the parties to the dispute), had the same force as a unanimous report of the Council.

In all, the Covenant did not abolish the right of States to resort to war. Subject to specific prohibitions, detailed in the articles cited, war remained lawful. If looked at from a complementary angle of vision, one could easily discern a number of "gaps" in the legal fence installed by the Covenant around the right of States to resort to war. The "gaps" opened the legal road to war in the following circumstances:

(a) The most blatant case in which the liberty to plunge into war was kept intact resulted from Article 15(7). In the absence of unanimity in the Council or a proper majority in the Assembly, excluding the votes of parties to the dispute, the parties retained their freedom of action.

(b) In light of Article 15(8), the Council (or the Assembly) was incompetent to reach a recommendation if in its judgment the matter came within the domestic jurisdiction of a party to the dispute. Since no recommendation would be adopted, the parties preserved their freedom of action. Thus, paradoxically, an international war could be triggered by a dispute that was ostensibly non-international in character.

(c) It was implied in Article 12 that, if the Council (or the Assembly) did not arrive at a recommendation within six months—or, alternatively, if either an arbitral award or a judicial decision was not delivered within reasonable time—the parties would be free to take any action that they deemed fit.

(d) Articles 13 and 15 forbade going to war against a State complying with an arbitral award, a judicial decision, a unanimous recommendation of the Council, or an Assembly recommendation based on the required majority. In conformity with Article 12, no war could be undertaken within three months of the award, decision or recommendation. The upshot was that, after three months, war could be started against a State failing to comply with the award, decision or recommendation.

(e) Naturally, all the limitations on the freedom of war applied to the relations between League Members *inter se*. The Covenant did not, and could not, curtail that freedom in the relations between non-Members and Members (and *a fortiori* between non-Members among themselves). Article 17 provided that, in the event of a dispute between a Member and a non-Member or between non-Members, the non-Member(s) should be invited to accept the obligations of membership for the purposes of the dispute, and then the stipulations of Articles 12 ff would apply. It goes without saying that non-Members had an option to accede to such an invitation or to decline it.

Shortly after the entry into force of the Covenant, initiatives were taken to close these "gaps." The most famous attempt was made in the Geneva Protocol on the Pacific Settlement of International Disputes, which was adopted by the Assembly of the League in 1924, but never entered into force. The capstone of the Protocol was Article 2, whereby the contracting parties agreed "in no case to resort to war," except in resistance to aggression or with the consent of the League's Council or Assembly. Article 2 was intended to abolish the general right to go to war. Yet, since the Protocol remained abortive, war did not become illegal in principle until the Kellogg-Briand Pact of 1928.

■ Notes

1. C. Eagleton, *International Government,* 3rd ed. (1957), p. 455.

2. Q. Wright, "Changes in the Conception of War," *American Journal of International Law* 18 (1924), pp. 755, 756.

3. J. L. Brierly, *The Outlook for International Law* (1944), p. 22.

4. C. A. Pompe, *Aggressive War an International Crime* (1953), p. 140.

5. H. W. Briggs, *The Law of Nations,* 2nd ed. (1952), p. 976.

6. See J. L. Kunz, "The Law of Nations, Static and Dynamic," *American Journal of International Law* 27 (1933), pp. 630, 634.

7. A. S. Hershey, *The Essentials of International Public Law* (1912), p. 349.

8. Q. Wright, "The Present Status of Neutrality," *American Journal of International Law* 34 (1940), pp. 391, 399.

9. Ibid., p. 400.

10. I. Brownlie, *International Law and the Use of Force by States* (1963), p. 19.

11. C. R. Rossi, "*Jus ad Bellum* in the Shadow of the 20th Century," *New York Law School Journal of International and Comparative Law* 15 (1994–1995), pp. 49, 60.

5.3 ——

Resort to Coercion

Myres S. McDougal and Florentino P. Feliciano

▣ From the Covenant to the Charter

The Covenant of the League of Nations represented the first significant break with the theory of traditional international law. The Covenant set forth a broad undertaking of members to "respect . . . the territorial integrity and existing political independence" of each other. The specific obligations it imposed upon its members were, however, less comprehensive. "Resort to war" was, under the terms of the Covenant, unlawful in four cases: when made without prior submission of the dispute to arbitration or judicial settlement or to inquiry by the Council of the League; when begun before the expiration of three months after the arbitral award or judicial decision or Council report; when commenced against a member which had complied with such award or decision or recommendation of a unanimously adopted Council report; and, under certain circumstances, when initiated by a non-member state against a member state.

It was of course no mere historical accident that the break with traditional theory and the re-establishment of a distinction between permissible and nonpermissible resort to coercion coincided with the first attempt at a permanent, institutionalized organization of the community of states. The necessity for such organization was underscored by the collapse of the nineteenth-century system of power-balancing in Europe, a system that had become increasingly unstable and precarious as the number of effective territorial units of power gradually diminished. The bloodletting of World War I, the first conflict since the Napoleonic Wars to assume the proportions of "total war," generated widespread revulsion over the use of violence to secure national goals. Thus, promoting recourse to nonviolent procedures of change was a principal purpose infusing the prescriptions of the Covenant. In fact, prior recourse to nonviolent procedures was made a test of permissible coercion. . . .

From *Law and Minimum World Public Order: The Legal Regulation of International Coercion* by Myres S. McDougal and Florentino P. Feliciano. New Haven: Yale University Press, 1961. Used by permission of W. Michael Reisman. Excerpt from chap. 3 ("Resort to Coercion").

The formally modest limitations which the Covenant of the League placed on the *jus ad bellum* of traditional international law were sought to be extended, and the so-called "gaps" in the Covenant closed, by the General Treaty for the Renunciation of War of 1928. This Pact of Paris (Kellogg-Briand Pact) condemned "recourse to war for the solution of international controversies" and set out comprehensive undertakings to renounce "war as an instrument of national policy" and to seek the resolution of "all disputes or conflicts, of whatever nature or whatever origin they may be" exclusively by "pacific means." The policy objectives of preventing violence and promoting noncoercive methods of adjustment were thus much more ambitiously formulated than in the League Covenant. That the Pact of Paris left intact the freedom of states to exercise violence in self-defense has at times been noted with some aspersion, as though that in some way impaired the Pact's prohibition of "recourse to war." The fact is, of course, that self-defense is recognized in even the most advanced municipal public orders, and is indispensable in an arena as ineffectively organized as that of the present world. . . .

It is true, however, that the Pact, by retaining "war" as a term of art, failed to quiet the continued debate as to the permissibility of force that participants might verbally describe as a "measure short of war." It was left to the Charter of the United Nations to resolve and make moot that debate by discarding the term "war" and employing in its stead the multiple references to "threat or use of force," "threat to the peace," "breach of the peace," and "act of aggression." Taken collectively, these phrases refer to a whole spectrum of degrees of intensity of coercion, including (so far as force is concerned) not only "war," understood as extensive armed hostilities or the highest degree of destructive use of the military instrument, but also all those applications of force of a lesser intensity or magnitude that in the past had been characterized as "short of war." The Charter sought also to centralize the process of characterizing, for purposes of requiring or authorizing enforcement action, a particular exercise of coercion as permissible or nonpermissible, and to vest that function in the organized community itself. . . .

■ The Conception of Impermissible Resort to Coercion: The Debate About Definitions

The decision of the framers of the United Nations Charter to leave such terms as "threat to the peace," "breach of the peace," and "act of aggression" ambiguous and comprehensive was a deliberate one. In recent years, however, the failure of the optimistic hopes for great power cooperation and intensifying expectations of violence have caused renewed agitation for the clarification and elaboration of basic concepts. The continuing debates today, like those within the League of Nations, have centered principally on the question of "defining aggression." Unfortunately, the efforts of the First and Sixth Committees, the political and legal committees, of the General Assembly, the International Law Commission, and the 1953 and 1956 Special Committees on Defining Aggression to formulate a generally acceptable "definition of aggression" have not been blessed with conspicuous success. Representatives of nation-states engaged in the enterprise of defining aggression conceive of too many implications, real and unreal, for national security to permit much consensus either on any particular proposed verbalization of the conception of aggression or even on the utility of attempts at definition.

The principal formulations proposed have generally assumed one or the other, or a combination, of two main forms. The first consists of a more or less lengthy catalogue of stereotypes of aggressive acts. The formulation vigorously propounded by the Soviet Union—a formulation which grew from the five-item closed list of overt military acts incorporated in the 1933 London Conventions for the Definition of Aggression to an open-ended fifteen-item inventory of acts of military, "indirect," "economic," and "ideological" aggression in 1956—is perhaps the best-known species of this genus of definitions. The point of such an inventory is that the state "which first commits" one of the listed acts is to be declared the aggressor. More distinctively, the Soviet formulation includes a list of negative criteria, of acts which are not to be characterized as aggression and internal conditions which do not justify the commission of any act catalogued as aggressive. The most basic defect of the Soviet and other comparable definitions is an overemphasis on material acts of coercion and on a mechanistic conception of priority; concomitantly, they fail to take into account other factors which rationally are equally relevant, factors such as the nature of the objectives of the initiating and responding participants and the character or intensity of the coercion applied.

The second major type of definition exhibits a different approach which rejects the technique of specific enumeration and seeks instead the construction of a broad and general formula that would comprehend all possible instances of aggression. Perhaps the broadest of these formulas was that submitted by Sr. Alfaro to the International Law Commission:

> Aggression is the threat or use of force by a State or Government against
> another State, in any manner, whatever the weapons employed and
> whether openly or otherwise for any reason or for any purpose other than
> individual or collective self-defense or in pursuance of a decision or rec-
> ommendation by a competent organ of the United Nations.[1]

This formulation emphasizes the complementarity of aggression on the one hand and self-defense and collective peace enforcement on the other. It is, however, little more than a posing, in highest level abstraction, of the general problem involved, and offers no index for the guidance of decision-makers who must apply it in specific cases. . . . In further illustration of this second major type of definition, the formulation incorporated in the Act of Chapultepec signed by all the American republics on March 8, 1945, may be noted. The act provides that

> Any attempt on the part of a non-American state against the integrity or inviolability of the territory, the sovereignty or the political independence of an American State shall be considered an act of aggression against all the American States.

. . . [T]his act offers some indication of the character of the perspectives that make coercion and violence unlawful. It exhibits, however, little effort to clarify what operations, "attempts," when moved by these perspectives, may be characterized as aggression.

A third type of definition, the so-called "mixed" definition, seeks to combine both the enumerative and "broad-formula" approaches by appending an illustrative but nonexhaustive list of specific examples of aggression to a relatively abstract statement of general policy. . . . The draft definition submitted by Iran and Panama at the ninth session of the General Assembly is representative:

> 1. Aggression is the use of armed force by a State against another State for any purpose other than the exercise of the inherent right of individual or collective self-defense or in pursuance of a decision or recommendation of a competent organ of the United Nations.
> 2. In accordance with the foregoing definition, in addition to any other acts which such international bodies as may be called upon to determine the aggressor may declare to constitute aggression, the following are acts of aggression in all cases:
> (a) Invasion by the armed forces of a State of territory belonging to another State or under the effective jurisdiction of another State;
> (b) Armed attack against the territory, population or land, sea or air forces of a State by the land, sea or air forces of another State;
> (c) Blockade of the coast or ports or any other part of the territory of a State by the land, sea or air forces of another State;
> (d) The organization, or the encouragement of the organization, by a State, of armed bands within its territory or any other territory for incursions into the territory of another State, or the toleration of the organization of such bands in its own territory, or the toleration of the use by such armed bands of its territory as a base of operations or as a point of departure for incursions into the territory of another State, as well as direct participation in or support of such incursions. . . .

▪ The Conception of Permissible Coercion

. . . [T]he conception of permissible coercion may usefully be assigned a threefold reference. First, there is a relatively low-level coercion which is "normal" and perhaps ineradicable in the ordinary value processes taking place across state boundaries and which includes all coercion not accelerated to the levels of intensity and magnitude that signal impermissible coercion. Secondly, there is the coercion of relatively great scope and intensity, including the most intense and extensive violence, that is exercised in necessary response to and defense against impermissible coercion by others. Lastly, there are police measures of varying degrees of comprehensiveness and intensity applied by or under the authorization of the organized community of states.

Admittedly, various specific acts encompassed in the first type of coercion, "ordinary coercion," may constitute international wrongs other than aggression which legitimatize responses in the form of denying reciprocities and imposing retaliations other than destructive uses of the military instrument. Such acts may contravene community prescriptions and policies other and less fundamental than those concerned with the securing of minimum public order and the promotion of peaceful modalities of international change. . . .

The specific contexts of interstate conflict which may confront authoritative decision-makers commonly include both measures of coercion and measures of counter or opposing coercion. These processes of coercion and counter coercion give rise to opposed claims that, on the one hand, the coercion applied is unlawful, initiating coercion and that, on the other, the coercion is lawful self-defense. When the respective contending participants are viewed in turn, each may be seen commonly to assert both claims simultaneously: that its opponent has unlawfully initiated coercion and that it is itself responding with coercion in self-defense. Obviously, an external decision-maker must make coordinated inquiry into and assessment of both the coercion claimed to be prohibited aggression and the coercion claimed to be permissible defense. The theme of complementarity is thus a dominant one manifesting itself both in the contraposition of claims asserted in practice and in the necessities of rational analysis by decision-makers.

▪ Self-Defense Distinguishable from Other Exercises of Coercion

For clarity in thought, that coercion which is claimed to be in defense against unlawful attack or threat against independence or territorial integrity must be distinguished sharply from certain other types of asserted coercion which differ greatly in modality, purpose, specific context, and relevant community policy but which also are frequently put forward under the name of self-defense. The claims with which we are primarily concerned here are claims to exercise highly intense coercion in response to what is alleged to be unlawfully initiated coercion. The other distinguishable types of assertions include claims by one belligerent that it is lawful to apply coercion against a nonparticipant state in response to or anticipation of some operation by the opposing belligerent in the nonparticipant's territory. . . .

Claims of Self-Defense

The first type—claims to employ highly intense coercion in defense against allegedly impermissible coercion—may be conveniently subcategorized according to the imminence and intensity of the coercion to which response is to be made. Most conspicuous perhaps are claims to respond with force to intense coercion that is immediate and current and that may be of varying degrees of comprehensiveness and continuity. Such is the claim which a target state makes when reacting violently to military blows initiated and delivered against it; the United States' declaration of war following the attack by Japanese air forces on Pearl Harbor is a familiar example. Claims to resort to force in anticipation and prevention of intense coercion are only slightly less prominent. The coercion anticipated may, in the expectations of the claimant, be of varying degrees of imminence or remoteness. Claims have been made, for instance, to initiate preemptive violence under allegedly high expectations of imminent or impending military attack. Israel's claim that its invasion of Egyptian territory in 1956 was defensive in character being, among other things, in anticipation of an "all-out attempt to eliminate Israel by force"[2] presents one contemporary illustration. The notion of anticipatory defense has at times been given extravagant unilateral interpretation by claimant states. In the past, states have asserted claims to pre-empt and counter by armed force not only imminently expected eruptions of military violence but also more or less remote possibilities of attack. They have asserted, in other words, the need to preclude a context of "conditions which, if allowed to develop, might become in time a source of danger."[3] What states have in effect claimed in these assertions, sometimes under an invocation of "self-preservation," is a competence forcibly to protect their values by forestalling processes which, they argue, may in the future develop into highly intense coercion or violence. Hence they seek to strike while these processes still embody only a low level of coercion.

Assertions of Coercion Against Third States

Claims by a belligerent to use force against a third state—a nonparticipant in the original conflict—in order to prevent or counter some anticipated hostile operation by the opposing belligerent in the territory of the third state, have been made under differing words: "self-defense," "self-preservation," "right of necessity," "necessity in self-preservation" and so on. The force employed against the third state under these assertions has varied widely in intensity, scope, and continuity, from isolated acts to full-scale invasion and occupation of the third state's territory. The classic illustration of a single limited application of force was the seizure of the Danish fleet in 1807 by British naval forces, following a severe bombardment of Copenhagen, to prevent acquisition of the fleet by Napoleon. A comparable instance arose in 1940 when the British destroyed the French fleet at Mers-el-Kebir and Oran to preclude capture of the fleet by German forces. Assertion of more comprehensive claims of this type may be documented by reference to the German invasions of Belgium in World War I and of Norway in World War II. In 1914, in its ultimatum demanding permission for German troops to march through Belgium, Germany declared that it was "essential for [her] self-defense that she should anticipate" what was alleged to be a French intention to mount an attack through Belgian territory. In 1946, it was contended by the defense at Nuremberg that "Germany was compelled to attack Norway to forestall an Allied invasion and [that] her action was therefore preventive."[4] Another comprehensive (though less extravagant) claim was the Anglo-Soviet occupation of Iran in 1941 to prevent further German infiltration and "fifth column" activities. . . .

■ Self-Defense

. . . The principal requirements which the "customary law" of self-defense makes prerequisite to the lawful assertion of these claims are commonly summarized in terms of necessity and proportionality. For the protection of the general community against extravagant claims, the standard of required necessity has been habitually cast in language so abstractly restrictive as almost, if read literally, to impose paralysis. Such is the clear import of the classical peroration of Secretary of State Webster in the *Caroline* case—that there must be shown a "necessity of self defense, instant, overwhelming, leaving no choice of means and no moment for deliberation."[5] The requirement of proportionality, which . . . is but another application of the principle of economy in coercion, is frequently expressed in equally abstract terms. . . . There is, however, increasing recognition that the requirements of necessity and proportionality . . . can be subjected only to that most comprehensive and fundamental test of all law, reasonableness in particular context. . . .

Conditions and the Expectation of Necessity

Inquiry may next be directed to the conditions under which coercion claimed to be in self-defense is exercised. The conditions we noted as relevant for scrutinizing allegedly unlawful coercion, conditions including both the general elements pervasive in power processes in the world arena and certain particular conditions of more direct significance, are, again, of equal relevance for reviewing assertions of self-defense. The most important condition that must be investigated is the degree of necessity—as that necessity is perceived and evaluated by the target-claimant and incorporated in the pattern of its expectations—which, in the particular instance, impels the claim to use intense responding coercion. . . .

The exacting standard of customary law. The structure of traditional prescription has established a standard of justifying necessity commonly referred to in exacting terms. A high degree of necessity . . . was prerequisite to a characterization of coercion as "legitimate self-defense." Necessity that assumed the shape of an actual and current application of violence presented little difficulty. It was of course the purpose of high requirements of necessity to contain and restrict the assertion of claims to apply preemptive violence, that is when the necessity pleaded consisted of alleged expectations of an attack which had yet actually to erupt. In the *Caroline* case . . . , the British claim with which Secretary of State Webster was confronted was an assertion of anticipatory defense. There is a whole continuum of degrees of imminence or remoteness in future time, from the most imminent to the most remote, which, in the expectations of the claimant of self-defense, may characterize an expected attack. Decision-makers sought to limit lawful anticipatory defense by projecting a customary requirement that the expected attack exhibit so high a degree of imminence as to preclude effective resort by the intended victim to nonviolent modalities of response.

One illustration of the application of the customary-law standard of necessity for anticipatory defense is offered in the judgment of the International Military Tribunal for the Far East in respect of the war waged by Japan against the Netherlands. Japan contended that "inasmuch as the Netherlands took the initiative in declaring war on Japan, the war which followed [could] not be described as a war of aggression by Japan."[6] The Netherlands declared war on Japan on December 8, 1941, before the actual invasion of the Netherlands East Indies by Japanese troops and before the issuance of the Japanese declaration of war against the Netherlands, both of which took place on January 11, 1942. The evidence showed, however, that as early as November 5, 1941, the Imperial General Headquarters had issued to the Japanese Navy operational orders for the attacks upon the Netherlands East Indies, as well as the Philippines and British Malaya, and that on December 1, 1941, an Imperial Conference had formally decided that Japan would "open hostilities against the United States, Great Britain and the Netherlands."[7] The Tribunal held that the Netherlands, "being fully apprised of the imminence of the attack," had declared war against Japan "in self defense."[8] Similarly, the International Military Tribunal at

Nuremberg, in rejecting a defense argument that the German invasion of Norway was "preventive" in character and designed to anticipate an Allied landing in Norway, pointed out that the German plans for invasion were not in fact made to forestall an "imminent" Allied landing, and that, at best, such plans could only prevent an Allied occupation "at some future time."[9] The documentary evidence submitted to the Tribunal did indicate that there was a "definite" Allied plan to occupy harbors and airports in Norway. The Tribunal found, however, that the expectations of Germany at the time of launching the invasion did not as a matter of fact include a belief that Britain was about to land troops in Norway. . . .

Effects and the Proportionality of Responding Coercion

We turn, finally, to appraisal of the effects of coercion claimed to be in self-defense. The principal reference here is to the degree of intensity and scope exhibited in this coercion—factors long recognized to be of special relevance in judgments about the lawfulness of particular claims to self-defense. It is primarily in terms of its magnitude and intensity—the consequentiality of its effects—that alleged responding coercion must be examined for its "proportionality." "Proportionality" which, like "necessity," is customarily established as a prerequisite for characterizing coercion as lawful defense, is sometimes described in terms of a required relation between the alleged initiating coercion and the supposed responding coercion: the (quantum of) responding coercion must, in rough approximation, be reasonably related or comparable to the (quantum of) initiating coercion. It is useful to make completely explicit that concealed in this shorthand formulation of the requirement of proportionality are references to both the permissible objectives of self-defense and the condition of necessity that evoked the response in coercion. Proportionality in coercion constitutes a requirement that responding coercion be limited in intensity and magnitude to what is reasonably necessary promptly to secure the permissible objectives of self-defense. For present purposes, these objectives may be most comprehensively generalized as the conserving of important values by compelling the opposing participant to terminate the condition which necessitates responsive coercion. Put a little differently, the objective is to cause the initiating participant to diminish its coercion to the more tolerable levels of "ordinary coercion." This is the import of Secretary of State Webster's somewhat cryptic statement that "nothing unreasonable or excessive [must be done], since the act, justified by the necessity of self defense, must be limited by that necessity and kept clearly within it." Thus articulated, the principle of proportionality is seen as but one specific form of the more general principle of economy in coercion and as a logical corollary of the fundamental community policy against change by destructive modes. Coercion that is grossly in excess of what, in a particular context, may be reasonably required for conservation of values against a particular attack, or that is obviously irrelevant or unrelated to this purpose, itself constitutes an unlawful initiation of coercive or violent change. . . .

■ Notes

1. UN Doc. No. A/CN.4/L.31, p. 27 (1951).

2. See the statements of the Israeli representative in the General Assembly. UN Gen. Ass., *Off. Rec.,* 1st Emer. Spec. Sess. 61 (1956), pp. 22–23. The "inherent right of self-defense" was explicitly invoked by the same representative.

3. Fenwick, *International Law,* 3d ed. (1948), p. 231.

4. Office of US Chief of Counsel for Prosecution of Axis Criminality, *Nazi Conspiracy and Aggression, Opinion and Judgment* (1947), p. 86.

5. Mr. Webster to Mr. Fox, April 24, 1841, in 29 *British and Foreign State Papers* (1840–1841), pp. 1129, 1138.

6. *Judgment of the International Military Tribunal for the Far East* (1948), p. 994.

7. Ibid., pp. 976–978.

8. Ibid., p. 995.

9. Office of US Chief of Counsel for Prosecution of Axis Criminality, *Nazi Conspiracy and Aggression, Opinion and Judgment* (1947), p. 57.

5.4 ————

Charter of the United Nations

■ Chapter I: Purposes and Principles

Article 1
The Purposes of the United Nations are:

1. To maintain international peace and security, and to that end: to take effective collective measures for the prevention and removal of threats to the peace, and for the suppression of acts of aggression or other breaches of the peace, and to bring about by peaceful means, and in conformity with the principles of justice and international law, adjustment or settlement of international disputes or situations which might lead to a breach of the peace;

2. To develop friendly relations among nations based on respect for the principle of equal rights and self-determination of peoples, and to take other appropriate measures to strengthen universal peace;

3. To achieve international co-operation in solving international problems of an economic, social, cultural, or humanitarian character, and in promoting and encouraging respect for human rights and for fundamental freedoms for all without distinction as to race, sex, language, or religion; and

4. To be a centre for harmonizing the actions of nations in the attainment of these common ends.

Article 2
The Organization and its Members, in pursuit of the Purposes stated in Article 1, shall act in accordance with the following Principles.

1. The Organization is based on the principle of the sovereign equality of all its Members.

2. All Members, in order to ensure to all of them the rights and benefits resulting from membership, shall fulfill in good faith the obligations assumed by them in accordance with the present Charter.

3. All Members shall settle their international disputes by peaceful

means in such a manner that international peace and security, and justice, are not endangered.

4. All Members shall refrain in their international relations from the threat or use of force against the territorial integrity or political independence of any state, or in any other manner inconsistent with the Purposes of the United Nations.

5. All Members shall give the United Nations every assistance in any action it takes in accordance with the present Charter, and shall refrain from giving assistance to any state against which the United Nations is taking preventive or enforcement action.

6. The Organization shall ensure that states which are not Members of the United Nations act in accordance with these Principles so far as may be necessary for the maintenance of international peace and security.

7. Nothing contained in the present Charter shall authorize the United Nations to intervene in matters which are essentially within the domestic jurisdiction of any state or shall require the Members to submit such matters to settlement under the present Charter; but this principle shall not prejudice the application of enforcement measures under Chapter VII. . . .

■ Chapter VII:
Action with Respect to Threats to the Peace, Breaches of the Peace, and Acts of Aggression

Article 39
The Security Council shall determine the existence of any threat to the peace, breach of the peace, or act of aggression and shall make recommendations, or decide what measures shall be taken in accordance with Articles 41 and 42, to maintain or restore international peace and security. . . .

Article 41
The Security Council may decide what measures not involving the use of armed force are to be employed to give effect to its decisions, and it may call upon the Members of the United Nations to apply such measures. These may include complete or partial interruption of economic relations and of rail, sea, air, postal, telegraphic, radio, and other means of communication, and the severance of diplomatic relations.

Article 42
Should the Security Council consider that measures provided for in Article 41 would be inadequate or have proved to be inadequate, it may take such action by air, sea, or land forces as may be necessary to maintain or restore

international peace and security. Such action may include demonstrations, blockade, and other operations by air, sea, or land forces of Members of the United Nations.

Article 43

1. All Members of the United Nations, in order to contribute to the maintenance of international peace and security, undertake to make available to the Security Council, on its call and in accordance with a special agreement or agreements, armed forces, assistance, and facilities, including rights of passage, necessary for the purpose of maintaining international peace and security.

2. Such agreement or agreements shall govern the numbers and types of forces, their degree of readiness and general location, and the nature of the facilities and assistance to be provided.

3. The agreement or agreements shall be negotiated as soon as possible on the initiative of the Security Council. They shall be concluded between the Security Council and Members or between the Security Council and groups of Members and shall be subject to ratification by the signatory states in accordance with their respective constitutional processes. . . .

Article 45

In order to enable the United Nations to take urgent military measures, Members shall hold immediately available national air-force contingents for combined international enforcement action. The strength and degree of readiness of these contingents and plans for their combined action shall be determined within the limits laid down in the special agreement or agreements referred to in Article 43, by the Security Council with the assistance of the Military Staff Committee.

Article 46

Plans for the application of armed force shall be made by the Security Council with the assistance of the Military Staff Committee.

Article 47

1. There shall be established a Military Staff Committee to advise and assist the Security Council on all questions relating to the Security Council's military requirements for the maintenance of international peace and security, the employment and command of forces placed at its disposal, the regulation of armaments, and possible disarmament.

2. The Military Staff Committee shall consist of the Chiefs of Staff of the permanent members of the Security Council or their representatives. Any Member of the United Nations not permanently represented on the Committee shall be invited by the Committee to be associated with it when

the efficient discharge of the Committee's responsibilities requires the participation of that Member in its work.

3. The Military Staff Committee shall be responsible under the Security Council for the strategic direction of any armed forces placed at the disposal of the Security Council. Questions relating to the command of such forces shall be worked out subsequently.

4. The Military Staff Committee, with the authorization of the Security Council and after consultation with appropriate regional agencies, may establish regional sub-committees. . . .

Article 51

Nothing in the present Charter shall impair the inherent right of individual or collective self-defence if an armed attack occurs against a Member of the United Nations, until the Security Council has taken measures necessary to maintain international peace and security. Measures taken by Members in the exercise of this right of self-defence shall be immediately reported to the Security Council and shall not in any way affect the authority and responsibility of the Security Council under the present Charter to take at any time such action as it deems necessary in order to maintain or restore international peace and security.

5.5 ——————

Resolution 3314:
Definition of Aggression
United Nations General Assembly

■ Definition of Aggression

Article 1
Aggression is the use of armed force by a State against the sovereignty, territorial integrity or political independence of another State, or in any other manner inconsistent with the Charter of the United Nations, as set out in this Definition.

Article 2
The first use of armed force by a State in contravention of the Charter shall constitute prima facie evidence of an act of aggression although the Security Council may, in conformity with the Charter, conclude that a determination that an act of aggression has been committed would not be justified in the light of other relevant circumstances, including the fact that the acts concerned or their consequences are not of sufficient gravity.

Article 3
Any of the following acts, regardless of a declaration of war, shall, subject to and in accordance with the provisions of article 2, qualify as an act of aggression:

(a) The invasion or attack by the armed forces of a State of the territory of another State, or any military occupation, however temporary, resulting from such invasion or attack, or any annexation by the use of force of the territory of another State or part thereof;

(b) Bombardment by the armed forces of a State against the territory of another State or the use of any weapons by a State against the territory of another State;

(c) The blockade of the ports or coasts of a State by the armed forces of another State;

(d) An attack by the armed forces of a State on the land, sea or air forces, or marine and air fleets of another State;

(e) The use of armed forces of one State which are within the territory of another State with the agreement of the receiving State, in contravention of the conditions provided for in the agreement or any extension of their presence in such territory beyond the termination of the agreement;

(f) The action of a State in allowing its territory, which it has placed at the disposal of another State, to be used by that other State for perpetrating an act of aggression against a third State;

(g) The sending by or on behalf of a State of armed bands, groups, irregulars or mercenaries, which carry out acts of armed force against another State of such gravity as to amount to the acts listed above, or its substantial involvement therein.

sanctions?

Article 4

The acts enumerated above are not exhaustive and the Security Council may determine that other acts constitute aggression under the provisions of the Charter.

Article 5

1. No consideration of whatever nature, whether political, economic, military or otherwise, may serve as a justification for aggression.

2. A war of aggression is a crime against international peace. Aggression gives rise to international responsibility.

3. No territorial acquisition or special advantage resulting from aggression is or shall be recognized as lawful.

Article 6

Nothing in this Definition shall be construed as in any way enlarging or diminishing the scope of the Charter, including its provisions concerning cases in which the use of force is lawful.

Article 7

Nothing in this Definition, and in particular article 3, could in any way prejudice the right to self-determination, freedom and independence, as derived from the Charter, of peoples forcibly deprived of that right and referred to in the Declaration on Principles of International Law concerning Friendly Relations and Cooperation among States in accordance with the Charter of the United Nations, particularly peoples under colonial and racist regimes or other forms of alien domination: nor the right of these peoples to struggle to that end and to seek and receive support, in accordance with the principles of the Charter and in conformity with the above-mentioned Declaration.

6 Preemption and Prevention

6.1

Introduction
The Editors

The term "preemption" is not specifically used by the classic architects of the just war tradition. It is, however, a logical extension of the right of a state to defend itself. Grotius lists fear as among the unjust causes of war. The simple fact that a state is enhancing its military might is not held to be justification for another state to attack it, even though this increase in military prowess might generate fear and anxiety in other states. "To maintain that the bare probability of some remote or future annoyance from a neighbouring state affords a just ground of hostile aggression, is a doctrine repugnant to every principle of equity." But Pufendorf notes an important qualification to this general view. Claiming that "an incipient injury, no less than a completed one, can sometimes be vindicated by war," Pufendorf supposes that if a state believes "with a morally evident certitude" that another state intends to attack or harm it in some way, it can take appropriate action, including military action, to avert the injury. This may now be considered the doctrine of preemption.

Under the rubric of self-defense, preemptive attacks by a state are justifiable under the morality of war only if an anticipated attack is imminent, and this view has now received acknowledgment in international law. As we show below, the rather strict formulation of legitimate preemption offered by Secretary of State Daniel Webster in the 1840s is often cited by diplomats in the modern era. At the same time, the decided ambiguity that surrounds Pufendorf's account of a justified preemptive attack is replicated in the contemporary language of imminence and its application to developing threats. Exactly when is an attack or injury imminent, and when is it not imminent? There is simply no easy or ready answer to this question, and since states may reasonably prefer to err on the side of caution, the notion of imminence may well be pushed back in practice toward the condition of fear. That seems to be the inclination of the Bush administration, which, in its 2002 National Security Strategy, announced that today's threats require that the traditional understanding of imminence be loosened.

One way to avoid this problem is to doubt the prudence, if not the morality, of the doctrine of preemption. Realists, for example, may be inclined to argue that rather than adopt a policy of preemptive action, states are better advised to enhance their own military capacity and indicate, as the United States did during the Cold War, that military aggression against them will be met with a swift and catastrophic retaliation. But this response is subject to two problems. First, it must be clear that states or nonstate aggressors are in fact likely to be deterred by a military response to aggression. Second, there must be a clear and vulnerable target (e.g., a specific and identifiable state with authority over a territory and its population) to retaliate against. The second condition now seems more problematic in a world where terrorist groups are exceptionally difficult to identify, locate, and reach with military assets. The US assault against the Taliban in Afghanistan, for example, succeeded in unseating the governing authority there, but it has not as yet brought an end to the activities of Al-Qaida.

Another way to resolve the problem of ambiguity is to articulate, as the Bush administration has done, a more expansive and less equivocal theory of justified anticipatory action against possible or potential attack and contend that military force may be used to defend against harmful actions even if they cannot be considered imminent. According to this view, states may initiate military action in order to prevent developments, like nuclear proliferation, that may ultimately lead to harmful actions against them, something that is now recognized as the doctrine of prevention. The doctrine of prevention has not as yet reached the status of international law, but it may do so at some point, as Mark Drumbl suggests. The crucial question it generates, however, is a moral one. Is the doctrine of preventive action a morally acceptable amendment to the morality of war?

Reflection on this question might begin by noting first that the distinction between preemption and prevention is not one of degree but of kind. Under the doctrine of prevention, states need not worry about or quibble over the imminence of the threat but focus instead on its realistic possibility. If states have reason to believe that they are subject to harmful attack, they may take steps to counter the threat. It is the presence of the threat and not its immediacy that matters. The US war against terrorism, for example, involves an effort to put an end to terrorist activity (or at least terrorist activity aimed at the United States), and not merely to disrupt or foil specific terrorist strikes against the United States, though of course the latter aim is contained in the former. What seems to justify suspending the requirement of immediacy is the fear that an attack, whenever and wherever it

out of
aggression

occurs, will have truly devastating consequences—the sort we might expect from the use of nuclear or other weapons of mass destruction (WMD).

If traditional deterrence strategy is likely to be ineffective because there is simply no obvious target of retaliation, a shift to a policy of prevention may make some sense in the course of dealing with certain kinds of threats. But there is a danger of taking such a policy too far. Fear, even justified fear, of state involvement or complicity in support of terrorist activity, for example, may legitimate preventive action under the doctrine of prevention, but a similar goal might just as easily be achieved by recourse to more traditional deterrence strategies. In the selection below, for example, John Mearsheimer and Stephen Walt argue that the putative reasons given to support the attack on Iraq by the United States, Great Britain, and other allies was hardly justified because Saddam Hussein was in fact quite deterrable. If deterrence can achieve the same goal as preventive action, it seems preferable from a moral (and not just a prudential) point of view because nonviolent strategies are morally superior to more violent ones. But of course arguments of this sort suffer from the traditional problem that haunts consequentialist reasoning. Can states be confident that their adversaries really are deterrable?

From the standpoint of classic just war theory, on the other hand, the prevention doctrine seems morally questionable. According to just war theory, it is the imminence of the threat, and not merely its existence, that matters. But just war theory was framed with the state system in mind and admits of an ambiguity when its strictures are applied in a world where harm and injury might be done by nonstate actors. Pufendorf implies, for example, that military action is justified to thwart an injury if the intent to harm is clear—again with "a morally evident certitude." The required evidence necessary to justify what we now think of as preemption would seem to involve something like the interception of orders from the leaders of a threatening state to prepare for attack, the mobilization of forces on one's border, and so forth. It is, however, evidence of the intent to do harm, for Pufendorf, that establishes imminence and not the actual preparation for hostilities. Within the setting of a state system, the latter condition is merely the evidence required to establish the existence of the former condition. If the intent is there, the imminence requirement is met.

If this reasoning is applied to nonstate actors like terrorists, it may be supposed that an initial attack, coupled with continued threats of more to come, justifies a conclusion that injury is imminent. Presumably, the intent is present and the terrorists are waiting only for the time to be right and some opportunity to present itself to attack. If this construction of the morality of anticipatory self-defense in the just war tradition is correct, then the underlying logic of just war theory would support a limited doctrine of prevention. In effect, the doctrine of prevention would collapse into the doctrine of preemption at home in just war reasoning. If, however, a state is the target of preventive action, as in the case of the US-led assault against Iraq, a clear connection between the state and those terrorist groups that intend the actual injury must be made. If the necessary nexus cannot be established, just war theory could not support preventive action against the state.

The difficulty is that the nature of the threat justifying preventive action—the threat of a devastating attack delivered covertly and without warning—may leave few visible traces as it is being prepared and executed. Indeed, this is why we do not have the luxury of waiting until the attack is imminent before striking preemptively. It is reasonable for the United States simply to assume that a nonstate actor, like Al-Qaida, is planning such an attack, will continue operating out of sight, and is not deterrable. The 9/11 attacks provide ample evidence of intent, as well as capability to deliver a blow. But because the sort of attack the United States fears depends on the acquisition of WMD, any state in a position to supply such weapons is a potential target of preventive action. Any states with clearly demonstrated WMD programs and links to global terrorism would top the list, of course, but what about states with primitive WMD programs and only tenuous links to terrorists? How certain must one be that the threat exists before taking preventive military action? And what about states with well-developed WMD programs and no links to terrorists, but characterized by political instability that may result in the government losing control over their weapons? At what point in this unraveling might preemptive strikes be justified?

The problem with the prevention doctrine, then, is not that states will never have a moral justification for striking first in order to avert a catastrophic attack, even a distant one. The problem is rather that the threshold for Pufendorf's "morally evident certitude" becomes more clouded by subjectivity and potential misjudgment the further we move away from the traditional requirement of imminence. That the traditional requirement has itself been open to dispute when invoked to justify or condemn particular preemptive acts of self-defense—for example, the US blockade during the Cuban Missile Crisis or the Israeli assault at the outset of the Six Day War—suggests that an international standard for legitimate preventive action is likely to remain elusive.

6.2 _____

The National Security Strategy of the United States of America

September 2002

The nature of the Cold War threat required the United States—with our allies and friends—to emphasize deterrence of the enemy's use of force, producing a grim strategy of mutual assured destruction. With the collapse of the Soviet Union and the end of the Cold War, our security environment has undergone profound transformation.

Having moved from confrontation to cooperation as the hallmark of our relationship with Russia, the dividends are evident: an end to the balance of terror that divided us; an historic reduction in the nuclear arsenals on both sides; and cooperation in areas such as counterterrorism and missile defense that until recently were inconceivable.

But new deadly challenges have emerged from rogue states and terrorists. None of these contemporary threats rival the sheer destructive power that was arrayed against us by the Soviet Union. However, the nature and motivations of these new adversaries, their determination to obtain destructive powers hitherto available only to the world's strongest states, and the greater likelihood that they will use weapons of mass destruction against us, make today's security environment more complex and dangerous.

In the 1990s we witnessed the emergence of a small number of rogue states that, while different in important ways, share a number of attributes. These states:

* brutalize their own people and squander their national resources for the personal gain of the rulers;
* display no regard for international law, threaten their neighbors, and callously violate international treaties to which they are party;
* are determined to acquire weapons of mass destruction, along with other advanced military technology, to be used as threats or offensively to achieve the aggressive designs of these regimes;
* sponsor terrorism around the globe; and

From *The National Security Strategy of the United States of America.* September 2002. Excerpt from chap. 5 ("Prevent Our Enemies from Threatening Us, Our Allies, and Our Friends with Weapons of Mass Destruction").

• reject basic human values and hate the United States and everything for which it stands.

At the time of the Gulf War, we acquired irrefutable proof that Iraq's designs were not limited to the chemical weapons it had used against Iran and its own people, but also extended to the acquisition of nuclear weapons and biological agents. In the past decade North Korea has become the world's principal purveyor of ballistic missiles, and has tested increasingly capable missiles while developing its own WMD arsenal. Other rogue regimes seek nuclear, biological, and chemical weapons as well. These states' pursuit of, and global trade in, such weapons has become a looming threat to all nations.

We must be prepared to stop rogue states and their terrorist clients before they are able to threaten or use weapons of mass destruction against the United States and our allies and friends. Our response must take full advantage of strengthened alliances, the establishment of new partnerships with former adversaries, innovation in the use of military forces, modern technologies, including the development of an effective missile defense system, and increased emphasis on intelligence collection and analysis.

Our comprehensive strategy to combat WMD includes:

• *Proactive counterproliferation efforts.* We must deter and defend against the threat before it is unleashed. We must ensure that key capabilities—detection, active and passive defenses, and counterforce capabilities—are integrated into our defense transformation and our homeland security systems. Counterproliferation must also be integrated into the doctrine, training, and equipping of our forces and those of our allies to ensure that we can prevail in any conflict with WMD-armed adversaries.

• *Strengthened nonproliferation efforts to prevent rogue states and terrorists from acquiring the materials, technologies, and expertise necessary for weapons of mass destruction.* We will enhance diplomacy, arms control, multilateral export controls, and threat reduction assistance that impede states and terrorists seeking WMD, and when necessary, interdict enabling technologies and materials. We will continue to build coalitions to support these efforts, encouraging their increased political and financial support for nonproliferation and threat reduction programs. The recent G-8 agreement to commit up to $20 billion to a global partnership against proliferation marks a major step forward.

• *Effective consequence management to respond to the effects of WMD use, whether by terrorists or hostile states.* Minimizing the effects of WMD use against our people will help deter those who possess such weapons and dissuade those who seek to acquire them by persuading enemies that they cannot attain their desired ends. The United States must also be prepared to respond to the effects of WMD use against our forces abroad, and to help friends and allies if they are attacked.

It has taken almost a decade for us to comprehend the true nature of this new threat. Given the goals of rogue states and terrorists, the United States can no longer solely rely on a reactive posture as we have in the past. The inability to deter a potential attacker, the immediacy of today's threats, and the magnitude of potential harm that could be caused by our adversaries' choice of weapons, do not permit that option. We cannot let our enemies strike first.

- In the Cold War, especially following the Cuban missile crisis, we faced a generally status quo, risk-averse adversary. Deterrence was an effective defense. But deterrence based only upon the threat of retaliation is less likely to work against leaders of rogue states more willing to take risks, gambling with the lives of their people, and the wealth of their nations.
- In the Cold War, weapons of mass destruction were considered weapons of last resort whose use risked the destruction of those who used them. Today, our enemies see weapons of mass destruction as weapons of choice. For rogue states these weapons are tools of intimidation and military aggression against their neighbors. These weapons may also allow these states to attempt to blackmail the United States and our allies to prevent us from deterring or repelling the aggressive behavior of rogue states. Such states also see these weapons as their best means of overcoming the conventional superiority of the United States.
- Traditional concepts of deterrence will not work against a terrorist enemy whose avowed tactics are wanton destruction and the targeting of innocents; whose so-called soldiers seek martyrdom in death and whose most potent protection is statelessness. The overlap between states that sponsor terror and those that pursue WMD compels us to action.

For centuries, international law recognized that nations need not suffer an attack before they can lawfully take action to defend themselves against forces that present an imminent danger of attack. Legal scholars and international jurists often conditioned the legitimacy of preemption on the existence of an imminent threat—most often a visible mobilization of armies, navies, and air forces preparing to attack.

We must adapt the concept of imminent threat to the capabilities and objectives of today's adversaries. Rogue states and terrorists do not seek to attack us using conventional means. They know such attacks would fail. Instead, they rely on acts of terror and, potentially, the use of weapons of mass destruction—weapons that can be easily concealed, delivered covertly, and used without warning.

The targets of these attacks are our military forces and our civilian population, in direct violation of one of the principal norms of the law of warfare. As was demonstrated by the losses on September 11, 2001, mass civilian casualties is the specific objective of terrorists and these losses would be exponentially more severe if terrorists acquired and used weapons of mass destruction.

The United States has long maintained the option of preemptive actions to counter a sufficient threat to our national security. The greater the threat, the greater is the risk of inaction—and the more compelling the case for taking anticipatory action to defend ourselves, even if uncertainty remains as to the time and place of the enemy's attack. To forestall or prevent such hostile acts by our adversaries, the United States will, if necessary, act preemptively.

The United States will not use force in all cases to preempt emerging threats, nor should nations use preemption as a pretext for aggression. Yet in an age where the enemies of civilization openly and actively seek the world's most destructive technologies, the United States cannot remain idle while dangers gather.

We will always proceed deliberately, weighing the consequences of our actions. To support preemptive options, we will:

• build better, more integrated intelligence capabilities to provide timely, accurate information on threats, wherever they may emerge;
• coordinate closely with allies to form a common assessment of the most dangerous threats; and
• continue to transform our military forces to ensure our ability to conduct rapid and precise operations to achieve decisive results.

The purpose of our actions will always be to eliminate a specific threat to the United States or our allies and friends. The reasons for our actions will be clear, the force measured, and the cause just.

6.3 _____

Preemption, Prevention, and *Jus ad Bellum*

Craig L. Carr and David Kinsella

There are two dimensions to the Bush Doctrine. The first, which is the main focus of our analysis, holds that the United States reserves the right to preempt threats to its national security using any amount of military force it deems necessary. The second dimension states that, in the war on terrorism, the United States will target both terrorists and those states that assist and harbor them. The two dimensions are linked because the Bush administration has determined that preventing terrorist attacks may require striking state sponsors; terrorists themselves often can escape detection, and therefore preemption, while the states that host or arm them cannot.

The preemption component of the Bush administration's doctrine has occasioned a heated debate within legal, academic, and policymaking circles. The most authoritative statement of the administration's position is presented in the *National Security Strategy of the United States of America* (NSS), released in September 2002, one year after the 9/11 attacks. As the NSS points out, "for centuries, international law recognized that nations need not suffer an attack before they can lawfully take action to defend themselves against forces that present an imminent danger of attack."[1] The subject of considerable dispute in the contemporary debate is: What constitutes "an imminent danger of attack"? Informed positions on this question range along a spectrum, both ends of which are identified in the NSS itself. "Legal scholars and international jurists often conditioned the legitimacy of preemption on . . . a visible mobilization of armies, navies, and air forces preparing to attack." This is the more restrictive end. The NSS, however, makes a case for locating US policy at the more permissive end. Acute threats to national security arising in an age of global terrorism and the proliferation of weapons of mass destruction obviate a policy of inaction. Faced with such threats, the United States shall take the necessary anticipatory action to defend itself "even if uncertainty remains as to the time and place of the enemy's attack."[2] Although critics of the Bush Doctrine assert that this position violates international standards for anticipatory self-defense, international law is, unfortunately, saddled with ambiguities on this very issue.

Before examining these, we ought to step back, briefly, and address the logically prior question of whether anticipatory self-defense of any sort is sanctioned under international law, for there are those who believe it is not. The United Nations Charter, in Chapter VII, empowers the UN Security Council to identify not only acts of aggression, but also "threats to the peace," and to undertake military action in order to maintain international peace and stability. While Article 51 reaffirms the state's "inherent right" to self-defense, this right seems limited to instances in which an "armed attack occurs," and only then until such time as the Security Council has made a final determination on the appropriate response. Thus, some interpret charter law as withdrawing the customary right of anticipatory self-defense from individual states and vesting the Security Council alone with the right of preemption.

It appears that most international legal scholars and jurists reject such an interpretation. Justice Stephen Schwebel, for instance, in his dissent from the majority opinion of the International Court of Justice in *Nicaragua v. United States,* disagreed with those who would read Article 51 as saying that states have the "inherent right of individual or collective self-defense if, *and only if,* an armed attack occurs."[3] (The majority did not adopt the contrary view; it simply declined to take up the question of anticipatory self-defense since neither party made it an issue in the case.) Others believe that charter law is perfectly compatible with customary law because an "armed attack" does not commence with the firing of the first shot; it begins before that, with the mobilization of forces for the purpose of attack. Preemptive (that is, interceptive) strikes by states are permitted because the armed attack is in fact under way. Still others characterize Article 51 as an "inept piece of draftsmanship." Myres McDougal and Florentino Feliciano contend that the article's main purpose, considering the *travaux préparatoires* (negotiating of history), was to preserve the ability of regional security organizations to take action when the Security Council was immobilized by one or more of its veto-wielding members.[4] Its purpose was not to strip states of their customary right of anticipatory self-defense.

We concur with the view that states retain the right of anticipatory self-defense, and we need not take a position on questions of legal consistency raised by Article 51 in order to proceed with our analysis. Virtually all contemporary discussions of preemption start by recognizing that the use of force in anticipatory self-defense is lawful under certain circumstances. How dire must those circumstances be? The restrictive end of the spectrum of views is anchored by the so-called Caroline standard. The British attack on the steamship *Caroline,* which was ferrying Canadian rebels and supplies from the New York side to the Canadian side of the Niagara River, was really a case of extraterritorial law enforcement. Nevertheless, what US secretary of state Daniel Webster wrote in 1841, nearly four years after the incident, became an international legal standard for anticipatory self-defense. In a letter to Henry Fox, the British minister in Washington,

Webster disputed the notion that the attack "can be justified by any reasonable application or construction of the right of self-defense under the law of nations . . . [for] nothing less than clear and absolute necessity can afford ground of justification." What the British could not show in this case was "a necessity of self-defense, instant, overwhelming, leaving no choice of means, and no moment for deliberation."[5]

Webster's formulation has been cited often in diplomatic forums, especially by those wanting to dispute the legitimacy of another state's claim of self-defense, as Webster himself had done. At Nuremberg, German defendants justified the invasion of Norway as an act of self-defense designed to forestall an Allied invasion preparatory to an attack on German positions. The military tribunal rejected this justification: "It must be remembered that preventive action in foreign territory is justified only in case of 'instant and overwhelming necessity for self-defense leaving no choice of means, and no moment of deliberation.' . . . When the plans for an attack on Norway were being made, they were not made for the purpose of forestalling an imminent Allied landing, but, at the most, that they might prevent an Allied occupation at some future date."[6] The Tokyo tribunal had to consider whether Japan was truly the aggressor when it attacked the Netherlands East Indies only after the Netherlands had declared war on December 8, 1941. But in the tribunal's judgment, "the fact that the Netherlands, being fully apprised of the imminence of the attack, in self defense declared war against Japan . . . cannot change that war from a war of aggression on the part of Japan into something other than that."[7]

Thus, both tribunals seem to have interpreted Webster's "instant" and "overwhelming" necessity to mean an armed attack, which if not preempted, would be instant and overwhelming, or nearly so. Similar interpretations were offered during the Security Council debate following Israel's bombardment of the Iraqi nuclear reactor at Osirak in 1981. Israel's representative, Yehuda Blum, asserted that "in destroying Osirak, Israel performed an elementary act of self-preservation, both morally and legally. In doing so, Israel was exercising its inherent right of self-defense as understood in general international law and as preserved in Article 51 of the Charter of the United Nations." Israel faced "the stark prospect that within a very short period of time Osirak would become critical."[8] Yet Israel's right to preemptively eliminate Iraq's nuclear weapons capability in this way was disputed by several delegates. Uganda's representative wondered how an Israeli air raid, planned and rehearsed for many months, could have met the requirements of self-defense "well established since the famous North American case of *The Caroline* in 1837."[9] Israel was not exercising self-defense, but rather aggression, said the representative of Niger, because it "was in no way facing an imminent attack, irrefutably proved and demonstrated."[10] Sierra Leone's delegate concurred: "the plea of self-defense is untenable where no armed attack has taken place or is imminent."[11] And the Irish representative noted that the premise behind Israel's claim went well beyond the right to preempt an imminent attack, for "it would replace the basic principle of the Charter . . . by a virtually unlimited concept of self-defense against all possible future dangers, subjectively assessed."[12]

The preemptive strike that began the Six Day War in 1967 came closer to meeting this "imminent attack" standard. In addressing the Security Council, Israeli foreign minister Abba Eban listed the signs that an Arab attack on Israel was coming: "the sabotage movement; the blockade of the port; and, perhaps more imminent than anything else, this vast and purposeful encirclement movement, against the background of an authorized presidential statement [by Nasser] announcing that the objective of the encirclement was to bring about the destruction and annihilation of a sovereign state."[13] Although there was considerable criticism of Israel at the time—though no formal Security Council condemnation—current discussions of anticipatory self-defense often cite the Israeli action as a case of legitimate preemption consistent with Webster's formulation. It is, however, one of few instances that commentators are inclined to mention with any degree of approval.

What many find worrisome about the Bush Doctrine is that it relaxes substantially Webster's requirements for anticipatory self-defense. The United States will preempt not only imminent threats, but also "sufficient threats" and "emerging threats." This is to move away from the restrictive end of the spectrum in the direction of permitting preventive or precautionary military action. If it is noticed that a state is actually preparing to attack another, then it is safe to infer that there is an intention to attack, even if this intention has not been specifically stated. Preventive or precautionary strikes, however, are normally understood to fall outside the Caroline standard. These strikes target states that are not yet in a position to launch a military attack, and may not even have stated an intention to do so. It may be possible to infer an intention to attack at some future point in time when those capabilities have been fully realized, but this inference is subject to substantially more uncertainty. International law places a premium on international peace and stability and thus far states have not wanted to legally sanction a practice that so clearly undermines that purpose. The Bush administration's view is different and rests on a risk assessment forged by the experience of 9/11. For those upholding the "imminent attack" standard for anticipatory self-defense, the risk of aggression, when unchecked by preemptive action, is acceptable in order to shore up a norm promoting the nonuse of force. For the Bush administration, however, the risk is far too high.

The administration argues that the country faces a "new threat," one that requires an adaptation of the customary standards for anticipatory self-defense. The threat is new, first, in terms of its magnitude. "As was demonstrated by the losses on September 11, 2001, mass civilian casualties . . . would be exponentially more severe if terrorists acquired and used weapons of mass destruction." Second, these weapons "can be easily concealed, delivered covertly, and used without warning."[14] Taken together, the two dimensions of this new threat render ineffective a policy that would preempt an attack only once it becomes visibly imminent. The threatened attack may remain invisible until it has actually been launched, at which point it would be too late to avert mass destruction.

There are no good historical parallels to the situation as described by the Bush administration—the threat is *new*, after all—but the Cuban Missile Crisis is instructive. During the crisis, the United States defended its use of a quarantine around Cuba as a collective security action sanctioned by the Organization of American States. Other members of the Security Council preferred to see it as a blockade, which is considered an act of war, and went on to ask whether the blockade was a justifiable act of self-defense. The representative of Ghana doubted there was, "in the words of a former American Secretary of State whose reputation as a jurist in this field is widely accepted, 'a necessity of self-defense, instant, overwhelming, leaving no choice of means and no moment for deliberation'?" What was missing, in his view, was "incontrovertible proof . . . as to the offensive character of military developments in Cuba."[15] By "offensive character of military developments," the Ghanaian delegate may have meant active preparations for an attack on US territory. But it is likely that what he really meant was something less daunting: the deployment of nuclear missiles with offensive *capability*. Would incontrovertible proof of the latter have been sufficient to show necessity of self-defense? This capability, if it materialized, would have introduced a threat of mass destruction, which could be delivered without warning. If the decision was made to launch such an attack and the attack became imminent, preemption would no longer be possible.

Of course, at the time of the Cuban Missile Crisis, there were many who believed that the Kennedy administration had embarked on a reckless course of action, regardless of the character of military developments in Cuba. Khrushchev was not suicidal, and probably neither was Castro, so it stood to reason that they had no intention of ever using nuclear missiles against the United States. Why push the crisis to the nuclear brink when the United States had the ability to deter an attack by holding the Soviet and Cuban populations hostage to a devastating retaliatory strike? Whether or not the Kennedy administration could have handled the Cuban Missile Crisis differently, the Bush Doctrine rests partly on the premise that "traditional concepts of deterrence will not work against a terrorist enemy . . . whose so-called soldiers seek martyrdom in death and whose most potent protection is statelessness."[16]

If deterrence won't work to check the new threat, and if preemption is not an option at the point of imminence, then anticipatory self-defense cannot be exercised except at an earlier point in time when the threat is visible and stoppable, and at a place where it is visible and stoppable. At this point and in this place, the threat is imminent, even if the attack is not. Here, following Webster, the necessity of self-defense is "instant" and "overwhelming"; preemptive military action is indeed the only available option ("no choice of means"), and it will not remain an option for much longer ("no moment for deliberation"). As Walter Slocombe puts it: "The right of anticipatory self-defense by definition presupposes a right to act while action is still possible. If waiting for 'imminence' means waiting until it is no longer possible to act effectively, the victim is left no alternative to suffering the first blow. So interpreted, the 'right' would be illusory."[17]

The logic of this argument is compelling. But critics of the Bush Doctrine have reason for skepticism. Although the Bush administration justified the 2003 Iraq War as an enforcement of previous Security Council resolutions, it also emphasized that Saddam Hussein's regime had (or was developing) WMD. Even if an Iraqi attack against US interests was unlikely, the regime was willing to provide them to terrorist groups like Al-Qaida, whose intent and capacity to strike the United States had already been demonstrated. Thus, Iraq seemed to be the first application of the Bush Doctrine of preemption. Nevertheless, a large portion of the international community, and a majority within the Security Council, did not believe that Iraq constituted a sufficient threat to the United States, or any other state. The information that came to light after the fall of the Ba'ath regime, especially regarding the absence of WMD programs, reinforced that view and further eroded the administration's credibility as a standard bearer for a revised conception of anticipatory self-defense.

Critics also see in the Bush Doctrine an attempt to provide a contemporary rationale for waging preventive or precautionary war, which even the most permissive reading of customary international law disallows. In the classic balance of power system, preventive wars were sometimes fought to head off disadvantageous power shifts among the major European states. This was Britain's motivation (vis-à-vis France) during the War of the Spanish Succession and Germany's motivation (vis-à-vis Russia) at the outset of World War I. Preventive war, Michael Walzer notes, presupposes a danger that "does not exist, as it were, on the ground; it has nothing to do with the immediate security of boundaries. . . . War is justified (as in Hobbes' philosophy) by fear alone and not by anything other states actually do or any signs they give of their malign intentions. Prudent rulers assume malign intentions."[18] It is not difficult to see why leading thinkers of the modern just war tradition, who sought to promote a normative order supportive of international peace and stability, would want to discredit such state practice. However, it is our contention that, despite certain similarities, the Bush Doctrine really does not amount to an assertion of the right to wage preventive war as understood here. While the doctrine may relax the customary standards for lawful preemption, the imminence of the threat (though not necessarily the attack) is what justifies military action as anticipatory self-defense. Historically, preventive wars have lacked this urgency. At the same time, when just war thinkers contemplated the conditions under which preventive action might be justified, they were inclined to introduce a notion of imminent threat not unlike the reconceptualization underpinning the Bush Doctrine of preemption.

Mark Drumbl suggests that the international community seems receptive to the idea that the traditional criteria for anticipatory self-defense need updating. "There is more going on here than the United States going its own way through the aspirations of one particular administration. For a variety of reasons, many states in diverse parts of the world support a more liberal use of violence to curb terrorists and mitigate the risk that rogue states may assist them."[19] The danger here, as illustrated by the Iraq War, is that an assessment of "the nature and motivations of these new adversaries," as the NSS puts it, and not just their active preparation to attack, becomes the smoking gun, a subjective criterion that is obviously open to abuse.[20] Little in just war doctrine or international law provides guidance for establishing evil intent, or the aiding and abetting of those with evil intent, aside from visible actions. The Bush Doctrine, while framed as a plea to adapt international law to more effectively deal with today's threats, also introduces ambiguity into the legal standards for the use of force in self-defense. "The United States seeks first to secure a preexisting claim," writes Michael Byers, "and then to stretch the resulting rule so as to render it highly ambiguous—thus enabling power and influence to determine where and when the rule applies."[21] In this arena, the preferences of the United States are more likely to prevail.

▪ Notes

1. *National Security Strategy of the United States of America,* September 2002, p. 15, available at www.whitehouse.gov/nsc/nss.html.
2. Ibid.
3. International Court of Justice, *Case Concerning Military and Paramilitary Activities in and Against Nicaragua (Nicaragua v. United States of America): Merits,* June 27, 1986, p. 347, available at www.icj-cij.org/icjwww/icases/inus/inus_ijudgment/inus_ijudgment_toc.htm (emphasis added).
4. Myres S. McDougal and Florentino P. Feliciano, *Law and Minimum World Public Order: The Legal Regulation of International Coercion* (New Haven, Conn.: Yale University Press, 1961), pp. 234–236.
5. Note from Daniel Webster to Henry Fox, April 24, 1842, available at The

Avalon Project, "Webster-Ashburton Treaty: The Caroline Case," www.yale.edu/lawweb/avalon/diplomacy/britain/br-1842d.htm.

6. International Military Tribunal, *The Trial of German Major War Criminals: Proceedings of the International Military Tribunal Sitting at Nuremberg, Germany* (London: 1946–1949), available at The Avalon Project, "Judgment: Invasion of Denmark and Norway," www.yale.edu/lawweb/avalon/imt/proc/juddenma.htm.

7. International Military Tribunal for the Far East, *The Tokyo War Crimes Trial* (New York: Garland, 1981), p. 994.

8. United Nations Security Council Official Records, 2280th meeting, June 12, 1981. UN Doc. no. S/PV.2280, pp. 8, 10.

9. United Nations Security Council Official Records, 2282th meeting, June 15, 1981. UN Doc. no. S/PV.2282, p. 2.

10. United Nations Security Council Official Records, 2284th meeting, June 16, 1981. UN Doc. no. S/PV.2284, p. 2.

11. United Nations Security Council Official Records, 2283rd meeting, June 15, 1981. UN Doc. no. S/PV.2283, p. 14.

12. Ibid., p. 3.

13. United Nations Security Council Official Records, 1348th meeting, June 6, 1967. UN Doc. no. S/PV.1348, p. 15.

14. *National Security Strategy,* p. 15.

15. United Nations Security Council Official Records, 1024th meeting, October 24, 1962. UN Doc. no. S/PV.1024, p. 19.

16. *National Security Strategy,* p. 15.

17. Walter B. Slocombe, "Force, Preemption and Legitimacy," *Survival* 45, no. 1 (Spring 2003), p. 125.

18. Michael Walzer, *Just and Unjust Wars: A Moral Argument with Historical Illustrations* (New York: Basic Books, 1977), pp. 75–76.

19. Mark A. Drumbl, "Self-Defense and the Use of Force: Breaking the Rules, Making the Rules, or Both?" *International Studies Perspectives* 4, no. 4 (November 2003), p. 424.

20. *National Security Strategy,* p. 13.

21. Michael Byers, "Preemptive Self-Defense: Hegemony, Equality and Strategies of Legal Change," *Journal of Political Philosophy* 11, no. 2 (2003), pp. 179–180.

6.4 _____

Self-Defense and the Use of Force

Mark A. Drumbl

The Charter of the United Nations (UN) (hereafter referred to as charter) admits two exceptions to its presumptive prohibition of the use of force. These are: (1) force authorized by the UN Security Council (charter, arts. 39, 42); and (2) force necessary in self-defense to an armed attack (charter, art. 51). According to the text of the charter, these two are the only exceptions. However, states have at times recognized the permissibility of the transnational use of force for other purposes: such as when invited by a state, when securing humanitarian protection, or when promoting democracy.

This legal background never is static. After all, international law derives from a number of dynamic sources. The two most important sources for the purposes of this analysis are international treaties negotiated by states (such as the charter) and international custom (also called customary international law). International custom derives from the behavior and practice of states undertaken out of a sense of legal obligation *(opinio juris)*. As such, customary international law can be empirically assessed by reviewing state behavior and practice, and the responses of states to the behavior and practice of others. States thus constitute a major force in the formulation of international law. Given the absence of a single international legislative authority, the actions and statements of states prompt change and reform in the international legal order. . . .

The international legal system is flexible and responsive to new developments. In this vein, the United States (along with many allies) has asserted and has been given considerable leeway in dealing with national security threats, particularly those emerging from nonstate terrorist actors, in the wake of the September 11, 2001, attacks. This leeway derives from the gravity of the attacks and mirrors the flexibility inherent in the charter: a living, breathing document . . . that did not initially contemplate the privatization of violence in the international system as effected by terrorist groups such as Al Qaeda. . . .

This increased flexibility in the *jus ad bellum*—the law regarding when a state can go to war—provides some backdrop to the use of force against Iraq. On March 19, 2003, the United States and the United Kingdom, with nominal troop assistance from Poland and Australia, invaded Iraq. This invasion proceeded without the explicit authorization of the Security Council. Rather, it was an initiative undertaken by two coalition partners, supported directly or indirectly by an ill-defined and fluctuating number of states. It was condemned by a significantly greater number of states and also by the secretary-general of the UN. . . .

■ The Law of Fear

The United States and the United Kingdom availed themselves of three legally distinct but politically overlapping arguments as part of their efforts to assert the legality of their invasion of Iraq. The U.S. and U.K. positions differ somewhat *inter se,* although both borrow—to varying degrees—from classic justifications for the exceptional use of force.

The central argument involved the Security Council. The United States and the United Kingdom argued that the Security Council had impliedly authorized the use of force to implement its resolutions regarding weapons inspections and decommissioning; and, closely connected thereto, both countries argued that Iraqi material breach of the decommissioning regime meant that the ceasefire that terminated the 1990–1991 Gulf War was to be set aside, thereby revitalizing the Security Council's 1990 explicit authorization to use force against Iraq.

A second argument relates to each nation's inherent right of self-defense. To different degrees, the United States and United Kingdom both argued that this right was exercisable against Iraq given potential threats Iraq posed to them and other nations owing to its purported possession of (or intent to possess) weapons of mass destruction (WMD, such as nuclear, biological, or chemical weapons), its refusal to decommission such weapons, and its links to international terrorists—such as Al Qaeda—who attacked the United States (and other targets) and continue to undertake and threaten further attacks. . . .

A tertiary argument asserted the necessity of force to liberate the Iraqi people—in particular, political opponents suffering torture and the nation's ethnic and religious minorities suffering violent persecution—from the abusive grasp of Saddam Hussein. The liberation argument gave the invasion its code name, Operation Iraqi Freedom. . . .

International law is both a dependent and an independent variable. It is informed by politics and it coincidentally informs politics; it derives from state behavior and it affects state behavior. Moreover, international law also has an important expressive function: it signals what we deem to be acceptable or unacceptable, appropriate or inappropriate, moral or immoral. To be sure, there has been frequent recourse to the use of force throughout the charter regime in ways that clearly infringed the charter. This has prompted some esteemed international lawyers to view the charter as aspirational rather than determinative (and perhaps even irrelevant). . . . On the other hand, the use of force against terrorists and the rogue—and often weak, if not failed—states that harbor them, such as Afghanistan, is discussed openly and presented as a needed change to the legal rules, rather than excused as a necessary transgression of those rules. Insofar as most states are concerned, this use of force constitutes an appropriate, acceptable, and morally justifiable way to do business in these more dangerous times in which we apparently live. Law transmits a message about our attitudes and expectations. We should reflect upon whether we now have fewer qualms about the use of force to protect ourselves, our way(s) of life, and our homeland(s) from actual or feared threats; and, if this is the case, why is this so. . . .

Divergent perceptions of fear regarding the dangerous times in which we live may go some way to explain the differing perceptions among states of the legality of preemptive force. In any event, a large number (80 percent, according to the president of the American Society of International Law) of international lawyers agree that the Iraq invasion was illegal under international law. According to this logic, the United States and the United Kingdom are rule-breakers. However, this is a simple conclusion focused singularly on the here-and-now. A multidimensional analysis would deem the present infringement (if assumed) to be an ancillary issue, the more important concern being whether the rule-breaking is deviant behavior or, rather, behavior that may animate the emergence of an inchoate rule. Breaking the law has much less effect than changing the law. There are plenty of times in law when the dissenting judgments of yesterday remain marginalized as wrong-headed; there are, however, other times when those judgments actually sowed the seeds of a new, and hopefully preferable, rule. This article posits that the United States' legal position, inasmuch as it invokes self-defense in regard to Iraq, should not be written off as terminally deviant. Nor is there any basis to state that it has transformed the preexisting law in the same way the military intervention in Afghanistan reconstituted, almost instantly, some precepts of the international law of self-defense. However, the justifications for the use of force in Iraq, in particular the notion of preemptive force against potential terrorists and their alleged hosts, might emerge as a normative framework that, either by the acquiescence or support of other states, could mold—for better or for worse—the future architecture of the *jus ad bellum*. . . .

■ Self-Defense and National (In)security

So long as they abide by the constraints of proportionality and necessity, states can use lethal force in self-defense to an armed attack. In fact, Article 51 of the charter recognizes self-defense as an inherent right of states. Thus, self-defense permits the use of force independently of Security Council authorization. Customary international law also recognizes self-defense (individual or collective). Whereas individual self-defense involves the state acting on behalf of its own interests, collective self-defense involves the right of a state or states to intervene militarily on behalf of a third (or others). . . .

International custom never is static and, in the case of self-defense, recently has been catalyzed by the September 11, 2001, terrorist attacks. A clear majority of states supported the use of armed force, as opposed to the criminal law, as an appropriate response to those attacks. Many states gave currency to the U.S. position that terrorism should be thwarted prospectively through the use of force and only secondarily through individualized—and often retrospective—criminal justice. . . .

Moreover, armed force has not been characterized "just" as a tool to incapacitate and obtain custody over alleged terrorists; rather, terrorists have been designated as fighters, in some cases, and unlawful combatants, in others, and subject to a military campaign in which they are to be destroyed or, if captured, detained until the war ends. . . .

It could be said that this invocation of self-defense is temporary and not norm-creating. If so, there would be cause to reflect upon the legal precedent, if any, established by the use of force against Afghanistan. Is the Afghan situation a unique event, or does it constitute state practice that redefines the contours of self-defense? I argue that the response to the September 11, 2001, attacks, although arising out of an exceptional set of circumstances, has not been treated as an exceptional one-time-only response. Rather, there have been active, albeit controversial, efforts to ensconce this response as legal precedent applicable to other places and spaces. In fact, I argue that, with specific regard to self-defense, the response of the international community to the September 11, 2001, attack has the potential to constitute a jurisgenerative event. Self-defense has become more elastic and fuzzy; it has quickly metamorphosed into something decidedly more ambiguous. Self-defense may be growing out of its original design as a provisional right, to be used temporarily, and subject to the review of the Security Council once the actual force defended against had been repulsed (charter, art. 51). . . .

Returning to the September 11, 2001, attacks, I argue that state practice and international organization statements in response thereto specifically have affected the content of the right of self-defense in five ways. They are:

1. Expanded the definition of "armed attack." Self-defense can only be justified if in response to an armed attack. Traditionally, armed attacks could only be launched by states. However, the use of force has become accepted as a way to defend against attacks from individuals connected to and receiving support from a nonstate actor, in the instant case Al Qaeda. Assuredly, these nonstate actors may present greater national security threats than do many states. . . .

2. Increased state responsibility for terrorist activities and the severity of the consequences when states default on that responsibility. The conduct of Al Qaeda was attributed to the Taliban, the government of Afghanistan (S.C. Res. 1378). This attribution justified attacking Afghanistan and deposing the Taliban. Going beyond Afghanistan, President Bush's position that the war on terrorism can be extended to states that harbor or support terrorists also reflects an attempt to expand state responsibility for the activities of nonstate actors. Traditionally at international law, a state was responsible only for the activities of those nonstate actors over which it exercised "effective" or "overall" control. Because it is unclear whether the new war on terrorism inquires whether the state in question has some "control" over the terrorists in question, it may well be that the level of state responsibility is moving in the direction of a strict liability standard while sanctions for default are expanding beyond financial reparations and countermeasures to include the extensive use of lethal force and regime destruction.

3. Internationalized internal insurrectionary groups. Although United States and United Kingdom forces launched attacks on Afghanistan, much of the military effort involved arming, supporting, financing, and aiding the Northern Alliance, which for years had been involved in an internal armed conflict with the Taliban. One of the concerns here is the extent to which the supporting powers can control the activities of the supported internal faction. In the case of the 2001 conflict in Afghanistan, there is considerable evidence that the Northern Alliance committed war crimes. . . . Is it appropriate for state responsibility to expand to cover the acts of nonstate actor terrorists without a similar expansion in the responsibility of other states for the acts of insurrectionary war criminals?

4. Diversified the spaces and places where lethal force can be used. Following September 11, 2001, some state practice supports a broad war on terrorism characterized by armed campaigns in multiple theatres of operation. These campaigns often are brief and discrete, for example the killing of individuals on terrorist lists by military action, as was the case in Yemen. Can self-defense cover isolated military incursions against individuals, such as the Yemeni killings, owing to their membership in Al Qaeda? . . . This challenges traditional principles of national sovereignty and nonintervention that are central to public international law. Moreover, can these opera-

tions be made consistent with the laws of war, namely the requirement to distinguish between civilian and combatant targets? Is it realistically possible to abide by the laws of war when armed force is used to kill individual fighters amid a civilian population?

5. Stretched the time-line. The United States and the United Kingdom initiated strikes against Afghanistan on October 7, 2001. Traditionally, under the celebrated *Caroline* precedent, the use of force in self-defense only is appropriate when the necessity of such force is "instant, overwhelming, and leaving no choice of means, and no moment for deliberation." This presupposes some sort of ongoing, armed attack or imminent threat thereof. Although at the time of the U.S. and U.K. strikes the prospect of ongoing terrorist violence was clearly foreseeable, it is unclear whether the stringent requirements of the *Caroline* test were satisfied. Nonetheless, state practice and international organization response to the strikes were largely supportive. As such, the imminence and necessity requirements of self-defense have been relaxed in light of the perceived dangers of terrorist attacks by nonstate actors.

▓ Fighting the Future: Toward Preemption

Among these changes, it is the fifth (the time-line expansion) that bears the most upon the Iraqi situation. Notwithstanding the significant factual differences between the threats from Afghanistan and those from Iraq, rigorous attempts arose to apply the precedent derived from the former to the latter. These were accompanied by attempts to generalize this precedent. One such attempt is the overt acknowledgment of preemptive self-defense as central to U.S. national security policy.

It is important to view the term "preemptive" self-defense as a tree with a number of branches. These branches are as follows: anticipatory self-defense, preventative self-defense, and precautionary self-defense. The three are distinguishable. Among the three, anticipatory self-defense bears the closest parallel to the type of action traditional international law would have allowed under the *Caroline* standard. Classically, self-defense can be permitted in response to an actual armed attack, and also to a case where a future armed attack is imminent. It took only a little help to extend this to the Afghanistan situation. . . . However, the language of self-defense in the Iraq case moved away from the imminence criteria toward a much more hypothetical threat. Self-defense was touted as necessary to prevent possible threats from arising in the future and, even if those threats do not appear to have materialized, as a precaution to ensure that they never materialize. . . . This no longer seems much like anticipatory self-defense. Whereas claims to anticipatory self-defense depend on palpable or imminent threats, claims to preventive or precautionary self-defense depend on contingent or possible threats. . . .

Let me be clear: there was no consensus among states supportive of the operationalization of self-defense for preventive or precautionary reasons through the use of force against Iraq outside of Security Council authorization. However, a not insubstantial number of states support the use of force against states alleged to have links with terrorists or those illegally seeking to acquire (or possessing) WMD. In fact, this number may be more substantial than opponents of the Iraq war may claim. Moreover, some states opposed to the Iraqi invasion, for instance the Russian Federation and Indonesia, advocate the use of lethal preemptive force against terrorists. All things considered, the situation is complex. The rub of my argument is as follows: few states support the use of preventative war to thwart the military development of other states or to promote "regime change," more states support the precautionary use of force against states deemed rogue that may have significant destructive capabilities, and many more states support the use of precautionary force against terrorists or states that support them.

The Bush administration's position is that this right of self-defense operates independently of whatever the Security Council might have to say on the subject. If normalized, this position would deregulate the locus of decision making regarding the use of force (even if alleged to be in the collective interest) and move it away from a centralized international institution. As there is more and more scope for self-defense, the importance of the nation-state rises and the influence of international institutions wanes in the decision whether or not to use force. This may well create a situation in which the deployment of lethal force in self-defense becomes inconsistent, perhaps even indeterminate. . . .

There are other concerns with the legality of launching preemptive strikes. One such concern is escalating instability within the international order. What prevents United States use of the Preemption Doctrine from constituting precedent for a variety of other countries in their regional conflicts, such as China in its confrontation with Taiwan, or India and its tensions with Pakistan, or Russia in its internal crackdowns in Chechnya? . . . Regardless of how broad this new dimension of preemption might become, states now successfully can assert a right to exercise armed force in self-defense to terrorist activity states deem to reach the level of an armed attack, whether coming from abroad or within.

For the moment, it is unclear whether the policy reforms pursued by the Bush administration will induce changes to the legal rules, or, on the other hand, form exceptions to still valid rules or, alternately, end up as unilateral actions that place one state above the rules. The point of this article is that the potential normative effects of these changes on the international legal system should be neither discounted nor dismissed. . . .

◼ Beyond the Breach

The military response to the September 11, 2001, attacks altered the *jus ad bellum,* the international law regarding the use of force. Principally, some elasticity—in time, space, and place—was imported into the legal understanding of self-defense. In this regard, our collective response to those terrorist attacks can be constructed as a jurisgenerative event—creating law, often times as a reaction, as we go along—that challenges a traditional, and perhaps naive, principle of international law, namely that order is to be pursued through peace. Instead, regarding terrorism, there is a sense that order is best pursued through force or, even, war. With this as a new *grundnorm,* some states are claiming additional entitlements regarding the use of force. The most aggressive expansionary entitlement—the U.S. Preemption Doctrine—posits that a state may have a right to attack another it thinks could otherwise attack it first, particularly should that other state be suspected of developing WMD, having links to terrorists, or both. For the moment, the Preemption Doctrine is far from norm-creating, given the widespread opposition to it around the world. . . .

Regardless whether it succeeds or not, which only can be assessed over the long term, the United States *wants* the law to change. . . . [T]he United States chafes at the charter's framework regarding the use of force. But the United States would prefer not to be a deviant. Rather, it wants to be a rule-maker, an agent for change, instead of a mere rule-breaker. Its actions are strategically undertaken to protect its national security while reshaping the international legal order to suit the interests of the single superpower. The United States would benefit considerably from the increased freedom with which it could pursue the military aspect of the war on terror. It would appear to gain from its ability to challenge rogue regimes that may one day threaten its interests. It could side-step the veto power of the permanent members of the Security Council along with the need to take matters to the Security Council in the first place. This, in turn, would obviate the need for self-defense to be limited on the facts to a threat, such as Iraq, that has been identified and sanctioned repeatedly through Security Council resolutions. . . . A case may even be made that the newly asserted right of preemptive self-defense is perceived by some states as serving the common interest. . . .

Yet there also is cause to fear the change sought by the United States. If the use of force emerges as a preferred method to police the proliferation of WMD, it would supplant other possible methods such as criminal sanctions, international treaties, and restrictions on the arms trade. This kind of policing creates a perverse incentive: it may accelerate the WMD arms race insofar as it can become rational for nations actually to acquire WMD if they are going to face military action simply based on the fact they are suspected of having WMD. Moreover, military conflict may encourage the distribution of WMD by state agents to nonstate actors and, thereby, aggravate the proliferation problem. Some analysts suspect that WMD in Iraq may have been removed (or stolen) from centralized state authority in the later stages of the war and disseminated into private hands. . . .

Developments in the *jus ad bellum* cannot be evaluated in isolation. Rather, they must be placed within the context of the increasingly fluid architecture of public international law, where changes are afoot in a number of corners. The war on terrorism also has been characterized by the restrictive application of the obligations imposed by international humanitarian law (the *jus in bello*), in particular the implementation of the Geneva Conventions on the Law of War. This creates a paradox: Whereas entitlements to use force are expanding under the *jus ad bellum,* entitlements to protections under the *jus in bello* are shrinking. . . . All in all, law and due process rhetorically have become cast as impediments to justice, as something to be feared in the war on terror. However, as it is unclear when and whether this war ever will come to an end, this diminished rights scrutiny may become a permanent fixture. . . .

6.5 _____

An Unnecessary War

John J. Mearsheimer and Stephen Walt

Should the United States invade Iraq and depose Saddam Hussein? If the United States is already at war with Iraq when this article is published, the immediate cause is likely to be Saddam's failure to comply with the new U.N. inspections regime to the Bush administration's satisfaction. But this failure is not the real reason Saddam and the United States have been on a collision course over the past year.

The deeper root of the conflict is the U.S. position that Saddam must be toppled because he cannot be deterred from using weapons of mass destruction (WMD). Advocates of preventive war use numerous arguments to make their case, but their trump card is the charge that Saddam's past behavior proves he is too reckless, relentless, and aggressive to be allowed to possess WMD, especially nuclear weapons. They sometimes admit that war against Iraq might be costly, might lead to a lengthy U.S. occupation, and might complicate U.S. relations with other countries. But these concerns are eclipsed by the belief that the combination of Saddam plus nuclear weapons is too dangerous to accept. . . .

Even many opponents of preventive war seem to agree deterrence will not work in Iraq. Instead of invading Iraq and overthrowing the regime, however, these moderates favor using the threat of war to compel Saddam to permit new weapons inspections. Their hope is that inspections will eliminate any hidden WMD stockpiles and production facilities and ensure Saddam cannot acquire any of these deadly weapons. Thus, both the hardline preventive-war advocates and the more moderate supporters of inspections accept the same basic premise: Saddam Hussein is not deterrable, and he cannot be allowed to obtain a nuclear arsenal.

One problem with this argument: It is almost certainly wrong. The belief that Saddam's past behavior shows he cannot be contained rests on distorted history and faulty logic. In fact, the historical record shows that the United States can contain Iraq effectively—even if Saddam has nuclear weapons—just as it contained the Soviet Union during the Cold War. . . .

◾ Is Saddam a Serial Aggressor?

Those who call for preventive war begin by portraying Saddam as a serial aggressor bent on dominating the Persian Gulf. The war party also contends that Saddam is either irrational or prone to serious miscalculation, which means he may not be deterred by even credible threats of retaliation. . . .

The facts, however, tell a different story. Saddam has dominated Iraqi politics for more than 30 years. During that period, he started two wars against his neighbors—Iran in 1980 and Kuwait in 1990. Saddam's record in this regard is no worse than that of neighboring states such as Egypt or Israel, each of which played a role in starting several wars since 1948. Furthermore, a careful look at Saddam's two wars shows his behavior was far from reckless. Both times, he attacked because Iraq was vulnerable and because he believed his targets were weak and isolated. In each case, his goal was to rectify Iraq's strategic dilemma with a limited military victory. Such reasoning does not excuse Saddam's aggression, but his willingness to use force on these occasions hardly demonstrates that he cannot be deterred.

The Iran-Iraq War, 1980–88

Iran was the most powerful state in the Persian Gulf during the 1970s. Its strength was partly due to its large population (roughly three times that of Iraq) and its oil reserves, but it also stemmed from the strong support the shah of Iran received from the United States. Relations between Iraq and Iran were quite hostile throughout this period, but Iraq was in no position to defy Iran's regional dominance. . . .

It is thus not surprising that Saddam welcomed the shah's ouster in 1979. Iraq went to considerable lengths to foster good relations with Iran's revolutionary leadership. Saddam did not exploit the turmoil in Iran to gain strategic advantage over his neighbor and made no attempt to reverse his earlier concessions, even though Iran did not fully comply with the terms of the 1975 agreement. Ruhollah Khomeini, on the other hand, was determined to extend his revolution across the Islamic world, starting with Iraq. By late 1979, Tehran was pushing the Kurdish and Shiite populations in Iraq to revolt and topple Saddam, and Iranian operatives were trying to assassinate senior Iraqi officials. . . .

Facing a grave threat to his regime, but aware that Iran's military readiness had been temporarily disrupted by the revolution, Saddam launched a limited war against his bitter foe on September 22, 1980. His principal aim was to capture a large slice of territory along the Iraq-Iran border, not to conquer Iran or topple Khomeini. . . .

Iran and Iraq fought for eight years, and the war cost the two antagonists more than 1 million casualties and at least $150 billion. Iraq received considerable outside support from other countries—including the United States,

Kuwait, Saudi Arabia, and France—largely because these states were determined to prevent the spread of Khomeini's Islamic revolution. Although the war cost Iraq far more than Saddam expected, it also thwarted Khomeini's attempt to topple him and dominate the region. War with Iran was not a reckless adventure; it was an opportunistic response to a significant threat.

The Gulf War, 1990–91

But what about Iraq's invasion of Kuwait in August 1990? Perhaps the earlier war with Iran was essentially defensive, but surely this was not true in the case of Kuwait. Doesn't Saddam's decision to invade his tiny neighbor prove he is too rash and aggressive to be trusted with the most destructive weaponry? And doesn't his refusal to withdraw, even when confronted by a superior coalition, demonstrate he is "unintentionally suicidal"?

The answer is no. Once again, a careful look shows Saddam was neither mindlessly aggressive nor particularly reckless. If anything, the evidence supports the opposite conclusion.

Saddam's decision to invade Kuwait was primarily an attempt to deal with Iraq's continued vulnerability. Iraq's economy, badly damaged by its war with Iran, continued to decline after that war ended. An important cause of Iraq's difficulties was Kuwait's refusal both to loan Iraq $10 billion and to write off debts Iraq had incurred during the Iran-Iraq War. Saddam believed Iraq was entitled to additional aid because the country helped protect Kuwait and other Gulf states from Iranian expansionism. To make matters worse, Kuwait was overproducing the quotas set by the Organization of Petroleum Exporting Countries, which drove down world oil prices and reduced Iraqi oil profits. Saddam tried using diplomacy to solve the problem, but Kuwait hardly budged. . . .

Saddam invaded Kuwait in early August 1990. This act was an obvious violation of international law, and the United States was justified in opposing the invasion and organizing a coalition against it. But Saddam's decision to invade was hardly irrational or reckless. Deterrence did not fail in this case; it was never tried.

But what about Saddam's failure to leave Kuwait once the United States demanded a return to the status quo ante? Wouldn't a prudent leader have abandoned Kuwait before getting clobbered? With hindsight, the answer seems obvious, but Saddam had good reasons to believe hanging tough might work. It was not initially apparent that the United States would actually fight, and most Western military experts predicted the Iraqi army would mount a formidable defense. These forecasts seem foolish today, but many people believed them before the war began. . . .

Saddam undoubtedly miscalculated when he attacked Kuwait, but the history of warfare is full of cases where leaders have misjudged the prospects for war. No evidence suggests Hussein did not weigh his options carefully, however. He chose to use force because he was facing a serious challenge and because he had good reasons to think his invasion would not provoke serious opposition. . . .

History provides at least two more pieces of evidence that demonstrate Saddam is deterrable. First, although he launched conventionally armed Scud missiles at Saudi Arabia and Israel during the Gulf War, he did not launch chemical or biological weapons at the coalition forces that were decimating the Iraqi military. Moreover, senior Iraqi officials . . . have said that Iraq refrained from using chemical weapons because the Bush Sr. administration made ambiguous but unmistakable threats to retaliate if Iraq used WMD. Second, in 1994 Iraq mobilized the remnants of its army on the Kuwaiti border in an apparent attempt to force a modification of the U.N. Special Commission's (UNSCOM) weapons inspection regime. But when the United Nations issued a new warning and the United States reinforced its troops in Kuwait, Iraq backed down quickly. In both cases, the allegedly irrational Iraqi leader was deterred.

■ Saddam's Use of Chemical Weapons

Preventive-war advocates also use a second line of argument. They point out that Saddam has used WMD against his own people (the Kurds) and against Iran and that therefore he is likely to use them against the United States. Thus, U.S. President George W. Bush recently warned in Cincinnati that the Iraqi WMD threat against the United States "is already significant, and it only grows worse with time." The United States, in other words, is in imminent danger.

Saddam's record of chemical weapons use is deplorable, but none of his victims had a similar arsenal and thus could not threaten to respond in kind. Iraq's calculations would be entirely different when facing the United States because Washington could retaliate with WMD if Iraq ever decided to use these weapons first. Saddam thus has no incentive to use chemical or nuclear weapons against the United States and its allies—unless his survival is threatened. . . .

Furthermore, if Saddam cannot be deterred, what is stopping him from using WMD against U.S. forces in the Persian Gulf, which have bombed Iraq repeatedly over the past decade? The bottom line: Deterrence has worked well against Saddam in the past, and there is no reason to think it cannot work equally well in the future.

President Bush's repeated claim that the threat from Iraq is growing makes little sense in light of Saddam's past record, and these statements should be viewed as transparent attempts to scare Americans into supporting a war. CIA Director George Tenet flatly contradicted the president in an

October 2002 letter to Congress, explaining that Saddam was unlikely to initiate a WMD attack against any U.S. target unless Washington provoked him. Even if Iraq did acquire a larger WMD arsenal, the United States would still retain a massive nuclear retaliatory capability. . . .

■ Saddam with Nukes

The third strike against a policy of containment, according to those who have called for war, is that such a policy is unlikely to stop Saddam from getting nuclear weapons. Once he gets them, so the argument runs, a host of really bad things will happen. For example, President Bush has warned that Saddam intends to "blackmail the world"; likewise, National Security Advisor Condoleezza Rice believes he would use nuclear weapons to "blackmail the entire international community." Others fear a nuclear arsenal would enable Iraq to invade its neighbors and then deter the United States from ousting the Iraqi army as it did in 1991. Even worse, Saddam might surreptitiously slip a nuclear weapon to al Qaeda or some like-minded terrorist organization, thereby making it possible for these groups to attack the United States directly.

The administration and its supporters may be right in one sense: Containment may not be enough to prevent Iraq from acquiring nuclear weapons someday. Only the conquest and permanent occupation of Iraq could guarantee that. Yet the United States can contain a nuclear Iraq, just as it contained the Soviet Union. None of the nightmare scenarios invoked by preventive-war advocates are likely to happen.

Consider the claim that Saddam would employ nuclear blackmail against his adversaries. To force another state to make concessions, a blackmailer must make clear that he would use nuclear weapons against the target state if he does not get his way. But this strategy is feasible only if the blackmailer has nuclear weapons but neither the target state nor its allies do.

If the blackmailer and the target state both have nuclear weapons, however, the blackmailer's threat is an empty one because the blackmailer cannot carry out the threat without triggering his own destruction. This logic explains why the Soviet Union, which had a vast nuclear arsenal for much of the Cold War, was never able to blackmail the United States or its allies and did not even try. . . .

■ What About a Nuclear Handoff?

Of course, now the real nightmare scenario is that Saddam would give nuclear weapons secretly to al Qaeda or some other terrorist group. Groups like al Qaeda would almost certainly try to use those weapons against Israel or the United States, and so these countries have a powerful incentive to take all reasonable measures to keep these weapons out of their hands.

However, the likelihood of clandestine transfer by Iraq is extremely small. First of all, there is no credible evidence that Iraq had anything to do with the terrorist attacks against the World Trade Center and the Pentagon or more generally that Iraq is collaborating with al Qaeda against the United States. Hawks inside and outside the Bush administration have gone to extraordinary lengths over the past months to find a link, but they have come up empty-handed.

The lack of evidence of any genuine connection between Saddam and al Qaeda is not surprising because relations between Saddam and al Qaeda have been quite poor in the past. Osama bin Laden is a radical fundamentalist (like Khomeini), and he detests secular leaders like Saddam. Similarly, Saddam has consistently repressed fundamentalist movements within Iraq. Given this history of enmity, the Iraqi dictator is unlikely to give al Qaeda nuclear weapons, which it might use in ways he could not control. . . .

Second, Saddam could hardly be confident that the transfer would go undetected. Since September 11, U.S. intelligence agencies and those of its allies have been riveted on al Qaeda and Iraq, paying special attention to finding links between them. If Iraq possessed nuclear weapons, U.S. monitoring of those two adversaries would be further intensified. To give nuclear materials to al Qaeda, Saddam would have to bet he could elude the eyes and ears of numerous intelligence services determined to catch him if he tries a nuclear handoff. This bet would not be a safe one.

But even if Saddam thought he could covertly smuggle nuclear weapons to bin Laden, he would still be unlikely to do so. Saddam has been trying to acquire these weapons for over 20 years, at great cost and risk. Is it likely he would then turn around and give them away? Furthermore, giving nuclear weapons to al Qaeda would be extremely risky for Saddam—even if he could do so without being detected—because he would lose all control over when and where they would be used. And Saddam could never be sure the United States would not incinerate him anyway if it merely suspected he had made it possible for anyone to strike the United States with nuclear weapons. . . .

In sum, Saddam cannot afford to guess wrong on whether he would be detected providing al Qaeda with nuclear weapons, nor can he afford to guess wrong that Iraq would be spared if al Qaeda launched a nuclear strike against the United States or its allies. And the threat of U.S. retaliation is not as far-fetched as one might think. The United States has enhanced its flexible nuclear options in recent years, and no one knows just how vengeful Americans might feel if WMD were ever used against the U.S. homeland. Indeed, nuclear terrorism is as dangerous for Saddam as it is for

Americans, and he has no more incentive to give al Qaeda nuclear weapons than the United States does—unless, of course, the country makes clear it is trying to overthrow him. Instead of attacking Iraq and giving Saddam nothing to lose, the Bush administration should be signaling it would hold him responsible if some terrorist group used WMD against the United States, even if it cannot prove he is to blame. . . .

7 Terrorism

7.1 _____

Introduction
The Editors

Not long ago it would have made little sense to include a section on terrorism in a reader on the morality of war. Needless to say, things have changed in the wake of 9/11 and the consequent claims by the United States that it would now wage war against terrorism. This challenge, along with the efforts of a seemingly increasing number of groups resorting to terrorism as a political strategy, has thrust the notion into the forefront of public consciousness. Nevertheless, it is difficult to see that terrorism raises any troubling issues from the standpoint of the morality of war. Domestic terrorism—terrorism practiced by the citizens of a state against the state itself or fellow citizens—is ordinarily understood to be an instance of domestic crime, and it is ordinarily treated accordingly. International terrorism—terrorism practiced against a state or its citizens by noncitizens—will likely occur within the legal jurisdiction of some state and, if so, it would appear to constitute a crime within that particular legal jurisdiction. Thus a concern for terrorism seems out of place in discussions of the morality of war. If, on the other hand, states, or groups acting in the interest of some state, practice terrorism in the course of prosecuting a war against a rival state, the morality of war should apply to these acts in the same way that it applies to more traditional combat.

But the obsession with terrorism that followed the events of 9/11 makes terrorism a worthy subject in its own right, and one that now demands to be placed in the perspective associated with the morality of war. In this regard, a host of questions arise that require critical scrutiny. Of these, two deserve special attention: What is terrorism? And, is terrorism ever morally justified? Related but ancillary questions quickly follow: Is terrorism in war possible, and, if so, is terrorism a legitimate strategy in warfare? Is it even possible to wage war against terrorist groups? Can states practice terrorism, or is it only possible for nonstate groups to do so? How does the current emphasis upon terrorism affect political thinking about the way some political strategies and activities are best conceptualized and understood?

The notion of terrorism, as a political tactic, can be traced back to postrevolutionary France and the efforts of the Jacobins to control the French population by means of a "reign of terror." Historically, the term was initially limited to efforts by states to control their own population through fear. In more recent times, however, the concept has been exploited by political actors in order to condemn violent acts against the state, its agents, or its interests. As a result, violent acts once viewed as merely criminal are now reconceptualized as terrorist and their perpetrators labeled terrorists. The actions of dissident groups in the 1960s, for example the bombings at ROTC buildings on college campuses, were not considered terrorist acts at the time. Today, however, they would likely be viewed as instances of domestic terrorism and condemned accordingly. This suggests that the notion of terrorism carries with it a particularly negative connotation, and effectively labeling some violent act as an instance of terrorism is now a good way to raise doubts about the moral propriety of the act.

This political use of the notion of terrorism now provides a good reason to take a more sober look at the idea of terrorism and to bring it into a clearer moral perspective. But this is no easy chore, for there is probably no very good definition of terrorism. The notion defies easy analysis because the concept itself is a matter of political and philosophical dispute. The construction of a viable concept of terrorism would involve offering a definition that covered all actions that qualify as terrorism without also including any actions that do not. But there is no common or settled agreement on just what these actions are; therefore, the most philosophical analysis can hope to do is to provide an account of terrorism that highlights certain aspects of the notion in a way that illustrates the source and nature of the confusion that surrounds popular thinking about it.

In this regard, it seems prudent to approach the analysis of terrorism by asking if the concept works descriptively or if, instead, it is fundamentally a normative term. Does terrorism identify or label some type of action that is then subject to independent moral critique, or is moral critique a fundamental element of the definition of the term? That is, does terrorism work like the concept "killing" (the taking of human life) or the concept "murder" (the unjustified taking of human life)? Both Virginia Held and Igor Primoratz, in the selections that follow, think that terrorism is a descriptive notion; they think that a satisfactory definition of terrorism still leaves open the additional question about its moral character. David Rodin, on the other hand, takes the concept to be normative in nature, and links the moral question of whether terrorism is justified to the definitional issue about what terrorism is.

No doubt there are some definitional features about terrorism that will receive near universal assent. Terrorist acts are invariably violent and clandestine, and they typically have a specific political purpose. Held, among others, also thinks terrorist acts are necessarily coercive; they are intended to compel others to accede to the political goals of the terrorists. If, however, terrorists are presumed to have a distinctive political agenda and if terrorist acts are perceived to be a means to the realization of political ends, terrorism as a political tactic must be inspired either by the fact that some state or group thinks terrorism is a more efficient method than, say, traditional warfare for realizing their political ends or that more traditional political strategies are not available to them. If so, then terrorism is a strategy states or groups use to achieve politically desirable ends when the more traditional means (e.g., traditional warfare) of achieving these ends are unlikely to succeed, or when they are unable to avail themselves of these means.

This last point, however, is terribly controversial, for it suggests that violent, clandestine, and coercive actions performed by states in the process of prosecuting a war cannot qualify, by definition, as terrorist, and this will seem wrong to anyone who thinks states can and do resort to terrorism in warfare. Consider, for example, the use of nuclear weapons by the United States during World War II. The attacks against Hiroshima and Nagasaki were violent, to say the least, and clandestine (unannounced), and they were done in an effort to coercively force Japan to surrender. According to the accounts of terrorism offered by Held and Primoratz, and perhaps also by Rodin, the attacks would qualify as acts of terrorism. But they were hardly considered such at the time, and it is not clear that they are considered such today by many Americans, in spite of the fact that their moral propriety under the morality of war may still be in doubt.

Definitional problems aside, the question of the moral legitimacy of terrorism is equally, if not more, challenging. Two strategies are available to anyone who wants to critique the moral justification of some action. First, one can suppose that the moral legitimacy of an action rides with its consequences. According to consequentialist argument, an action is morally justified if it promotes the greater good in some way, perhaps by advancing the public interest or promoting the general welfare of some group. Second, an action is morally justified on deontological grounds if it respects, furthers, or promotes individual rights and/or the requirements of justice.

Consequentialist arguments are necessarily suspect because it is terribly difficult, if not impossible, for anyone to know in advance the consequences of their actions. This is particularly troubling when it comes to terrorism because those states that are the typical targets of contemporary terrorist activities are unlikely to accede to the desires of terrorist groups. Instead, these states are likely to redouble their efforts to deal with the terrorist threat in ways that simply make things worse for the terrorist. This suggests not only that terrorist acts against powerful states are unlikely to ever be justified on consequentialist grounds, but also that terrorism as a political strategy under these circumstances isn't terribly effective.

It also seems difficult to justify terrorism on deontological grounds if and when terrorism targets private individuals and results in their death or great physical harm. Terrorist activities of this sort violate the rights of the private parties involved, and from a deontological point of view this seems wrong in principle. It could be argued, of course, that it is important to distinguish at this point between combatants and noncombatants; terrorist acts directed against combatants may be justified under appropriate circumstances while similar acts against noncombatants cannot be justified on deontological grounds.

The distinction, however, doesn't seem overly helpful, and not just because of the difficulty in distinguishing combatants from noncombatants. In the absence of declared war, everyone is a noncombatant, and if terrorism is a political alternative to war, it could then not be justified on deontological grounds. If, however, we allow for the possibility of terrorist acts in war, then the distinction between noncombatant and combatant status inherent in the morality of war provides the normative background that permits reasonable conclusions about the moral justification of the acts. Rodin's discussion of the legitimacy of terrorist acts in war, for example, may profitably be read as an important comment upon the principle of double effect in the morality of war that really has little to do with the issue of terrorism.

Held, on the other hand, provides an intriguing deontological defense of the legitimacy of terrorism. She argues that if terrorist acts advance the rights of some group whose rights have previously been compromised, the acts are morally justified on the grounds of the just distribution of rights, even if the rights of some others, whose rights were not previously compromised, are violated in the process (as they must be if the acts are to qualify as terrorism). Primoratz, however, objects to this argument on the grounds that one's right to life cannot be traded off in this manner. He doesn't think, in effect, that it makes sense to compromise Smith's right to life in order to realize for Jones and Brown other rights that have been denied them. Primoratz takes a strong stand on the notion of human rights and insists that a right to life can be compromised only in the name of self-defense or justified punishment.

Perhaps ironically, Primoratz's argument may justify the very terrorist acts he intends to condemn, for terrorists may suppose that their actions constitute a form of collective self-defense or even visit a justified punishment against an oppressor or an aggressor. On the other hand, Held's argument may not amount to much in practice. While she avoids a consequentialist position by insisting that her defense of terrorism involves the promotion of a more just distribution of rights and not the pursuit of some sense of the good, she must still address the problem, inherent in consequentialist argument, of anticipated outcomes. Terrorism is justifiable, in her view, only if terrorist acts will have the intended outcome, and it is hard to imagine that anyone can be confident of this in advance or that a more just distribution of rights will result from terrorist activity.

7.2

Terrorism, Rights, and Political Goals
Virginia Held

▓ Usage and Definition

An examination of usage is particularly unhelpful in deciding what terrorism is and whether it can be justified. Usage characteristically applies the term to violent acts performed by those of whose positions and goals the speaker disapproves, and fails to apply it to similar acts by those with whose positions and goals the speaker identifies. And usage much more frequently applies the term to those who threaten established conditions and governments than to those using similar kinds of violence to uphold them. There is a tendency to equate terrorism with the *illegal* use of violence, but of course the questions who can decide what is illegal and on what grounds are often the questions at issue. . . .

Much recent philosophical discussion of the term "terrorism" provides sufficient clarification, and demands sufficient consistency, to make persuasive the view that terrorism is not committed only by those opposed to governments and their policies. "Terrorism" must be understood in such a way that states and governments, even friendly or democratic ones, can be held to engage in acts of terrorism, along with those who challenge the authority of and disrupt the order of such states and governments. But an adequate definition has not yet emerged in the philosophical literature. . . .

One of the most useful recent discussions is that of C. A. J. Coady, though I shall disagree with his definition. He defines terrorism as "the tactic or policy of engaging in terrorist acts," and a terrorist act as "a political act, ordinarily committed by an organized group, which involves the intentional killing or other severe harming of non-combatants or the threat of the same."[1] The crucial component of terrorism, in his view, is intentionally targeting noncombatants. He does not think the intent to spread fear should be part of the definition of terrorism. Among his reasons is that, instead of spreading fear and demoralization, the terrorist act may give rise to defiance and a strengthening of resolve. . . .

A difficulty with confining terrorism to those acts involving the intentional harming of noncombatants is that doing so will exclude actions that seem among leading candidates for inclusion, such as the blowing up of the marine barracks in Lebanon in October 1983. In this attack, in which a truck with explosives was driven into a marine compound and exploded, 241 persons, most of them American marines, were killed. The drivers of the truck were killed as well. The marines were clearly the intended target. On Coady's definition, this act could not be an act of terrorism, and this seems arbitrary. . . .

Another difficulty here is the drawing of the distinction between combatant and noncombatant itself. Coady calls various claims that one cannot distinguish the two "absurd and obscene," but he unfairly loads his own descriptions of the distinctions. He is surely right that inconsistency often operates here, as those who deny that the distinction can be made among their enemies in wartime fail to accept a comparable argument made by revolutionaries about *their* enemies. Still, the distinction is considerably more difficult to make, on both sides, than Coady admits, for reasons that will be touched on later. . . .

My own view of what terrorism is remains . . . close to what it was in an article I published in 1984, in which I focused on violence, rather than on terrorism itself. I there defended the view that violence is "action, usually sudden, predictably and coercively inflicting injury upon or damage harming a person."[2] And I saw terrorism as a form of violence to achieve political goals where creating fear is usually high among the intended effects. For reasons similar to those subsequently argued by others, I limited violence and terrorism to harm to persons rather than to property; sometimes, though not always, one harms persons by harming their property, but the intention to harm persons must be present. . . .

I now think that we should probably not construe either the intention to spread fear or the intention to kill noncombatants as necessary for an act of political violence to be an act of terrorism. It does seem that both are often present, but not always. And there do not seem to be good reasons to make the latter a part of the definition while dismissing the former. . . .

▨ The Justifiability of Terrorism

A second way in which usage and much popular and some academic discussion have been unhelpful in illuminating the topic of terrorism is that they have frequently built a judgment of immorality or nonjustifiability into the definition of terrorism, making it impossible even to question whether given acts of terrorism might be justified. Thus news reports frequently equate terrorism with evildoing. . . .

Arguments against building unjustifiability into the definition of terrorism can follow similar arguments against holding that violence is by definition morally wrong. Not only is violence often used in ways usually accepted, as in upholding law, but one can easily cite examples of violence used against governmental authority where it makes sense to ask whether such uses of violence were morally wrong or not. The 1944 bomb plot against Hitler is one obvious candidate. Even if examples of possibly justifiable acts of terrorism, as distinct from other forms of violence, are for many persons harder to acknowledge, we should still be able to *consider* the justifiability of terrorist acts. We should be able to treat such questions as open, and this requires that we not imagine them to be answerable merely by appealing to a definition.

Many of those who use "terrorist" as a term of denunciation apply it, as noted before, to their opponents and refuse to apply it to the acts of their own government, or of governments of which they approve, even when such governmental action is as clearly violent, intended to spread fear, or expectably productive of the killing of noncombatants. But one cannot effectively criticize the terrorism of those Third World revolutionaries who consider various terrorist acts to be admirable unless one also criticizes the terrorist acts of campaigns of counterterrorism carried out by one's government and the governments of states one considers "friendly." . . .

Some of those who define terrorism as the intentional harming of noncombatants conclude that therefore, either by definition or not, terrorism is always wrong. Since we can rule out as inadequate the view that terrorism is by definition always wrong, let us consider only those cases where the judgment is not one of definition but independently arrived at. Then, is intentionally harming noncombatants always wrong, and terrorism always wrong because it involves this?

Let us consider some objections to the position that it is never justifiable to harm noncombatants. First let us take up the question of harming noncombatants in wartime, and focus on a recent example. Reports suggest that the Iran-Iraq war may have cost some 1 million dead, 1.7 million wounded, and more than 1.5 million refugees. It is also suggested that Iran's decision to accept UN Resolution 598 calling for an end of the fighting was partly the result of a demoralization within Iran brought about by the Iraqi bombing of Iranian cities.

Certainly, from a moral point of view, the war ought not to have been fought and other means to achieve this outcome should have been found. Iraq was at fault in starting the war and in violation of international law in its use of poison gas. But once the war was under way, was violence used against noncombatants beyond the possibility of moral justification, if it did in fact hasten the cessation of violence? . . .

An argument can be made that no absolute right of noncombatants to immunity from the violence suffered by combatants should be granted, especially when many of the combatants have been conscripted or misled into joining the armed forces. Recent reports indicate that many who serve in armies around the world are children. Iran's conscription age was lowered to thirteen, the Contra rebels in Nicaragua recruited boys as young as twelve, and these are not isolated examples. . . . Such "combatants" hardly seem legitimate targets while the "civilians" who support the war in which they fight are exempt.

Now let us apply this objection to terrorism. Is violence that kills young persons whose economic circumstances made military service seem to be almost their only option very much more plausibly justifiable than violence attacking well-off shoppers in a mall, shoppers whose economic comfort is enjoyed at the expense of the young persons who risk their lives in order to eat and thereby defend the shoppers? It is hard to see here a deep moral distinction between combatant and noncombatant. If the combatant is a conscript, the distinction between combatant and "ordinary person" is often difficult to draw. And although one may certainly hold that any child is innocent, it is still not clear why the children of one group should be granted an absolute right of exemption from the risk of violence where no such right is granted to the children of an opposing group, *if* the violence is justified on other grounds. . . .

This is not to suggest that we should simply abandon the distinction between combatant and noncombatant. It is certainly harder to justify harming noncombatants than it is to justify harming combatants, other things being equal, and we can try to combine this distinction with usefully drawn notions of "those responsible." . . .

Many of those who most bitterly denounce terrorism are entirely willing to sacrifice the innocent lives of hostages to uphold the principle that one should never negotiate with hostage takers. They judge that in the long run fewer lives will be lost if one upholds this principle. But this risks harm to innocent hostages and may rest on justifications quite comparable to those of hostage takers, who are willing to risk harming innocent persons to bring about a political goal on the theory that in the long run, fewer lives overall will be lost if the goal is achieved than if intolerable oppression continues. . . .

*   *   *

Burleigh Wilkins in a recent article argues that consequentialism provides weak defenses against terrorism. To a consequentialist, terrorism would have to be justifiable if, on balance, it brings about better consequences than its alternatives. And though such consequentialists considered by Wilkins as Hare and Kai Nielsen think that terrorism is hardly ever justified, their arguments depend on empirical estimates that terrorism almost always produces results that are worse on consequentialist grounds than their alternatives. Others find the empirical claims on which such judgments rest to be questionable. . . .

It may be almost impossible to predict whether an act of terrorism will in fact have its intended effect of hastening some political goal sought by the terrorists, or whether it will in fact do the terrorists' cause more harm than good. But as Wilkins asks, "Is there something special about acts of violence which makes them different from other acts where judgments about their consequences are concerned? We frequently do many things where the outcome is uncertain." If existing conditions are terrible, "they might prompt a prospective terrorist to reason that *any* chance of altering these states of affairs is worth the risk of failure and the near certainty of harm to property or persons that violence involves."[3]

Furthermore, states use violence and the threat of violence to uphold their laws, and some use terrorism. Many theorists still define the state in terms of its monopoly on the use of violence considered legitimate. But if violence can be condemned on consequentialist grounds it can be condemned in unjustified state behavior as well as in the behavior of a state's opponents. On the other hand, if violence or terrorism by the state *can* be justified, it may be as impossible to predict its success as to predict the success of the violence or terrorism of its opponents. . . .

■ Terrorism and Rights

In my view we cannot adequately evaluate social action in consequentialist terms alone. The framework of rights and obligations must also be applied, and in the case of terrorism it is certainly relevant to ask: Are rights being violated, and can this be justified? . . .

The use of violence directed at noncombatants is judged justifiable on utilitarian grounds if carried out by one's own or a friendly state, as in many evaluations of the justifiability of bombing raids in wartime in which civilians can be expected to be killed. At the same time, when revolutionaries and rebels use violence that harms noncombatants, such acts are judged on nonutilitarian grounds to be unjustifiable violations of prohibitions on how political goals are to be pursued. . . . [C]onsistency can be achieved either by applying utilitarian evaluations to both sides or by applying nonutilitarian evaluations to both sides. . . . My own suggestion is for a nonutilitarian comparison of rights violations. . . .

One of the most difficult problems for political philosophy is the problem of how to evaluate situations where human rights are not being respected. What are persons justified in doing to bring about such respect, and how should these actions be judged? Should "bringing about increased respect for human rights" be evaluated in consequentialist terms? But then how should this consequence be weighed against any violations of rights necessitated by the action to achieve this consequence? If we say that no violations of rights are justified, even in this case, this can become a disguised recipe for maintaining the status quo. If we permit violations, we risk undermining the moral worth of the very rights for which we are striving to achieve respect.

My suggestion is that we not yield to a merely consequentialist evaluation, but that we strive for reasonable comparative judgments. In a well-developed scheme of assured rights, rights should not be traded off against one another, or judged in comparative terms. We do not usefully speak of more of a right to vote or less of a right to vote, but of a right to vote. And we do not usefully try to determine whether a right to vote is more or is less important than a right to nondiscrimination in employment. Where rights conflict, we may order them by priorities or stringency; this, however, is not a matter of maximizing, but of seeking consistency. Some rights may be deemed to have priority over others, or to be more basic than others, but our aim is not to engage in trade-offs. . . .

In a defective society, on the other hand, where rights are not in fact being respected, we should be able to make comparative judgments about which and whose rights violations are least justifiable. Is it more important, for instance, for blacks in South Africa to gain assurance of rights to personal safety than it is for white South Africans to continue to enjoy their property rights undisturbed? While blacks are denied respect for their most basic rights, it seems worse to continue these violations than to permit some comparable violations of the rights of whites participating in this denial.

Such an evaluation is not a consequentialist calculation, but it does allow us to compare rights violations. It requires us not to ignore the violations involved in maintaining an existing system, since of course charges of rights violation should not be applied only to those seeking change, while those upholding an existing system are exempt.

I shall use the expression "effective respect for rights" to mean that an existing legal system recognizes the rights in question and effectively upholds respect for them. Of course this does not mean that violations never occur; no legal system can secure perfect compliance with its norms. It means that violations are on the whole prevented by adequate education, socialization, and police protection, and that those who commit such violations are apprehended and dealt with to a sufficient degree to make respect for the rights in question generally high. There is no escape from the fact that effective respect for rights is a matter of degree, but it is quite possible to make an accurate empirical judgment that it is absent when a legal system does not even recognize a right in question as a legal right. When using the expression "effective respect for rights," we should specify the type of rights in question; this can be done.

Let's consider the case where a certain type of right is recognized as a human right by the major international documents and bodies establishing international norms concerning rights. When such a right is not recognized as a legal right for a certain group of persons in a given legal system, there will clearly then be no effective respect for those rights of those persons in that legal system. . . .

Now let us ask whether it can be morally justifiable to violate some rights to achieve effective respect for other rights. First, an aside: If there are legal rights in conflict with human rights such that we can judge that these legal rights ought not to exist, then what appears to be a violation of them will probably not be morally unjustified. That kind of case will not present the moral difficulties I wish to consider.

The difficult case is when achieving effective respect for the fundamental human rights of the members of one group, which rights ought to be respected, requires the violation of the fundamental human rights of the members of another group, which are also rights that seemingly ought to be respected. If terrorism can ever be justified, it would seem to present this kind of problem. Where there is a lack of effective respect for the fundamental human rights of the members of one group, and *if* there is a reasonable likelihood that limited terrorism will significantly contribute to bringing about such effective respect, and no other effective means are available, can it be justifiable to violate the fundamental human rights of those who will suffer from such terrorism? Their rights to "life, liberty and security of person," as specified in article 3 of the Universal Declaration, are likely to be violated by any act of terrorism. Can this possibly be justified?

Let us specify two situations. In the first, S_1, the members of group A have a human right to x and they enjoy effective respect for this right in a given legal system, while the members of group B also have a human right to x, but suffer a lack of effective respect for this right. In situation S_2, in contrast, both the members of A and the members of B have a human right to x and they enjoy effective respect for that right. Obviously S_2 is a morally better situation than S_1. It is the process of getting from S_1 to S_2 that is in question. . . .

If a judgment is made, especially in special circumstances, that nonviolence cannot succeed, but that terrorism will be effective in moving a society from S_1 to S_2, can engaging in terrorism be better than refraining from it? Given that it will involve a violation of human rights, can it be better to violate rights through terrorism than to avoid this violation? . . .

Alternative 1 is to maintain S_1 and to refrain from terrorism; alternative 2 is to employ terrorism and to achieve S_2. Both alternatives involve rights violations. The questions are: Can they be compared and can either be found to be less unjustifiable?

It has often been pointed out, in assessing terrorism, that we can almost never accurately predict that an outcome such as S_2 will be achieved as a result of the terrorism in question. But I am trying to deal with the moral issues *given* certain empirical claims. And *if* the empirical judgment is responsibly made that the transition is likely to achieve S_2, which situation is clearly morally better than S_1, and that no other means can do so, can alternative 2 be better than alternative 1? Rights will be violated in either case. Are there any grounds on which the violations in alternative 2 are morally less unjustifiable than the violations in alternative 1?

It seems reasonable, I think, that on grounds of justice, it is better to equalize rights violations in a transition to bring an end to rights violations than it is to subject a given group that has already suffered extensive rights violations to continued such violations, if the degree of severity of the two violations is similar. And this is the major argument of this essay: If we must have rights violations, a more equitable distribution of such violations is better than a less equitable distribution.

If the severity of the violations is very dissimilar, then we might judge that the more serious violations are to be avoided in favor of the less serious, regardless of who is suffering them, although this judgment could perhaps be overridden if, for instance, many different though less serious violations were suffered by the members of group B, a situation that could outweigh a serious violation for the members of group A. But generally, there would be a prima facie judgment against serious violations, such as those of rights to life, to bring about respect for less serious rights, such as those to more equitable distributions of property above what is necessary for the satisfaction of basic needs.

The case on which I focus, however, involves serious violations among both groups. The human rights to personal safety of oppressed groups are, for instance, frequently violated. If a transition to a situation such as S_2 involves violations of the rights to personal safety of the oppressing groups, why would this violation be less unjustifiable than the other? Fairness would seem to recommend a sharing of the burden of rights violation, even if no element of punishment were appealed to. If punishment is considered, it would seem more appropriate for those who have benefited from the rights violations of the members of a given group to suffer, in a transition, any necessary rights violations than to allow the further rights violations of those who have already been subjected to them. . . .

That justice itself often requires a concern for how rights violations are distributed seems clear. We can recognize that some distributions are unfair, and seek to make them less so. Consider the following: The right to personal security, of freedom from unlawful attack, can be fully recognized as a right in a given legal community, and yet of course some assaults will occur. The community's way of trying to assure respect for such rights is likely to include the deployment of police forces. But if almost all the police forces are deployed in high-income white neighborhoods and almost none in low-income black neighborhoods, so that the risk of assault for inhabitants of the latter is many times greater than the risk for inhabitants of the former, we can judge without great difficulty that the deployment is unfair. Or if we take any given level of effort to protect persons from assault, and if cuts in protection are then necessary for budgetary reasons, and the cuts are all made in areas already suffering the greatest threats of attack, we can judge that such cuts are being made unfairly.

The basis for such judgments must be a principle of justice with respect to the distribution of rights violations, or of risks of such violations. This is the principle to which I am appealing in my argument concerning terrorism, and it seems clear that it is a relevant principle that we should not ignore.

What all this may show is that terrorism cannot necessarily be ruled out as unjustifiable on a rights-based analysis, any more than it can on a consequentialist one. Depending on the severity and extent of the rights violations in an existing situation, a transition involving a sharing of rights violations, if this and only this can be expected to lead to a situation in which rights are more adequately respected, may well be less morally unjustifiable than continued acceptance of ongoing rights violations.

■ Notes

1. C. A. J. Coady, "The Morality of Terrorism," *Philosophy,* vol. 60 (January 1985), p. 52.

2. Virginia Held, "Violence, Terrorism, and Moral Inquiry," *Monist,* vol. 67, no. 4 (October 1984), p. 606.

3. Burleigh Wilkins, "Terrorism and Consequentialism," *Journal of Value Inquiry,* vol. 21, no. 2 (1987), p. 150.

7.3 ⸻

The Morality of Terrorism

Igor Primoratz

■ I

In an ethical context terrorism is best defined as the deliberate use of violence, or the threat of its use, against innocent people, with the aim of intimidating some other people into a course of action they otherwise would not take. With regard to this definition, the following points should be noted:

(a) Terrorism has a certain structure. It targets two different persons or groups of people. One is the primary, the other the secondary target. The latter target is directly hit, but the aim is to get at the former, to intimidate them into doing something they otherwise would not do.

(b) The secondary target, which is directly attacked, is innocent people. In the context of war or insurgency, this means persons who are neither members of the armed forces or security services, nor persons who supply these with arms and ammunition, nor political officials involved in the conflict. Terrorism is thus distinguished from war in general (and guerrilla war in particular), and from political violence. This, of course, does not mean that an army cannot employ terrorism; many armies have done that. . . .

(c) The etymological connection of "terrorism" with "terror" and "terrorising" is preserved.

(d) The definition covers both political and non-political (such as religious or criminal) terrorism.

(e) With regard to political terrorism, the definition makes it possible to speak both of state and anti-state terrorism, revolutionary and counterrevolutionary terrorism, terrorism of the left and of the right. The definition is politically neutral.

(f) It is also morally neutral, at least at the most basic level of discussion. I believe it captures the elements of terrorism that cause many of us to view it with utmost moral repugnance: *violence* (or threat of violence) against the *innocent,* for the purpose of *intimidation* and *coercion.* But it is not an attempt at prejudging a *moral* decision by means of a *definition:* it does not make moral condemnation of terrorism analytically true and thus trivial, nor its moral defence analytically false, a contradiction in terms, nor the question of its moral status a self-answering one.

(g) When compared to the use of the word "terrorism" in ordinary language, this definition may appear both too narrow in some respects and too wide in others. One might object that it is too narrow, since it implies that attacks of insurgents on soldiers or police officers, which the media as a rule depict as terrorism, should not be called that, but rather political violence or guerrilla war. On the other hand, it might also be objected that it is too wide, for it follows from it that the bombing of Dresden and Hamburg in World War Two, or recent Israeli Army incursions into Lebanon, were cases of terrorism, or that some of the violence whereby the mafia forces the unwilling population to collaborate is also terroristic. But if we can agree that paradigmatic cases of terrorism do not involve the four morally problematic components the definition singles out—violence (or threat of its use) against innocent people, for the sake of intimidation and coercion—we may be willing to accept these, admittedly significant, deviations from ordinary usage.

(h) By focusing on the innocent as the victims of terrorism, the definition connects debates about the morality of terrorism with the traditional discussion of just war theory. For the main provision of that theory with regard to *jus in bello* is the prohibition on attacking noncombatants.

II

When queried about the morality of their actions, some terrorists turn out to be amoralists. Others try to come up with a moral justification of terrorism. Indeed, there is a tradition of moral apologetics of political terrorism employed by the radical left, from Bakunin and Nechaev in the nineteenth century to Trotsky and Marcuse in the twentieth. All these apologies have an unmistakably consequentialist character.

From the consequentialist point of view, terrorism, just as everything else, is not morally wrong or impermissible in itself; it all depends on the consequences it is going to have in the circumstances given. When its consequences are bad, terrorism is, or course, impermissible. But when its consequences are good enough, terrorism, just like everything else, is given moral consecration. For a consequentialist, the question of the moral status of terrorism is solely the question of its consequences. . . .

Many find this lack of any opposition to terrorism *as such* on the part of the consequentialist rather disturbing. Many find it difficult to accept that the use of violence, or threat of it, against innocent people, with the aim of intimidating some other people into doing something they would not otherwise do, is morally right and proper whenever its consequences are good enough. This is only a particular case of what is generally seen as the main problem with consequentialism: the much too great willingness of the theory to permit and indeed call for, various actions that would be considered morally wrong in themselves, i.e. wrong even when they would produce good results. . . .

Many remain unimpressed by the consequentialist defense of terrorism in terms of its good consequences. They feel that the consequentialist account is incomplete. There are other considerations that need to be taken into account—considerations that have great moral weight, and tend to show that terrorism is morally unacceptable even when it does have good consequences. These considerations are the following.

The Separateness of Persons

A terrorist who justifies his actions in consequentialist terms has one paramount goal: to bring about the state of affairs to which he accords the highest value. That can be the good, just, truly free and humane society, or the liberation of the homeland and establishment of an independent state, or the victory of the one true faith, or whatever. Since his commitment is to the highest value, that value overrides all other values that might conflict with it, all considerations that might stand in the way of its realization. He may also have certain beliefs about society according to which the way to bring about the desired state of affairs is, or includes, terrorism. It is sometimes said terrorism is indiscriminate violence, but that is certainly not true if taken literally. The terrorist does not strike blindly, left and right, but rather plans his actions carefully, considering the situation and the resources at his disposal, and trying for the course of action likely to be most effective in the circumstances. . . .

Respect for Persons

Since the terrorist does not take the separateness of persons seriously, she is not in a position to show respect for persons. The principle of respect for persons can be construed in more than one way; but the terrorist is bound to offend against it on any plausible construal. On one interpretation, the principle enjoins respect for the core of individuality of each and every person, a concern for seeing things from the point of view of the other person, in terms of his or her character of "ground project." This is the direct opposite of the impersonal, objective, calculatory way in which the terrorist relates to her victims. According to another interpretation, the principle demands that we recognize and respect certain basic human rights of every human being, which safeguard a certain area of personal freedom; persons are to be respected as holders of rights. There is no way the terrorist can do this; for if I have any basic rights at all, the right not to be killed or maimed in order that the terrorist's cause be promoted is surely one of them. On still another interpretation, the principle prohibits using another person as a mere means. The Kantian account of the principle is not as clear as could be desired; but at a minimum, it requires that the other person be able to "share in the end" of one's action, that is, to consent to it. This is just what the terrorist's victim is not in a position to do. . . .

Guilt and Innocence

The distinction between guilt and innocence is generally considered one of the most fundamental moral distinctions. We tend to accord it central significance when war and other types of violence are to be judged and circumscribed from the moral point of view. Terrorists deliberately and systematically attack, kill and otherwise severely harm innocent people; this, and the aim of intimidation and coercion they seek to achieve by doing this, are what make them terrorists. . . .

Moral Dialogue

We often hope for moral dialogue with those whose moral views differ from ours. In particular, we feel a need for such a dialogue with those who propose to do to us something we find extremely objectionable. We want to hear how they can justify their actions *to us*. In general, it seems that, other things being equal, a theory of punishment that goes some way in convincing the person punished that the punishment is justified is better than a theory that does not try to address her in particular; a moral justification of progressive taxation that appeals to the rich is better than one that remains on the most abstract level, and does nothing in particular to convince those who are to pay the highest price when it is put into effect. The terrorist does not, and is not in a position to, try to justify her actions *to* her victims in a free and equal dialogue with them.

Moral Equality

We hope for moral dialogue with others because we believe in basic moral equality of humans. We believe that every mature and sane human being, *qua* human being, is qualified to exercise moral judgment and to reason with us on an equal footing. We accept that there are experts on certain factual questions involved in moral issues; but we acknowledge no *moral* experts. We admire certain individuals as morally saintly or heroic; but we do not believe in *moral elites*. Terrorists who justify their actions in utilitarian terms see themselves as members of such an elite, and relegate us to the status of lesser beings, to whom they need not, and indeed, cannot, try to explain and justify their actions. . . .

Secrecy

With respect to eminently other-regarding action, with certain narrowly circumscribed exceptions, we tend to be morally suspicious of actions and policies that have to be kept secret. With regard to moral principles, in particular, we insist on publicity; we want them to be such that they can be publicly proclaimed, and that their import, validity and application can be publicly debated. No terrorist could satisfy this requirement and succeed nor, indeed, remain in business for long. Secrecy is a *sine qua non* of his action, as well as of his principles of action. . . .

▓ IV

If we are looking for a moral justification of terrorism, we should look for it in consequentialist ethics; deontological theory can be expected to judge it as wrong in itself, even when it has good consequences.

Still, in recent philosophy there is one important attempt at moral justification of terrorism from a deontological point of view. I am referring to Virginia Held's paper "Terrorism, Rights and Political Goals." The main thesis of the paper is that terrorism can be justified under certain circumstances in terms of basic human rights.

Held begins by emphasizing that social action in general cannot be properly judged solely in the light of its consequences; we must also apply the concepts of rights and duties. When dealing with terrorism, we must focus on the fact that terrorists violate rights, and ask whether such violations can be morally justified.

What may we do in order to secure respect of rights? May we, in order to ensure that the rights of one person or group are respected violate the rights of another person or group? "If we say that no violations of rights are justified, even in this case, this can become a disguised recipe for maintaining the status quo. If we permit violations, we risk undermining the moral worth of the very rights for which we are striving to achieve respect."[1] . . .

According to Held, the question of the moral justification of terrorism is a particular case of the general question whether we may violate certain rights in order to ensure the respect of other rights. Terrorism violates basic human rights of its victims. But what if a limited use of terrorism is the only way of securing effective respect of the basic human rights of all in a society?

In Held's view, in such a society resort to terrorism would still not be justified. But it would become justified, if an additional condition were met: that of *distributive justice*. If, in a society, (a) the basic human rights of a part of the population are effectively respected, while the same rights of another part of the population are violated; (b) if the only way of overcoming this state of affairs, and ensuring the effective respect of the basic human rights of all, is a limited use of terrorism, i.e. violating basic human rights of those who end up as its victims; finally, (c) if terrorism is directed *against members of the first group,* that terrorism will be justified. . . .

The justification of terrorism offered by Held is original and interesting. It is quite different from the usual consequentialist justification that refers to the good consequences of terrorism: to the fact that its use in certain circumstances maximises the common good, promotes the general interest, satisfies the preferences of all. For this is a justification of terrorism in terms of *rights.* It is also different from a justification of terrorism in terms of consequentialism of rights. Consequentialism of rights will allow resort to terrorism when that is the only way of maximizing the respect of rights, or minimizing their violations. Held does not simply refer to rights, but to a *just distribution* of violation of rights. The crucial part of her justification of terrorism is the argument of distributive *justice.*

Is this justification convincing? . . .

A candidate for a victim of a terrorist attack, faced with the usual consequentialist justification of terrorism, will most likely say that she finds it unacceptable to be killed or maimed for the sake of maximizing the satisfaction of everyone's preferences, promoting the general interest, realizing the common good. She has a *right* to life and bodily integrity, and this right must not be violated merely in order to promote the general interest, the common good. Considerations of rights have in principle greater weight than those of consequences. When offered a justification of the attack couched in terms of consequentialism of rights, she will likely say that she finds that justification unacceptable too. For that justification, too, does not take seriously the separateness of persons, and sacrifices *her* basic human rights for the sake of the greatest possible degree of respect of rights of a certain *group* of people.

I believe that such a person, faced with the justification of terrorism offered by Held—the justification that invokes basic human rights, *and* applies distributive justice to violations of such rights—might well make a similar retort. She might say that she finds the justification unconvincing and unacceptable; for it too does not take seriously the separateness of persons, but rather sacrifices *her* basic human rights for the sake of a more just distribution of violations of such rights within a group of people in the course of the transition to a stage where these rights would be generally respected.

Is this retort convincing? The answer to this question will depend on the view of rights one espouses. If one views rights as almost absolute side constraints on our pursuit of individual and collective aims, the way Robert Nozick does,[2] one is likely to find this retort quite appropriate, and to reject the justification of terrorism advanced by Held. But this view of rights has been criticized as much too radical, and as one that prevents us from making certain obviously relevant moral distinctions. In Nozick's theory, says H. L. A. Hart, "the basic rights which fill the moral landscape and express the inviolability of persons are few in number but are all equally stringent."[3] As a result, the theory has unacceptable implications:

> How can it be right to lump together, and ban as equally illegitimate, things so different in their impact on individual life as taking some of a man's income to save others from some great suffering and killing him or taking one of his vital organs for the same purpose? [. . .] Can one man's great gain or relief from great suffering not outweigh a small loss of income imposed on another to provide it?[4]

On the other hand, if, in order to avoid these implications of Nozick's radical account, one opts for a more moderate view of rights, Held's argument may appear quite attractive.

However, although Nozick's view of rights is indeed much too radical if one applies it across the board—that is, to property rights, as to the rights to life and to bodily integrity, the way Nozick does—this view no longer looks quite as exaggerated if we recall *just what rights* the terrorist typically violates. Are my rights not to be killed or maimed (except in self-defence or as deserved punishment) almost absolute, or rights that may be sacrificed for the sake of a more just distribution of violations of the same rights within a group in a transition to a stage where they will be generally respected?

Faced with the prospect of being killed or maimed on the grounds of this last justification, might I not draw on Nozick's view of rights, and say that I am a person in my own right, that my life is the only life I have and all I have, and that nobody may take it away, nor ruin it by making me a cripple, for the sake of a more just distribution of, and subsequently more general respect for, the right to life and bodily security within a group of people. My life and at least some of my basic human rights amount to more than mere membership in a group of holders of rights. The value and significance of my life is not derived from my membership in a group. Nobody may sacrifice it to the group.

If so, then Virginia Held's attempt to justify terrorism from a deontological point of view does not succeed. Nozick's radical view of rights as almost absolute side constraints on our pursuit of individual and collected goals is not *too radical* when the rights at stake are the rights the terrorist typically violates: the rights of the individual not be killed or maimed (except in self-defence or as deserved punishment). If it is not, if these rights are indeed almost absolute, then the considerations of rights and distributive justice to which Held appeals cannot override them after all.

■ V

If our preferred ethical theory is consequentialism, then we will accept terrorism in certain circumstances. . . . On the other hand, . . . we cannot accept that in morality everything depends on the consequences of actions, but rather believe that some actions are wrong, obligatory or prohibited, in themselves, and if we take seriously the separateness of persons and the value of personhood, the difference between guilt and innocence, and the ideas of moral equality, moral dialogue, and publicity of moral principles and action, our stand on terrorism is likely to be clearly and strongly negative. If my critique of Virginia Held's attempt at a deontological justification of terrorism is valid, terrorism remains almost absolutely wrong.

■ Notes

1. Virginia Held, "Terrorism, Rights, and Political Goals," in *Violence, Terrorism and Justice,* ed. R. G. Frey and C. W. Morris (Cambridge: Cambridge University Press, 1991), p. 73.

2. See Robert Nozick, *Anarchy, State, and Utopia* (Oxford: Blackwell, 1974), pp. 28–33.

3. H. L. A. Hart, "Between Utility and Rights," in *The Idea of Freedom: Essays in Honour of Isaiah Berlin,* ed. A. Ryan (Oxford: Oxford University Press, 1979), p. 81.

4. Ibid., p. 84.

7.4 ⸻

Terrorism Without Intention

David Rodin

In this article, I present a unified way of understanding the moral significance of terrorism. I begin by briefly identifying four different strategies for
defining terrorism. I then introduce a definition of terrorism which locates
its moral significance in the object of attack—terrorism is given its distinctive moral character by the fact that it uses force against those who should
not have force used against them. In the idiom of the just war theory, it uses
force against noncombatants.

It has sometimes been claimed that certain military actions of key
Western powers such as the United States, NATO, and Israel are properly
described as acts of terrorism because they cause the death of a large number of noncombatants. This is a counterintuitive claim. But by examining
the doctrine of double effect and contrasting it with the categories of reckless and negligent harming, I will argue that there are good reasons for
thinking that these claims may sometimes be correct. . . .

■ Defining Terrorism

The concept of terrorism has been so deformed by rhetorical usage that it is
probably not possible to provide a full analysis of its use in common language. At best what we can discern is a loose family resemblance. I shall
suggest, however, that it is possible to provide a moral definition of the term.
By this I mean an analysis of the features of acknowledged core instances of
terrorism which merit and explain the moral reaction which most of us have
toward them. These reactions are undeniably negative; most of us regard acts
of terrorism with abhorrence. This in turn raises the question of whether the
moral definition of a pejorative concept makes the specified act wrong by
definition. There is certainly truth in the thought that wrongness is part of the
meaning of terrorism—in this respect the concept is more like that of murder
than it is of killing. Yet it is not the case that establishing a moral definition

trivializes the task of morally assessing terrorism by turning it into a matter of simple definition. This is because, first, it is part of the function of a moral definition to *explain why* the class of actions is wrong. The strategy I employ in this article is to explain an explicitly normative concept through definitional elements that are at least less normative. Second, once we have discovered the set of features that accounts for our negative moral reaction to a class of action, it is still an open question whether there exist cases in which the act so defined may be justified or excused (e.g., because of overwhelming consequentialist considerations). . . .

Many philosophers and theorists of various kinds have attempted to define terrorism. These attempted definitions are too numerous to review here in detail, but they may be usefully classified as making appeal to four different sets of consideration. . . .

1. *Tactical and operational definition.* This may be phrased in terms of the weapons deployed; for example, Carlos Marighela, the Brazilian revolutionary, defined terrorism simply as "the use of bomb attacks."[1] Clearly this is too narrow. Any such definition would have to be enlarged to include a range of further operational modalities, some of which are distinctive to terrorism (such as plane hijacking), but others may include more familiar military practices. Another form of operational definition focuses not on the weapon systems themselves but on the mode of their employment. Michael Walzer claims that "randomness is the crucial feature of terrorist activity."[2] The point here is not that terrorist attacks are unplanned or untargeted but rather that the violence appears random from the perspective of the victim. . . .

2. *Teleological definition.* This focuses on the ends or goals of violence. Many writers claim that terrorism must be a political act. The definition of the U.K. Terrorism Act 2000 is somewhat broader, specifying that it be "for the purpose of advancing a political, religious or ideological cause." Beyond this, some authors have argued that a necessary feature of terrorism is that it is coercive, aiming to get people or groups to do things they would not otherwise do. Finally, "terrorism" is etymologically connected to "terror," and some authors have argued that the creation of terror among a given community is definitional of terrorism.

3. *Agent-focused definition.* In contrast to tactical and teleological definitions which focus on the nature of the act, this approach focuses on the nature of the actor. . . . Unsurprisingly, such a definition which excludes state action from the definition of terrorism has been enthusiastically endorsed by states themselves: for example, the U.S. State Department definition of "terrorism" restricts it to "violence perpetrated . . . by sub-national groups or clandestine agents."[3]

4. *Object-focused definition.* Finally, terrorism has been defined as attacks against a particular class of target variously described as "innocent," "neutral," "civilian," or "non-combatant." . . .

What are we to make of this multiplicity of definitional elements? The first thing to note is that it is plausible that each of these definitional features may have utility in different contexts. For example, for the purposes of a military-strategic, or sociological, or psychological investigation it may be highly relevant to distinguish between violence committed by state and nonstate actors, between different tactical modalities, and between violence directed to different teleological aims. However, it will be my argument that for the purposes of a moral definition of terrorism, the crucial factor is the fourth element—the object against which force is used. The key to a moral understanding of terrorism is that it consists in the use of force against those who should not have force used against them. . . .

With this in mind, I propose to introduce the following moral definition: *terrorism is the deliberate, negligent, or reckless use of force against noncombatants, by state or nonstate actors for ideological ends and in the absence of a substantively just legal process.* Like all definitions, this one contains a number of suppressed arguments, and it is important that we make them explicit in order to see what is doing the moral and conceptual work. The aspect of my definition which is likely to be most controversial is the claim that terrorism may include negligent and reckless as well as deliberate uses of force, and this will be defended in a separate section below. Before doing this I propose to explain each clause of the definition in some detail.

Use of force. This is a deliberately broader notion than that of violence, with its connotations of wild and explosive physical harming. Clearly the kinds of force used and the methods of its deployment must be interpreted widely. Use of conventional weapons, weapons of mass destruction, hostage taking, poisoning, systematic incidences of rape, and destruction of property may all be terroristic. . . .

Ideological ends. The term "ideological" is used here in its broadest sense to signify "a systematic scheme of ideas, usually relating to politics or society, or to the conduct of a class or group, and regarded as justifying actions."[4] It is meant only to signify a commitment to some systematic and socially directed end beyond the motives of fear, anger, lust, and personal enrichment, which are the typical motives of common violent crimes.

This teleological element is required in the definition to distinguish terrorism from common crime. Though terrorism is a species of crime, it is distinguished from common murder, rape, and destruction of property by the fact it is directed toward a broader agenda. . . .

Noncombatants. Clearly this clause of the definition contains the crux of the moral argument. It is designed to capture the intuition that terrorism has the significance it does in our moral thinking because the targets it attacks are morally inappropriate. Put simply, terrorism involves the use of force against those who should not have force used against them, and to do so is a moral crime. . . .

Now to characterize terrorism in this way is implicitly to invoke some principled way of distinguishing those who are morally liable to the use of force and those who are not. In the Western tradition the most widely accepted way of doing this in the context of political conflict is by reference to the principle of discrimination within the just war theory. This stipulates that the only appropriate objects of force in a conflict are combatants—those who are engaged in fighting and are therefore either individually or collectively offering harm to the putative agent of force or to another. All others are to be regarded as noncombatants and excluded from attack.

The just war principle of discrimination is not without its critics. It has been doubted, for example, whether the notion of a combatant really identifies sufficient conditions for being an appropriate object of force. For being a combatant or offering harm is a material fact about the agent; it need say nothing about his moral responsibility for the fact that he is offering harm. . . . But for our present purposes we need make no judgment about the soundness of the permissive side of the principle of discrimination. . . .

The term "noncombatant" is preferable to the related term "civilian" often employed in international law. The reason for this can be seen from consideration of the bomb attack on the American destroyer USS *Cole* in the port of Aden in October 2000. . . . The crew members killed were uniformed servicemen and therefore not civilians, but they were noncombatants in the morally relevant sense. . . .

State or nonstate actor. Strictly this element is superfluous to the definition—it has been inserted only to make the universality of the definition explicit. . . .

Substantively just legal process. The purpose of this clause is to create a qualified exception to the definition. The exception is required because without it the use of force by agents of the state to enforce the law would be classed as terrorism. That cannot be right. Proper enforcement of the law by state agents is not an instance of terrorism; indeed it is a paradigm of morally justified use of force. . . .

One further element of my definition is operative by way of omission. I have made no mention of the further teleological and agent-focused features which some authors have thought definitional of terrorism: the claim that it is coercive, the claim that there is a necessary distinction between direct and indirect targets, and the link between terrorism and terror. Jenny Teichman says "we will look pretty silly if we do not mention terror in our account of terrorism."[5] . . .

Well, is it silly to omit mention of terror in a moral definition of terrorism? . . . Only in the most extreme cases do terrorist attacks cause a genuine terror or panic in the population as a whole. Shocking as the attacks may be, ordinary people generally get on with their lives and think about the threat only when personally affected or when the violence is reported in the news. . . .

It does not seem to be the case that terrorism invariably has the effect of causing terror in a population. On the contrary, there have been instances in which communities have grown stronger and more resilient as a result of terrorist attacks. . . .

■ The Doctrine of Double Effect and the Distinction Between Terror Bombing and Tactical Bombing

The final element of my definition is intended to be somewhat more revisionary than the preceding analysis. Because the definition includes "negligent and reckless" uses of force, it implicitly entails that some harms unintentionally inflicted on noncombatants in the course of war are a form of terrorism. The issue arises particularly in the case of aerial bombardment against targets within or adjacent to civilian populations which is almost certain to generate noncombatant casualties. Although new targeting technologies have significantly increased the bombing accuracy of Western air forces, the number of noncombatant casualties in modern air campaigns such as Kosovo, Afghanistan, and Iraq remains high in absolute terms. . . .

According to traditional moral theory, such "collateral casualties" are considered the regrettable but generally permissible side effect of legitimate military activity and are strongly distinguished from terrorism. In what follows I aim to cast doubt on this assessment. Doing so will entail examining a feature of moral theory which has long been thought to support it: the doctrine or principle of double effect. A standard formulation of the principle of double effect is as follows. One may never intentionally bring about an evil, either as an end in itself, or as a means to some greater good. Nonetheless, one may use neutral or good means to achieve a good end which one foresees will have evil consequences provided that (i) the evil consequences are not disproportionate to the intended good, (ii) the action is necessary in the sense that there is no less costly way of achieving the good.

The double-effect principle has traditionally been taken to ground a moral distinction between the deliberate targeting of noncombatants, often called terror bombing, and tactical bombing, which aims at military targets but may cause collateral damage among noncombatants. In terror bombing, so the argument goes, the agent intends the death of noncombatants as a means to his ends. This is always wrong, though the goodness and viability of the ends may be very great indeed. In tactical bombing, on the other hand, the agent intends only to strike at legitimate military targets. The death of noncombatants, while it is a foreseen consequence of the action, is not intended either as a means or as an end. . . . Provided the requirements of necessity and proportionality are met, therefore, the action, together with its foreseen consequences, is not impermissible. . . .

I would like to raise a . . . set of questions about the principle of double effect by contrasting it with two considerations that explain how legal and moral culpability may exist in the absence of direct intention: these are the concepts of recklessness and negligence. Recklessness may be characterized as the culpable bringing about of unintentional evil consequences (or the risk thereof) that are in fact unreasonable and unjustified in the circumstances. . . . In law there are two forms of recklessness, subjective recklessness, which requires that the agent consciously foresaw the risk of evil consequences, and objective recklessness, in which the agent did not foresee the risk but where a reasonable person would have done so. Objective recklessness is very similar in content to negligence, which is the failure to take reasonable precautions in the face of a foreseeable risk. . . .

Judgments involving negligence and recklessness sit uncomfortably with the principle of double effect. Take the case of a motorist who drives across a crowded school yard to deliver a sick person to a hospital. The motorist certainly has no direct intention to harm the children—he aims at their death neither as a means nor as an end. His conduct may be necessary in the context, and if we imagine that the risk of death to his passenger and to the children are roughly balanced, then it will also be proportionate. Yet if he strikes and kills a child he will be held liable, in law and in morality, for manslaughter because of the recklessness of his actions. . . .

One might object that there can be no tension between the concepts of recklessness and negligence on the one hand, and the doctrine of double effect on the other, because reckless and negligent risks must be such that they are in fact unreasonable in the circumstances. But we have already said that actions that pass the double-effect test must be necessary and proportionate, and surely action that is necessary and proportionate is ipso facto reasonable. To construe the notion of reasonableness in this way, however, is to miss a crucial point. Persons have rights against being harmed or used for the benefit of others, rights which can only be alienated in very specific ways, usually having to do with actions and decisions they have freely and responsibly taken. Because of this there is an additional element to the reasonableness test which goes beyond the necessity and proportionality requirements, namely: is it justifiable to inflict such a risk upon this particular person? What motivates our intuition in the case of driving to the hospital through the school yard . . . is that those who are being forced to bear the risk have a right not to have such grave risks inflicted upon them. The fact that the risks are necessary (from the perspective of the beneficiaries of the risky activity) and proportionate (from the impersonal perspective of the world at large) is not sufficient to defeat the personal right not to be endangered or used in this way.

Now these observations about negligence and recklessness do not strictly contradict the doctrine of double effect because that doctrine, on its traditional interpretation, does not purport to identify sufficient conditions for innocence, only sufficient conditions for guilt. Nonetheless, there is clearly a tension here. The principle is supposed to show how the absence of a direct intention on the part of the agent can materially affect the permissibility of acts with harmful consequences. The concepts of negligence and recklessness, on the other hand, approach the idea of permissibility by drawing on the idea of a requirement to observe a reasonable standard of care in one's actions and not to undertake unreasonable risks. But one may fail to observe a reasonable standard of care either by possessing a direct intention to cause harm, by possessing an oblique intention to cause harm, or by possessing no intentional attitude toward the harm at all, as when one fails to foresee a harmful consequence of one's action that one could have been reasonably expected to foresee and avoid. Considerations of recklessness and negligence threaten not to disprove the principle of double effect but rather in certain contexts to render it irrelevant. . . .

■ Recklessness and Negligence as Mens Rea for Terrorism

Even if one is not persuaded that standards of care in the course of military operations are as high as I have suggested, one will have to accept that there is *some* standard of care incumbent on soldiers engaged in military operations and that when harm is caused as a consequence of their action falling below this standard, those harms will be culpable by reason of negligence or recklessness. The question then arises whether such reckless and negligent harming of noncombatants may properly be regarded as terrorist. Under the moral definition which I have been defending, there is strong reason to suppose that it may, for both share an underlying moral structure with more familiar forms of terrorism. Both constitute a culpable use of force for ideological ends, by a state or nonstate actor, against noncombatants, and without substantively just legal process. . . .

There is no denying, however, that such an analysis is at odds with the current common usage of the term, which generally restricts terrorism to acts of intentional harming. This may lead one to the following response: why should we meddle with the moral definition of terrorism, when we already possess an adequate set of conceptual tools for dealing with the issues raised in this article, in the form of the proportionality requirement within the laws of war? Military action which causes unacceptable unintended harm to noncombatants can be condemned as disproportionate use of force. What is significant about the arguments I have presented here is that they show that the hurdle for proportionate use of force is much higher than has been commonly believed. But the appropriate way to deal with this is to strengthen the proportionality requirement, not to deform the ordinary meaning of terrorism.

There are two reasons why I think this response is not adequate. The first has to do with a general observation about the proportionality requirement in the laws of war. The notion of proportionality has its most natural application in the domestic sphere. If I kill an assailant who was about to kill me, it is easy to see that this is a proportionate use of force, just as it is easy to see that killing someone to defend my prize apple pie from premature and wrongful consumption is a disproportionate use of force. But in the context of war the proportionality requirement is much more difficult to interpret. The *jus in bello* proportionality requirement states that the harm done in the course of a military operation must not be disproportionate to the concrete military advantage likely to be gained. But it is not at all obvious that the two values of military advantage and harm against noncombatants are morally commensurable. Exactly what metric is one supposed to use to determine the level of military advantage required to offset the foreseeable deaths of a given number of noncombatants? . . .

The second and deeper reason for the inadequacy of the proportionality response is that it rests on a misunderstanding of the reasons why the unintended infliction of harm or risk upon noncombatants is morally problematic. The proportionality requirement is most naturally interpreted as a quasi-consequentialist principle which states that there is a moral limit upon prima facie justified actions which is triggered when such actions do more harm than good. The doubts about collateral damage which I have been raising in this article have an entirely different source. They derive rather from a conception of persons as beings with rights against being harmed, or exposed to risk of harm, in the absence of justifying conditions relating specifically to their autonomous actions and decisions. . . .

If the only way I can flee an assailant is to kill or impose a significant risk of death upon an innocent bystander, such action would certainly be proportionate on any reasonable interpretation of proportionality. But most people would view such action as wrong, and the reason for this is that there is no relevant moral fact about the bystander which could justify inflicting this . . . harm upon him or her. In the same way, the conclusion that much collateral damage caused by military operations is negligent or reckless is not motivated only by the thought that the force is disproportionate (though it may well be that also). It is rather motivated by the thought that it is inflicted upon those who should not have force inflicted upon them—those who because they are noncombatants have no liability to have force (not even proportionate force) used against them. Proportionality, therefore, is not the appropriate locus for the kind of moral issue I have been raising. . . .

■ Notes

1. Quoted in C. A. J. Coady, "The Morality of Terrorism," *Philosophy,* vol. 60 (1985), p. 47.

2. Michael Walzer, *Just and Unjust Wars: A Moral Argument with Historical Illustrations* (New York: Basic, 1977), p. 197.

3. Quoted in George Lopez and Neve Gordon, "Terrorism in the Arab-Israeli Conflict," in *Ethics in International Affairs,* ed. Andrew Valls (Lanham, Md.: Rowman & Littlefield, 2000), p. 103.

4. *Oxford English Dictionary,* 2d ed.

5. Jenny Teichman, "How to Define Terrorism," *Philosophy,* vol. 64 (1989), p. 511.

8 Intervention

8.1

Introduction
The Editors

As we have seen in earlier chapters, defense against aggression is considered a just cause for war and it is widely accepted that self-defense may be preemptive, and perhaps even preventive under certain conditions. Thus, it is sometimes the case that the aggressor is not the state that first resorts to military force. There is another exception, falling under the rubric of what is commonly referred to as "armed intervention," and that is the subject of the readings in this chapter. Armed intervention is the use of military force, short of full-scale war, intended to change the domestic conditions within another state. There is a long history of states undertaking military interventions for purely political purposes, typically to bring about the collapse of an unfriendly regime. Those are clearly cases of aggression. But there are other cases where a state forcibly intervenes to prevent or mitigate widespread human suffering. There is little in international law that sanctions such "humanitarian intervention," but the moral ground for intervention of this type is sufficiently firm that states are increasingly called upon to use force in response to man-made humanitarian disasters.

One of the strongest statements against intervention of any type is the UN General Assembly's 1970 Declaration on Principles of International Law Concerning Friendly Relations and Co-operation Among States (Resolution 2625). The Annex to the Declaration states that "No State or group of States has the right to intervene, directly or indirectly, for any reason whatever, in the internal or external affairs of any other State." All armed interventions are said to be violations of international law. The UN Charter seems to provide more room for maneuver; Article 2 states that nothing in the charter authorizes intervention into "matters which are essentially within the jurisdiction of any state." Although there was a time that the principle of sovereignty was understood to allow state leaders free rein in the conduct of their internal affairs, this is no longer accepted. Some types of behavior, like systematic human rights abuses, are considered illegitimate—that is, they are not *essentially* within the jurisdiction of any state. A state's territorial integrity and political independence are not violated, arguably, by armed intervention if the intervening force has no territorial ambitions and intends that the sovereignty of the target state will be restored once the humanitarian emergency has passed. The argument is unlikely to carry much water with the regime against whom the intervention is directed, but international law recognizes states, not regimes, as legal entities.

The British philosopher John Stuart Mill, writing in the latter part of the 1850s, was reluctant to provide a moral justification for armed intervention in support of a people fighting against a tyrannical government. Mill felt that generally outsiders should not interfere in peoples' "arduous struggle to become free by their own efforts"; liberty must be earned through hardship and sacrifice. Mill admits an exception to his nonintervention principle when the government the people are struggling against is being supported by another state. Under these circumstances, there is an externally imposed imbalance, which he believed could be redressed by a corresponding intervention on behalf of the freedom fighters.

Mill's argument is consequentialist: the justice or injustice of armed intervention depends on the likely impact on the domestic balance of forces. But an alternative view has been put forward by Terry Nardin and other advocates of humanitarian intervention. Nardin draws attention to a "common morality" undergirding relations between all human beings, as distinct from the morality shared by members of particular communities. This notion of a common morality is at the core of cosmopolitan thought in international relations. When the behavior of a state transgresses the limits of this common morality—for example, when genocide against a minority group is unleashed—state sovereignty provides no moral barrier to armed intervention by outsiders to rescue the regime's victims. Indeed, if states, collectively or individually, can intervene at acceptable costs, our common morality obligates this action.

Gareth Evans and Mohamed Sahnoun, as well as Nardin, would prefer that humanitarian intervention take the form of collective action under the auspices of the UN. There have been two impediments to timely and effective humanitarian rescue by the UN. First, the Cold War so immobilized the Security Council that it never developed the military capability necessary for rapid and robust deployment. The peacekeeping capabilities that did develop during the Cold War years are generally not up to the task of armed humanitarian intervention, as demonstrated in Rwanda and Bosnia during the mid-1990s. Second, Chapter VII of the UN Charter limits the council's role to the maintenance of international, not domestic, peace and security.

These obstacles to UN involvement in humanitarian intervention have not proven insurmountable, however. In recent years, the Security Council has determined that humanitarian crises within states have the potential to undermine regional peace and security. This was how the council judged the situation in Iraq in 1991 (when Saddam Hussein's regime was moving against the Kurds in the north), in Bosnia and Somalia in 1992, and in Rwanda in 1994. The council, mindful of the UN's limited military capability, has shown a willingness to grant certain member states with the lead role in mounting military relief operations, as the United States did in Somalia and the French did in Rwanda (the relative success of these missions is another matter).

In the introduction to Chapter 5, we suggested that the *jus ad bellum* requirement of just cause, under international law, has been substantially narrowed to self-defense against aggression. The idea, put forward by Aquinas and other canonical thinkers, that war could serve as a means of righting wrongs and punishing evildoers, while surely not completely gone from the minds of statesmen, does not find much support among international legal theorists. Yet the emerging willingness of the international community to sanction armed intervention against regimes that deliberately and systematically trample the basic human rights of their citizens suggests some movement, however tentative, in the direction of the natural law tradition once rejected by legal positivists whose views shaped the development of the contemporary law of nations.

Two other *jus ad bellum* criteria seem especially relevant to the current debate over armed humanitarian intervention. In addition to just cause, Aquinas maintained that war must be authorized by a *proper authority,* which in his day typically meant the monarch. This was intended less as an empowerment of the monarch and more as a protection for the monarch's subjects. A war declared by the highest authority in the realm was more likely to be in pursuit of the common good than was one declared by lesser authorities, who might be in search of private gain. War was an instrument available to the sovereign, and only the sovereign, by which the well-being of the realm was to be secured and promoted. When cosmopolitans look to the UN to authorize humanitarian intervention, they do so because that body is more likely to be guided by a conception of the common good—that is, the good of humanity—than a single state acting unilaterally would be.

Aquinas, following St. Augustine, was also concerned that war be guided by *right intention.* It was recognized that wars undertaken for just cause may nevertheless become unjust wars motivated by self-aggrandizement and cruelty. For Aquinas, the ultimate aim of war should always be the establishment of peace and justice. This, of course, is also the aim of humanitarian intervention, but realists do not have much faith that right intention will prevail over calculations of self-interest, and are therefore reluctant to support the deployment of military force for such purposes. The uncertainty with which the international community has confronted humanitarian emergencies is due in large part to the continued influence of realist thought.

In recent years, the cause of humanitarian intervention has been taken up by some who otherwise do not subscribe to all aspects of the cosmopolitan perspective. In the United States, they are drawn from the neoconservative movement and their views are reflected in the foreign policy of the George W. Bush administration. Like cosmopolitans, they believe in a common morality from which universal principles of human rights and good governance derive. But like realists, they lack confidence in the UN as an institutional mechanism for responding to the humanitarian abuses (and other dangers) perpetrated by rogue states. Instead, the United States, acting alone or in coalition with other like-minded nations, should be prepared to confront these rogue states and their agents with military force if necessary. Doing so requires that the United States maintain and enhance its military capabilities and also that its freedom of action remain unencumbered by treaty and other international legal obligations.

The US-led invasion and occupation of Iraq in 2003 illuminated the contending perspectives on humanitarian intervention. The war split both the realist and liberal camps. Those realists who supported the war did so because they perceived a threat to US interests that could only be addressed by the force of arms. Realists who opposed the war felt that the threat posed by Saddam Hussein's regime was sufficiently contained and did not warrant the resort to war with its attendant costs. And many liberals agreed with them. But other liberals, those with a cosmopolitan bent, had come to believe that the existing policy of containment was imposing too many hardships on the Iraqi population, segments of which continued to be brutalized by the Ba'athist regime. They would have preferred a UN-sanctioned military response, and were critical of the Bush administration's heavy-handed diplomatic maneuverings, but it was imperative that something be done to alleviate the widespread human suffering in Iraq.

8.2 _____

A Few Words on Non-Intervention

John Stuart Mill

. . . There seems to be no little need that the whole doctrine of non-interference with foreign nations should be reconsidered, if it can be said to have as yet been considered as a really moral question at all. We have heard something lately about being willing to go to war for an idea. To go to war for an idea, if the war is aggressive, not defensive, is as criminal as to go to war for territory or revenue; for it is as little justifiable to force our ideas on other people as to compel them to submit to our will in any other respect. But there assuredly are cases in which it is allowable to go to war, without having been ourselves attacked, or threatened with attack; and it is very important that nations should make up their minds in time as to what these cases are. There are few questions which more require to be taken in hand by ethical and political philosophers, with a view to establish some rule or criterion whereby the justifiableness of intervening in the affairs of other countries, and (what is sometimes fully as questionable) the justifiableness of refraining from intervention, may be brought to a definite and rational test. Whoever attempts this will be led to recognize more than one fundamental distinction, not yet by any means familiar to the public mind, and, in general, quite lost sight of by those who write in strains of indignant morality on the subject. There is a great difference (for example) between the case in which the nations concerned are of the same, or something like the same, degree of civilization, and that in which one of the parties to the situation is of a high, and the other of a very low, grade of social improvement. To suppose that the same international customs, and the same rules of international morality, can obtain between one civilized nation and another, and between civilized nations and barbarians, is a grave error, and one which no statesman can fall into, however it may be with those, who, from a safe and unresponsible position, criticise statesmen. Among many reasons why the same rules cannot be applicable to situations so different, the two following are among the most important. In the first place, the rules of ordinary international morality imply reciprocity. But barbarians will not reciprocate. They

From *Dissertations and Discussions: Political, Philosophical, and Historical* by John Stuart Mill. New York: Henry Holt, 1882. Excerpt from "A Few Words on Non-Intervention."

cannot be depended on for observing any rules. Their minds are not capable of so great an effort, nor their will sufficiently under the influence of distant motives. In the next place, nations which are still barbarous have not got beyond the period during which it is likely to be for their benefit that they should be conquered and held in subjection by foreigners. Independence and nationality, so essential to the due growth and development of a people further advanced in improvement, are generally impediments to theirs. The sacred duties which civilized nations owe to the independence and nationality of each other are not binding towards those to whom nationality and independence are either a certain evil, or, at best, a questionable good. The Romans were not the most clean-handed of conquerors; yet would it have been better for Gaul and Spain, Numidia and Dacia, never to have formed part of the Roman Empire? To characterize any conduct whatever towards a barbarous people as a violation of the law of nations, only shows that he who so speaks has never considered the subject. A violation of great principles of morality it may easily be; but barbarians have no rights as a *nation,* except a right to such treatment as may, at the earliest possible period, fit them for becoming one. The only moral laws for the relation between a civilized and a barbarous government are the universal rules of morality between man and man. . . .

But among civilized peoples, members of an equal community of nations, like Christian Europe, the question assumes another aspect, and must be decided on totally different principles. It would be an affront to the reader to discuss the immorality of wars of conquest, or of conquest even as the consequence of lawful war; the annexation of any civilized people to the dominion of another, unless by their own spontaneous election. Up to this point, there is no difference of opinion among honest people; nor on the wickedness of commencing an aggressive war for any interest of our own, except when necessary to avert from ourselves an obviously impending wrong. The disputed question is that of interfering in the regulation of another country's internal concerns—the question whether a nation is justified in taking part, on either side, in the civil wars or party contests of another; and, chiefly, whether it may justifiably aid the people of another country in struggling for liberty; or may impose on a country any particular government or institutions, either as being best for the country itself, or as necessary for the security of its neighbors.

Of these cases, that of a people in arms for liberty is the only one of any nicety, or which, theoretically at least, is likely to present conflicting moral considerations. The other cases which have been mentioned hardly admit of discussion. Assistance to the government of a country in keeping down the people, unhappily by far the most frequent case of foreign intervention, no one writing in a free country needs take the trouble of stigmatizing. A government which needs foreign support to enforce obedience from its own citizens is one which ought not to exist; and the assistance given to it by foreigners is hardly ever any thing but the sympathy of one despotism with another. A case requiring consideration is that of a protracted civil war, in which the contending parties are so equally balanced, that there is no probability of a speedy issue; or, if there is, the victorious side cannot hope to keep down the vanquished but by severities repugnant to humanity, and injurious to the permanent welfare of the country. In this exceptional case it seems now to be an admitted doctrine, that the neighboring nations, or one powerful neighbor with the acquiescence of the rest, are warranted in demanding that the contest shall cease, and a reconciliation take place on equitable terms of compromise. Intervention of this description has been repeatedly practised during the present generation, with such general approval, that its legitimacy may be considered to have passed into a maxim of what is called international law. The interference of the European Powers between Greece and Turkey, and between Turkey and Egypt, were cases in point. That between Holland and Belgium was still more so. The intervention of England in Portugal a few years ago, which is probably less remembered than the others, because it took effect without the employment of actual force, belongs to the same category. At the time, this interposition had the appearance of a bad and dishonest backing of the government against the people, being so timed as to hit the exact moment when the popular party had obtained a marked advantage, and seemed on the eve of overthrowing the government, or reducing it to terms. But, if ever a political act which looked ill in the commencement could be justified by the event, this was: for, as the fact turned out, instead of giving ascendancy to a party, it proved a really healing measure; and the chiefs of the so-called rebellion were, within a few years, the honored and successful ministers of the throne against which they had so lately fought.

With respect to the question, whether one country is justified in helping the people of another in a struggle against their government for free institutions, the answer will be different according as the yoke which the people are attempting to throw off is that of a purely native government, or of foreigners; considering as one of foreigners every government which maintains itself by foreign support. When the contest is only with native rulers, and with such native strength as those rulers can enlist in their defence, the answer I should give to the question of the legitimacy of intervention is, as a general rule, No. The reason is, that there can seldom be any thing approaching to assurance, that intervention, even if successful, would be for the good of the people themselves. The only test possessing any real value, of a people's having become fit for popular institutions, is, that they, or a sufficient portion of them to prevail in the contest, are willing to brave labor and danger for their liberation. I know all that may be said. I know it may be urged, that the virtues of freemen cannot be learnt in the school of slavery; and that, if a people are not fit for freedom, to have any chance of becoming so they must first be free. And this would be conclusive, if the intervention recommended would really give them freedom. But the evil is, that, if they have not sufficient love of liberty to be able to wrest it from merely domestic oppressors, the liberty which is bestowed on them by other hands than their own will have nothing real, nothing permanent. No people ever was and remained free, but because it was determined to be so; because neither its rulers nor any other party in the nation could compel it to be otherwise. If a people—especially one whose freedom has not yet become prescriptive—does not value it sufficiently to fight for it, and maintain it against any force which can be mustered *within* the country, even by those who have the command of the public revenue, it is only a question in how few years or months that people will be enslaved. Either the government which it has given to itself, or some military leader or knot of conspirators who contrive to subvert the government, will speedily put an end to all popular institutions; unless, indeed, it suits their convenience better to leave them standing, and be content with reducing them to mere forms: for, unless the spirit of liberty is strong in a people, those who have the executive in their hands easily work *any* institutions to the purposes of despotism. There is no sure guaranty against this deplorable issue, even in a country which has achieved its own freedom; as may be seen in the present day by striking examples both in the Old and New Worlds: but, when freedom has been achieved *for* them, they have little prospect indeed of escaping this fate. When a people has had the misfortune to be ruled by a government under which the feelings and the virtues needful for maintaining freedom could not develop themselves, it is during an arduous struggle to become free by their own efforts that these feelings and virtues have the best chance of springing up. Men become attached to that which they have long fought for, and made sacrifices for; they learn to appreciate that on which their thoughts have been much engaged; and a contest in which many have been called on to devote themselves for their country is a school in which they learn to value their country's interest above their own.

It can seldom, therefore—I will not go so far as to say never—be either judicious or right, in a country which has a free government; to assist, otherwise than by the moral support of its opinion, the endeavors of another to extort the same blessing from its native rulers. We must except, of course, any case in which such assistance is a measure of legitimate self-defence. If (a contingency by no means unlikely to occur) this country, on account of its freedom, which is a standing reproach to despotism everywhere, and an encouragement to throw it off, should find itself menaced with attack by a coalition of Continental despots, it ought to consider the popular party in every nation of the Continent as its natural ally: the Liberals should be to it what the Protestants of Europe were to the Government of Queen Elizabeth.

So, again, when a nation, in her own defence, has gone to war with a despot, and has had the rare good fortune, not only to succeed in her resistance, but to hold the conditions of peace in her own hands, she is entitled to say that she will make no treaty, unless with some other ruler than the one whose existence as such may be a perpetual menace to her safety and freedom. . . .

But the case of a people struggling against a foreign yoke, or against a native tyranny upheld by foreign arms, illustrates the reasons for non-intervention in an opposite way; for, in this case, the reasons themselves do not exist. A people the most attached to freedom, the most capable of defending and of making a good use of free institutions, may be unable to contend successfully for them against the military strength of another nation much more powerful. To assist a people thus kept down is not to disturb the balance of forces on which the permanent maintenance of freedom in a country depends, but to redress that balance when it is already unfairly and violently disturbed. The doctrine of non-intervention, to be a legitimate principle of morality, must be accepted by all governments. The despots must consent to be bound by it as well as the free States. Unless they do, the profession of it by free countries comes but to this miserable issue—that the wrong side may help the wrong, but the right must not help the right. Intervention to enforce non-intervention is always rightful, always moral, if not always prudent. Though it be a mistake to *give* freedom to a people who do not value the boon, it cannot but be right to insist, that, if they do value it, they shall not be hindered from the pursuit of it by foreign coercion. . . .

8.3 _____

The Moral Basis of Humanitarian Intervention

Terry Nardin

Humanitarian intervention is usually discussed as an exception to the nonintervention principle. According to this principle, states are forbidden to exercise their authority, and certainly to use force, within the jurisdiction of other states. The principle finds firm support in the United Nations Charter, which permits a state to defend itself from attack but forbids the use of armed force against the territorial integrity or political independence of other states. Taken literally, these provisions prohibit armed intervention, including intervention to protect human rights. And in general, humanitarian intervention finds scant support in modern international law.

There is, however, a much older tradition in which the use of force is justified not only in self-defense but also to punish wrongs and protect the innocent. This tradition is in some tension with modern international law and especially with the UN Charter. It holds that armed intervention is permissible to enforce standards of civilized conduct when rulers violate those standards, and finds expression today in the widely held opinion that states, acting unilaterally or collectively, are justified in enforcing respect for human rights. It is this enduring tradition, not current international law, that best explains the moral basis of humanitarian intervention. . . .

■ Humanitarian Intervention in Early Modern Natural Law

In twentieth-century international law, a just war is above all a war of self-defense. But sixteenth- and seventeenth-century European moralists justified war as a way to uphold law and protect rights, of which self-defense was only one. Rulers, these moralists argued, have a right and sometimes a duty to enforce certain laws beyond their realms. Some of these belong to the "law of nations" *(ius gentium)*, understood not as international law but as general principles of law recognized in many different communities. This law of nations is an inductively established body of norms common to all or most peoples. But the most important class of universally enforceable law is "natural law," understood as comprising precepts that can be known by reason and are binding on all rational beings. What the law of nations and natural law have in common is that each identifies principles more general than the often-idiosyncratic norms of particular communities. And in many respects, their principles are similar, though there are glaring exceptions. . . .

The medieval literature on just war, like that of modern times, is concerned with wrongs done by one community to another. When Aquinas suggests that a "just cause" is required for resorting to war, he is thinking of situations in which one community acts to punish another. "Those who are attacked," he says, "should be attacked because they deserve it on account of some fault."[1] And he goes on to quote Augustine, for whom a just war is one that "avenges wrongs"—for example, when a state "has to be punished for refusing to make amends for the wrongs inflicted by its subjects or to restore what it has unjustly seized."[2] To get to the idea of humanitarian intervention, we must shift our attention from wrongs done by one community to another to those done by a government to its own subjects, either directly or by permitting mistreatment. And if the justification of war is to prevent or punish wrongdoing, it is not hard to make this shift. . . . In the absence of a norm of nonintervention, no special justification for humanitarian intervention is needed. Even those who treat "the liberation of an oppressed people" as needing further justification will have an easier time making their case if the core justification for war is to "avenge wrongs." . . .

The Protestant Hugo Grotius is a key figure in debates over intervention to uphold natural law. The international morality he defends is one that permits such intervention but does not demand it. Grotius's "thin" or minimal morality requires human beings to refrain from injuring one another but does not require that they help one another. The basis of this morality, which he expounds in an unpublished early work, is self-preservation. Because the desire for self-preservation is inherent in their nature, human beings cannot be blamed for acting on it. And if they have a right to preserve themselves, they must also have the right to acquire the things needed for life and to defend their lives and possessions. These presocial rights, which are the foundation of natural law, are enjoyed not only by natural persons but also by artificial persons, like states, that coexist in a condition of nature. In such a condition, the first imperative is self-preservation, the law that governs this condition, the law of nature, is a law that prescribes mutual forbearance, not beneficence. Natural law requires only that we leave one another alone; it does not demand that we assist or protect one another. But we *may* assist or protect one another. It would contravene the teaching of

Christ, Grotius argues, to say that Christians have nothing in common with non-Christians, for the injunction to love one's neighbor means that a Christian must love every human being. It follows that "the protection of infidels from injury (even from injury by Christians) is never unjust."[3] . . .

In a subsequent work, Grotius asks whether a sovereign can rightly wage war to punish violations of natural law that do not affect him or his subjects. His answer is that sovereigns have the right to punish any acts that "excessively violate the law of nature or of nations in regard to any persons whatsoever." He invokes Innocent IV against those who argue that punishment is a civil power and therefore that a government has no right to wage war to defend persons over whom it has no legal jurisdiction. If we accept this view, Grotius argues, no sovereign would be able to punish another for harming him or his subjects. The right to punish is based not on civil power but on the law of nature, which existed before there were civil societies. Therefore, wars are justly waged on those who "sin against nature" by engaging in cannibalism, piracy and other barbaric practices. . . .[4]

According to the new understanding of international relations that was emerging along with the idea of the sovereign state, any government has the right to enforce natural law against any other government that is guilty of violating it. In the "state of nature" postulated by Grotius and other seventeenth-century natural law theorists, there is no enforcing power superior to that of the sovereign of each. Because in the state of nature unpunished violations of natural law by one sovereign harm every other sovereign by undermining natural law, any sovereign can punish such violations. A sovereign is even justified in punishing crimes that another commits against his own subjects, provided the offense is "very atrocious and very evident."[5] This general "right of punishment" owned by every sovereign in the international state of nature therefore justifies humanitarian intervention, at least in some situations.

The noninterventian principle, which was increasingly important in international law during the eighteenth and nineteenth centuries, can be understood as a reaction against the view that every state has a right to enforce natural law. The chief objection to this doctrine was made by Samuel Pufendorf in works published during the 1670s. "We are not to imagine," Pufendorf writes, "that every man, even they who live in the liberty of nature, has a right to correct and punish with war any person who has done another an injury," for it is "contrary to the natural equality of mankind for a man to force himself upon the world for a judge and decider of controversies. . . . Any man might make war upon any man upon such a pretense."[6] Nevertheless, any person may justly assist any victim of oppression who invites assistance. "Kinship alone"—"may suffice for us to go to the defense of an oppressed party who makes a plea for assistance, so far as we conveniently may."[7] For Pufendorf, to come to the aid of the oppressed is not only a right but in some cases a duty. It is, however, an "imperfect duty"—not a specific obligation like that prescribed by a contract but a duty of beneficence to be performed insofar as it can be performed without disproportionate inconvenience. The proviso that the victim must have invited assistance cannot, however, bear the weight Pufendorf gives it in distinguishing justifiable humanitarian intervention from unjustifiable interference by a sovereign who has usurped the office of judge over other sovereigns. Morally speaking, it is the act of oppression, not a request for assistance, that justifies an intervention.

The natural law argument for humanitarian intervention continued to erode during the eighteenth and nineteenth centuries as the view that international law is "positive law" based on the will of states emerged. The enlightenment philosopher Christian von Wolff and his popularizer, Emmerich de Vattel, are among the last to treat international law as part of natural law (that is, as belonging in effect to morality rather than to positive law), and both dismiss the classic argument justifying humanitarian intervention. According to Wolff, "A punitive war is not allowed against a nation for the reason that it is very wicked, or violates dreadfully the law of nature, or offends against God." And he explicitly asserts the principle of nonintervention, even when a sovereign abuses his subjects.[8] Vattel agrees, though he adds a qualification: if "by his insupportable tyranny" a prince "brings on a national revolt against him," any foreign power "may rightfully give assistance to an oppressed people who ask for its aid."[9] But in the absence of armed rebellion intervention must be condemned; to say that one nation can use force to punish another for grave moral abuses is to open the door to war motivated by religious zealotry or economic ambition. Here we have a new principle, added to Pufendorf's requirement that the victims of oppression must request outside assistance: they must mount their own armed resistance. By the middle of the nineteenth century, this principle was being used to argue *against* humanitarian intervention. In his essay "A Few Words on Non-intervention," J. S. Mill argues that the subjects of an oppressive ruler must win their own freedom, without outside assistance, and they must suffer the consequences if their struggle is unsuccessful. Not even bloody repression can justify armed intervention by foreign powers, for were such intervention permissible, the idea of "self-determination," which Mill thinks is basic to political community, would be meaningless.[10]

Though he is a moralist, not an international lawyer, Mill perfectly articulates the view of humanitarian intervention we find in mainstream nineteenth-century international law. W. E. Hall, the author of a standard English work on international law at the end of that century, treats humanitarian intervention under the heading "Interventions in Restraint of Wrongdoing," a precise title, morally speaking. He argues that tyrannical oppression by a government of its own subjects, including religious persecution or massacres and brutality in a civil war, have nothing to do with relations between states. And he insists that we must not confuse outraged public opinion with the requirements of law. Some commentators, he writes, hold that states can lawfully intervene "to put an end to crimes and slaughter," but in the absence of consensus on this point, their judgment is not law.[11] If there is any legal basis for humanitarian intervention, it must rest not on principles of international morality but on agreement among states to recognize such principles as law. Hall here invokes the doctrine—a keynote of legal positivism—that international law is enacted by the joint will of sovereign states. Just as legislation is the criterion of law within each state, so agreement between states is the criterion of international law. The age of natural law had come to an end.

■ Common Morality and the Duty to Protect

Though banished from the realm of positive law, natural law did not simply disappear. It continued to march under the banner of morality. To distinguish this latter-day natural law, stripped of its religious and legal connotations, from the mores of particular communities, we may speak of a "common morality" binding on all human beings. Common morality assumes that human beings are thinking, choosing agents, and that everyone has an equal right to think and choose. It therefore requires us to recognize the inherent capacity of each person to make choices of his or her own. The foundation of common morality, then, is the principle that each person must respect the agency of every other. This is Kant's "principle of respect."[12] The more specific precepts of common morality are interpretations of this basic principle.

We must distinguish common morality from the mores of particular communities. Its principles constitute a common moral world in which human beings have rights not as members of this or that community but as members of the human community. Common morality rests neither on positive laws nor on custom. It is, rather, the product of critical reflection on laws and customs, and in this sense may be said to be known by "reason." . . .

The principles of common morality—like those that prohibit murder and deliberate harm to innocents and teach friendship, cooperation, and fairness—are basic to civilized life and are in fact recognized in most communities and traditions. This broad recognition is of immense practical importance, for it means that in appealing to common morality the moralist is appealing to principles whose authority has already been granted, implicitly if not explicitly, by a great many people. There are certainly people who do not belong to the common moral world, but one should not underestimate the degree to which its principles are generally acknowledged. It is important to emphasize, however, that although the principles of common morality may be "common" in the sense that they are recognized in different communities, their validity does not depend on such recognition. They are required by a conception of the person and of what is owed to persons, not by convention. Common morality is a critical morality possessing wider authority than the moral practices of particular communities, and for this reason it provides a standard by which to criticize these practices. Like the idea of human rights, the idea of common morality is opposed to communitarian ethical theories that ground moral duties on custom and consent.

The relevance of common morality to humanitarian intervention should by now be apparent. Humanitarian intervention is a response to grave human rights violations, and the most basic human rights are universal moral rights—rights, in other words, that rest on the principles of common morality. There are, then, good reasons for grounding the ethics of humanitarian intervention in common morality and not in particular religious or national moralities, or even in international law, which rests on custom and agreement, not moral reasoning. . . .

Common morality forbids us to use other human beings coercively to achieve our ends. Using force, without good reason, violates the principle of respect. This explains not only why murder and slavery are wrong but also why self-defense is morally justifiable. But common morality does not limit the use of force to self-defense. It also permits us to defend the rights of others when those rights are threatened. We are therefore justified in using force to thwart violence against other persons, provided those persons are morally "innocent"—that is, not themselves engaged in unjust violence. Using force to resist those who attack the innocent does not violate the attackers' rights as free persons because they have, by their own actions, lost the moral right to act as they choose. It is even permitted to kill attackers, if necessary, to protect their victims. We are justified in using as much force as is needed to thwart the attack, but not more—bearing in mind that precise calculations about such matters are impossible.[13]

Though derived ultimately from the principle of respect, the right to use force to defend the innocent from violence rests more immediately on the idea of beneficence, which is the idea that human beings should support one another in appropriate ways. To respect other human beings as rational agents means not only that we must not interfere with their freedom but also that we should assist them in achieving their ends. Common morality is at its core a morality of constraint, but its precepts are not limited to those that constrain us. It also asks us to advance the well-being of others—by being cooperative, helpful, charitable, and the like—in ways that are morally permissible and not disproportionately costly. In other words, in helping others we are forbidden to do wrong for their sake and we are not required to do more than we can reasonably afford.

Given the principle of beneficence, common morality may require us to act when others are in danger of serious injury, whether by accident or as victims of wrongdoing. This requirement is expressed in the parable of the Good Samaritan and, more pointedly, in the divine command that you must not stand idly by the blood of your neighbor. The principle of beneficence, which this command invokes, leaves us free to decide how to promote the well-being of others. Nevertheless, if we are able to provide immediate assistance to someone who needs it, we should provide that assistance. And this implies that we must not allow anyone to be harmed by violence if we can reasonably prevent it. In short, assuming that the costs are not too high, it is "not merely permissible but a duty to employ force against the violent if their victims cannot otherwise be protected."[14] This is the fundamental principle underlying humanitarian intervention. . . .

When Is Humanitarian Intervention Permissible?

. . . If humanitarian intervention means acting to protect human rights, there are many such rights besides the right to life that might be threatened, including rights against torture, arbitrary detention, and racial discrimination. But usually only the gravest violations, like genocide and ethnic cleansing, are held to justify armed intervention. Such acts affect the lives of many people and the fate of entire communities. In the classic phrase, they "shock the conscience of mankind."

It is consistent with common morality to argue that humanitarian intervention is justified, in principle, in a wide range of situations, but that practical considerations usually override this justification. But one can also justify limiting intervention to the gravest abuses by invoking considerations that arise from the aims of civil association. The state as a coercive institution is morally justifiable because, in principle, it enables human beings to fulfill their potentialities by living together according to common rules. But once a state has been established, its citizens must obey the laws it adopts for this purpose, assuming these laws are not substantially unjust. And a substantially just state is entitled to respect by other states, which are morally barred from interfering with its government. The nonintervention principle is therefore basic to relations between states. It is not a mere custom of the international system. There are moral reasons why a state must be recognized as having rights, in particular the right that outsiders respect its independence and boundaries. But the same principles that justify the nonintervention principle justify exceptions to that principle. If a government seriously violates the moral rights of those it governs, others may defend those rights, using force if necessary. The nonintervention principle is not a shield behind which an unjust state can hide while it violates the moral rights of its subjects. Such violations, if serious enough, permit forcible humanitarian intervention and may even demand it. But respect for the rights of a political community requires that those violations be truly grave. . . .

Who Should Intervene?

Humanitarian intervention is traditionally defined as the use of force by states to protect human rights. This definition presumes that it is states that should do the intervening. It is sometimes argued that the traditional definition is obsolete because humanitarian intervention is increasingly a matter of collective action under UN auspices, not action undertaken by states acting on their own authority. But to say that humanitarian intervention *should* be collective is simply to offer a different answer to the question of who should intervene. The moral principle is general: *You* shall not stand idly by, whoever you are, if you can provide effective assistance at reasonable cost and without neglecting other duties. There are practical reasons for suggesting that the international community should authorize humanitarian interventions. Such interventions may, for example, be more likely than unilateral actions to benefit from collective wisdom and to gain wide support. But to insist on such authorization is to presume a degree of justice and effectiveness at the supranational level that the world has not yet achieved.

There are, however, moral reasons why states should adhere to international law and therefore why unilateral intervention should be condemned if international law forbids it. It is regrettable that NATO's decision to intervene in Kosovo had to be made outside the framework of the UN and in a manner not explicitly provided for by its own charter, which requires its members to defend one another if attacked, but says nothing about intervention or peacekeeping that is unrelated to collective defense. But if unilateral intervention is illegal and procedures exist for collective action, and yet the international community as a whole is unable to act effectively, must individual states also "stand idly by"? As Secretary-General Annan implies in discussing the world's failure to act in Rwanda, to say yes is to repudiate common morality.

Some moralists argue that only a government that respects human rights is entitled to intervene to protect human rights. There are reasons for favoring such a requirement in many cases, but the principle is not part of common morality. A murderer is not forbidden to save a drowning child. The objectionable character of the Vietnamese government in 1979 does not mean that its intervention in Cambodia, which ended the genocide there, was morally wrong.

What Means of Protection Are Called For?

Common morality prescribes that we must not stand idly by when human lives are threatened, but this is a very broad injunction. As we have seen, coercive action is not immoral if it is aimed at those who are themselves acting immorally, and provided we do not pursue good ends by immoral means. Clearly this means that forces conducting humanitarian interventions must comply with the laws of war, as these laws are understood both in the just war tradition and in international law. It means in particular that such forces must respect the principle of noncombatant immunity, which is that innocent persons may not be directly attacked either as an end or as a means to an end, and that the costs of indirect injury must not be unfairly distributed.

The responses we might choose are not limited to those requiring military force. War is an extreme remedy. The label "humanitarian intervention" is sometimes applied to transnational charitable efforts to relieve human suffering as well as forcible interventions to protect human rights. Those who see armed intervention as a kind of just war sometimes protest that using a common label muddies the waters by linking modes of international assistance that raise different issues and should be handled in different ways. Common morality certainly recognizes as morally relevant the distinction between coercive and noncoercive assistance. But it also prescribes assisting fellow human beings in any effective and morally permissible manner. It therefore allows a wide range of responses to situations in which lives are endangered, while recognizing that responses involving the use of force require additional justification. It reminds us, too, that military action cannot be assumed to be effective and that the only force that is morally justifiable is the minimum necessary to accomplish its purpose.

In considering what to do, an intervening state is not barred from weighing the costs and from deciding not to act if those costs are too high. Although beneficence is a duty, it is what moralists sometimes call an imperfect duty. Like an individual person, a state is not obligated to intervene at great cost to itself. Risking all to save others may be praiseworthy, even saintly, but common morality does not demand it. But if no country can be asked to seriously harm its own interests to assist another, what can we reasonably ask it to do? If I save someone's life, I am not supposed to have taken on a long-term obligation to care for that person. But the injunction to "save" my neighbor, if my neighbor is a community, might entail continued involvement. Armed intervention to halt a massacre is likely to be only the first of many measures needed to restore order to a chaotic society and prevent subsequent massacres. If prevention is important, the challenge for humanitarian policy is to move from responding to humanitarian crises to forestalling them. And if common morality requires civil association and the rule of law, a policy of progressively strengthening civil institutions at the international level may itself be morally required, as Kant long ago argued in *Perpetual Peace*. It is perhaps no coincidence that the greatest theorist of common morality was also concerned with the conditions of a just and peaceful international order. . . .

Decisions about whether and how to intervene will always involve a wide range of contingencies, for states have no duty to intervene unless they can do so successfully and at reasonable cost to themselves and to others. It follows that selectivity in the choice of occasions for intervention is both inevitable and potentially justifiable. These conclusions are neither novel nor especially controversial. This should be taken as an encouraging sign, suggesting that the contribution of common morality to the debate over humanitarian intervention is to help us clarify the rational foundation of views whose cogency is already widely acknowledged. Its contribution is to indicate from the standpoint of a carefully articulated and intellectually powerful position, where, morally speaking, arguments over particular interventions can and cannot go. . . .

▓ Notes

1. Saint Thomas Aquinas, *Summary of Theology* II-II, Q.40, a.1, in *On Law, Morality, and Politics,* ed. William P. Baumgarth and Richard J. Regan, S. J. (Indianapolis: Hackett Publishing Company, 1988), p. 221.
2. Augustine, *Questions on the Heptateuch* 6.10, quoted by Aquinas, *On Law, Morality, and Politics,* p. 221.
3. Hugo Grotius, *De jure praedae* (1604), published in English as *Commentary on the Law of Prize and Booty,* trans. Gwaldys L. Williams (Oxford: Clarendon Press, 1950), p. 315.
4. Hugo Grotius, *De jure belli ac pacis* (1625), *On the Law of War and Peace,* 1656 edition trans. Francis W. Kelsey (Oxford: Oxford University Press, 1925), pp. 504–506.
5. Ibid., p. 508.
6. Samuel von Pufendorf, *Of the Law of Nature and Nations* (1672), trans. C. H. Oldfather and W. A. Oldfather (Oxford: Clarendon Press, 1934), p. 847.
7. Samuel von Pufendorf, *On the Duty of Man and Citizen,* ed. James Tully (Cambridge: Cambridge University Press, 1991), p. 170.
8. Christian von Wolff, *The Law of Nations Treated According to a Scientific Method* (1748), trans. Joseph D. Drake (Oxford: Oxford University Press, 1934) section 637; sections 258 and 1011.
9. Emmerich de Vattel, *The Law of Nations, or Principles of Natural Law Applied to the Conduct and Affairs of Nations and Sovereigns* (1758), trans. Charles G. Fenwick (Washington, D.C.: Carnegie Institution, 1916), p. 131; see also p. 340.
10. J. S. Mill, *Dissertations and Discussions,* 2d ed. (London: Longmans, 1867), vol. 3, pp. 153–178. The essay was first published in 1859.
11. William Edward Hall, *A Treatise on International Law,* 6th ed. (Oxford: Oxford University Press, 1909), pp. 284, 287–288, 285n.
12. Immanuel Kant, *Foundations of the Metaphysics of Morals* (1785), trans. Lewis White Beck (Indianapolis: Bobbs-Merrill, 1959), pp. 66–67.
13. Alan Donagan, *The Theory of Morality* (Chicago: University of Chicago Press, 1979), pp. 85–87.
14. Ibid., p. 86.

8.4

The Responsibility to Protect

Gareth Evans and Mohamed Sahnoun

◼ Revisiting Humanitarian Intervention

The international community in the last decade repeatedly made a mess of handling the many demands that were made for "humanitarian intervention": coercive action against a state to protect people within its borders from suffering grave harm. There were no agreed rules for handling cases such as Somalia, Bosnia, Rwanda, and Kosovo at the start of the 1990s, and there remain none today. Disagreement continues about whether there is a right of intervention, how and when it should be exercised, and under whose authority.

Since September 11, 2001, policy attention has been captured by a different set of problems: the response to global terrorism and the case for "hot preemption" against countries believed to be irresponsibly acquiring weapons of mass destruction. These issues, however, are conceptually and practically distinct. There are indeed common questions, especially concerning the precautionary principles that should apply to any military action anywhere. But what is involved in the debates about intervention in Afghanistan, Iraq, and elsewhere is the scope and limits of countries' rights to act in self-defense—not their right, or obligation, to intervene elsewhere to protect peoples other than their own.

Meanwhile, the debate about intervention for human protection purposes has not gone away. And it will not go away so long as human nature remains as fallible as it is and internal conflict and state failures stay as prevalent as they are. The debate was certainly a lively one throughout the 1990s. Controversy may have been muted in the case of the interventions, by varying casts of actors, in Liberia in 1990, northern Iraq in 1991, Haiti in 1994, Sierra Leone in 1997, and (not strictly coercively) East Timor in 1999. But in Somalia in 1993, Rwanda in 1994, and Bosnia in 1995, the UN action taken (if taken at all) was widely perceived as too little too late, misconceived, poorly resourced, poorly executed, or all of the above. During NATO's 1999 intervention in Kosovo, Security Council members were

---

sharply divided; the legal justification for action without UN authority was asserted but largely unargued; and great misgivings surrounded the means by which the allies waged the war.

It is only a matter of time before reports emerge again from somewhere of massacres, mass starvation, rape, and ethnic cleansing. And then the question will arise again in the Security Council, in political capitals, and in the media: What do we do? This time around the international community must have the answers. Few things have done more harm to its shared ideal that people are all equal in worth and dignity than the inability of the community of states to prevent these horrors. In this new century, there must be no more Rwandas.

Secretary-General Kofi Annan, deeply troubled by the inconsistency of the international response, has repeatedly challenged the General Assembly to find a way through these dilemmas. But in the debates that followed his calls, he was rewarded for the most part by cantankerous exchanges in which fervent supporters of intervention on human rights grounds, opposed by anxious defenders of state sovereignty, dug themselves deeper and deeper into opposing trenches.

If the international community is to respond to this challenge, the whole debate must be turned on its head. The issue must be reframed not as an argument about the "right to intervene" but about the "responsibility to protect." And it has to be accepted that although this responsibility is owed by all sovereign states to their own citizens in the first instance, it must be picked up by the international community if that first-tier responsibility is abdicated, or if it cannot be exercised.

■ Sovereignty as Responsibility

Using this alternative language will help shake up the policy debate, getting governments in particular to think afresh about what the real issues are. Changing the terminology from "intervention" to "protection" gets away from the language of "humanitarian intervention." The latter term has always deeply concerned humanitarian relief organizations, which have hated the association of "humanitarian" with military activity. Beyond that, talking about the "responsibility to protect" rather than the "right to intervene" has three other big advantages. First, it implies evaluating the issues from the point of view of those needing support, rather than those who may be considering intervention. The searchlight is back where it should always be: on the duty to protect communities from mass killing, women from systematic rape, and children from starvation. Second, this formulation implies that the primary responsibility rests with the state concerned. Only if that state is unable or unwilling to fulfill its responsibility to protect, or is itself the perpetrator, should the international community take the responsibility to act in its place. Third, the "responsibility to protect" is an umbrella concept, embracing not just the "responsibility to react" but the "responsibility to prevent" and the "responsibility to rebuild" as well. Both of these dimensions have been much neglected in the traditional humanitarian-intervention debate. Bringing them back to center stage should help make the concept of reaction itself more palatable.

At the heart of this conceptual approach is a shift in thinking about the essence of sovereignty, from control to responsibility. In the classic Westphalian system of international relations, the defining characteristic of sovereignty has always been the state's capacity to make authoritative decisions regarding the people and resources within its territory. The principle of sovereign equality of states is enshrined in Article 2, Section 1, of the UN Charter, and the corresponding norm of nonintervention is enshrined in Article 2, Section 7: a sovereign state is empowered by international law to exercise exclusive and total jurisdiction within its territorial borders, and other states have the corresponding duty not to intervene in its internal affairs. But working against this standard has been the increasing impact in recent decades of human rights norms, bringing a shift from a culture of sovereign impunity to one of national and international accountability. The increasing influence of the concept of human security has also played a role: what matters is not just state security but the protection of individuals against threats to life, livelihood, or dignity that can come from within or without. In short, a large and growing gap has been developing between international behavior as articulated in the state-centered UN Charter, which was signed in 1946, and evolving state practice since then, which now emphasizes the limits of sovereignty.

Indeed, even the strongest supporters of state sovereignty will admit today that no state holds unlimited power to do what it wants to its own people. It is now commonly acknowledged that sovereignty implies a dual responsibility: externally, to respect the sovereignty of other states, and internally, to respect the dignity and basic rights of all the people within the state. In international human rights covenants, in UN practice, and in state practice itself, sovereignty is now understood as embracing this dual responsibility. Sovereignty as responsibility has become the minimum content of good international citizenship. Although this new principle cannot be said to be customary international law yet, it is sufficiently accepted in practice to be regarded as a de facto emerging norm: the responsibility to protect.

■ Military Intervention: Setting the Bar

The responsibility to protect implies a duty to react to situations in which there is compelling need for human protection. If preventive measures fail to resolve or contain such a situation, and when the state in question is unable or unwilling to step in, then intervention by other states may be required. Coercive measures then may include political, economic, or judicial steps. In extreme cases—but only extreme cases—they may also include military action. But what is an extreme case? Where should we draw the line in determining when military intervention is defensible? What other conditions or restraints, if any, should apply in determining whether and how that intervention should proceed? And, most difficult of all, who should have the ultimate authority to determine whether an intrusion into a sovereign state, involving the use of deadly force on a potentially massive scale, should actually go ahead? These questions have generated an enormous literature and much competing terminology, but on the core issues there is a great deal of common ground, most of it derived from "just war" theory. To justify military intervention, six principles have to be satisfied: the "just cause" threshold, four precautionary principles, and the requirement of "right authority."

■ Operation Just Cause

As for the "just cause" threshold, our starting point is that military intervention for human protection purposes is an extraordinary measure. For it to be warranted, civilians must be faced with the threat of serious and irreparable harm in one of just two exceptional ways. The first is large-scale loss of life, actual or anticipated, with genocidal intent or not, which is the product of deliberate state action, state neglect, inability to act, or state failure. The second is large-scale "ethnic cleansing," actual or anticipated, whether carried out by killing, forced expulsion, acts of terror, or rape.

Why does the bar for just cause need to be set so high? There is the conceptual reason that military intervention must be very exceptional. There is also a practical political rationale: if intervention is to happen when it is most necessary, it cannot be called on too often. In the two situations identified as legitimate triggers, we do not quantify what is "large scale" but make clear our belief that military action can be legitimate as an anticipatory measure in response to clear evidence of likely large-scale killing or ethnic cleansing. Without this possibility, the international community would be placed in the morally untenable position of being required to wait until genocide begins before being able to take action to stop it. The threshold criteria articulated here not only cover the deliberate perpetration of horrors such as in the cases of Bosnia, Rwanda, and Kosovo. They can also apply to situations of state collapse and the resultant exposure of the population to mass starvation or civil war, as in Somalia. Also potentially covered would be overwhelming natural or environmental catastrophes, in which the state concerned is either unwilling or unable to help and significant loss of life is occurring or threatened. What are not covered by our "just cause" threshold criteria are human rights violations falling short of outright killing or ethnic cleansing (such as systematic racial discrimination or political oppression), the overthrow of democratically elected governments, and the rescue by a state of its own nationals on foreign territory. Although deserving of external action—including in appropriate cases political, economic, or military sanctions—these are not instances that would seem to justify military action for human protection purposes.

■ Precautionary Principles

Of the precautionary principles needed to justify intervention, the first is "right intention." The primary purpose of the intervention, whatever other motives intervening states may have, must be to halt or avert human suffering. There are a number of ways of helping ensure that this criterion is satisfied. One is to have military intervention always take place on a collective or multilateral basis. Another is to look at the extent to which the intervention is actually supported by the people for whose benefit the intervention is intended. Yet another is to look to what extent the opinion of other countries in the region has been taken into account and is supportive. Complete disinterestedness may be an ideal, but it is not likely always to be a reality: mixed motives, in international relations as everywhere else, are a fact of life. Moreover, the budgetary cost and risk to personnel involved in any military action may make it imperative for the intervening state to be able to claim some degree of self-interest in the intervention, however altruistic its primary motive.

The second precautionary principle is "last resort": military intervention can be justified only when every nonmilitary option for the prevention or peaceful resolution of the crisis has been explored, with reasonable grounds for believing lesser measures would not have succeeded. The responsibility to react with military coercion can be justified only when the responsibility to prevent has been fully discharged. This guideline does not necessarily mean that every such option must literally have been tried and failed; often there is simply not enough time for that process to work itself out. But it does mean that there must be reasonable grounds for believing that, given the circumstances, other measures would not have succeeded.

The third principle is "proportional means": the scale, duration, and intensity of the planned military intervention should be the minimum necessary to secure the defined objective of protecting people. The scale of action taken must be commensurate with its stated purpose and with the magnitude of the original provocation. The effect on the political system of the country targeted should be limited to what is strictly necessary to accomplish the intervention's purpose. Although the precise practical implications of these strictures are always open to argument, the principles involved are clear enough.

Finally, there is the principle of "reasonable prospects": there must be a reasonable chance of success in halting or averting the suffering that has justified the intervention; the consequences of action should not be worse than the consequences of inaction. Military action must not risk triggering a greater conflagration. Applying this precautionary principle would, on purely utilitarian grounds, likely preclude military action against any one of the five permanent members of the Security Council, even with all other conditions for intervention having been met. Otherwise, it is difficult to imagine a major conflict being avoided or success in the original objective being achieved. The same is true for other major powers that are not permanent members of the Security Council. This raises the familiar question of double standards, to which there is only one answer: The reality that interventions may not be plausibly mounted in every justifiable case is no reason for them not to be mounted in any case.

■ Whose Authority?

The most difficult and controversial principle to apply is that of "right authority." When it comes to authorizing military intervention for human protection purposes, the argument is compelling that the United Nations, and in particular its Security Council, should be the first port of call. The difficult question—starkly raised by the Kosovo war—is whether it should be the last.

The issue of principle here is unarguable. The UN is unquestionably the principal institution for building, consolidating, and using the authority of the international community. It was set up to be the linchpin of order and stability, the framework within which members of the international system negotiate agreements on the rules of behavior and the legal norms of proper conduct to preserve the society of states. The authority of the UN is underpinned not by coercive power but by its role as the applicator of legitimacy. The concept of legitimacy acts as the connecting link between the exercise of authority and the recourse to power. Attempts to enforce authority can be made only by the legitimate agents of that authority. Nations regard collective intervention blessed by the UN as legitimate because a representative international body duly authorized it, whereas unilateral intervention is seen as illegitimate because it is self-interested. Those who challenge or evade the authority of the UN run the risk of eroding its authority in general and undermining the principle of a world order based on international law and universal norms.

The task is not to find alternatives to the Security Council as a source of authority, but to make the council work better than it has. Security Council authorization should, in all cases, be sought prior to any military intervention being carried out. Those advocates calling for an intervention should formally request such authorization, ask the council to raise the matter on its own initiative, or demand that the secretary-general raise it under Article 99 of the UN Charter. The Security Council should deal promptly with any request for authority to intervene where there are allegations of large-scale loss of life or ethnic cleansing. It should, in this context, also seek adequate verification of facts or conditions on the ground that might support a military intervention. And the council's five permanent members should agree to not exercise their veto power (in matters where their vital state interests are not involved) to block resolutions authorizing military intervention for human protection purposes for which there is otherwise majority support. We know of at least one that will so agree.

If the Security Council is unable or unwilling to act in a case crying out for intervention, two institutional solutions are available. One is for the General Assembly to consider the matter in an emergency special session under the "Uniting for Peace" procedure, used in the cases of Korea in 1950, Egypt in 1956, and Congo in 1960. Had it been used, that approach could well have delivered a speedy majority recommendation for action in the Rwanda and Kosovo cases. The other is action within an area of jurisdiction by regional or subregional organizations under Chapter VIII of the UN Charter, subject to their seeking subsequent authorization from the Security Council; that is what happened with the West African interventions in Liberia in the early 1990s and in Sierra Leone in 1997. But interventions by ad hoc coalitions (or individual states) acting without the approval of the Security Council, the General Assembly, or a regional or subregional grouping do not find wide international favor. As a matter of political reality, then, it would simply be impossible to build consensus around any set of proposals for military intervention that acknowledged the validity of any intervention not authorized by the Security Council or General Assembly.

There are many reasons to be dissatisfied with the role that the Security Council usually plays: its generally uneven performance, its unrepresentative membership, and its inherent institutional double standards with the permanent-five veto power. But there is no better or more appropriate body than the Security Council to deal with military intervention issues for human protection purposes. The political reality—quite apart from the force of the argument in principle—is that if international consensus is ever to be reached about how military intervention should happen, the Security Council will clearly have to be at the heart of that consensus.

But what if the Security Council fails to discharge its own responsibility to protect in a conscience-shocking situation crying out for action, as was the case with Kosovo? A real question arises as to which of two evils is the worse: the damage to international order if the Security Council is bypassed, or the damage to that order if human beings are slaughtered while the Security Council stands by. The answer to this dilemma is twofold, and these messages have to be delivered loud and clear. First, if the Security Council does fail to discharge its responsibility in such a case, then concerned individual states simply may not rule out other means to address the gravity and urgency of the situation. It follows that there will be a risk that such interventions, without the discipline and constraints of UN authorization, will not be conducted for the right reasons or with the right commitment to the necessary precautionary principles. Second, if the council does fail to act and a military intervention by an ad hoc coalition or individual state follows and respects all the necessary threshold and precautionary criteria—and if that intervention succeeds and is seen by the world to have succeeded—this outcome may have enduringly serious consequences for the stature of the UN itself. This is essentially what happened with the NATO intervention in Kosovo. The UN cannot afford to drop the ball too many times on that scale. . . .

Part 3

Conduct of War
(Jus in Bello)

9 Combatant Rights

9.1 _____

Introduction
The Editors

Just war doctrine demands two separate judgments: under what circumstances may a state resort to war, and how should a state's military conduct itself on the battlefield. As the chapters in Part 2 of this volume suggest, the *jus ad bellum* constraints derived from just war theory are very much in contention and are far from being settled in international law. The society of states still lacks a consensus on what exactly constitutes aggression, and therefore legitimate self-defense, and the challenges posed by modern terrorism and humanitarian crisis have disinclined states to foreswear the first use of military force. When it comes to appropriate conduct on the battlefield, the situation is rather different. As a moral matter, the core elements of *jus in bello* command widespread agreement. As a legal matter, the law of armed conflict—a subset of international humanitarian law—is extensively codified, notably in the Hague Conventions, the Geneva Conventions, and their protocols. This is not to say that these moral and legal limits are not transgressed; they most certainly are. It is simply easier to spot the transgressions when the boundaries between what is just and unjust in war are relatively settled in the moral and legal discourse.

Although war is the most primitive form of conflict resolution, there are rules. Foremost among them is that military actions should discriminate between combatants and noncombatants. The readings in Chapters 10, 11, and 12 take up the issue of noncombatant rights, but the rights (and, of course, the responsibilities) of combatants, the subject of this chapter, derive from similar moral principles. Soldiers are expected to engage in military operations without targeting civilian populations and so as to allow the opposing military to do the same. Soldiers do this by distinguishing themselves as combatants, that is, legitimate objects of attack. Such conduct on the battlefield is supposed to limit war's participants to those who are licensed to kill and be killed.

Alas, fighters do not always behave nobly and the law of war attempts to identify them and deny them the "privileges" otherwise enjoyed by combatants. The Hague Law (the 1899 and 1907 Hague Conventions and protocols) first identified as qualified combatants those organized within a chain of command, wearing distinctive insignia, carrying their arms openly, and conforming their conduct to the law of war. It was taken for granted that states' regular militaries satisfied these criteria. Militias and various irregular forces may also satisfy them, in which case those fighters are recognized as lawful combatants. Among other things, [all lawful combatants must be treated as prisoners of war if they are captured by opposing forces.]

The excerpts from the Third Geneva Convention included in this chapter detail the rights to be afforded to POWs. Some protections are the standard ones: prisoners may not be killed, maimed, or tortured (physically or mentally); they may not be subject to arbitrary punishment; they must be released when hostilities have ended. Other POW rights may seem rather extravagant (and, in fact, often are not observed in contemporary armed conflicts): POWs should be detained in quarters comparable to those of their detainers of similar rank; allowances should be made for prisoners' religious practices; they should not be insulted or placed on public display. Unlawful combatants are not entitled to POW rights if they are captured. They do, however, retain their "fundamental rights" as human beings: murder, mutilation, torture, rape, and other outrages upon their personal dignity are prohibited.

Consequently, designating one's opponents as lawful or unlawful combatants is not idle rhetoric, but may have serious implications for prescribed treatment when these individuals are captured on the battlefield and imprisoned. During and after the US invasion of Afghanistan in 2001, for example, the Bush administration had to classify prisoners from that conflict, many of whom were moved to a detention facility established at the US Naval base at Guantánamo Bay, Cuba. Although it was determined that the military conflict with the Taliban was governed by the Geneva Convention, Taliban fighters were considered by the administration to be unlawful combatants. Taliban detainees, therefore, were not accorded POW privileges, although the administration maintained that they were being treated humanely nonetheless, as stipulated in Geneva Law (the four Geneva Conventions of 1949, plus the two 1977 protocols).

The administration adopted a three-part rationale for classifying Taliban forces as unlawful combatants: the Taliban regime was a failed state and was not recognized by most other members of the international community; its military forces were therefore irregulars; as irregulars, they did not fulfill the requirements of lawful combatancy—in particular, they wore no distinctive insignia distinguishing them from noncombatants. This was disputed by many legal scholars, who regarded the Taliban as the de facto government of Afghanistan. After all, it was the Taliban government that the Bush administration went to with its ultimatum to turn over Osama bin Laden and his lieutenants. If soldiers in the Taliban army failed to distinguish themselves as combatants, they should not be denied their status as lawful combatants, but rather should be tried for war crimes as provided in Geneva Law.

Global terrorism and states' efforts to confront and contain it, especially by means of the so-called war on terrorism, pose significant challenges for the application of *jus in bello* principles. As we saw in Chapter 7, terrorist acts themselves are defined largely by the rejection of the moral argument upholding noncombatant immunity. That the perpetrators of terrorism should enjoy none of the rights enjoyed by lawful combatants in traditional wars is a sentiment widely held today. The Bush administration made clear early on in the war on terrorism that the conflict with Al-Qaida, in Afghanistan and elsewhere, falls outside the confines of Geneva Law and, by implication, the theory of just war from which it derives. If unlawful combatants enjoy no rights in captivity except the "fundamental right" to be treated humanely, what rights are enjoyed by those, like Al-Qaida detainees, who do not qualify even as unlawful combatants?

The Guantánamo detentions and the prisoner abuse at the Abu Ghraib detention center in Iraq, as well as the apprehension of terrorist masterminds Ramzi bin al-Shibh and Khalid Sheikh Mohammed, generated the sort of public debate on the pros and cons of torture that was taboo before 9/11. Alan Dershowitz, who was perhaps most responsible for bringing the discussion to the surface, has floated the idea of a court-issued "torture warrant" allowing the application of extreme force, medically supervised, designed to extract information from a "ticking bomb terrorist"—an individual who has set in motion an attack that will kill a large number of innocent civilians and who possesses the information necessary to avert it. If asked, many of us (probably more than care to admit it) would affirm the use of torture in such cases. But even among those willing to see torture used to stop this kind of attack, the notion of a court-issued warrant causes some unease.

One reason for the unease is the presence of the moral dilemma sometimes referred to as "dirty hands." Torture is bad; most countries, including the United States, have signed an international convention saying so and have pledged not to do it. Bombing innocent civilians is also bad, and we may be prepared to tolerate one evil to prevent another, but are we prepared to license it? Dershowitz believes we are hypocrites if we do not make some attempt to regulate by law what we all suspect has gone on in places like Camp X-Ray at Guantánamo, Abu Ghraib, Bagram Air Base in Afghanistan, and other detention centers doubling as outposts for the collection of intelligence. "Rendering" suspected terrorists to other countries, like Egypt or Pakistan, whose intelligence services may have fewer qualms about the use of torture is not, morally speaking, any better. Should we elect to look away and ignore the torture taking place, we are saying, in effect, that torture is not categorically wrong; it depends on the circumstances, which we hope are rare, and the likelihood that interrogators will get the information they need. Now we can leave it to the intelligence services to determine the circumstances and estimate the likelihood of success, in which case we continue to look the other way. Dershowitz believes we can lessen the hypocrisy in evidence here by creating a system that allows a judicial magistrate to make the final call by issuing, or refusing to issue, a torture warrant.

✈ Critics of Dershowitz's proposal worry about the slippery slope: if today we are willing to license torture in situations of extreme emergency, then tomorrow we may want to use it to confront less extreme dangers; and if today we are willing to torture the "ticking bomb terrorist," then tomorrow we may try it on the probable terrorist, or the probable terrorist's loved ones. But a criticism from the standpoint of "dirty hands" is somewhat different. Torture is wrong, always. If we are forced by emergency circumstances to resort to torture, so be it; but that does not make it right, even under those circumstances. Perhaps we have managed to save many innocent lives, but we still have dirty hands, and that should bother us. Any form of legal sanction, torture warrants included, permits us to be unbothered, to do bad things with clean hands.

The Bush administration has chosen the term "war" to describe its effort to contain and defeat global terrorism, so as to emphasize that something more is required than law enforcement. Yet the moral issues that confront us in this kind of war are not easily within the confines of traditional just war theory. Those who plot and fight on behalf of Al-Qaida and other terrorist networks are surely not lawful combatants with rights defined in Geneva Law. How far we are willing to go in stripping them of the sorts of basic human rights that Geneva Law reserves for unlawful combatants remains to be seen.

9.2 _____

Third Geneva Convention Relative to the Treatment of Prisoners of War
Signed: August 12, 1949
In Force: October 21, 1950

■ Part II: General Protection of Prisoners of War

Article 13
Prisoners of war must at all times be humanely treated. Any unlawful act or omission by the Detaining Power causing death or seriously endangering the health of a prisoner of war in its custody is prohibited, and will be regarded as a serious breach of the present Convention. In particular, no prisoner of war may be subjected to physical mutilation or to medical or scientific experiments of any kind which are not justified by the medical, dental or hospital treatment of the prisoner concerned and carried out in his interest.

Likewise, prisoners of war must at all times be protected, particularly against acts of violence or intimidation and against insults and public curiosity.

Measures of reprisal against prisoners of war are prohibited.

Article 14
Prisoners of war are entitled in all circumstances to respect for their persons and their honor.

Women shall be treated with all the regard due to their sex and shall in all cases benefit by treatment as favorable as that granted to men.

Prisoners of war shall retain the full civil capacity which they enjoyed at the time of their capture. The Detaining Power may not restrict the exercise, either within or without its own territory, of the rights such capacity confers except in so far as the captivity requires. *define captivity*

■ Part III, Section I: Beginning of Captivity

Article 17
Every prisoner of war, when questioned on the subject, is bound to give only his surname, first names and rank, date of birth, and army, regi-

mental, personal or serial number, or failing this, equivalent information. . . .

No physical or mental torture, nor any other form of coercion, may be inflicted on prisoners of war to secure from them information of any kind whatever. Prisoners of war who refuse to answer may not be threatened, insulted, or exposed to unpleasant or disadvantageous treatment of any kind. Prisoners of war who, owing to their physical or mental condition, are unable to state their identity, shall be handed over to the medical service. The identity of such prisoners shall be established by all possible means, subject to the provisions of the preceding paragraph. . . .

▣ Section II, Chapter II:
Quarters, Food and Clothing of Prisoners of War

Article 25
Prisoners of war shall be quartered under conditions as favorable as those for the forces of the Detaining Power who are billeted in the same area. The said conditions shall make allowance for the habits and customs of the prisoners and shall in no case be prejudicial to their health.

The foregoing provisions shall apply in particular to the dormitories of prisoners of war as regards both total surface and minimum cubic space, and the general installations, bedding and blankets.

The premises provided for the use of prisoners of war individually or collectively, shall be entirely protected from dampness and adequately heated and lighted, in particular between dusk and lights out. All precautions must be taken against the danger of fire.

In any camps in which women prisoners of war, as well as men, are accommodated, separate dormitories shall be provided for them. . . .

▣ Chapter V:
Religious, Intellectual and Physical Activities

Article 34
Prisoners of war shall enjoy complete latitude in the exercise of their religious duties, including attendance at the service of their faith, on condition that they comply with the disciplinary routine prescribed by the military authorities.

Adequate premises shall be provided where religious services may be held. . . .

■ Section VI, Chapter III:
Penal and Disciplinary Sanctions

Article 84
A prisoner of war shall be tried only by a military court, unless the existing laws of the Detaining Power expressly permit the civil courts to try a member of the armed forces of the Detaining Power in respect of the particular offence alleged to have been committed by the prisoner of war.

In no circumstances whatever shall a prisoner of war be tried by a court of any kind which does not offer the essential guarantees of independence and impartiality as generally recognized, and, in particular, the procedure of which does not afford the accused the rights and means of defence provided for in Article 105. . . .

Article 99
No prisoner of war may be tried or sentenced for an act which is not forbidden by the law of the Detaining Power or by international law, in force at the time the said act was committed.

No moral or physical coercion may be exerted on a prisoner of war in order to induce him to admit himself guilty of the act of which he is accused.

No prisoner of war may be convicted without having had an opportunity to present his defence and the assistance of a qualified advocate or counsel. . . .

Article 105
The prisoner of war shall be entitled to assistance by one of his prisoner comrades, to defence by a qualified advocate or counsel of his own choice, to the calling of witnesses and, if he deems necessary, to the services of a competent interpreter. He shall be advised of these rights by the Detaining Power in due time before the trial. . . .

■ Part IV, Section I: Direct Repatriation
and Accommodation in Neutral Countries

Article 109
Subject to the provisions of the third paragraph of this Article, Parties to the conflict are bound to send back to their own country, regardless of number or rank, seriously wounded and seriously sick prisoners of war, after having cared for them until they are fit to travel, in accordance with the first paragraph of the following Article.

Throughout the duration of hostilities, Parties to the conflict shall endeavour, with the cooperation of the neutral Powers concerned, to make arrangements for the accommodation in neutral countries of the sick and wounded prisoners of war referred to in the second paragraph of the following Article. They may, in addition, conclude agreements with a view to the direct repatriation or internment in a neutral country of able-bodied prisoners of war who have undergone a long period of captivity.

No sick or injured prisoner of war who is eligible for repatriation under the first paragraph of this Article, may be repatriated against his will during hostilities. . . .

■ Section II: Release and Repatriation of Prisoners of War at the Close of Hostilities

Article 118

Prisoners of war shall be released and repatriated without delay after the cessation of active hostilities.

In the absence of stipulations to the above effect in any agreement concluded between the Parties to the conflict with a view to the cessation of hostilities, or failing any such agreement, each of the Detaining Powers shall itself establish and execute without delay a plan of repatriation in conformity with the principle laid down in the foregoing paragraph. . . .

9.3

Protocol I to the Geneva Conventions of 1949

Signed: 1977
In Force: December 7, 1979

■ Part III, Section I: Methods and Means of Warfare

Article 35: Basic Rules
1. In any armed conflict, the right of the Parties to the conflict to choose methods or means of warfare is not unlimited.
2. It is prohibited to employ weapons, projectiles and material and methods of warfare of a nature to cause superfluous injury or unnecessary suffering.
3. It is prohibited to employ methods or means of warfare which are intended, or may be expected, to cause widespread, long-term and severe damage to the natural environment. . . .

Article 37: Prohibition of Perfidy
1. It is prohibited to kill, injure or capture an adversary by resort to perfidy. Acts inviting the confidence of an adversary to lead him to believe that he is entitled to, or is obliged to accord, protection under the rules of international law applicable in armed conflict, with intent to betray that confidence, shall constitute perfidy. The following acts are examples of perfidy:
(a) The feigning of an intent to negotiate under a flag of truce or of a surrender;
(b) The feigning of an incapacitation by wounds or sickness;
(c) The feigning of civilian, non-combatant status; and
(d) The feigning of protected status by the use of signs, emblems or uniforms of the United Nations or of neutral or other States not Parties to the conflict.
2. Ruses of war are not prohibited. Such ruses are acts which are intended to mislead an adversary or to induce him to act recklessly but which infringe no rule of international law applicable in armed conflict and which are not perfidious because they do not invite the confidence of an adversary with respect to protection under that law. The following are examples of such ruses: the use of camouflage, decoys, mock operations and misinformation. . . .

Article 41: Safeguard of an Enemy Hors de Combat

1. A person who is recognized or who, in the circumstances, should be recognized to be hors de combat shall not be made the object of attack.

2. A person is hors de combat if:

(a) He is in the power of an adverse Party;

(b) He clearly expresses an intention to surrender; or

(c) He has been rendered unconscious or is otherwise incapacitated by wounds or sickness, and therefore is incapable of defending himself; provided that in any of these cases he abstains from any hostile act and does not attempt to escape.

3. When persons entitled to protection as prisons of war have fallen into the power of an adverse Party under unusual conditions of combat which prevent their evacuation as provided for in Part III, Section I, of the Third Convention, they shall be released and all feasible precautions shall be taken to ensure their safety. . . .

Article 43: Armed Forces

1. The armed forces of a Party to a conflict consist of all organized armed forces, groups and units which are under a command responsible to that Party for the conduct of its subordinates, even if that Party is represented by a government or an authority not recognized by an adverse Party. Such armed forces shall be subject to an internal disciplinary system which, inter alia, shall enforce compliance with the rules of international law applicable in armed conflict.

2. Members of the armed forces of a Party to a conflict (other than medical personnel and chaplains covered by Article 33 of the Third Convention) are combatants, that is to say, they have the right to participate directly in hostilities.

3. Whenever a Party to a conflict incorporates a paramilitary or armed law enforcement agency into its armed forces it shall so notify the other Parties to the conflict.

Article 44: Combatants and Prisoners of War

1. Any combatant, as defined in Article 43, who falls into the power of an adverse Party shall be a prisoner of war.

2. While all combatants are obliged to comply with the rules of international law applicable in armed conflict, violations of these rules shall not deprive a combatant of his right to be a combatant or, if he falls into the power of an adverse Party, of his right to be a prisoner of war, except as provided in paragraphs 3 and 4.

3. In order to promote the protection of the civilian population from the effects of hostilities, combatants are obliged to distinguish themselves from the civilian population while they are engaged in an attack or in a military

operation preparatory to an attack. Recognizing, however, that there are situations in armed conflicts where, owing to the nature of the hostilities an armed combatant cannot so distinguish himself, he shall retain his status as a combatant, provided that, in such situations, he carries his arms openly:

(a) During each military engagement, and

(b) During such time as he is visible to the adversary while he is engaged in a military deployment preceding the launching of an attack in which he is to participate.

Acts which comply with the requirements of this paragraph shall not be considered as perfidious within the meaning of Article 37, paragraph 1 (c).

4. A combatant who falls into the power of an adverse Party while failing to meet the requirements set forth in the second sentence of paragraph 3 shall forfeit his right to be a prisoner of war, but he shall, nevertheless, be given protections equivalent in all respects to those accorded to prisoners of war by the Third Convention and by this Protocol. This protection includes protections equivalent to those accorded to prisoners of war by the Third Convention in the case where such a person is tried and punished for any offences he has committed.

5. Any combatant who falls into the power of an adverse Party while not engaged in an attack or in a military operation preparatory to an attack shall not forfeit his rights to be a combatant and a prisoner of war by virtue of his prior activities. . . .

Article 45:
Protection of Persons Who Have Taken Part in Hostilities

1. A person who takes part in hostilities and falls into the power of an adverse Party shall be presumed to be a prisoner of war, and therefore shall be protected by the Third Convention, if he claims the status of prisoner of war, or if he appears to be entitled to such status, or if the Party on which he depends claims such status on his behalf by notification to the detaining Power or to the Protecting Power. Should any doubt arise as to whether any such person is entitled to the status of prisoner of war, he shall continue to have such status and, therefore, to be protected by the Third Convention and this Protocol until such time as his status has been determined by a competent tribunal.

2. If a person who has fallen into the power of an adverse Party is not held as a prisoner of war and is to be tried by that Party for an offence arising out of the hostilities, he shall have the right to assert his entitlement to prisoner-of-war status before a judicial tribunal and to have that question adjudicated. Whenever possible under the applicable procedure, this adjudication shall occur before the trial for the offence. The representatives of the Protecting Power shall be entitled to attend the proceedings in which that question is adjudicated, unless, exceptionally, the proceedings are held in

camera in the interest of State security. In such a case the detaining Power shall advise the Protecting Power accordingly.

3. Any person who has taken part in hostilities, who is not entitled to prisoner-of-war status and who does not benefit from more favorable treatment in accordance with the Fourth Convention shall have the right at all times to the protection of Article 75 of this Protocol. In occupied territory, any such person, unless he is held as a spy, shall also be entitled, notwithstanding Article 5 of the Fourth Convention, to his rights of communication under that Convention.

Article 46: Spies

1. Notwithstanding any other provision of the Conventions or of this Protocol, any member of the armed forces of a Party to the conflict who falls into the power of an adverse Party while engaging in espionage shall not have the right to the status of prisoner of war and may be treated as a spy.

2. A member of the armed forces of a Party to the conflict who, on behalf of that Party and in territory controlled by an adverse Party, gathers or attempts to gather information shall not be considered as engaging in espionage if, while so acting, he is in the uniform of his armed forces. . . .

Article 47: Mercenaries

1. A mercenary shall not have the right to be a combatant or a prisoner of war.

2. A mercenary is any person who:

(a) Is specially recruited locally or abroad in order to fight in an armed conflict;

(b) Does, in fact, take a direct part in the hostilities;

(c) Is motivated to take part in the hostilities essentially by the desire for private gain and, in fact, is promised, by or on behalf of a Party to the conflict, material compensation substantially in excess of that promised or paid to combatants of similar ranks and functions in the armed forces of that Party;

(d) Is neither a national of a Party to the conflict nor a resident of territory controlled by a Party to the conflict;

(e) Is not a member of the armed forces of a Party to the conflict; and

(f) Has not been sent by a State which is not a Party to the conflict on official duty as a member of its armed forces. . . .

Article 75: Fundamental Guarantees

1. In so far as they are affected by a situation referred to in Article 1 of this Protocol, persons who are in the power of a Party to the conflict and who do not benefit from more favorable treatment under the Conventions or

under this Protocol shall be treated humanely in all circumstances and shall enjoy, as a minimum, the protection provided by this Article without any adverse distinction based upon race, color, sex, language, religion or belief, political or other opinion, national or social origin, wealth, birth or other status, or on any other similar criteria. Each Party shall respect the person, honor, convictions and religious practices of all such persons.

2. The following acts are and shall remain prohibited at any time and in any place whatsoever, whether committed by civilian or by military agents:

(a) Violence to the life, health, or physical or mental well-being of persons, in particular: (i) Murder; (ii) Torture of all kinds, whether physical or mental; (iii) Corporal punishment; and (iv) Mutilation;

(b) Outrages upon personal dignity, in particular humiliating and degrading treatment, enforced prostitution and any form of indecent assault;

(c) The taking of hostages;

(d) Collective punishments; and

(e) Threats to commit any of the foregoing acts.

9.4 _____

Should the Ticking Bomb Terrorist Be Tortured?

Alan M. Dershowitz

■ How the Current Torture Debate Began

Before September 11, 2001, no one thought the issue of torture would ever reemerge as a topic of serious debate in this country. Yet shortly after that watershed event, FBI agents began to leak stories suggesting that they might have to resort to torture to get some detainees, who were suspected of complicity in al-Qaeda terrorism, to provide information necessary to prevent a recurrence. An FBI source told the press that because "we are known for humanitarian treatment" of arrestees, we have been unable to get any terrorist suspects to divulge information about possible mature plans. "We're into this thing for 35 days and nobody is talking," he said in obvious frustration. "Basically we're stuck." A senior FBI aide warned that "it could get to the spot where we could go to pressure . . . where *we won't have a choice,* and we are probably getting there."[1] But in a democracy there is always a choice. . . .

Constitutional democracies are, of course, constrained in the choices they may lawfully make. The Fifth Amendment prohibits compelled self-incrimination, which means that statements elicited by means of torture may not be introduced into evidence against the defendant who has been tortured. But if a suspect is given immunity and then tortured into providing information about a future terrorist act, his privilege against self-incrimination has not been violated. (Nor would it be violated if the information were elicited by means of "truth serum," as Judge William Webster, the former head of the FBI and the CIA, has proposed—as long as the information and its fruits were not used against him in a criminal trial.) Nor has his right to be free from "cruel and unusual punishment," since that provision of the Eighth Amendment has been interpreted to apply solely to punishment after

---

From *Why Terrorism Works: Understanding the Threat, Responding to the Challenge* by Alan M. Dershowitz. Copyright © 2002 by Yale University Press. Used by permission of Yale University Press. Excerpt from chap. 4 ("Should the Ticking Bomb Terrorist Be Tortured? A Case Study in How a Democracy Should Make Tragic Choices").

conviction. The only constitutional barriers would be the "due process" clauses of the Fifth and Fourteenth Amendments, which are quite general and sufficiently flexible to permit an argument that the only process "due" a terrorist suspected of refusing to disclose information necessary to prevent a terrorist attack is the requirement of probable cause and some degree of judicial supervision.

In addition to possible constitutional constraints, we are also limited by our treaty obligations, which have the force of law. The Geneva Convention Against Torture prohibits all forms of torture and provides for no exceptions. It defines torture so broadly as to include many techniques that are routinely used around the world, including in Western democracies:

> For the purposes of this Convention, the term "torture" means any act by which severe pain or suffering, whether physical or mental, is intentionally inflicted on a person for such purposes as obtaining from him or a third person information or a confession, punishing him for an act he or a third person has committed or is suspected of having committed, or intimidating or coercing him or a third person, or for any reason based on discrimination of any kind, when such pain or suffering is inflicted by or at the instigation of or with the consent or acquiescence of a public official or other person acting in an official capacity.

Many nations that routinely practice the most brutal forms of torture are signatories to this convention, but they hypocritically ignore it. The United States adopted the convention, but with a reservation: we agreed to be bound by it "only to the extent that it is consistent with . . . the Eighth Amendment." Decisions by U.S. courts have suggested that the Eighth Amendment may not prohibit the use of physical force to obtain information needed to save lives; so if the United States chose to employ nonlethal torture in such an extreme case it could arguably remain in technical compliance with its treaty obligation. . . .

In any event, there are legal steps we could take, if we chose to resort to torture, that would make it possible for us to use this technique for eliciting information in dire circumstances. Neither the presence nor the absence of legal constraints answers the fundamental moral question: should we? This is a choice that almost no one wants to have to make. Torture has been off the agenda of civilized discourse for so many centuries that it is a subject reserved largely for historians rather than contemporary moralists. . . .

▪ The Case for Torturing the Ticking Bomb Terrorist

The arguments in favor of using torture as a last resort to prevent a ticking bomb from exploding and killing many people are both simple and simpleminded. Bentham constructed a compelling hypothetical case to support his utilitarian argument against an absolute prohibition on torture:

> Suppose an occasion were to arise, in which a suspicion is entertained, as strong as that which would be received as a sufficient ground for arrest and commitment as for felony—a suspicion that at this very time a considerable number of individuals are actually suffering, by illegal violence inflictions equal in intensity to those which if inflicted by the hand of justice, would universally be spoken of under the name of torture. For the purpose of rescuing from torture these hundred innocents, should any scruple be made of applying equal or superior torture, to extract the requisite information from the mouth of one criminal, who having it in his power to make known the place where at this time the enormity was practising or about to be practised, should refuse to do so? To say nothing of wisdom, could any pretence be made so much as to the praise of blind and vulgar humanity, by the man who to save one criminal, should determine to abandon 100 innocent persons to the same fate?[2]

If the torture of one guilty person would be justified to prevent the torture of a hundred innocent persons, it would seem to follow—certainly to Bentham—that it would also be justified to prevent the murder of thousands of innocent civilians in the ticking bomb case. Consider two hypothetical situations that are not, unfortunately, beyond the realm of possibility. In fact, they are both extrapolations on actual situations we have faced.

Several weeks before September 11, 2001, the Immigration and Naturalization Service detained Zacarias Moussaoui after flight instructors reported suspicious statements he had made while taking flying lessons and paying for them with large amounts of cash. The government decided not to seek a warrant to search his computer. Now imagine that they had, and that they discovered he was part of a plan to destroy large occupied buildings, but without any further details. They interrogated him, gave him immunity from prosecution, and offered him large cash rewards and a new identity. He refused to talk. They then threatened him, tried to trick him, and employed every lawful technique available. He still refused. They even injected him with sodium pentothal and other truth serums, but to no avail. The attack now appeared to be imminent, but the FBI still had no idea what the target was or what means would be used to attack it. We could not simply evacuate all buildings indefinitely. An FBI agent proposes the use of nonlethal torture—say, a sterilized needle inserted under the fingernails to produce unbearable pain without any threat to health or life, or the method used in the film *Marathon Man,* a dental drill through an unanesthetized tooth.

The simple cost-benefit analysis for employing such nonlethal torture seems overwhelming: it is surely better to inflict nonlethal pain on one guilty terrorist who is illegally withholding information needed to prevent an act of terrorism than to permit a large number of innocent victims to die. Pain is a lesser and more remediable harm than death; and the lives of a thousand innocent people should be valued more than the bodily integrity of one guilty person. If the variation on the Moussaoui case is not sufficiently compelling to make this point, we can always raise the stakes. Several weeks after September 11, our government received reports that a ten-kiloton nuclear weapon may have been stolen from Russia and was on its way to New York City, where it would be detonated and kill hundreds of thousands of people. The reliability of the source, code named Dragonfire, was uncertain, but assume for purposes of this hypothetical extension of the actual case that the source was a captured terrorist—like the one tortured by the Philippine authorities—who knew precisely how and where the weapon was being brought into New York and was to be detonated. Again, everything short of torture is tried, but to no avail. It is not absolutely certain torture will work, but it is our last, best hope for preventing a cataclysmic nuclear devastation in a city too large to evacuate in time. Should nonlethal torture be tried? Bentham would certainly have said yes.

The strongest argument against any resort to torture, even in the ticking bomb case, also derives from Bentham's utilitarian calculus. Experience has shown that if torture, which has been deemed illegitimate by the civilized world for more than a century, were now to be legitimated—even for limited use in one extraordinary type of situation—such legitimation would constitute an important symbolic setback in the worldwide campaign against human rights abuses. Inevitably, the legitimation of torture by the world's leading democracy would provide a welcome justification for its more widespread use in other parts of the world. . . .

Bentham's own justification was based on *case* or *act* utilitarianism—a demonstration that in a *particular case* the benefits that would flow from the limited use of torture would outweigh its costs. The argument against any use of torture would derive from *rule* utilitarianism—which considers the implications of establishing a precedent that would inevitably be extended beyond its limited case utilitarian justification to other possible evils of lesser magnitude. Even terrorism itself could be justified by a case utilitarian approach. Surely one could come up with a singular situation in which the targeting of a small number of civilians could be thought necessary to save thousands of other civilians—blowing up a German kindergarten by the relatives of inmates in a Nazi death camp, for example, and threatening to repeat the targeting of German children unless the death camps were shut down.

The reason this kind of single-case utilitarian justification is simpleminded is that it has no inherent limiting principle. If nonlethal torture of one person is justified to prevent the killing of many important people, then what if it were necessary to use lethal torture—or at least torture that posed a substantial risk of death? What if it were necessary to torture the suspect's mother or children to get him to divulge the information? What if it took threatening to kill his family, his friends, his entire village? Under a simple-minded quantitative case utilitarianism, anything goes as long as the number of people tortured or killed does not exceed the number that would be saved. This is morality by numbers, unless there are other constraints on what we can properly do. These other constraints can come from rule utilitarianism or other principles of morality, such as the prohibition against deliberately punishing the innocent. Unless we are prepared to impose some limits on the use of torture or other barbaric tactics that might be of some use in preventing terrorism we risk hurtling down a slippery slope into the abyss of amorality and ultimately tyranny. . . .

▨ The Three—or Four—Ways

. . . The modern resort to terrorism has renewed the debate over how a rights-based society should respond to the prospect of using nonlethal torture in the ticking bomb situation. In the late 1980s the Israeli government appointed a commission headed by a retired Supreme Court justice to look into precisely that situation. The commission concluded that there are "three ways for solving this grave dilemma between the vital need to preserve the very existence of the state and its citizens, and maintain its character as a law-abiding state." The first is to allow the security services to continue to fight terrorism in "a twilight zone which is outside the realm of law." The second is "the way of the hypocrites: they declare that they abide by the rule of law, but turn a blind eye to what goes on beneath the surface." And the third, "the truthful road of the rule of law," is that the "law itself must insure a proper framework for the activity" of the security services in seeking to prevent terrorist acts.

There is of course a fourth road: namely to forgo any use of torture and simply allow the preventable terrorist act to occur. After the Supreme Court of Israel outlawed the use of physical pressure, the Israeli security services claimed that, as a result of the Supreme Court's decision, at least one preventable act of terrorism had been allowed to take place, one that killed several people when a bus was bombed. Whether this claim is true, false, or somewhere in between is difficult to assess. But it is clear that if the preventable act of terrorism was of the magnitude of the attacks of September 11, there would be a great outcry in any democracy that had deliberately refused to take available preventive action, even if it required the use of torture. . . . The real issue, therefore is not whether some torture would or would not be used in the ticking bomb case—it would. The question is whether it would be done openly, pursuant to a previously established legal procedure, or whether it would be done secretly, in violation of existing law.

Several important values are pitted against each other in this conflict. The first is the safety and security of a nation's citizens. Under the ticking bomb scenario this value may require the use of torture, if that is the only way to prevent the bomb from exploding and killing large numbers of civilians. The second value is the preservation of civil liberties and human rights. This value requires that we not accept torture as a legitimate part of our legal system. . . . Former presidential candidate Alan Keyes took the position that although torture might be necessary in a given situation it could never be right. He suggested that a president should authorize the torturing of a ticking bomb terrorist, but that this act should not be legitimated by the courts or incorporated into our legal system. He argued that wrongful and indeed unlawful acts might sometimes be necessary to preserve the nation, but that no aura of legitimacy should be placed on these actions by judicial imprimatur.

This understandable approach is in conflict with the third important value: namely, open accountability and visibility in a democracy. "Off-the-book actions below the radar screen" are antithetical to the theory and practice of democracy. Citizens cannot approve or disapprove of governmental actions of which they are unaware. . . . Perhaps the most extreme example of such a hypocritical approach to torture comes—not surprisingly—from the French experience in Algeria. The French army used torture extensively in seeking to prevent terrorism during a brutal colonial war from 1955 to 1957. An officer who supervised this torture, General Paul Aussaresses, wrote a book recounting what he had done and seen, including the torture of dozens of Algerians. "The best way to make a terrorist talk when he refused to say what he knew was to torture him," he boasted. Although the book was published decades after the war was over, the general was prosecuted—but not for what he had done to the Algerians. Instead, he was prosecuted for revealing what he had done, and seeking to justify it.

In a democracy governed by the rule of law, we should never want our soldiers or our president to take any action that we deem wrong or illegal. A good test of whether an action should or should not be done is whether we are prepared to have it disclosed—perhaps not immediately, but certainly after some time has passed. No legal system operating under the rule of law should ever tolerate an "off-the-books" approach to necessity. Even the defense of necessity must be justified lawfully. The road to tyranny has always been paved with claims of necessity made by those responsible for the security of a nation. Our system of checks and balances requires that all presidential actions, like all legislative or military actions, be consistent with governing law. If it is necessary to torture in the ticking bomb case, then our governing laws must accommodate this practice. If we refuse to change our law to accommodate any particular action, then our government should not take that action.

Only in a democracy committed to civil liberties would a triangular conflict of this kind exist. Totalitarian and authoritarian regimes experience no such conflict, because they subscribe to neither the civil libertarian nor the democratic values that come in conflict with the value of security. The hard question is: which value is to be preferred when an inevitable clash occurs? One or more of these values must inevitably be compromised in making the tragic choice presented by the ticking bomb case. If we do not torture, we compromise the security and safety of our citizens. If we tolerate torture, but keep it off the books and below the radar screen, we compromise principles of democratic accountability. If we create a legal structure for limiting and controlling torture, we compromise our principled opposition to torture in all circumstances and create a potentially dangerous and expandable situation. . . .

We associate torture with the Inquisition, the Gestapo, the Stalinist purges, and the Argentine colonels responsible for the "dirty war." We recall it as a prelude to death, an integral part of a regime of gratuitous pain leading to a painful demise. We find it difficult to imagine a benign use of nonlethal torture to save lives. . . . Yet there was a time in the history of Anglo-Saxon law when torture was used to save life, rather than to take it, and when the limited administration of nonlethal torture was supervised by judges. . . .

In his book on legalized torture during the sixteenth and seventeenth centuries, *Torture and the Law of Proof,* Langbein demonstrates the trade-off between torture and other important values. Torture was employed for several purposes. First, it was used to secure the evidence necessary to obtain a guilty verdict under the rigorous criteria for conviction required at the time—either the testimony of two eyewitnesses or the confession of the accused himself. Circumstantial evidence, no matter how compelling, would not do. As Langbein concludes, "no society will long tolerate a legal system in which there is no prospect in convicting unrepentant persons who commit clandestine crimes. Something had to be done to extend the system to those cases. The two-eyewitness rule was hard to compromise or evade, but the confession invited 'subterfuge.'"[3] The subterfuge that was adopted permitted the use of torture to obtain confessions from suspects against whom there was compelling circumstantial evidence of guilt. The circumstantial evidence, alone, could not be used to convict, but it was used to obtain a torture warrant. That torture warrant was in turn used to obtain a confession, which then had to be independently corroborated—at least in most cases (witchcraft and other such cases were exempted from the requirement of corroboration).

Torture was also used against persons already convicted of capital crimes, such as high treason, who were thought to have information necessary to prevent attacks on the state.

Langbein studied eighty-one torture warrants, issued between 1540 and 1640, and found that in many of them, especially in "the higher cases of treason, torture is used for discovery, and not for evidence." Torture was "used to protect the state" and "mostly that meant preventive torture to identify and forestall plots and plotters."[4] It was only when the legal system loosened its requirement of proof (or introduced the "black box" of the jury system) and when perceived threats against the state diminished that torture was no longer deemed necessary to convict guilty defendants against whom there had previously been insufficient evidence, or to secure preventive information. . . .

In deciding whether the ticking bomb terrorist should be tortured, one important question is whether there would be less torture if it were done as part of the legal system, as it was in sixteenth- and seventeenth-century England, or off the books, as it is in many countries today. The Langbein study does not definitively answer this question, but it does provide some suggestive insights. The English system of torture was more visible and thus more subject to public accountability, and it is likely that torture was employed less frequently in England than in France. "During these years when it appears that torture might have become routinized in English criminal procedure, the Privy Council kept the torture power under careful control and never allowed it to fall into the hands of the regular law enforcement officers," as it had in France. In England "no law enforcement officer . . . acquired the power to use torture without special warrant." Moreover, when torture warrants were abolished, "the English experiment with torture left no traces."[5] Because it was under centralized control, it was easier to abolish than it was in France, where it persisted for many years.

It is always difficult to extrapolate from history, but it seems logical that a formal, visible, accountable, and centralized system is somewhat easier to control than an ad hoc, off-the-books, and under-the-radar-screen nonsystem. I believe, though I certainly cannot prove, that a formal requirement of a judicial warrant as a prerequisite to nonlethal torture would decrease the amount of physical violence directed against suspects. At the most obvious level, a double check is always more protective than a single check. In every instance in which a warrant is requested, a field officer has already decided that torture is justified and, in the absence of a warrant requirement, would simply proceed with the torture. Requiring that decision to be approved by a judicial officer will result in fewer instances of torture even if the judge rarely turns down a request. Moreover, I believe that most judges would require compelling evidence before they would authorize so extraordinary a departure from our constitutional norms, and law enforcement officials would be reluctant to seek a warrant unless they had compelling evidence that the suspect had information needed to prevent an imminent terrorist attack. A record would be kept of every warrant granted, and although it is certainly possible that some individual agents might torture without a warrant, they would have no excuse, since a warrant procedure would be available. They could not claim "necessity," because the decision as to whether the torture is indeed necessary has been taken out of their hands and placed in the hands of a judge. In addition, even if torture were deemed totally illegal without any exception, it would still occur, though the public would be less aware of its existence.

I also believe that the rights of the suspect would be better protected with a warrant requirement. He would be granted immunity, told that he was now compelled to testify, threatened with imprisonment if he refused to do so, and given the option of providing the requested information. Only if he refused to do what he was legally compelled to do—provide necessary information, which could not incriminate him because of the immunity—would he be threatened with torture. Knowing that such a threat was authorized by the law, he might well provide the information. If he still refused to, he would be subjected to judicially monitored physical measures designed to cause excruciating pain without leaving any lasting damage.

There are other, somewhat more subtle, considerations that should be factored into any decision regarding torture. There are some who see silence as a virtue when it comes to the choice among such horrible evils as torture and terrorism. It is far better, they argue, not to discuss or write about issues of this sort, lest they become legitimated. And legitimation is an appropriate concern. Justice Jackson, in his opinion in one of the cases concerning the detention of Japanese-Americans during World War II, made the following relevant observation:

> Much is said of the danger to liberty from the Army program for deporting and detaining these citizens of Japanese extraction. But a judicial construction of the due process clause that will sustain this order is a far more subtle blow to liberty than the promulgation of the order itself. A military order, however unconstitutional, is not apt to last longer than the military emergency. Even during that period a succeeding commander may revoke it all. But once a judicial opinion rationalizes such an order to show that it conforms to the Constitution, or rather rationalizes the Constitution to show that the Constitution sanctions such an order, the Court for all time has validated the principle of racial discrimination in criminal procedure and of transplanting American citizens. . . . A military commander may overstep the bounds of constitutionality, and it is an incident. But if we review and approve, that passing incident becomes the doctrine of the Constitution. There it has a generative power of its own, and all that it creates will be in its own image.[6]

A similar argument can be made regarding torture: if an agent tortures, that is "an incident," but if the courts authorize it, it becomes a precedent.

There is, however, an important difference between the detention of Japanese-American citizens and torture. The detentions were done openly and with presidential accountability; torture would be done secretly with official deniability. Tolerating an off-the-book system of secret torture can also establish a dangerous precedent.

A variation on this "legitimation" argument would postpone consideration of the choice between authorizing torture and forgoing a possible tactic necessary to prevent an imminent act of terrorism until after the choice—presumably the choice to torture—has been made. In that way, the discussion would not, in itself, encourage the use of torture. If it were employed, then we could decide whether it was justified, excusable, condemnable, or something in between. The problem with that argument is that no FBI agent who tortured a suspect into disclosing information that prevented an act of mass terrorism would be prosecuted—as the policemen who tortured the kidnapper into disclosing the whereabouts of his victim were not prosecuted. In the absence of a prosecution there would be no occasion to judge the appropriateness of the torture.

I disagree with these more passive approaches and believe that in a democracy it is always preferable to decide controversial issues in advance, rather than in the heat of battle. . . . Even if government officials decline to discuss such issues, academics have a duty to raise them and submit them to the marketplace of ideas. There may be danger in open discussion, but there is far greater danger in actions based on secret discussion, or no discussion at all.

■ Notes

1. Walter Pincus, "Silence of 4 Terror Probe Suspects Poses a Dilemma for FBI," *Washington Post,* 21 October 2001 (emphasis added).
2. Quoted in W. L. Twining and P. E. Twining, "Bentham on Torture," *Northern Ireland Legal Quarterly,* vol. 24 (Autumn 1973), p. 347.
3. John Langbein, *Torture and the Law of Proof* (Chicago: University of Chicago Press, 1977), p. 7.
4. Ibid., p. 9, quoting Bacon.
5. Ibid., pp. 136–137, 139.
6. *Korematsu v. United States,* 323 U.S. 214, 245-46 (1944) (Jackson, J., dissenting).

10 Noncombatant Rights

10.1 ____

Introduction
The Editors

Noncombatant immunity, or *discrimination,* is the most fundamental stricture of *jus in bello* and is firmly established in the international law of war. In an earlier era when battles were fought far from population centers, it was much easier to conduct military operations in conformity with this rule than it is today. Still, professional militaries in modern times rarely target civilian populations directly, and usually take care to minimize unintentional civilian deaths. Many civilians died during the wars of the twentieth century, however, due both to targeted attacks and to the collateral effects of attacks on legitimate military targets, and contemporary wars continue to impose heavy costs on those not directly engaged in the fighting. Noncombatant immunity has been (and continues to be) violated, even if that is not the norm, and it is difficult to justify the large numbers of civilians killed and displaced during wartime with the plea that these are unintended outcomes of wars otherwise rightly fought.

During the US Civil War, Professor Francis Lieber of Columbia University drafted a set of guidelines for proper conduct on the battlefield. These were revised by Army officers and issued by President Lincoln as General Orders No. 100. The so-called Lieber Code stated that "the unarmed citizen is to be spared in person, property, and honor as much as the exigencies of war will admit." The Lieber Code also introduced the concept of "military necessity," defined in reference to "measures which are indispensable for securing the ends of the war, and which are lawful according to the modern law and usages of war." In other words, in war (unlike love), all is *not* fair. The conduct of military operations must be necessary *and* legitimate means toward legitimate military ends.

241

In the just war tradition, the moral basis for discrimination is not the question of guilt or innocence. When a state resorts to war unjustly, its soldiers are not considered complicit in the crime of aggression, and its civilians are not assumed to be innocent. Immunity from attack, as James Turner Johnson explains, derives instead from the simple fact that noncombatants cannot do physical harm to an opposing army. Those who can do harm, soldiers, may be targeted—even though some may strenuously object to the war they are fighting, as is often the case. This same principle of discrimination affords combatants a set of rights once they are taken prisoners of war, as detailed in the last chapter. Because POWs can no longer do harm, they may not be killed while captive and must be released when the war comes to an end. The war they fought before being taken prisoner may have been a war of aggression, but they are not responsible for that crime. If they are lawful combatants, if their conduct on the battlefield conforms to the laws of war, then the principle of discrimination gives them the right to surrender—in effect, to become noncombatants immune from attack. Injured soldiers, those who can no longer do harm, acquire this same immunity.

Jus in bello also requires *proportionality*. In almost any war, some civilians will unavoidably be killed if military targets are hit, and just war theorists accept some number of civilian deaths as a byproduct of striking a military target. But civilians are not to be killed without limit, even unintentionally. In war, the good sought and the harm done must be proportionate, suggesting that discrimination alone—*targeting* only combatants—is not enough to make a military action morally acceptable. Lieber's notion of military necessity implies much the same thing; it seems to require both an absolutist and a consequentialist determination.

Discrimination and proportionality come together in the *jus in bello* concept of "double effect." Military actions undertaken during wartime have both good and bad effects. In order for those actions to be just, the good effect must outweigh the bad. Double effect requires that noncombatant immunity be observed—that the bad effect be unintended—but also requires that this unintended bad effect be proportional to the legitimate objective of the military action. The use of toxic defoliants by the United States in Vietnam probably violated the principle of double effect. The aim was legitimate: to reveal enemy forces, allowing them to be targeted by aerial bombardment. But the use of defoliants like Agent Orange caused long-term environmental damage and contamination. These bad effects were unintended, but we might ask whether destroying the enemy's cover was worth the adverse and foreseeable consequences for the civilian population.

Did the 2003 Iraq War, as prosecuted by the US and British militaries, meet the requirements of *jus in bello*? There can be little doubt the US and British forces went to great lengths to discriminate between combatants and noncombatants. That meant avoiding targets like roads, bridges, and other public works, as well as hospitals, schools, and mosques. It also meant relying heavily on precision-guided munitions. Despite these and other precautions, it is likely that the order of magnitude of civilian deaths reached into the thousands. High-end estimates, not surprisingly, included figures released by various antiwar groups and were in the tens of thousands. Most estimates of war deaths count only direct and immediate fatalities from violence. They do not include deaths that may occur even years after the war, from disease, malnutrition, the plight of refugees, and the destruction of health, water, and sanitation services. These indirect and long-term deaths may be ten or twenty times as numerous. Whatever the actual tally, it surely provides a sharp contrast to the comparatively low number of US and British combat deaths during the invasion and (so far) the postinvasion period.

The ethical question of whether due care was exercised in shielding the civilian population from collateral damage will dog the war's defenders as long as the most commonly accepted fatality estimates remain in the high thousands. The *political* problem of civilian casualties, on the other hand, was rather effectively addressed by what some called "the weaponization of reporters." Correspondents embedded with military units leading the invasion provided a steady stream of information about the conduct of combat operations, and virtually none of it showed US or British soldiers deliberately killing or otherwise abusing civilians (aside from some manhandling during house-to-house searches). It could be that the "embeds" provided a deterrent to improper conduct. But it is also the case that their reporting put on display the fairly impressive moral and legal restraints indoctrinated in the course of modern military training. Either way, most of the criticism derived from *jus in bello* thinking is likely to be reserved for the air campaign. This never became a political problem because its effects were much less visible to US and other Western audiences—whose opinions, frankly, counted for more—than was the conduct of the ground campaign.

In the introduction to the last chapter, we mentioned the moral dilemma known as "dirty hands," and suggested that it confounds the effort to fight a war on global terrorism according to the dictates of just war theory. But the dilemma is not new; it has frequently presented itself in the more familiar context of interstate war. Michael Walzer's example—like Dershowitz's in the last chapter, a controversial one—is the Allied bombing of German cities during World War II. Walzer argues that from 1940 to 1942 Britain faced a "supreme emergency." The emergency existed because the prospect of Britain's defeat by German forces was clear and present; British defenses were on the verge of collapse. The emergency was supreme because, from the perspective of those contemplating defeat, the anticipated disaster of a Nazi victory was "literally beyond calculation, immeasurably awful." That compound prospect, the disaster of Nazi victory and its imminence, left the

[handwritten note: Chemical warfare? ↳ lasting effects]

British no other choice but to bomb German cities, an unambiguous viola-tion of *jus in bello*. Walzer's position is that a supreme emergency may pro-vide an excuse for the commission of a wrongful act, but not a justification. Those who justify such acts fail to see their dirty hands.

Critics of Walzer's position on the Allied bombings either refuse to admit exceptions to noncombatant immunity or dispute, as an empirical matter, his assessment of the Nazi danger. As a principle, though, supreme emergency sets the bar very high. The US bombing of Japanese cities did not clear it, in Walzer's view, nor did the Allied bombing of German cities after 1942 when Britain's defeat no longer loomed. It is when entire politi-cal communities are in jeopardy that we have a supreme threat. Only then is Walzer willing to abandon the absolute prohibition on targeting civilians and base military necessity on a consequentialist calculation that seeks to preserve one political community at the expense of members of another.

James Turner Johnson, in the first of a two-part analysis included in this volume, highlights characteristics of contemporary armed conflicts that have served to undermine noncombatant immunity. One is that group identi-ties are important to those fighting each other, to the point where everyone sharing the identity (ethnic, tribal, religious, etc.) of one's enemy becomes a target, whether or not they are engaged in actual fighting. Another feature of these conflicts is that they are often fought not just by professional soldiers, but also by paramilitaries, volunteer corps, and roving gangs, and the disci-pline and military training, including training in the law of war, can be lim-ited or nonexistent for the latter groups. These aspects of many modern con-flicts conspire to make them especially brutal and indiscriminate. Fighters may be little concerned about differentiating between combatants and non-combatants, and in fact may target civilian populations intentionally to ter-rorize them or, in the most extreme cases, to displace or destroy them as a group. The campaigns of ethnic cleansing and genocide witnessed during the 1990s in Yugoslavia and in Rwanda showed that *jus in bello* restraints continue to be violated, often blatantly. They also showed that the interna-tional community can be rather unprepared, or unwilling, to do much to stop what everyone recognizes as a gross subversion of international moral-ity and law.

10.2 _____

Protocol I to the Geneva Conventions of 1949

Signed: 1977
In Force: December 7, 1979

■ **Part IV, Section I, Chapter 1:
Basic Rule and Field of Application**

Article 48: Basic Rule

In order to ensure respect for and protection of the civilian population and civilian objects, the Parties to the conflict shall at all times distinguish between the civilian population and combatants and between civilian objects and military objectives and accordingly shall direct their operations only against military objectives. . . .

■ **Chapter 2: Civilians and Civilian Populations**

Article 50: Definition of Civilians and Civilian Population

1. A civilian is any person who does not belong to one of the categories of persons referred to in Article 4 A (1), (2), (3) and (6) of the Third Convention and in Article 43 of this Protocol. In case of doubt whether a person is a civilian, that person shall be considered to be a civilian.

2. The civilian population comprises all persons who are civilians.

3. The presence within the civilian population of individuals who do not come within the definition of civilians does not deprive the population of its civilian character.

Article 51: Protection of the Civilian Population

1. The civilian population and individual civilians shall enjoy general protection against dangers arising from military operations. To give effect to this protection, the following rules, which are additional to other applicable rules of international law, shall be observed in all circumstances.

2. The civilian population as such, as well as individual civilians, shall not be the object of attack. Acts or threats of violence the primary purpose of which is to spread terror among the civilian population are prohibited.

3. Civilians shall enjoy the protection afforded by this Section, unless and for such time as they take a direct part in hostilities.

4. Indiscriminate attacks are prohibited. Indiscriminate attacks are:

(a) Those which are not directed at a specific military objective;

(b) Those which employ a method or means of combat which cannot be directed at a specific military objective; or

(c) Those which employ a method or means of combat the effects of which cannot be limited as required by this Protocol; and consequently, in each such case, are of a nature to strike military objectives and civilians or civilian objects without distinction.

5. Among others, the following types of attacks are to be considered as indiscriminate:

(a) An attack by bombardment by any methods or means which treats as a single military objective a number of clearly separated and distinct military objectives located in a city, town, village or other area containing a similar concentration of civilians or civilian objects; and

(b) An attack which may be expected to cause incidental loss of civilian life, injury to civilians, damage to civilian objects, or a combination thereof, which would be excessive in relation to the concrete and direct military advantage anticipated.

6. Attacks against the civilian population or civilians by way of reprisals are prohibited.

7. The presence or movements of the civilian population or individual civilians shall not be used to render certain points or areas immune from military operations, in particular in attempts to shield military objectives from attacks or to shield, favor or impede military operations. The Parties to the conflict shall not direct the movement of the civilian population or individual civilians in order to attempt to shield military objectives from attacks or to shield military operations.

8. Any violation of these prohibitions shall not release the Parties to the conflict from their legal obligations with respect to the civilian population and civilians, including the obligation to take the precautionary measures provided for in Article 57. . . .

Article 54: Protection of Objects
Indispensable to the Survival of the Civilian Population

1. Starvation of civilians as a method of warfare is prohibited.

2. It is prohibited to attack, destroy, remove or render useless objects indispensable to the survival of the civilian population, such as foodstuffs, agricultural areas for the production of foodstuffs, crops, livestock, drinking water installations and supplies and irrigation works, for the specific purpose of denying them for their sustenance value to the civilian population or to the adverse Party, whatever the motive, whether in order to starve out civilians, to cause them to move away, or for any other motive.

3. The prohibitions in paragraph 2 shall not apply to such of the objects covered by it as are used by an adverse Party:

(a) As sustenance solely for the members of its armed forces; or

(b) If not as sustenance, then in direct support of military action, provided, however, that in no event shall actions against these objects be taken which may be expected to leave the civilian population with such inadequate food or water as to cause its starvation or force its movement.

4. These objects shall not be made the object of reprisals.

5. In recognition of the vital requirements of any Party to the conflict in the defence of its national territory against invasion, derogation from the prohibitions contained in paragraph 2 may be made by a Party to the conflict within such territory under its own control where required by imperative military necessity.

10.3 _____

Fourth Geneva Convention Relative to the Protection of Civilian Persons in Time of War

Signed: August 12, 1949
In Force: October 21, 1950

■ Part I: General Provisions

Article 4

Persons protected by the Convention are those who, at a given moment and in any manner whatsoever, find themselves, in case of a conflict or occupation, in the hands of a Party to the conflict or Occupying Power of which they are not nationals.

Nationals of a State which is not bound by the Convention are not protected by it. Nationals of a neutral State who find themselves in the territory of a belligerent State, and nationals of a co-belligerent State, shall not be regarded as protected persons while the State of which they are nationals has normal diplomatic representation in the State in whose hands they are. . . .

■ Part III, Section I: Provisions Common to the Territories of the Parties to the Conflict and to Occupied Territories

Article 27

Protected persons are entitled, in all circumstances, to respect for their persons, their honor, their family rights, their religious convictions and practices, and their manners and customs. They shall at all times be humanely treated, and shall be protected especially against all acts of violence or threats thereof and against insults and public curiosity.

Women shall be especially protected against any attack on their honor, in particular against rape, enforced prostitution, or any form of indecent assault.

Without prejudice to the provisions relating to their state of health, age and sex, all protected persons shall be treated with the same consideration by the Party to the conflict in whose power they are, without any adverse distinction based, in particular, on race, religion or political opinion.

However, the Parties to the conflict may take such measures of control and security in regard to protected persons as may be necessary as a result of the war.

Article 28

The presence of a protected person may not be used to render certain points or areas immune from military operations.

Article 29

The Party to the conflict in whose hands protected persons may be, is responsible for the treatment accorded to them by its agents, irrespective of any individual responsibility which may be incurred. . . .

▧ Section III: Occupied Territories

Article 50

The Occupying Power shall, with the cooperation of the national and local authorities, facilitate the proper working of all institutions devoted to the care and education of children.

The Occupying Power shall take all necessary steps to facilitate the identification of children and the registration of their parentage. It may not, in any case, change their personal status, nor enlist them in formations or organizations subordinate to it.

Should the local institutions be inadequate for the purpose, the Occupying Power shall make arrangements for the maintenance and education, if possible by persons of their own nationality, language and religion, of children who are orphaned or separated from their parents as a result of the war and who cannot be adequately cared for by a near relative or friend. . . .

Article 51

The Occupying Power may not compel protected persons to serve in its armed or auxiliary forces. No pressure or propaganda which aims at securing voluntary enlistment is permitted.

The Occupying Power may not compel protected persons to work unless they are over eighteen years of age, and then only on work which is necessary either for the needs of the army of occupation, or for the public utility services, or for the feeding, sheltering, clothing, transportation or health of the population of the occupied country. Protected persons may not be compelled to undertake any work which would involve them in the obligation of taking part in military operations. The Occupying Power may not compel protected persons to employ forcible means to ensure the security of the installations where they are performing compulsory labor. . . .

Article 53

Any destruction by the Occupying Power of real or personal property belonging individually or collectively to private persons, or to the State, or to other public authorities, or to social or cooperative organizations, is prohibited, except where such destruction is rendered absolutely necessary by military operations. . . .

Article 55

To the fullest extent of the means available to it, the Occupying Power has the duty of ensuring the food and medical supplies of the population; it should, in particular, bring in the necessary foodstuffs, medical stores and other articles if the resources of the occupied territory are inadequate.

The Occupying Power may not requisition foodstuffs, articles or medical supplies available in the occupied territory, except for use by the occupation forces and administration personnel, and then only if the requirements of the civilian population have been taken into account. Subject to the provisions of other international Conventions, the Occupying Power shall make arrangements to ensure that fair value is paid for any requisitioned goods. . . .

Article 56

To the fullest extent of the means available to it, the public Occupying Power has the duty of ensuring and maintaining, with the cooperation of national and local authorities, the medical and hospital establishments and services, public health and hygiene in the occupied territory, with particular reference to the adoption and application of the prophylactic and preventive measures necessary to combat the spread of contagious diseases and epidemics. Medical personnel of all categories shall be allowed to carry out their duties. . . .

Article 58

The Occupying Power shall permit ministers of religion to give spiritual assistance to the members of their religious communities.

The Occupying Power shall also accept consignments of books and articles required for religious needs and shall facilitate their distribution in occupied territory.

Article 59

If the whole or part of the population of an occupied territory is inadequately supplied, the Occupying Power shall agree to relief schemes on behalf of the said population, and shall facilitate them by all the means at its disposal.

Such schemes, which may be undertaken either by States or by impartial humanitarian organizations such as the International Committee of the Red Cross, shall consist, in particular, of the provision of consignments of foodstuffs, medical supplies and clothing. . . .

Article 63

Subject to temporary and exceptional measures imposed for urgent reasons of security by the Occupying Power: (a) recognized National Red Cross (Red Crescent, Red Lion and Sun) Societies shall be able to pursue their activities in accordance with Red Cross principles, as defined by the International Red Cross Conferences. Other relief societies shall be permitted to continue their humanitarian activities under similar conditions; (b) the Occupying Power may not require any changes in the personnel or structure of these societies, which would prejudice the aforesaid activities.

The same principles shall apply to the activities and personnel of special organizations of a non-military character, which already exist or which may be established, for the purpose of ensuring the living conditions of the civilian population by the maintenance of the essential public utility services, by the distribution of relief and by the organization of rescues.

Article 64

The penal laws of the occupied territory shall remain in force, with the exception that they may be repealed or suspended by the Occupying Power in cases where they constitute a threat to its security or an obstacle to the application of the present Convention.

Subject to the latter consideration and to the necessity for ensuring the effective administration of justice, the tribunals of the occupied territory shall continue to function in respect of all offences covered by the said laws.

The Occupying Power may, however, subject the population of the occupied territory to provisions which are essential to enable the Occupying Power to fulfill its obligations under the present Convention, to maintain the orderly government of the territory, and to ensure the security of the Occupying Power, of the members and property of the occupying forces or administration, and likewise of the establishments and lines of communication used by them. . . .

Article 70

Protected persons shall not be arrested, prosecuted or convicted by the Occupying Power for acts committed or for opinions expressed before the occupation, or during a temporary interruption thereof, with the exception of breaches of the laws and customs of war.

Nationals of the Occupying Power who, before the outbreak of hostilities, have sought refuge in the territory of the occupied State, shall not be arrested, prosecuted, convicted or deported from the occupied territory, except for offences committed after the outbreak of hostilities, or for offences under common law committed before the outbreak of hostilities which, according to the law of the occupied State, would have justified extradition in time of peace. . . .

Article 77

Protected persons who have been accused of offences or convicted by the courts in occupied territory, shall be handed over at the close of occupation, with the relevant records, to the authorities of the liberated territory.

10.4 ⎯⎯⎯

Supreme Emergency

Michael Walzer

▓ The Nature of Necessity . . .

. . . If we are to adopt or defend the adoption of extreme measures, the danger must be of an unusual and horrifying kind. Such descriptions, I suppose, are common enough in time of war. One's enemies are often thought to be—at least they are often said to be—unusual and horrifying. Soldiers are encouraged to fight fiercely if they believe that they are fighting for the survival of their country and their families, that freedom, justice, civilization itself are at risk. But this sort of thing is only sometimes plausible to the detached observer, and one suspects that its propagandistic character is also understood by many of the participants. War is not always a struggle over ultimate values, where the victory of one side would be a human disaster for the other. It is necessary to be skeptical about such matters, to cultivate a wary disbelief of wartime rhetoric, and then to search for some touchstone against which arguments about extremity might be judged. We need to make a map of human crises and to mark off the regions of desperation and disaster. These and only these constitute the realm of necessity, truly understood. Once again, I am going to use the experience of World War II in Europe to suggest at least the rough contours of the map. For Nazism lies at the outer limits of exigency, at a point where we are likely to find ourselves united in fear and abhorrence.

That is what I am going to assume, at any rate, on behalf of all those people who believed at the time and still believe a third of a century later that Nazism was an ultimate threat to everything decent in our lives, an ideology and a practice of domination so murderous, so degrading even to those who might survive, that the consequences of its final victory were literally beyond calculation, immeasurably awful. We see it—and I don't use the phrase lightly—as evil objectified in the world, and in a form so potent and apparent that there could never have been anything to do but fight against it. I obviously cannot offer an account of Nazism in these pages. But such an account is hardly necessary. It is enough to point to the historical experience of Nazi rule. Here was a threat to human values so radical that its imminence would surely constitute a supreme emergency; and this example can help us understand why lesser threats might not do so. . . .

[T]he survival and freedom of political communities—whose members share a way of life, developed by their ancestors, to be passed on to their children—are the highest values of international society. Nazism challenged these values on a grand scale, but challenges more narrowly conceived, *if they are of the same kind,* have similar moral consequences. They bring us under the rule of necessity (and necessity knows no rules). I want to stress . . . , however, that the mere recognition of such a threat is not itself coercive; it neither compels nor permits attacks on the innocent, so long as other means of fighting and winning are available. Danger makes only half the argument; imminence makes the other half. Now let us consider a time when the two halves came together: the terrible two years that followed the defeat of France, from the summer of 1940 to the summer of 1942, when Hitler's armies were everywhere triumphant.

■ Overriding the Rules of War

The Decision to Bomb German Cities

There have been few decisions more important than this one in the history of warfare. As a direct result of the adoption of a policy of terror bombing by the leaders of Britain, some 300,000 Germans, most of them civilians, were killed and another 780,000 seriously injured. No doubt, these figures are low when compared to the results of Nazi genocide; but they were, after all, the work of men and women at war with Nazism, who hated everything it stood for and who were not supposed to imitate its effects, even at lagging rates. And the British policy had further consequences: it was the crucial precedent for the fire-bombing of Tokyo and other Japanese cities and then for Harry Truman's decision to drop atomic bombs on Hiroshima and Nagasaki. The civilian death toll from Allied terrorism in World War II must have exceeded half a million men, women, and children. How could the initial choice of this ultimate weapon ever have been defended?

The history is a complex one. . . . I can review it only briefly, attending especially to the arguments put forward at the time by Churchill and other British leaders, and always remembering what sort of a time it was. The decision to bomb cities was made late in 1940. A directive issued in June of that year had "specifically laid down that targets had to be identified and aimed at. Indiscriminate bombing was forbidden." In November, after the

German raid on Coventry, "Bomber Command was instructed simply to aim at the center of a city." What had once been called indiscriminate bombing (and commonly condemned) was now required, and by early 1942, aiming at military or industrial targets was barred: "the aiming points are to be the built-up areas, not, for instance, the dockyards or aircraft factories."[1] The purpose of the raids was explicitly declared to be the destruction of civilian morale. Following the famous minute of Lord Cherwell in 1942, the means to this demoralization were specified: working-class residential areas were the prime targets. Cherwell thought it possible to render a third of the German population homeless by 1943.

Before Cherwell provided his "scientific" rationale for the bombing, a number of reasons had already been offered for the British decision. From the beginning, the attacks were defended as reprisals for the German blitz. This is a very problematic defense, even if we leave aside the difficulties of the doctrine of reprisals. . . . First of all, it appears possible, as one scholar has recently argued, that Churchill deliberately provoked the German attacks on London—by bombing Berlin—in order to relieve pressure on R.A.F. installations, until then the major *Luftwaffe* target. Nor was it Churchill's purpose, once the blitz began, to deter the German attacks or to establish a policy of mutual restraint.[2]

> We ask no favor of the enemy. We seek from them no compunction. On the contrary, if tonight the people of London were asked to cast their votes whether a convention should be entered into to stop the bombing of all cities, the overwhelming majority would cry, "No, we will mete out to the Germans the measure, and more than the measure, that they have meted out to us."

Needless to say, the people of London were not in fact asked to vote on such a convention. Churchill assumed that the bombing of German cities was necessary to their morale and that they wanted to hear (what he told them in a radio broadcast of 1941) that the British air force was making "the German people taste and gulp each month a sharper dose of the miseries they have showered upon mankind."[3] . . .

We must concentrate now on the military justifications for terror bombing, which were presumably paramount in Churchill's mind, whatever he said on the radio. I can discuss these only in a general way. There was a great deal of dispute at the time, some of it technical, some of it moral in character. The calculations of the Cherwell minute, for example, were sharply attacked by a group of scientists whose opposition to terrorism may well have had moral grounds, but whose position, to the best of my knowledge, was never stated in moral terms. Explicit moral disagreement developed most importantly among the professional soldiers involved in the decisionmaking process. These disagreements are described, in characteristic fashion, by a strategic analyst and historian who has studied the British escalation: "The . . . debate had been beclouded by emotion on one side of the argument, on the part of those who as a matter of moral principle objected to making war on civilians."[4] The focus of these objections seems to have been some version of the doctrine of double effect. . . . At the height of the blitz, many British officers still felt strongly that their own air attacks should be aimed only at military targets and that positive efforts should be made to minimize civilian casualties. They did not want to imitate Hitler, but to differentiate themselves from him. Even officers who accepted the desirability of killing civilians still sought to maintain their professional honor: such deaths, they insisted, were desirable "only insofar as [they] remained a by-product of the primary intention to hit a military target. . . ."[5] A tendentious argument, no doubt, yet one that would drastically have limited the British offensive against cities. But all such proposals ran up against the operational limits of the bomber technology then available.

Early in the war, it became clear that British bombers could fly effectively only at night and, given the navigational devices with which they were equipped, that they could reasonably aim at no target smaller than a fairly large city. A study made in 1941 indicated that of those planes that actually succeeded in attacking their target (about two-thirds of the attacking force), only one-third dropped their bombs within five miles of the point aimed at.[6] Once this was known, it would seem dishonest to claim that the intended target was, say, this aircraft factory and that the indiscriminate destruction around it was only an unintended, if foreseeable, consequence of the justified attempt to stop the production of planes. What was really unintended but foreseeable was that the factory itself would probably escape harm. If any sort of strategic bombing offensive was to be maintained, one would have to plan for the destruction that one could and did cause. Lord Cherwell's minute was an effort at such planning. In fact, of course, navigational devices were rapidly improved as the war went on, and the bombing of specific military targets was an important part of Britain's total air offensive, receiving top priority at times (before the June 1944 invasion of France, for example) and cutting into the resources allowed for attacks on cities. Today many experts believe that the war might have ended sooner had there been a greater concentration of air power against targets such as the German oil refineries. But the decision to bomb cities was made at a time when victory was not in sight and the specter of defeat ever present. And it was made when no other decision seemed possible if there was to be any sort of military offensive against Nazi Germany.

Bomber Command was the only offensive weapon available to the British in those frightening years, and I expect there is some truth to the notion that it was used simply because it was there. "It was the only force in the West," writes Arthur Harris, chief of Bomber Command from early 1942 until the end of the war, "which could take offensive action . . . against Germany, our only means of getting at the enemy in a way that would hurt at all."[7] Offensive action could have been postponed until (or in hope of) some more favorable time. That is what the war convention would require, and there was also considerable military pressure for postponement. Harris was hard-pressed to keep his Command together in the face of repeated calls for tactical air support—which would have been coordinated with ground action largely defensive in character, since the German armies were still advancing everywhere. Sometimes, in his memoirs, he sounds like a bureaucrat defending his function and his office, but obviously he was also defending a certain conception of how the war might best be fought. He did not believe that the weapons he commanded should be used because he commanded them. He believed that the tactical use of bombers could not stop Hitler and that the destruction of cities could. Later in the war, he argued that only the destruction of cities could bring the fighting to a quick conclusion. The first of these arguments, at least, deserves a careful examination. It was apparently accepted by the Prime Minister. "The bombers alone," Churchill had said as early as September 1940, "provide the means of victory."[8]

The bombers alone—that poses the issue very starkly, and perhaps wrongly, given the disputes over strategy to which I have already referred. Churchill's statement suggested a certainty to which neither he nor anyone else had any right. But the issue can be put so as to accommodate a degree of skepticism and to permit even the most sophisticated among us to indulge in a common and a morally important fantasy: suppose that I sat in the seat of power and had to decide whether to use Bomber Command (in the only way that it could be used systematically and effectively) against cities. Suppose further that unless the bombers were used in this way, the probability that Germany would eventually be defeated would be radically reduced. It makes no sense at this point to quantify the probabilities; I have no clear notion what they actually were or even how they might be calculated given our present knowledge; nor am I sure how different figures, unless they were very different, would affect the moral argument. But it does seem to me that the more certain a German victory appeared to be in the absence of a bomber offensive, the more justifiable was the decision to launch the offensive. It is not just that such a victory was frightening, but also that it seemed in those years very close; it is not just that it was close, but also that it was so frightening. Here was a supreme emergency, where one might well be required to override the rights of innocent people and shatter the war convention.

Given the view of Nazism that I am assuming, the issue takes this form: should I wager this determinate crime (the killing of innocent people) against that immeasurable evil (a Nazi triumph)? Obviously, if there is some other way of avoiding the evil or even a reasonable chance of another way, I must wager differently or elsewhere. But I can never hope to be sure; a wager is not an experiment. Even if I wager and win, it is still possible that I was wrong, that my crime was unnecessary to victory. But I can argue that I studied the case as closely as I was able, took the best advice I could find, sought out available alternatives. And if all this is true, and my perception of evil and imminent danger not hysterical or self-serving, then surely I must wager. There is no option; the risk otherwise is too great. My own action is determinate, of course, only as to its direct consequences, while the rule that bars such acts is founded on a conception of rights that transcends all immediate considerations. It arises out of our common history; it holds the key to our common future. But I dare to say that our history will be nullified and our future condemned unless I accept the burdens of criminality here and now.

This is not an easy argument to make, and yet we must resist every effort to make it easier. Many people undoubtedly found some comfort in the fact that the cities being bombed were German and some of the victims Nazis. In effect, they applied the sliding scale and denied or diminished the rights of German civilians so as to deny or diminish the horror of their deaths. This is a tempting procedure, as we can see most clearly if we consider again the bombing of occupied France. Allied fliers killed many Frenchmen, but they did so while bombing what were (or were thought to be) military targets. They did not deliberately aim at the "builtup areas" of French cities. Suppose such a policy had been proposed. I am sure that we would all find the wager more difficult to undertake and defend if, through some strange combination of circumstances, it required the deliberate slaughter of Frenchmen. For we had special commitments to the French; we were fighting on their behalf (and sometimes the bombers were flown by French pilots). But the status of the civilians in the two cases is no different. The theory that distinguishes combatants from noncombatants does not distinguish Allied from enemy noncombatants, at least not with regard to the question of their murder. I suppose it makes sense to say that there were more people in German than in French cities who were responsible (in some fashion) for the evil of Nazism, and we may well be reluctant to extend to them the full range of civilian rights. But even if that reluctance is justified, there is no way for the bombers to search out the right people. And for all the others, terrorism only reiterates the tyranny that the Nazis had already established. It assimilates ordinary men and women to their government as if the two really made a totality, and it judges them in a totalitarian way. If one is forced to bomb cities, it seems to me, it is best to acknowledge that one has also been forced to kill the innocent.

Once again, however, I want to set radical limits to the notion of necessity even as I have myself been using it. For the truth is that the supreme emergency passed long before the British bombing reached its crescendo. The greater number by far of the German civilians killed by terror bombing were killed without moral (and probably also without military) reason. The decisive point was made by Churchill in July of 1942:[9]

> In the days when we were fighting alone, we answered the question: "How are you going to win the war?" by saying: "We will shatter Germany by bombing." Since then the enormous injuries inflicted on the German Army and manpower by the Russians, and the accession of the manpower and munitions of the United States, have rendered other possibilities open.

Surely, then, it was time to stop the bombing of cities and to aim, tactically and strategically, only at legitimate military targets. But that was not Churchill's view: "All the same, it would be a mistake to cast aside our original thought . . . that the severe, ruthless bombing of Germany on an ever-increasing scale will not only cripple her war effort . . . but will create conditions intolerable to the mass of the German population." So the raids continued, culminating in the spring of 1945—when the war was virtually won—in a savage attack on the city of Dresden in which something like 100,000 people were killed. Only then did Churchill have second thoughts. "It seems to me that the moment has come when the question of bombing German cities simply for the sake of increasing the terror, though under other pretexts, should be reviewed. . . . The destruction of Dresden remains a serious query against the conduct of Allied bombing."[10] Indeed it does, but so does the destruction of Hamburg and Berlin and all the other cities attacked simply for the sake of terror.

The argument used between 1942 and 1945 in defense of terror bombing was utilitarian in character, its emphasis not on victory itself but on the time and price of victory. The city raids, it was claimed by men such as Harris, would end the war sooner than it would otherwise end and, despite the large number of civilian casualties they inflicted, at a lower cost in human life. Assuming this claim to be true (I have already indicated that precisely opposite claims are made by some historians and strategists), it is nevertheless not sufficient to justify the bombing. It is not sufficient, I think, even if we do nothing more than calculate utilities. For such calculations need not be concerned only with the preservation of life. There is much else that we might plausibly want to preserve: the quality of our lives, for example, our civilization and morality, our collective abhorrence of murder, even when it seems, as it always does, to serve some purpose. Then the deliberate slaughter of innocent men and women cannot be justified simply because it saves the lives of other men and women. I suppose it is possible to imagine situations where that last assertion might prove problematic, from a utilitarian perspective, where the number of people involved is small, the proportions are right, the events hidden from the public eye, and so on. Philosophers delight in inventing such cases in order to test out our moral doctrines. But their inventions are somehow put out of our minds by the sheer scale of the calculations necessary in World War II. To kill 278,966 civilians (the number is made up) in order to avoid the deaths of an unknown but probably larger number of civilians and soldiers is surely a fantastic, godlike, frightening, and horrendous act. . . .

▓ The Limits of Calculation

Hiroshima

. . . [T]he President and his advisors believed the Japanese to be fighting an aggressive war and, moreover, to be fighting it unjustly. Thus Truman's address to the American people on August 12, 1945:

> We have used [the bomb] against those who attacked us without warning at Pearl Harbor, against those who have starved and beaten and executed American prisoners of war, against those who have abandoned all pretense of obeying international laws of warfare. We have used it in order to shorten the agony of war. . . .

Here again, the sliding scale is being used to open the way for utilitarian calculations. The Japanese have forfeited (some of) their rights, and so they cannot complain about Hiroshima so long as the destruction of the city actually does, or could reasonably be expected to, shorten the agony of war. But had the Japanese exploded an atomic bomb over an American city, killing tens of thousands of civilians and thereby shortening the agony of war, the action would clearly have been a crime, one more for Truman's list. This distinction is only plausible, however, if one renders a judgment not only against the leaders of Japan but also against the ordinary people of Hiroshima and insists at the same time that no similar judgment is possible against the people of San Francisco, say, or Denver. I can find . . . no way of defending such a procedure. How did the people of Hiroshima forfeit their rights? Perhaps their taxes paid for some of the ships and planes used in the attack on Pearl Harbor; perhaps they sent their sons into the navy and air force with prayers for their success; perhaps they celebrated the actual event, after being told that their country had won a great victory in the face of an imminent American threat. Surely there is nothing here that makes these people liable to direct attack. (It is worth noting, though the fact is not relevant in judging the Hiroshima decision, that the raid on Pearl Harbor was directed entirely against naval and army installations: only a few stray bombs fell on the city of Honolulu.)

But if Truman's argument on August 12 was weak, there was a worse one underlying it. He did not intend to apply the sliding scale with any precision, for he seems to have believed that, given Japanese aggression, the Americans could do anything at all to win (and shorten the agony of war). Along with most of his advisors, he accepted the "war is hell" doctrine; it is a constant allusion in defenses of the Hiroshima decision. Thus Henry Stimson:[11]

> As I look back over the five years of my service as Secretary of War, I see too many stern and heartrending decisions to be willing to pretend that war is anything else but what it is. The face of war is the face of death; death is an inevitable part of every order that a wartime leader gives.

And James Byrnes, Truman's friend and his Secretary of State:[12] " . . . war remains what General Sherman said it was." And Arthur Compton, chief scientific advisor to the government:[13]

> When one thinks of the mounted archers of Ghengiz Khan . . . the Thirty Years War . . . the millions of Chinese who died during the Japanese invasion . . . the mass destruction of western Russia . . . one realizes that in whatever manner it is fought, war is precisely what General Sherman called it.

And Truman himself:[14] "Let us not become so preoccupied with weapons that we lose sight of the fact that war itself is the real villain."

War itself is to blame, but also the men who begin it . . . while those who fight justly merely participate in the hell of war, choicelessly, and there are no moral decisions for which they can be called to account. This is not, or not necessarily, an immoral doctrine, but it is radically one-sided; it evades the tension between *jus ad bellum* and *jus in bello;* it undercuts the need for hard judgments; it relaxes our sense of moral restraint. When he was choosing a target for the first bomb, Truman reports, he asked Stimson which Japanese cities were "devoted exclusively to war production."[15] The question was reflexive; Truman did not want to violate the "laws of war." But it wasn't serious. Which American cities were devoted exclusively to war production? It is possible to ask such questions only when the answer doesn't matter. If war is hell however it is fought, then what difference can it make how we fight it? And if war itself is the villain, then what risks do we run (aside from the strategic risks) when we make decisions? The Japanese, who began the war, can also end it; only they can end it, and all we can do is fight it, enduring what Truman called "the daily tragedy of bitter war." I don't doubt that that was really Truman's view; it was not a matter of convenience but of conviction. But it is a distorted view. It mistakes the actual hellishness of war, which is particular in character and open to precise definition, for the limitless pains of religious mythology. The pains of war are limitless only if we make them so—only if we move, as Truman did, beyond the limits that we and others have established. Sometimes, I think, we have to do that, but not all the time. Now we must ask whether it was necessary to do it in 1945.

The only possible defense of the Hiroshima attack is a utilitarian calculation made without the sliding scale, a calculation made, then, where there was no room for it, a claim to override the rules of war and the rights of Japanese civilians. I want to state this argument as strongly as I can. In 1945, American policy was fixed on the demand for the unconditional surrender of Japan. The Japanese had by that time lost the war, but they were by no means ready to accept this demand. The leaders of their armed forces expected an invasion of the Japanese main islands and were preparing for a last-ditch resistance. They had over two million soldiers available for the fighting, and they believed that they could make the invasion so costly that the Americans would agree to a negotiated peace. Truman's military advisors also believed that the costs would be high, though the public record does not show that they ever recommended negotiations. They thought that the war might continue late into 1946 and that there would be as many as a million additional American casualties. Japanese losses would be much higher. The capture of Okinawa in a battle lasting from April to June of 1945 had cost almost 80,000 American casualties, while virtually the entire Japanese garrison of 120,000 men had been killed (only 10,600 prisoners were taken).[16] If the main islands were defended with a similar ferocity, hundreds of thousands, perhaps millions, of Japanese soldiers would die. Meanwhile, the fighting would continue in China and in Manchuria, where a Russian attack was soon due. And the bombing of Japan would also continue, and perhaps intensify, with casualty rates no different from those anticipated from the atomic attack. For the Americans had adopted in Japan the British policy of terrorism: a massive incendiary raid on Tokyo early in March 1945 had set off a firestorm and killed an estimated 100,000 people. Against all this was set, in the minds of American decision-makers, the impact of the atomic bomb—not materially more damaging but psychologically more frightening, and holding out the promise, perhaps, of a quick end to the war. "To avert a vast, indefinite butchery . . . at the cost of a few explosions," wrote Churchill in support of Truman's decision, "seemed, after all our toils and perils, a miracle of deliverance."[17]

"A vast indefinite butchery" involving quite probably the deaths of several million people: surely this is a great evil, and if it was imminent, one could reasonably argue that extreme measures might be warranted to avert it. Secretary of War Stimson thought it was the sort of case I have already described, where one had to wager; there was no option. "No man, in our position and subject to our responsibilities, holding in his hand a weapon of such possibilities for . . . saving those lives, could have failed to use it."[18]

This is by no means an incomprehensible or, on the surface at least, an outrageous argument. But it is not the same as the argument I suggested in the case of Britain in 1940. It does not have the form: if we don't do *x* (bomb cities), they will do *y* (win the war, establish tyrannical rule, slaughter their opponents). What Stimson argued is very different. Given the actual policy of the U.S. government, it amounts to this: if we don't do *x, we* will do *y.* The two atomic bombs caused "many casualties," James Byrnes admitted, "but not nearly so many as there would have been had our air force continued to drop incendiary bombs on Japan's cities."[19] Our purpose, then, was not to avert a "butchery" that someone else was threatening, but one that we were threatening, and had already begun to carry out. Now, what great evil, what supreme emergency, justified the incendiary attacks on Japanese cities?

Even if we had been fighting in strict accordance with the war convention, the continuation of the struggle was not something forced upon us. It had to do with our war aims. The military estimate of casualties was based not only on the belief that the Japanese would fight almost to the last man, but also on the assumption that the Americans would accept nothing less than unconditional surrender. The war aims of the American government required either an invasion of the main islands, with enormous losses of American and Japanese soldiers and of Japanese civilians trapped in the war zones, or the use of the atomic bomb. Given that choice, one might well reconsider those aims. Even if we assume that unconditional surrender was morally desirable because of the character of Japanese militarism, it might still be morally undesirable because of the human costs it entailed. But I would suggest a stronger argument than this. The Japanese case is sufficiently different from the German so that unconditional surrender should never have been asked. Japan's rulers were engaged in a more ordinary sort of military expansion, and all that was morally required was that they be defeated, not that they be conquered and totally overthrown. Some restraint upon their war-making power might be justified, but their domestic authority was a matter of concern only to the Japanese people. In any case, if killing millions (or many thousands) of men and women was militarily necessary for their conquest and overthrow, then it was morally necessary—in order not to kill those people—to settle for something less. . . . If people have a right not to be forced to fight, they also have a right not to be forced to continue fighting beyond the point when the war might justly be concluded. Beyond that point, there can be no supreme emergencies, no arguments about military necessity, no cost-accounting in human lives. To press the war further than that is to re-commit the crime of aggression. In the summer of 1945, the victorious Americans owed the Japanese people an experiment in negotiation. To use the atomic bomb, to kill and terrorize civilians, without even attempting such an experiment, was a double crime.

These, then, are the limits of the realm of necessity. Utilitarian calculation can force us to violate the rules of war only when we are face-to-face not merely with defeat but with a defeat likely to bring disaster to a political community. But these calculations have no similar effects when what is at stake is only the speed or the scope of victory. They are relevant only to the conflict between winning and fighting well, not to the internal problems of combat itself. Whenever that conflict is absent, calculation is stopped short by the rules of war and the rights they are designed to protect. Confronted by those rights, we are not to calculate consequences, or figure relative risks, or compute probable casualties, but simply to stop short and turn aside.

■ Notes

1. Noble Frankland, *Bomber Offensive: The Devastation of Europe* (New York: Ballantine Books, 1970), p. 41.

2. Quoted in George Quester, *Deterrence Before Hiroshima: The Airpower Background of Modern Strategy* (New York: Wiley, 1966), p. 141.

3. Quoted in Angus Calder, *The People's War, 1939–1945* (New York: Pantheon Books, 1969), p. 491.

4. F. M. Sallagar, "The Road to Total War: Escalation in World War II," Rand Corporation Report (1969), p. 127.

5. Ibid., p. 128.

6. Frankland, *Bomber Offensive*, pp. 38–39.

7. Arthur Travers Harris, *Bomber Offensive* (London: Collins, 1947), p. 74.

8. Calder, *The People's War*, p. 229.

9. Winston S. Churchill, *The Second World War*, vol. 4: *The Hinge of Fate* (New York: Houghton Mifflin, 1950), p. 770.

10. Quoted in Quester, *Deterrence Before Hiroshima*, p. 156.

11. "The Decision to Use the Atomic Bomb," *Harpers Magazine* (February 1947), repr. in *The Atomic Bomb: The Great Decision*, ed. Paul R. Baker (New York: Holt Rinehart, 1968), p. 21.

12. James F. Byrnes, *Speaking Frankly* (New York: Harper, 1947), p. 261.

13. Arthur Holly Compton, *Atomic Quest, a Personal Narrative* (New York: Oxford University Press, 1956), p. 247.

14. Harry S. Truman, *Mr. Citizen* (New York: Random House, 1960), p. 267.

15. Robert C. Batchelder, *The Irreversible Decision, 1939–1950* (Boston: Houghton Mifflin, 1962), p. 159.

16. Ibid., p. 149.

17. Winston S. Churchill, *The Second World War*, vol. 6: *Triumph and Tragedy* (Boston: Houghton Mifflin, 1962), p. 639.

18. "The Decision to Use the Atomic Bomb," p. 21.

19. Byrnes, *Speaking Frankly*, p. 264.

10.5 _____

Maintaining the Protection
of Non-Combatants (Part 1)

James Turner Johnson

■ The Problem of Warfare on Non-Combatants

All warfare imposes a burden of harm on non-combatants. This burden may be relatively light, as when the citizens of a nation engaged in a faraway war fought by mercenaries are taxed to support that war. The weight is heavier when the soldiers are drawn from the same population that is at war, whether by volunteering or by a draft. And of course it is heaviest of all on people caught up in the swirl of war, whose lives and livelihoods are disrupted, whose property may be damaged, destroyed, or taken away, and who may have no say in their ultimate fate as their nation's boundaries are changed or even obliterated by the outcome of the war. These burdens increase as the magnitude of war itself increases. Modern warfare has often been criticized because of its scale: the numbers of people drawn into its armies, the destructive power of its weapons, its global reach.

Still, these burdens are of a different kind from those imposed by warfare in which either or both belligerent parties consciously make no distinction between non-combatants and combatants or, worse yet, in which one or both belligerents target non-combatants directly as a method of war. Either sort of warfare tends to place a disproportionately heavy load on non-combatants, for a variety of reasons: military personnel may be better sheltered from armed attack, while non-combatants are more exposed and vulnerable; military personnel may have preferred access to good food and medical care; military personnel are able to fight back, a fact that may deter attacks on them while redirecting an attacking force to the softer targets represented by non-combatants. When no distinction is made between enemy combatants and enemy non-combatants, the non-combatants suffer disproportionately. When non-combatants are chosen as preferred targets, this burden of suffering becomes heaviest of all.

In these comments, I make two assumptions which are of fundamental moral importance and are central to the argument of this article. The first is that it is right and morally necessary to distinguish between non-combatants and combatants in a society at war. This would perhaps seem obvious to many people; yet it has often been challenged theoretically by people who argue that this distinction is meaningless in modern wars and, directly to the point of the present article, it is often denied both in theory and in practice in contemporary armed conflicts, especially those involving ethnic, religious, or other similar differences. The second assumption from which I am proceeding is that it is right and morally necessary to distinguish direct, intended harm toward non-combatants from indirect, unintended harm. This is the concept usually called the "rule of double effect" in moral discussions. In the following sections, I examine both of these assumptions—and the challenges to them—in some detail, and I depend on them throughout the discussion below. . . .

The Moral Basis of the Combatant–Non-Combatant Distinction: Challenges to That Distinction

In moral terms, in war it is the enemy's engagement in activity that aims to do me harm that gives me the right to do harm to him. That is, it is actions, not hostile sympathies or simple membership of a group with which one's own is in conflict, that justify the use of force: force is justified as a response to threat or use of force. Of course, much more needs to be said that qualifies and restricts this right, and just war tradition as a whole defines such qualifications and restrictions. In the present context, though, it is important to observe that the distinction between combatants and non-combatants follows directly from the above rationale: in the most basic terms, this is the distinction between those members of the enemy society or party who are engaged in such activity and those who are not. We may examine this concept more closely by considering three lines of challenge to the combatant–non-combatant distinction found in contemporary discussion.

First, some critics argue that, in modern societies, the degree of integration between civilian and military functions is so tight that whatever the theoretical difference, no practical distinction can be made between the two. The employee of the electric power company, it is observed, serves civilian and military users alike, as does the operator for the telephone company. So does the worker on the factory line who cans fruits and vegetables. All these, and others in other tasks all across the society, are argued to be implicitly contributing to the military effort of a country at war. By extension, so are those people who support them physically and emotionally, such as members of their families.

This line of argument has a certain plausibility, but it goes too far in its claims. In its effort to draw military and non-military activities as closely together as possible, it overlooks or collapses all possibility of distinctions having to do with degree of cooperation in specifically military activities. Yet not only is it in fact possible to make such distinctions, but they are also morally meaningful. There really is a difference between, for example, a worker in a munitions factory and one engaged in processing food that is distributed alike to the civilian population and members of the military forces. While there may be some cases of ambiguity, these do not justify a general decision that warfare today must be indiscriminate. As Paul Ramsey once observed, in thinking about how to wage modern war morally, the distinction between combatants and non-combatants does not have to be clear on a person-by-person basis: "We do not need to know *who* or *where* the non-combatants are" but only "*that* there are non-combatants—even 'only small children and the helpless, sick and aged'—in order to know the basic moral difference between limited and total war."[1]

Another line of attack goes still further in denying the idea of a distinction between non-combatants and combatants. This argument is that among one's enemies, all—regardless of age, relative health or helplessness, or degree of involvement in political decisionmaking or military activity— may be assumed to support the war, and thus all may be rightly targeted. This kind of argument identifies the entire enemy society or party, and not just its armed forces or its responsible political leadership, as the foe. While it takes different forms, perhaps the most virulent is the identification of all members of another ethnic or linguistic group, tribe, or religion as equally the enemy. When to this is added the identification of one's own cause with ultimate right, and the contrary cause as ultimately wrong, then the members of the enemy group have lost all rights to fair treatment and even to life itself. The problem with this position is that it loses sight of what it is in war that confers the right on one person to do harm to another: the threat of harm that this person represents. Contrary beliefs or different ethnicities or languages or citizenship do not in themselves constitute such a threat.

A third line of challenge to the idea of a combatant–non-combatant distinction makes reference to the alleged inherent destructiveness and indiscriminate character of modern weaponry and thus of modern warfare as such. This argument has most flourished as a means of attack on nuclear weapons and on war itself in the age of such weapons. On this position, though the weapons of war have become so destructive that they are inherently indiscriminate, in order to fight wars, belligerents have to make use of them. Thus, modern wars *necessarily* can make no distinction between non-combatants and combatants.

There are three sorts of problems with this argument. First, it overgeneralizes: not all contemporary weapons are so grossly destructive as to be able to be called indiscriminate, but rather, some are exceedingly accurate and of relatively low yield, while others are hand weapons of the same sort that have been used in wars for centuries. The second problem is that this conception makes war into a kind of technological determinism in which human decisions have no role—for not all uses of grossly destructive weapons are indiscriminate, and not all uses of less destructive ones are discriminate; the difference is how belligerents choose to use them. The third problem is that it entirely misses the point of the indiscriminateness found in contemporary armed conflicts, in which the warfare waged against noncombatants makes use of knives, clubs, and handguns, which are not inherently indiscriminate.

Despite its problems, this line of argument does raise an important point: some means of war are in fact *mala in se*—i.e. their use is morally justified under no circumstances whatsoever. Their use constitutes, *prima facie,* a violation of the moral limits that should be observed in war, and such use may be a war crime. A considerable international consensus outlaws weapons of mass destruction for this reason. Yet it is morally important to keep in mind that mass destruction does not require such weaponry but can be achieved by quite ordinary arms, such as knives, clubs, and handguns or by deprivation of food, water, and shelter—methods widely exemplified in contemporary conflicts. Again, the central moral problem is how the available weapons of war are employed against the enemy and, because of this, it is fundamental to distinguish noncombatants from combatants.

All these arguments have positive and negative versions; that is, at one end of the spectrum of debate over morality and war, they are used to argue for a kind of warfare in which protection of non-combatants has no place, and at the other end of this spectrum they are used to argue that war itself has become so awful that it must be abolished. Taken together, these produce an argument from false alternatives: if there is to be war, it must be total war; if total war is to be avoided, then war as an institution must be abolished. There is, however, a third alternative: that the conduct of war can be subjected to moral limits. Distinguishing between non-combatants and combatants is a basic and necessary step in this direction.

Direct Versus Indirect, Intended Versus Unintended Harm

The second fundamental assumption I make in discussing the moral protection due non-combatants is between direct, intended harm to persons deserving such protection and harm that comes to them indirectly and unintentionally in the way of war. There are two qualifiers here, and both are important. The ideal would be an attack on a legitimate military target with a weapon able to be aimed accurately at it and of destructive power no greater than needed to destroy the intended target. It is possible, even in such a tightly construed case, that some harm to non-combatants might result from the attack. More realistically, since in war the ideal possibility is normally not the rule, a direct attack on a legitimate target by a weapon not *mala in se* and with the intention to destroy only that target will often produce collateral harm to non-combatants. Tragic though such harm may be, this is a different kind of case from one in which there is a direct attack on non-combatants (for example, if refugees are rounded up and shot) or when the intention includes the harming or killing of non-combatants (as when a conscious choice is made for a particular target because significant numbers of non-combatants live in the immediate vicinity). The difference between the former kind of case and these two latter kinds is explained by what moralists call the rule of double effect.

Michael Walzer provides an inclusive statement of this rule in terms of four conditions:

> (1) The act is good in itself or at least indifferent, which means, for our purposes, that it is a legitimate act of war;
> (2) The direct effect is morally acceptable—the destruction of military supplies, for example, or the killing of enemy soldiers;
> (3) The intention of the actor is good, that is, he aims only at the acceptable effect; the evil effect is not one of his ends, nor is it a means to his ends;
> (4) The good effect is sufficiently good to compensate for allowing the evil effect. . . .[2]

A major issue is how to measure the actor's intention. This may, in the first instance, be addressed by determining what orders were given, what targets were specified, and so on. The existence of orders to target non-combatants directly is clear evidence that harm suffered by them as a result was not indirect and unintended but direct and intended. But lacking such evidence, whether right intention is present can also be judged by considering whether the actual action is plausibly consistent with a good intention on the part of the agent. Thus, after further consideration, Walzer tightens the requirement as to intention, phrasing it in terms of a required "double intention" both not to do evil and to seek actively to minimize any evil done:

> (3) The intention of the actor is good, that is, he aims narrowly at the acceptable effect; the evil effect is not one of his ends, nor is it a means to his ends, and, aware of the evil involved, he seeks to minimize it, accepting costs to himself.[3]

What is important here is not only the specifying of a "double intention" but the recognition that intention may be judged by the form of the act. . . .

The Moral Obligation to
Non-Combatants: During Armed Conflict

. . . [T]he point is that not all the harm done in warfare, especially not all the killing that occurs during war, is morally the same. There are two real differences that matter morally: first, between harm done to non-combatants and harm done to combatants, and second, between direct, intentional harm to non-combatants and that which indirectly and unintentionally accompanies justifiable acts of war.

What is morally wrong about the practice of much contemporary warfare is that it denies these assumptions in one or another way, either treating the above differences as meaningless, as when all members of a particular ethnic group or religion are defined as equally the enemy and equally targets for armed force, or the even worse case of deliberate attacks on non-combatants as a way of defeating the enemy. . . .

▓ War on Non-Combatants . . .

While examples of intentional, direct targeting of non-combatants can be found in warfare from any period, such targeting has been characteristic of much recent armed conflict, and it has been particularly so in the forms that armed conflicts have taken since the end of the Cold War. As a century has ended in which impressive steps have been taken in defining legal protections for non-combatants during war, a pressing problem for the new century is how to ensure the actual protection from harm of non-combatants caught in the midst of such struggles.

Distinctive Features of Contemporary Armed Conflict
Contemporary armed conflicts have not, in the first place, been formally constituted wars between sovereign states, but conflicts of other sorts, often within the borders of existing states. In some contemporary conflicts (e.g. Rwanda), the struggle may be over dominance and rule within the state, while in other cases (e.g. Croatia, Bosnia) it may be over the secession of an element of an existing state in order to form a new one. In either case, the government (or governments in the case of conflicts over secession) of the state in question may be one of the parties to the fighting, but may not be sufficiently powerful to ensure protection of non-combatant citizens, or it may itself be a source of attacks directed against non-combatants.

A second feature of contemporary armed conflicts is that special importance has typically been attached to particular differences of identity between the parties fighting each other. These differences may or may not correspond to the categories of membership in "national, ethnical, racial or religious groups" specified in the Genocide Convention, but they function in much the same way, providing a basis for ascribing guilt by association to all persons whose identity marks them as enemies, regardless of whether they have any active involvement in the fighting or not.

A third characteristic typical of such conflicts is that they have been intensely territorial, becoming defined, by one or both parties, as zero-sum games in which the entire enemy group must be not only defeated militarily and/or dominated politically, but also killed or otherwise removed from one's own territory.

A fourth characteristic of such conflict, different in kind from the first three, is that the actual fighters may include a variety of kinds of individuals, armed groups, and paramilitary forces as well as soldiers theoretically subject to military discipline. It is through military discipline that states at war impose restraint on the conduct of their armed forces and can responsibly seek to enforce behavior in accord with the laws of armed conflict and of humanity. While a disciplined military force may of course be used as an instrument of warfare against enemy non-combatants, a special problem of contemporary armed conflict is that many of the persons under arms take part in the fighting for private reasons—for example, because of old feuds or to pursue criminal activities—and may operate essentially as they please in the areas through which they move. A further sort of problem is posed when paramilitary police are employed as part of a fighting force in a civil conflict, since many societies give more license to such forces in dealing with members of the general population than international law gives to military forces in dealing with non-combatants.

When the combatant–non-combatant distinction is ignored, and, more pointedly, when a non-combatant population is itself directly and intentionally targeted as a method of waging war, not only does the burden of the war shift decisively to them, but also the means of war more broadly shift toward being uncontrolled, as enemy soldiers engage in murder, rape, torture, pillage, and wanton destruction with the aim of creating terror among those persons who know they may be the next victims. In the worst cases, when such warfare aims not only to dominate the enemy population, but also to remove them entirely as a competitor, warfare against non-combatants may escalate to mass killings and even genocide.

All these characteristics have been present in different degrees throughout the range of recent armed conflict. In the following discussion, I examine warfare against non-combatants as exemplified in two recent conflicts, those in Rwanda-Zaire and the former Yugoslavia [see Chapter 11.2 of this volume], which provide important and highly visible examples of deliberate attacks on non-combatants as a means of waging war. I will focus on specific forms of assaults on non-combatants in each of these conflicts: in the case of Rwanda-Zaire, instigation of genocide and war against refugees; in the case of the former Yugoslavia, war against population centers.

Both these conflicts have taken place between rival groups with enmities entwined with their distinctive historical identities. In such cases, there is a temptation for both participants and outsiders to think of any single period of fighting as simply one stage in the much longer struggle, and to justify atrocious conduct today by referring to past atrocities. This has been the case in the conflicts in both Rwanda-Zaire and the former Yugoslavia. Yet while it is important to understand the history of a conflict, it is mistaken to press this into an argument that any particular conflict is somehow inevitable because of past enmity or that moral judgment on the conduct of present-day fighters must be relativized by consideration of past evils. To the contrary, historical rivals are in no way predestined to keep on fighting each other forever; rather, examples abound of past rivals overcoming their enmity and living together peacefully and cooperatively. Moreover, new conflicts may arise between peoples that have no history of rivalry or conflict, as historical conditions change. While knowledge of a history of rivalry or conflict can help to inform understanding of the group identities of particular parties to a new conflict, it would be shortsighted to blame such new conflict simply on those identities. Similarly, a history of rivalry and conflict in no way legitimizes atrocious conduct by participants in present-day conflicts in the name of past wrongs. To think morally about any given conflict, it must be seen in its own particularity; to think morally about the conduct of participants in such a conflict, their actions must be examined and judged in their own right by reference to common standards of morality, not by reference to the wrongs done by other persons in other periods of fighting in some time past.

War on Refugees in the Rwanda-Zaire Conflict

The first specific conflict with which we are concerned here is that which took place between Hutu and Tutsi in the territory of Rwanda and Eastern Zaire (now the Democratic Republic of Congo) between 1994 and 1997. Forms of warfare against non-combatants developed during two phases of this conflict: first at its inception, when the problem was of a generalized massacre of Rwandan citizens perpetrated along ethnic lines; the second, beginning somewhat later, when both sides in this conflict engaged in direct, intentional attacks on refugee camps. The attacks on non-combatants at the beginning of this conflict have already had much attention directed to them, and are the focus of ongoing war crimes investigations and prosecutions. My focus below is on the kind of warfare against non-combatants that developed later in the conflict, after a Tutsi military force operating from bases in Uganda had succeeded in retaking Rwanda and establishing a new government.

At this stage in the conflict, the critical development of the fighting shifted to Zaire, where approximately one million Hutu had fled the violence, including both non-combatant refugees and former militiamen who had sheltered themselves among the non-combatants during flight. Indeed, the Hutu combatants continued to shelter themselves in this way, even after they regained enough military strength to begin launching raids across the border back into Rwanda in 1996. Both the presence of masses of refugees and the military activity of the Hutu fighters led to sporadic conflict with the Zairian army. In October 1996, the ongoing war was widened when elements of the new Tutsi-dominated Rwandan army entered Zaire in response to the cross-border raids of the Hutu fighters. This became the nucleus of a larger force, which also included Zairian Tutsi and members of the smoldering Zairian rebellion led by Laurent Kabila. Thus, the cross-border fighting became a springboard to a broadened civil war in Zaire, one which culminated in the overthrow of the Mobutu government and the installation of Kabila as head of state of the country now renamed the Democratic Republic of Congo.

During this stage in this broad and changing conflict, a pattern of direct, intentional warfare against refugees developed. Since the radical Hutu militiamen were working from bases in the refugee camps and sheltering themselves by the presence of the refugees, the Rwandan incursion force initially directed its military actions against the camps near the border. While non-combatant refugees were sometimes harmed in these attacks, the repatriation of significant numbers of Hutu refugees into Rwanda under the eyes of Tutsi military and civilian officials (as well as those of UN and non-governmental organization observers involved in relief efforts) argues that, at this point in the conflict, a war directed at the refugees themselves had not yet begun. But as the conflict continued, the Hutu fighters in retreat moved large numbers of refugees with them, using the refugees both for support and as shields. Discrimination between the militiamen and their human shields became progressively more difficult, and at some point the refugees themselves began to be targeted. Thus, the initial action against the radical Hutu militiamen based in the refugee camps evolved into a war against the Hutu refugees as a whole. The process escalated as the war wore down: the worst reported atrocities occurred after the rebel victory in Zaire and the establishment of the Kabila government. According to reports from the war, the shift in targeting seems to have been a conscious policy choice. . . .

But the war against refugees did not remain one-sided. Bands of remaining Hutu fighters reconstituted themselves in the northeastern part of Congo, near the Rwandan border, strengthened by recruits from dominantly Hutu northwestern Rwanda. By the final months of 1997, these Hutu fighters had regained enough strength to engage in terrorist attacks from their bases in Congo across the border into northwestern Rwanda, specifically targeting refugee camps in that area inhabited by both Tutsi and repatriated Hutu non-combatants.

Serious moral issues are found at many stages in this developing conflict. While the radical Hutu militiamen bear moral blame for their actions throughout the conflict (for their initial and later violence against non-Hutu non-combatants and their later violation of the rights of Hutu non-combatants by intentionally coercing them and drawing them into the circle of harm), the deliberate killing of Hutu refugees in mass by Rwandan and Zairian forces is blameworthy in itself and was not justified by earlier radical Hutu actions. Furthermore, any conscious policy decision to pursue the deaths of the refugee masses as such would in itself have been a serious violation of the moral and legal obligations of the opposing military forces and the rights of the non-combatants in morality and international law. The later reconstitution of Hutu militia bands in Zaire/Congo and their own attacks into Rwanda against both Tutsi and repatriated Hutu refugees added a further dimension to the pattern of warfare against refugees, but do not alter the moral issues.

Can these attacks on non-combatants be justified in any way? First, it must be asked whether the attacks on the refugee camps (by both sides in this conflict) were cases in which the rule of double effect applies. Such moral reasoning fits the initial limited attacks by Rwandan forces against the Hutu camps in Zaire, where the Hutu fighters had intentionally based themselves among genuine refugees, and no attack could be made against them without secondary, unintended harm to the non-combatants in the camps. But, subsequently, the camps as such became the object of attack, with all their inhabitants targeted indiscriminately for death; here, the deaths of the Hutu non-combatants were directly intended, not an undesired secondary effect of an otherwise legitimate military action. It is equally clear that the attacks by Hutu militiamen against refugee settlements in Rwanda (similar to the original violence against non-Hutus in 1994) were directly intended. Both sorts of attacks have involved face-to-face killing of individuals one by one, by other individuals armed with hand weapons. No effort was made by the combatants on either side to spare non-combatants; to the contrary, the evidence is that they were deliberately targeted as victims.

Three other possible mitigations must also be examined. First, can the targeting of refugees in this conflict be regarded as justified retaliation for earlier atrocities? The answer must be no: acts of retaliation in armed conflicts should respect the same moral (and legal) restraints that bear on all military actions. Second, does the fact that, during the Zairian phase of the conflict, the Hutu non-combatant refugees in some respects served the purposes of the Hutu fighters excuse military action against them? Again the answer must be no, because the refugees had no real say in this; they were not complicit by choice but out of coercion. The possibility of complicity in any case does not apply to the Hutu militia's attacks on refugee camps in Rwanda beginning in 1997, since these refugees were segregated in their own non-defended compounds. They were chosen as targets precisely because they were unable to fight back. Third, does the fact that the non-combatants on both sides may be assumed to have sympathized with the goals of the fighters of their own ethnic group justify their being targeted? No, because even if they did have such sympathies (by no means obvious, and impossible to prove), mere sympathy or shared ethnic identity does not make one a combatant.

In short, while there are moral considerations that may allow some harm to non-combatants during war, none of these excuse what took place in this conflict. Not only the initial massacre of non-Hutu Rwandans which initiated this conflict in 1994, but also the later attacks against refugees after the war had spread into Zaire during 1996–97, violated the moral immunity from direct, intended harm owed to non-combatants and the rules of international law providing for the protection of non-combatants. Both at its beginning and at its end, this was a conflict in which the killing of non-combatants was not incidental and undesired but a deliberately chosen means of carrying on the war. . . .

■ Notes

1. Paul Ramsey, *The Just War: Force and Political Responsibility* (New York: Charles Scribner's Sons, 1968), emphasis in original.

2. Michael Walzer, *Just and Unjust Wars: A Moral Argument with Historical Illustrations* (New York: Basic Books, 1977), p. 153.

3. Ibid., p. 155.

11 Blockades and Sanctions

11.1

Introduction
The Editors

Considerable conceptual and practical confusion surrounds the subject of sanctions and the related use of the tactics of blockade and siege. At law, a sanction is normally understood to be a punishment; to violate a criminal law, for example, is to be liable to sanction or punishment. Moreover, the severity of the sanction ordinarily rides with the gravity of evil linked to the criminal violation. It is a commonplace of jurisprudence to suppose that the punishment should fit the crime, and criminal law usually stipulates the range of penalty to which one is liable upon a finding of criminal responsibility or culpability.

Things are neither so clear nor so straightforward in international law and politics, however, where the notion of a sanction has become connected to both punishment and to a form of what might be called diplomatic or even military coercion. Reliance upon the use of sanctions to pressure states to change certain policies deemed immoral or intolerable by those states employing such measures is generally considered preferable to open warfare. But the use of the strategies of blockade and siege are often considered in international law to be acts of war. Both blockade and siege are strategies that might be applied in war, but they might also be applied as a coercive measure to pressure a state into some sort of policy change without a formal declaration of war. Whether such use constitutes an act of war, particularly if it is undertaken unilaterally by one state against another, remains a matter of some dispute. As an alternative to war, the use of sanctions is often thought justifiable on the grounds that it is an effective way to pressure states into compliance with moral norms short of the horrors associated with war.

Actions that qualify as sanctions short of war usually involve an economic policy designed and intended to pressure the sanctioned state into compliance with morally desirable norms by imposing an economic hardship on the targeted state. They may be extended to blockades and sieges as a way of making economic sanctions effective and meaningful. There are, however, a few distinctions of some importance that should be made to clarify the moral legitimacy and propriety of the use of sanctions short of war.

First, it is important to be clear on whether a sanction violates the sovereign integrity of the targeted state or whether it falls within the range of legitimate interstate action. When sanctions function as a form of coercion, which they often do, they are morally suspect in principle. But purported sanctions that fall within the realm of legitimate interstate action are, from a moral point of view, reasonable methods of pursuing a state's foreign policy. Suppose, for example, the United States withholds Most-Favored-Nation trading status from China on the grounds that it opposes what it considers to be Chinese human rights violations. This might be regarded as a sanction against China premised upon its disregard for human rights, and it may be inspired by the US desire to see the Chinese change their policy on this score. While such unilateral action might seem coercive, it is really not so since the United States is not under any obligation to extend Most-Favored-Nation trading status to China or any other state, though it may have economic and political reasons for wanting to do so. This, in short, is a legitimate form of interstate behavior; the United States is at liberty to decide for itself with whom it will trade on a Most-Favored-Nation basis. Actions of a state that conform to the sovereign rights of the state in its dealings with others thus qualify as sanctions in only the most nominal sense.

We move to a different level of moral difficulty, however, when purported state sanctions extend beyond the reach of legitimate interstate activity. The US blockade of Cuba during the Cuban Missile Crisis offers a salient example. By sealing off Cuban waters the United States effectively ̀interfered with the right of Cuba to engage in interstate trade with third parties, and while the United States hoped to pressure the Soviet Union into removing its missiles from Cuba by its actions, the coerciveness of its measures may still be a cause for moral concern.

The moral legitimacy of the use of sanctions as a form of arm-twisting diplomacy may have its strongest moral justification when it is done under the auspices of some international or regional authority, like the United Nations, and for the purpose of pressuring an offending state into compliance with international moral norms. Though coercive diplomacy is inherently suspect, it offers a reasonable alternative to warfare, particularly when undertaken in a multilateral fashion, to bring about desirable moral ends. Yet even here there are causes for concern. Economic sanctions, and perhaps more particularly blockades and sieges, are likely to bring rather indiscriminate harm to citizens and noncombatants in the targeted states. From a moral point of view, then, there is reason to question whether the end that prompts the sanctions justifies the use of a means that may, and likely will, cause harm to innocent others, and whether the end is in fact achievable by the use of such means.

In defense of the legitimate use of sanctions as an alternative to warfare, Drew Christiansen and Gerard Powers propose five criteria that should be met before sanctions are justified. First, the sanctions should be a response to a "grave injustice." Second, those states that impose the sanction should have "reasonable prospects" for an acceptable political settlement. Third, sanctions should be imposed only when less coercive strategies for achieving a desirable outcome have been exhausted. Fourth, those states imposing sanctions should "make provision for basic human needs." And finally, the sanctions imposed should be proportionate, that is, the harm they produce should not exceed the good to be achieved by them. To this, they add the recommendation that sanctions be multilaterally imposed rather than unilaterally imposed.

Of these basic conditions, the fourth is perhaps the most problematic. The condition requires the extension of humanitarian aid to guarantee that sanctions do not deprive innocent citizens of basic human needs or create conditions that might generate disease, malnutrition, or otherwise endanger the welfare of the general population of the targeted state. The great difficulty here is that economic sanctions are a blunt instrument for achieving desired political reform; their effects almost invariably fall indiscriminately upon the population of the targeted state. It may prove extremely difficult for those states imposing such sanctions to recognize either the extent or the gravity of the impact their actions will have on innocent populations. In the event sanctions do cause death, starvation, or disease amongst innocent populations, it is certainly reasonable to insist that sanctioning states change their practices and policies. But by this point, the damage has already been done.

Practical questions about the ability to satisfy the fourth condition introduced by Christiansen and Powers raise the possibility that the use of sanctions will prove ineffective. If humanitarian conditions are introduced to minimize the suffering of innocent populations, it remains an open question whether the sanctions, suitably qualified, will have any chance of achieving their desired objective. But it would seem that practical political efficacy should also be a condition of the justified use of sanctions. If sanctions have no, or an extremely small, chance of success, their use can hardly be justified in the face of the harm they cause. If mitigating the harm to innocents reduces the chances that the sanctions will succeed in having the desired outcome, the harm they might still cause would be difficult to justify on consequentialist grounds.

Of course, there is also no necessary guarantee that sanctions causing more extreme and unmitigated forms of human suffering will achieve their desired end either. The belief that sanctions that cause reasonably severe harm to a state's population may have a greater chance of bringing about compliance with the desires of the states imposing the sanction may simply underestimate the extent to which government officials actually care about the welfare of their citizens and/or the ability of the citizenry to pressure their government into acceding to international demands.

In addition to these practical difficulties, there is the additional moral concern that derives from the fact that sanctions invariably impose hardships on innocents not necessarily implicated in the wrongful behavior of their state. The just war distinction between combatants and noncombatants is of importance in this regard. If noncombatants ought not be harmed during warfare, why should they become legitimate subjects of harm by means of the use of coercive sanctions, in the name of finding an alternative to warfare? The crudeness of sanctions, as a coercive device, again raises difficulties. While Christiansen and Powers correctly note that a state's citizen population may at times be implicated in the wrong perpetrated by its government, this is not necessarily, perhaps not even typically, the case. If this population could not be justifiably harmed in open warfare, why then should it be subjected to harm in the name of avoiding the evils of warfare?

Concern for the welfare of noncombatants is reason, as James Turner Johnson argues, to qualify the use of the strategies of blockade and siege during wartime. Noncombatants should have an opportunity to avoid or escape the harm caused by such drastic measures. But the logic of this argument would seem to extend to the use of sanctions as a strategy to avert warfare as well. Yet this might reduce significantly the effectiveness of such strategies, thus rendering the use of sanctions as a form of coercive diplomacy rather pointless.

11.2 ___

Maintaining the Protection
of Non-Combatants (Part 2)

James Turner Johnson

■ War on Non-Combatants

Forms of Warfare Against Non-Combatants
in the Conflicts in Bosnia and Kosovo

Attacks on groups of refugees have also been a prominent feature of the conflicts in the former Yugoslavia, but here I wish to focus on another form of direct, intentional warfare on non-combatants: attacks on population centers. I will discuss two forms of such warfare: the conduct of sieges against Bosnian cities and, much more briefly, the destruction of towns and villages in Kosovo.

Siege warfare raises particular and pressing moral problems, but it is largely ignored in recent writing on the ethics of war. Among contemporary theorists, Michael Walzer has been the only major contributor to ethical analysis of war to have directly treated the subject of sieges. Many of the concerns arising from strategic air bombing arise also in sieges, and it is possible to extrapolate moral reasoning from the one to the other; yet there are also moral questions specific to sieges, and these deserve to be examined directly. Military theory, similar to moral analysis, has largely ignored siege warfare or treated it only indirectly. International law, as noted above, has sought to prevent certain kinds of military actions that might be employed in sieges, notably bombardment of undefended places and damage to cultural property. But, as in moral thought, the focus of concern has not been sieges as such, and the provisions set in place do not address the full range of moral problems raised by siege warfare.

What is morally critical in siege warfare, as in other forms of war, is the degree to which non-combatants in the besieged place are themselves directly and intentionally targeted by the besiegers. Siege warfare is not inherently war on non-combatants. Walzer makes this point early in his discussion of sieges, employing two examples from Jewish history. The first, Josephus's account of the Roman siege of Jerusalem in AD 72, tells of horrific suffering and death in a sealed-off city deprived of food. Josephus comments, "that is what [a siege] is meant to be like," and explains what he means: "The death of the ordinary inhabitants of the city is expected to force the hand of the civilian or military leadership. The goal is surrender; the means is not the defeat of the enemy army, but the fearful spectacle of the civilian dead."[1] This is a depiction of siege warfare as direct, intentional warfare on non-combatants. But Walzer does not give Josephus the last word. Rather, he turns to a normative counter-example, the Talmudic law of sieges as summarized by Maimonides in the 12th century: "When siege is laid to a city for the purpose of capture, it may not be surrounded on all four sides, but only on three, in order to give an opportunity for escape to those who would flee to save their lives."[2] This is a quite different understanding of a siege, one in which the besiegers intentionally seek to allow non-combatants the opportunity to avoid harm from attacks on the city's defenses. Though this may increase the risk to the besieging army (since the same opening allows for supply and reinforcement, if any is available), it is in line with the requirements of double-effect reasoning applied to non-combatant protection. Nor is increased risk a foregone conclusion: it is also possible that the defending force may use the same route to withdraw, giving the objective to the besiegers at less cost to themselves.

In any case, this conception of the proper conduct of siege warfare is strikingly different from that of Josephus, in which causing the suffering and death of non-combatants is itself the means of conducting the siege. The Talmudic model, by contrast, seeks deliberately to protect non-combatants from such suffering and death during the course of a siege. Those who remain may be harmed by the besiegers' efforts to take the city, but this harm should not be aimed at them directly and should not be intentional on the part of the besiegers. Those non-combatants who do not leave the besieged place are simply in the way of legitimate acts of war.

But this is not the entire story, as Walzer's discussion also recognizes. Non-combatants who remain in the city, where they are in the way of harm, may be there for various reasons, and these reasons are morally important. The purest case for moral analysis using the double-effect rule is that of non-combatants who freely decide to remain, perhaps because this is, after all, where they live. These remain non-combatants, and they may not be targeted directly and intentionally, though it is not morally wrong if they are harmed indirectly and unintentionally by military actions from the besiegers. But there are other reasons why civilians may be present. If the civilians in the besieged place participate materially in its defense, whether voluntarily or involuntarily (for example, by digging a ditch or building a wall to assist the defense), they lose their non-combatant status while they are at this work, but not when they are going about their regular lives at home, in their civilian work, or in civilian shelters. A further possibility is that inhabitants of the besieged place have been prevented from leaving by the defending force, which has forced them to remain to be used as shields, as labor, or as a source of supply for the soldiers (a case similar to that of the Hutu refugees discussed above); in this case, the defending force bears a measure of the blame for harm to the non-combatants, but the attackers still have an obligation, both in morality and in the law of war, to avoid targeting them directly and intentionally. Finally, there is the possibility that the non-combatants cannot realistically leave the besieged place. This may be because the besiegers have closed the circle around the place and driven back everyone who tries to leave (the possibility that most closely matches what Josephus took to be the normative way of carrying on a siege), or else they have so devastated the surrounding countryside that would-be refugees know they could not survive if they left. Related to this last possibility is another, not mentioned by Walzer, that the non-combatant population remaining in the besieged place has been enlarged by refugees driven in by the attacks of the besiegers and is unable to leave for the same reason. In trapping the inhabitants and driving in refugees, the besiegers bear the entire responsibility for harm to these non-combatants, since they could choose to provide a way to leave for those who wish to do so.

A siege is warfare against non-combatants, then, in any one of three cases. The first is what Josephus described and what we have just discussed: when the besiegers encircle the besieged place and prevent non-combatants from leaving as a way to weaken and ultimately defeat the defenders by causing harm to the non-combatants present. This targets the defenders through the non-combatants, effectively reversing the logic of double-effect reasoning. In the second place, a siege is also warfare against non-combatants when the besiegers adopt disproportionately destructive means that utterly devastate the city, with the aim of causing the defenders to yield the place in order to save it from such devastation. This second case exemplifies what international lawyer Tom Farer calls the "master principle" of "no Carthaginian peace": no destruction that strikes at the basis of non-combatant life after the conflict is over, when all are non-combatants.[3] The moral reasoning here recognizes that protection due non-combatants in war includes not only their persons, but also the circumstances on which non-combatant life depends. Direct, intentional devastation of that which is necessary for non-combatant life is itself a form of warfare against non-combatants, a violation of the moral principle of discrimination on which non-combatant immunity is based. If siege warfare proceeds by means of such devastation, it is warfare against non-combatants. The third case is that in which the non-combatants in the besieged place are directly targeted, as when their homes, schools, hospitals, or other public places are intentionally bombarded, or when individual non-combatants going about their daily lives are subjected to sniper fire. As we shall see, the sieges of the Bosnian cities provide examples of all three of these forms of warfare against non-combatants.

In mid-1995, when the Bosnian Serb forces' attacks on the eastern cities of Gorazde, Zepa, and Srebrenica began, they already had encircled these places and put them under siege. As government-held enclaves in the midst of enemy-held territory, these cities had become refugee centers for non-combatants who had been intentionally and directly made refugees by the policy of "ethnic cleansing" in smaller towns and rural areas. The designation of the eastern cities as "safe havens" by the UN, together with the presence of nominal forces of UN peacekeepers, was intended to neutralize these places for the purposes of the conflict. Yet the reality was a great deal more ambiguous: the UN forces, small and lightly equipped, were mainly a symbolic presence, and were not actually able to control or defend the areas assigned to them. Moreover, these same cities harbored Bosnian government forces, who by their presence compromised the supposedly neutral status of the cities, and the UN peacekeepers lacked sufficient capability to police them. Thus, despite the formal "safe haven" status of these areas, their real character was mixed due to the continuing presence and activity of pro-government forces. Had they not been there, the areas in question would have been militarily more vulnerable, but their non-combatant status would have been unambiguous. The presence of the pro-government forces gave the Serb forces their rationale for attacking the enclaves, though this was an excuse rather than a serious reason, since the government fighters, cut off from the main government-held areas, posed little, if any, offensive threat and turned out not even to have enough strength to defend the cities from capture when attacked. Moreover, given the policy of "ethnic cleansing" on the part of the Bosnian Serb forces, it is not likely that the "safe havens" would have been left inviolate even without the presence of government forces in them. For this had already proved to be a war carried on significantly by direct, intentional actions against non-combatants. The attacks on the eastern enclaves followed the reverse double-effect logic that I identified above as a mark of immoral conduct of war: not to allow only collateral harm to non-combatants while aiming at the fighters (the standard meaning of double-effect reasoning in war) but, just the opposite, to strike at the fighters *through* harm done to the non-combatants.

The offensives against the enclaves followed patterns set earlier in the war. First, there was an increase in artillery fire, directed not at the defending forces but at the center of the city, where the non-combatants were gathered; the infantry attack and takeover followed. After the capture of Srebrenica and Zepa, males from approximately 10 years of age upwards were separated out and taken prisoner, being treated indiscriminately as combatants, while the women and other children were driven out into other government-held areas already heavily burdened by refugees. Nor did these go unmolested; women from the enclaves told stories of rape and mistreatment, as well as of seeing the bodies of dead men hung from trees. In all, some 23,000 Bosnian Muslim women and children were expelled from Srebrenica, and thousands of men and older boys were captured and executed. Red Cross figures list 6,456 persons missing from Srebrenica after its capture; most of the names are those of men.[4]

Several characteristics of war against non-combatants stand out here: direct firing on areas where non-combatants were concentrated, lack of effort to distinguish combatants from non-combatants in the treatment of men and boys, sexual violence against women, forced expulsion of all non-combatants, even those who had been residents of the fallen cities, and efforts to terrorize pro-government non-combatants by various means. The sieges of the eastern Bosnian cities exemplify war against non-combatants not only in the conduct of the sieges, but also in the behavior of the victors after the enclaves had fallen.

The case of Sarajevo allows a closer look at the practice of war against non-combatants during a siege in progress. In this siege, non-combatants were routinely fired on to keep them from leaving the city or bringing in supplies; apartment blocks, schools, religious buildings, hospitals, and market places were shelled, often at times chosen for maximum presence of members of the population. A random reading of Zlatko Dizdarevic's *Sarajevo: A War Journal* provides a day-by-day sampler of ways in which the conduct of the siege directly targeted the city's non-combatant population: snipers taking shots at "everything that moves"; the gradual improvement of conditions so that "now only a few children get killed every day"; the point at which the snipers began using silencers and dum-dum bullets; the shelling of the building housing his newspaper; the mortar shelling of a downtown Sarajevo street between major streetcar stops, killing 6 people and wounding 20; the hanging of a huge banner from a downtown Sarajevo hotel in order to blind snipers who otherwise would shoot at anyone walking on the street below; shelling for no other purpose than "to obliterate what has already been destroyed"; the intentional cutting off of electricity and water, then firing on the besieged inhabitants as they try to restore the supply or get water from the limited sources left.[5]

All these examples have to do with the harming of non-combatants but, more to the point, they exemplify the direct, intentional targeting of non-combatants in their own right. Some efforts seem more calculated than others: shooting at "everything that moves" is indiscriminate and thus bad enough, but other kinds of actions by the besiegers were clearly aimed specifically at causing civilian harm. One of these is the shelling of a busy downtown street between tram stops in a city in which the streetcar system served the non-combatant population, not the defending forces. Another is the deliberate restriction of water supplies so that people would have to seek water from the remaining sources, where they were targeted by snipers or mortar fire.

Thinking more closely about this last kind of case, it is important to observe that cutting off water and power supplies during sieges is as old as the practice of sieges, and that such actions are allowed, in traditional moral reasoning, by the rule of double effect. Properly, such actions aim at the defenders, even though everyone inside the besieged place is equally harmed by the action. But restricting water, leaving it available only in exposed places, and then firing on non-combatants seeking it is a very different matter. The firing is a plain violation of their non-combatant status, arguing that the original action against the water supply was part of an effort directly and intentionally to target the non-combatants in the city. The whole train of action thus represents a direct and intentional attack on non-combatants, the opposite of the protection they are due.

While a siege, no matter how indiscriminately carried out, ultimately aims at the control of the besieged place by the besiegers for their purposes, a sharper form of war against population centers aims at the complete destruction of such places or at rendering them utterly uninhabitable. In such cases, there is no question of possible double effect; the direct, intended target is the population of the places attacked, and the purpose is to kill the inhabitants or drive them out and make it impossible for them to return. Such means have been employed for the end of "ethnic cleansing" in all stages of the armed conflicts following the breakup of Yugoslavia, and they are exemplified by Dizdarevic's reference to shelling "to obliterate what has already been destroyed"; more recently, both in the months leading up to and during the NATO bombing of Yugoslavia in 1999, the complete destruction of population centers has been a preferred means of war employed by Yugoslav Serb forces against the ethnic Albanian population of Kosovo. . . .

[T]urning non-combatants out of their homes and communities as refugees may be done only as a secondary, not directly intended, effect of action against a justified military target. To carry on a war through directly seeking to create refugees and/or kill members of the enemy's civilian population is another matter entirely: this is warfare against non-combatants, pure and simple. While the sieges of the Bosnian cities discussed above involve elements of such warfare, this has been the main character of the conflict in Kosovo. In *prima facie* terms, it rises to the level of the legal definition of genocide: the people targeted have been chosen because they are Albanians, members of a specific national and religious group; the methods involve three of the kinds of actions forbidden in the Genocide Convention—killing, causing serious bodily or mental harm, and deliberately inflicting conditions of life calculated to bring about the group's destruction in whole or in part. As in the case of the Rwandan killings discussed above, and even without a formal designation of this form of warfare as genocide, direct attacks aimed at destroying population centers so as to kill or drive out their inhabitants violate fundamental moral obligations to persons in an area of conflict who, whatever their sympathies, are simply attempting to live their daily lives in as normal a manner as possible. Such attacks are no less than a form of direct, intentional warfare against non-combatants.

■ Reflections

The increase in the magnitude, deliberateness, and variety of harm to non-combatants in present-day armed conflicts poses a special irony, since this same century has witnessed impressive developments in international law designed to protect non-combatants, as well as intense and sustained moral argument on behalf of such protection. Though I have focused on Western moral tradition in this article, concern to distinguish non-combatants from combatants and to protect them from harm during armed conflict is by no means unique to the West but is recognized in the major moral traditions of other world cultures as well. Nor is the rejection of such warfare limited to elites: media accounts and public consciousness react strongly to violence directed against non-combatants. The problem is not that the need for such protection is poorly realized and not widely accepted, or even that the protections due non-combatants are ill defined; indeed, the irony is that exactly the opposite is the case.

At the same time, however, as noted toward the beginning of this article, arguments persist that the combatant–non-combatant distinction is meaningless in modern warfare, or meaningless in wars over ideology, ethnicity, and religion, or cannot be made a standard for the actual conduct of war because of the great destructive power of modern weapons. If it were only war criminals who made these arguments, they would be of little account; yet, in fact, they are common among well-meaning, highly moral people who see them as supporting their principled opposition to all war. Modern war, they argue, cannot be conducted so as to honor moral distinctions and restraints; therefore war as such must be abolished. Such an argument does not explain why it is presumably possible to abolish war entirely, yet impossible to restrain it within moral limits. Whatever the long-term prospect, in the present day, war has not disappeared, and it does not seem likely to do so in the foreseeable future. This poses an immediate moral obligation: so long as there continue to be armed conflicts, there remains an urgent need to hold fast to the moral and legal restraints defining non-combatant status and seeking to protect non-combatants during such conflict. In reflecting on this need, I want to return to the various arguments against special status and protection for non-combatants identified at the beginning of this article in order to consider further the case against those arguments.

As to whether it is meaningful any more to distinguish non-combatants from combatants during warfare, it is well to recall Paul Ramsey's extensive and careful efforts to explain the moral distinction between the two.[6] The need for care in making this distinction reflects the fact that non-combatants are often mixed with combatants in the way of war, but the moral obligations and permissions toward them differ radically. The line distinguishing non-combatants from combatants may move about from time to time, and there have always been ambiguous cases: particular exceptions may need to be made in any general list of who qualifies as a non-combatant. Moreover, careful attention needs to be paid to uses of the terms "civilian" and "non-combatant" (or "soldier" and "combatant"). They are not, at bottom, interchangeable. The moral issue is the functional role of combatancy or non-combatancy. That functional role of civilians in war has differed not only over history, but also from culture to culture and even, within a culture, from one armed force to another, depending on its structure; it will continue to change according to context. To admit such variations is not to say that the concept of non-combatancy is meaningless or irrelevant today but that it needs to be understood and applied with care and precision in every war in any age, both by combatants and by others—for example, the media and moral analysts—who comment on particular wars. The point of the distinction, after all, is to require active moral effort to identify *who* are non-combatants so as to spare them from direct, intentional harm. When the effort is made for exactly the opposite reason—to identify non-combatants as "soft targets" who can be attacked with impunity as a means of injuring the enemy's ability to fight—then this utterly reverses the moral purpose behind the combatant–non-combatant distinction. In the examples from the conflicts in Rwanda-Zaire and the former Yugoslavia, there is evidence not only of a disregard of non-combatant status and protection, but also of an effort that is just the reverse of what it should be: to target non-combatants directly and intentionally *as non-combatants*.

As to whether the weapons of modern war make it inherently incapable of combatant–non-combatant discrimination, I have focused here on the conflicts in Rwanda, Zaire and the former Yugoslavia precisely because these have *not* involved such weapons. In these conflicts, the weapons used—from sticks to knives to rifles to artillery fire—became indiscriminate in their effects only because the persons using them, or their commanders, made the conscious choice to use them in this way. That choice and the resulting action are immoral in any and every war in any and every time, past, present, or future. Of course, weapons of mass destruction are rightly rejected as *mala in se;* this is because their inherent purpose is to target non-combatants. But even clubs, knives, and bullets become weapons of mass destruction when they are used intentionally and directly to kill masses of people. The point of insisting on a distinction between non-combatants and combatants is exactly to avoid this.

Another justification for attacks against non-combatants is often offered in contemporary warfare and is involved directly in raising the question of genocide: all the members of the opposing group are equally enemies because of ideology, religious belief, ethnicity, or some other cultural factor, so that the combatant–non-combatant distinction does not matter in conflict with them. From the standpoint of moral tradition and international law on war, this is not so much a counter-argument as a denial of the fundamental perspective of both morality and law. This perspective holds that common moral rules apply even in war; the rejection consists in the claim that war is necessarily total. The rationale for distinguishing non-combatants and for treating them differently in war was well put by the 18th-century philosopher, diplomat, and jurist Emmerich de Vattel, who spoke both for the just war tradition he had inherited and for the positive international law whose development he influenced:

> Women, children, the sick and aged, are in the number of enemies. And there are rights with regard to them as belonging to the nation with which one is at war, and the rights and pretensions between nation and nation affect the body of the society, together with all its members. *But these are enemies who make no resistance, and consequently give us no right to treat their persons ill, or use any violence against them, much less to take away their lives.*[7]

In moral terms, the argument that allows warfare to be intentionally directed against ethnically or religiously different non-combatants in such conflicts as those in the former Yugoslavia and Rwanda-Zaire is simply wrong. Only what persons *do* makes them morally liable to have armed force used against them, not what they *believe* religiously or who they are ethnically or culturally.

Holding to the combatant–non-combatant distinction is basic to the moral conduct of war, but moral tradition and international law also seek to limit the means of war so that they do not cause destruction out of proportion to the justified goal. What is wrong to do to combatants certainly should never be done against non-combatants: the rule protecting the former also covers the latter. Consider some examples: combatants rendered helpless are to be made prisoners of war and treated humanely, not killed or tortured; non-combatants, by definition helpless, deserve no less. The use of poison gas or chemical or biological agents against combatants is prohibited in the law of armed conflicts and, more generally, poison is prohibited as *mala in se* in the moral tradition; thus, such means may also not be used against non-combatants. To use means calculated to cause unnecessary suffering against combatants is forbidden in the law of armed conflicts; similarly, such means are forbidden in dealing with non-combatants. These are all examples of the principle of proportionality, and they apply apart from concerns having directly to do with the distinction between non-combatants and combatants. Moreover, proportionality imposes the positive obligation to seek to accomplish justified military objectives by the least destructive means overall. When the distinction between non-combatants and combatants is relatively easy to make in practice, this implies an effort to minimize the harm done to non-combatants in the way of the objective (as in Walzer's "double intention" argument), but even when non-combatants and combatants are inextricably mingled, or even when the idea of a distinction between them is denied, there remains the separate obligation imposed by proportionality: for example, not to destroy a town completely or drive all the inhabitants from an area in order to possess it.

Why should parties to a conflict observe such restrictions on their means of fighting, if their goal is to win? Posing the question this way assumes in advance that winning requires total war. But the moral tradition of just war and the law of armed conflict reject this assumption. They do so not simply as expressions of abstract ideals with no connection to the real demands of warfare or political action; rather, both the moral tradition and the law reflect a rich and varied historical experience of war and of statecraft and, in the case of the law, the rules laid down also express formal agreements by states working out of their own interests and values. Fundamentally, the limits set on the conduct of war by morality and the law of war aim at ensuring that warfare does not destroy everything that is worth living for in peacetime, or make it hard or impossible to return to peace after the end of armed conflict. "[W]e go to war that we may have peace," and not simply for the sake of war, wrote Augustine. He continued with this counsel for the conduct of war: "Be peaceful, therefore, in warring, so that you may vanquish those whom you war against, and bring them to the prosperity of peace."[8] The underlying point, seen clearly by Augustine, is that the way a war is fought determines whether peace can be created once again and, if so, what kind of a peace it can be. Unjust conduct in war works against the achievement of a just peace, that is, a genuine peace. Bringing a conflict to a close in which the parties are able to reach reconciliation and cooperate in rebuilding their society or societies depends importantly on how they fought each other during the armed phase of their dispute.

Thus, both because it is inherently wrong to make war on non-combatants and because of the goal of peace and stability in domestic and international affairs, it is vitally important to maintain the restraints on the conduct of war found in moral tradition and in international law on war. Doing so affects everyone, and so does failure to do so.

▓ Notes

1. Michael Walzer, *Just and Unjust Wars: A Moral Argument with Historical Illustrations* (New York: Basic Books, 1977), p. 161.
2. Ibid., p. 168.
3. Tom J. Farer, *The Laws of War 25 Years After Nuremberg.* International Conciliation, No. 583 (New York: Carnegie Endowment for International Peace, 1971), pp. 16, 53.
4. Jan Willem Honig and Norbert Both, *Srebrenica: Record of a War Crime* (New York: Penguin, 1997), pp. xviii, 65.
5. Zlatko Dizdarevic, *Sarajevo: A War Journal* (New York: Henry Holt, 1994), pp. 104, 108, 119, 130, 131, 138, 144–146.
6. Paul Ramsey, *The Just War: Force and Political Responsibility* (New York: Charles Scribner's Sons, 1968), pp. 153–156.
7. Emmerich de Vattel, *The Law of Nations; or Principles of the Law of Nature* (London, 1740), section 145 (emphasis added).
8. Augustine, *Letter clxxix, To Boniface,* cited in Aquinas, *Summa Theologica,* vols. 1–3 (London: R & T Washbourne; New York: Benziger Brothers), IIa-Ilae, q. 40, a. 1.

11.3 ⸺

Economic Sanctions and the Just-War Doctrine

Drew Christiansen and Gerard F. Powers

■ Consequentialism, Deontology, and the Political Function of Sanctions

It is useful for purposes of moral analysis to distinguish five broad purposes of sanctions: (1) to induce or compel a country to change its domestic polices or even its government, (2) to defend against or prevent illegal or aggressive action, (3) to renounce complicity in illegal or immoral actions, (4) to punish a country, and (5) to symbolically signal disapproval with a country's policies. Much of the commentary on economic sanctions evaluates sanctions solely in terms of how effective they are in achieving the first two objectives. Such commentary represents a purely consequentialist or utilitarian approach to the moral problem of sanctions. . . . [W]hile the moral analysis of economic sanctions ought not be reduced to questions of effectiveness, such treatment will frequently intersect with political appraisals where consequential judgments are salient, as they are when sanctions are imposed to achieve specific changes in government or policy.

Because the last three objectives of sanctions—noncomplicity in evil, punishment of an offending nation, and symbolic disapproval for violation of international standards—are less directly intended to effect specific behaviors of the target country, they raise a set of questions that differentiate the moral from the political arguments about sanctions. If forcing a change in policy or deterring aggression are objectives concerned with efficacy these latter three seek integrity. If the first two objectives call for standard forms of political argument about consequences, the latter three objectives involve primarily deontological justifications, that is, stands based on moral principle with less regard to actual or potential consequences. To be

From "Economic Sanctions and the Just-War Doctrine" by Drew Christiansen, S. J., and Gerard F. Powers. In *Economic Sanctions: Panacea or Peacebuilding in a Post–Cold War World,* ed. David Cortright and George A. Lopez. Copyright © 1995 by Westview Press. Used by permission of Westview Press, a member of Perseus Books, L.L.C.

sure, contemporary schools of ethics, both secular and religious, differ over whether at least some ethical principles are unconditioned and, therefore, are immune from the casuistry of consequential analysis. There are nonetheless significant schools of thought that adhere to deontology. In practice, moreover, individual activists and social movements engaged in influencing social and public policy, groups which political analysis should not overlook, are inclined to be purists who will initiate proposals for deontological reasons and will oppose compromise in attaining solutions. . . .

The third objective uses sanctions to avoid complicity in immoral policies. Characteristically public ethics deals with the morality of acts or policies (e.g., apartheid, massacres, genocide, exploitation), but both ethical theory and common practice also concern themselves with moral agency. When the results are grave enough, states, like people, are held accountable for the indirect consequences of their actions. One traditional moral category is that of complicity or material cooperation—the notion that, even when one is not immediately responsible for a grave moral offense, one is forbidden from cooperating in an act that aids and abets that evil. For example, the denial of Most-Favored-Nation trading status to China as a response to the use of slave labor may be justified on the grounds of noncomplicity in an immoral practice. The deontological concern for renouncing complicity in evil is closely aligned with the use of sanctions to give expression to moral censure for grave and pervasive moral and legal offenses by governments. Campaigns to bring about corporate disengagement from South Africa, in the face of objections that sanctions would be ineffective, may be viewed as moral protests of this sort. They constituted a form of social conduct that demonstrated public condemnation of apartheid.

In the case of punishment, we meet a form of deontological reasoning where acting-on-principle is not exclusively symbolic, as consequentialist critics tend to allege, but also possesses a practical dimension. When used to punish an egregious offense against international order and common morality, sanctions may express international revulsion for certain classes of crimes. On a deontological analysis, for example, some would justify sanctions against Serbia as a punitive expression of international repugnance for ethnic cleansing without regard to its role in reducing the conflict or bringing about a political settlement. Thus, when sanctions are imposed wholly or in part because strong action is regarded as an appropriate response to a grave moral offense—one so abhorrent that it must be punished as a matter of natural justice—the motive (and justification) inclines to the side of acting-on-principle. It is done because it is the morally required response (Greek: *deon*, "it is necessary") in the situation. In other words, some acts (e.g., systematic rape) are simply so abhorrent that they must be punished as a matter of natural justice. A strictly moral (i.e., duty-based) function of sanctions involves a principled concern for the character of a people, namely, to assert a people's human dignity and rights in the face of unjust policies. Gandhi's protest of the salt tax and boycott of British textiles would fall in this category. The Organization of American States' sanctions against Haiti may be regarded as a reaction of the democratic states of the hemisphere against a government imposed by military coup. The sanctions were a collective expression under the Santiago Agreement of the governments' common commitment to democracy.

Even the first two objectives (influencing policy or deterring aggression) may have a deontological dimension. Outside parties may join in rejection of a policy by indigenous groups out of reasons of solidarity, that is, to lend support to groups struggling against some form of injustice. Boycotts, whether of domestic lettuce and grapes or of Salvadorian coffee, are conducted out of motives of solidarity. Effectiveness may or may not be relevant to such protests. Even without results, identification with a just cause may satisfy the protesting party. Solidarity, of course, is more frequently a motive of activist social groups, and less frequently among governments. When interest groups are strong enough, solidaristic commitments can become government policy as well. Pressures brought on the former Soviet Union for the emigration of Jews may be seen as an instance of a solidaristic use of coercive diplomacy at the international level.

In politics, deontologically motivated and justified policies are seldom found in their pure form. Policies undertaken without regard to consequences may prove to have desirable consequences. In democratic political practice, policy design and implementation will inevitably entail doing business with those who have purely consequentialist outlooks. Indeed many activists will themselves have a mixture of deontological and consequentialist ways of thinking. Just-war theory, with its mixture of hard principles and consequentialist reasoning, is one example of this practical complexity. The operative distinction between basic human rights and other less-basic rights, or in UN practice, that between rights of bodily integrity and human rights generally, is another. In the same way, the practical demands of implementing a just-sanctions regime will require moving back and forth between deontological and consequential considerations. The ethical analysis of sanctions must include both a deontological view of public policy choices and consequentialist assessments of effectiveness.

▓ Sanctions: Alternative to War or Alternate Form of War?

Scholars often treat economic sanctions as analogous with acts of war. At times, international law has regarded sanctions as a *casus belli,* and moralists and legal scholars sometimes treat them, along with blockades and sieges, as acts of war. Indeed they do constitute a form of coercive diplomacy, sometimes undertaken as part of a war effort or a prelude to war and other times as an alternative to war. While many of the ethical issues which sanctions raise parallel those found in contemporary just-war analyses, it would be misleading to apply the criteria of just war, without qualification, to the sanctions question. Especially in the cases of concern here—comprehensive sanctions imposed by the United Nations or regional institutions as an alternative to the use of military force—ethicists and policy analysts should be prepared to examine the moral issues of this new phenomenon on their own terms, and be cautious about applying the pre-existing schema used to evaluate wartime blockades. They need to be alert to the limits of analogy and the unique and emergent features of sanctions as a moral phenomenon.

Sanctions as War: Sieges and Blockades

Most contemporary cases use economic embargoes as an alternative to war, but some do not. The widespread use of siege tactics in Bosnia-Herzegovina is evidence of the continued relevance of a just-war analysis when economic coercion is a means of war. The just-war tradition, including the international law of armed combat, is an effort to establish restraints on the use of force and prevent the downward spiral of conflict into "total war." A primary way in which restraint has been established in the conduct of war has been the principle of noncombatant or civilian immunity. In wartime, only military personnel are liable to direct attack because only they bear arms. Civilians and other noncombatants, because they are considered innocent and threaten no one, are immune from direct attack. Just-war analysts generally extend the immunity of civilians in wartime to cases of economic coercion in which the lives of civilians are placed at risk. When wartime blockades are employed, just-war theorists tend to presume that they constitute a long step on the road to total war because they intensify the conflict by making noncombatants, who have no possibility of escape, the victims of attack. As Michael Walzer argues, these blockades, like saturation bombing, may be aimed at the political and military authorities, but they are aimed through the civilian population. From a moral point of view, Walzer contends, the besieger "can risk incidental deaths, but he cannot kill civilians simply because he finds them between himself and his enemies."[1] According to Walzer, noncombatants must be afforded free exit or another form of protection from the indiscriminate effects of sieges and blockades. Such humanitarian provision is, in fact, required by international laws of war.

Sanctions Without War

A plausible case can be made for extending the prohibition on wartime blockades to the kinds of sanctions imposed by the international community against Iraq, Serbia, and Haiti. After all, comprehensive sanctions, in or out of war, can do what just-war theory regards as immoral: inflict serious harm on an entire population to affect political and military authorities. To the extent that sanctions do in fact try to effect change in the policies of a government by inflicting suffering on its people, our moral analysis shares with just-war reasoning a strong presumption against economic coercion unless adequate humanitarian provision is made for the civilian population. Nonetheless, while the analysis of wartime blockades provides a helpful point of departure for thinking about sanctions, dissimilarities in the two cases make it an ultimately inadequate paradigm for moral analysis of comprehensive sanctions. The siege-and-blockade model is even an impediment to evaluating sanctions imposed in a nonwar context. The international community, following Woodrow Wilson, persists in seeing sanctions as different from wartime sieges and blockades.

Let us be clear, the search for an alternative model is not a convenient way to clear the obstacles to a policy we may want, in any case, to carry out. An alternative model is necessary for an explicitly moral reason: for the international community to correct a grave evil in a way that will be less destructive than war. We might then conceptualize economic sanctions in a way that enables us to reason about them as a potentially moral policy option by acknowledging that, while military force, sieges, economic sanctions, and diplomatic pressure are all forms of coercive diplomacy, the differences between these types of coercion are at least as important as the similarities.

We start, then, by considering three characteristics of sanctions that distinguish them from wartime blockades: (1) unlike wartime blockades, these sanctions are not imposed as a form of war but as an alternative to war; (2) some harms caused by sanctions may be justified, either because the affected population has consented to sanctions, or because it shares responsibility with its government for the injustices which warrant sanctions; and (3) with appropriate humanitarian provisos, the harm inflicted by sanctions is not as grievous as the harm of war. We then consider the problem of effectiveness: do sanctions offer a realistic prospect for avoiding war?

Sanctions as an alternative to war. It helps to think of economic sanctions as a policy option independent of active hostility between states or between the international community and an offending state. In this "pure" form, sanctions possess three defensible goals, all of which have foundation in international law and the practice of states: (1) to affirm international standards of conduct; (2) to deter, correct, or punish a grave infraction of the international order; and (3) to do so without recourse to armed force.

In this revised model, what distinguishes economic sanctions from sieges and blockades in wartime is the intention to avoid the use of armed force, as opposed to an intention to multiply the effects of war. Economic sanctions allow for more deliberation and negotiation while avoiding the abrupt lethal and maiming effects of warfare. The availability of sanctions, therefore, increases the nonmilitary options policymakers have at hand, and so raises the threshold for resort to force, thereby strengthening the just-war standard of "last resort." As we discuss below, it is necessary to assess whether, in fact, sanctions do less harm than armed conflict and whether they are effective in achieving their objectives. Nonetheless, the intention to avoid the use of force is, morally speaking, a desirable one. It distinguishes sanctions from wartime blockades, where there is no such intention.

In light of increasing doubts about the efficacy, political viability, and morality of war, the intention to avoid force gains added importance. Military analysts themselves sometimes question the utility of force in contemporary international affairs. If, as some commentators claim, military force is no more than dubiously effective in attaining political ends, then the uncertainty of the nonviolent coercion would be more tolerable morally than the destructiveness of ineffective armed conflict. Moreover, as U.S. military doctrine of overwhelming and decisive force makes the use of force at once less available as a policy tool and morally problematic in terms of the strategies this doctrine justifies, sanctions become not only a moral tool for the conduct of foreign policy, but a practicable one as well. Finally, though the contention is much debated, religious leaders and moralists question the morality of modern warfare on grounds of the disproportionate harm it often entails. Thus, the development of economic sanctions as a tool for the enforcement of international policy in matters of fundamental human importance seems not only desirable, but necessary.

Economic sanctions and the suffering of innocents. Sanctions may be intended and conceived as an alternative to war, but if the harm they cause is like that caused by war, are they, in fact, morally superior to war? And even if the harm caused does not compare with that caused by war, how can one justify imposing even a lesser harm on the civilian population? Skepticism about its effectiveness may be the major policy hurdle for justifying sanctions, but the harm sanctions inflict on the civilian population may be the major moral hurdle to legitimizing sanctions. Writing of the Gulf crisis, James Turner Johnson argues, the more "effective" sanctions were, "the greater their inherent impact on those persons most remote from the wrongdoing of their nation's leaders and least able to bring about change: the poor, the aged, children, the infirm. These are exactly the people who, in war, are regarded most clearly as noncombatants."[2] The case of Iraq, of course, is muddled by the interweaving of sanctions with the use of military force, but Johnson's point is valid in situations short of war as well. If sanctions impose the greatest harm on the most vulnerable in society and those most remote from the wrongdoing, something is wrong. A morally just sanctions regime must take account of the suffering it inflicts on these "innocents." As we shall argue, it can do so in two ways: (1) considering whether the population has assented to sanctions; (2) in the case of comprehensive sanctions, making effective humanitarian provision for the affected population; and (3) adopting a preference for using selective sanctions aimed at governing elites and others complicit in an offending policy.

The impact of sanctions on the civilian population varies in each case, depending upon several conditions: the type of sanctions imposed, the extent to which sanctions are being enforced, the degree to which the target country is self-sufficient in the production of basic commodities, whether adequate humanitarian exemptions are in place, whether the target government uses available resources to mitigate the suffering of its population, and whether the economy is strong. . . .

▓ Ensuring a Just-Sanctions Regime

Acknowledging the moral dilemmas posed by sanctions, we have argued that comprehensive sanctions may be considered as an alternative to war in terms of their intent, the nature of the harm they cause, and their effectiveness, although limited, in resolving problems without recourse to force. This is not to suggest, however, that sanctions may be given blanket moral approval. Far from it. We would propose that a morally legitimate sanctions regime should clearly meet several criteria.

First, imposing sanctions should be a response to a grave injustice committed. Because a comprehensive sanctions regime is a blunt and potent instrument of coercion, it should be imposed only in response to aggression or grave and ongoing injustice. Fundamental international norms must be at stake to warrant resort to this level of coercion. The violation need not be as serious as that necessary to justify the use of military force, but it must meet a high threshold.

Second, parties imposing sanctions should have a commitment to and reasonable prospects for reaching a political settlement. We have argued that the moral legitimacy of a sanctions regime depends, in part, on whether it is used as an alternative to war. That, in turn, requires that it be intended and pursued as an alternative to war; that it has a reasonable prospect of achieving legitimate objectives, instrumental or symbolic; and that it does not cause the grave or irremediable harm of the kind caused by war. It is imperative that any sanctions regime be tied to an abiding commitment to and a feasible strategy for finding a political solution to the problem that justified the imposition of sanctions. As Vatican Secretary of State Cardinal Angelo Sodano has said, "Sanctions—whether in the former Yugoslavia,

Haiti, or Iraq—must also be accompanied by an international commitment to negotiations in order to be legitimate."[3] Without the requisite political will and reasonable prospects for a political solution, sanctions lose much of their moral attractiveness. Sanctions then fail to serve as a tool of international diplomacy and become more like a war of attrition or an excuse for inaction or indifference. The requirement that sanctions be part of a feasible political strategy means that a sanctions regime should have clear and reasonable conditions set for their removal. If it becomes clear that existing sanctions have no reasonable prospect of achieving their objectives and are causing unacceptable harm, they should be lifted.

Third, sanctions should only be imposed when less coercive means have failed. The international community should impose sanctions only if less coercive measures have been tried or are not likely to succeed. If war is the last resort, comprehensive economic sanctions are the penultimate resort. Generally, therefore, sanctions should be pursued as an alternative to and before the use of military force. But sometimes, as in Somalia and Rwanda, the urgency of the situation and the likelihood that sanctions would not work could justify the limited use of military force without first applying economic sanctions. With respect to less coercive measures, this condition also places a twofold burden on the international community. In the short term, it must look to international monitoring, diplomacy, political sanctions, arms embargoes, and similar measures to deal with particular crises before it moves toward imposing economic sanctions. In the long term, the international community has an obligation to develop and strengthen the full range of its collective security mechanisms, so that it can better prevent conflicts and injustices before they arise, and better deal with those that do through means less onerous than sanctions.

Fourth, parties imposing sanctions should make provision for basic human needs. As noted earlier, a basic-rights approach to sanctions necessarily entails a humanitarian proviso. Humanitarian provision can be made by exempting basic commodities and providing humanitarian relief. Protection for the basic rights of citizens in offending countries remains a continuing responsibility of international authorities and other sanctioning parties. When humanitarian exemptions have proven insufficient to prevent the death by starvation or disease of citizens of the targeted country, sanctioning authorities are duty bound to redesign mechanisms for humanitarian provision to make them effective. Further failure to provide for the basic needs of the target-country population would require additional decisions, either to fall back on selected sanctions, to discontinue comprehensive sanctions as morally unworkable, or ultimately to resort to the use of force. Humanitarian exemptions should be defined broadly enough that there can be no threat to human health or life. Broader exemptions than those permitted under existing sanctions regimes could make the enforcement of sanctions more difficult and might diminish the effectiveness of sanctions, but due care for civilian populations seems to require that these added difficulties be accepted if adequate provision is to be made for civilians.

Fifth, sanctions must be proportionate. Another criterion is proportionality. Is the overall harm caused by sanctions outweighed by the good to be achieved by them? This criterion ensures that there always be a relationship between the objectives of sanctions and the kinds of sanctions imposed. The imposition of comprehensive sanctions arguably is a proportionate response to Iraqi aggression against Kuwait or genocide in Bosnia-Herzegovina. Continuance of comprehensive sanctions (as opposed to lesser ones) against Iraq, however, long after Kuwait has been freed, to gain compliance with the few remaining unmet conditions of the cease-fire resolution seems disproportionate. As in war, this condition is inherently difficult to assess. Nevertheless, the proportionality principle, which is firmly rooted in both moral and legal frameworks, places an important limit on what can be done in the name of sanctions. It forces us to look beyond the prospects for achieving our objectives and to assess carefully the harm sanctions are causing. Because the harm caused by sanctions tends to increase and become irreversible the longer sanctions remain in place, proportionality provides a check against imposing sanctions for interminable periods of time.

Finally, the imposition of multilateral sanctions is usually preferable to unilateral sanctions. That economic coercion has been used most effectively and historically by big powers to impose their will on weaker states should give any moralist pause. Our framework might well respond to the moral problem of means: ensuring that the blunt instrument of economic sanctions conforms to moral norms. But sanctions could be imposed in a moral way, yet still be subject to the worst kinds of abuse by unscrupulous states or misguided multilateral organizations. It is not at all surprising that the most vulnerable countries of the developing world have frequently sought international condemnation of boycotts and other forms of "economic warfare" in the name of principles of nonintervention, nondiscrimination, self-determination, and solidarity. As notions of sovereignty, nonintervention and other fundamental principles of international order are redefined and developed, the political and legal limits of sanctions should become clearer. Usually imposing sanctions multilaterally, especially within the collective security framework of the United Nations, tends to reduce the risk that sanctions will be used for unjust purposes. The more sanctions are employed by international institutions rather than individual states, the more there will be a procedural brake on any temptation to misuse sanctions to serve narrow interests of the powerful (as opposed to the interests of justice). That is not to say that multilateralism is a panacea. . . . The need to seek international legitimation can serve as an excuse for not acting when action is justified. It can also serve as a fig leaf for the interests of an uncompromising hegemonic power. Multilateralism for its own sake is not the answer. But multilateralism combined with a commitment to the principles of collective security could at least lower the risk that sanctions could be used by the powerful to bully the vulnerable. . . .

▨ Notes

1. Michael Walzer, *Just and Unjust Wars: A Moral Argument with Historical Illustrations* (New York: Basic Books, 1977), pp. 170–75.

2. James Turner Johnson, "Just-War Tradition and the War in the Gulf," *The Christian Century,* February 6–13, 1991, p. 134.

3. Cardinal Angelo Sodano, Vatican Secretary of State, quoted in *Catholic News Service,* April 7, 1994, p. 1.

11.4 _____

Economic Sanctions and the "Fearful Spectacle of Civilian Dead"

Joy Gordon

Economic sanctions are rapidly becoming one of the major tools of international governance of the post–Cold War era. The UN Security Council, empowered under Article 16 of the UN Charter to use economic measures to address "threats of aggression" and "breaches of peace," approved partial or comprehensive sanctions on only two occasions from 1945 to 1990. By contrast, since 1990 the Security Council has imposed sanctions on eleven nations, including the former Yugoslavia, Libya, Somalia, Liberia, Haiti, and several other nations. However, the U.S. has imposed sanctions, unilaterally or with other nations, far more frequently than any other nation in the world, or any multinational body in the world, including the United Nations. More than two-thirds of the sixty-plus sanctions cases between 1945 [and 1990] were initiated and maintained by the United States, and three-quarters of these cases involved unilateral U.S. action without significant participation by other countries. Thus, while the question of ethical legitimacy has implications for the UN strategies of international governance, it has far greater implications for the U.S., which uses sanctions more frequently and in many more contexts, from trade regimes and human rights enforcement to its efforts to maintain regional and global hegemony.

Sanctions seem to lend themselves well to international governance. They seem more substantial than mere diplomatic protests, yet they are politically less problematic, and less costly, than military incursions. They are often discussed as though they were a mild sort of punishment, not an act of aggression of the kind that has actual human costs. Consequently, sanctions have for the most part avoided the scrutiny that military actions would face, in the domains of both politics and ethics. . . .

Because it is now clear that sanctions can do fully as much human damage as warfare, it seems to me critical that we begin applying a higher level of scrutiny than has been the case since the end of World War I.

From "Economic Sanctions, Just War Doctrine, and the 'Fearful Spectacle of the Civilian Dead'" by Joy Gordon. _CrossCurrents,_ vol. 49, no. 3. Copyright © 1999 by _CrossCurrents._ Used by permission of _CrossCurrents._

Furthermore, because sanctions are themselves a form of violence, I would argue that they cannot legitimately be seen merely as a peacekeeping device, or as a tool for enforcing international law. Rather, I will suggest, they require the same level of justification as other acts of warfare. . . .

The principle of discrimination in Just War Doctrine requires the attacker to distinguish between combatants and noncombatants; between combatants who are injured and those who are uninjured; between combatants who are armed and those who have surrendered and are defenseless; etc. Under Just War Doctrine, there is no strict prohibition against killing civilians, or killing injured or unarmed combatants, when it is required by "military necessity" or as an unavoidable consequence of an attack on a legitimate military target. A common example is that an ammunition factory is a legitimate military target in wartime; if in bombing the factory, civilians who live nearby are also killed, no war crime has been committed. What is prohibited is to target civilians directly, or injured or defenseless combatants; or to bomb indiscriminately, where the deaths of civilians are foreseeable.

As Walzer notes, siege is the oldest form of war waged against both soldiers and civilians. In siege, noncombatants are not only exposed, but in fact are more likely to be killed than combatants, given that the goal of siege "is surrender, not by defeat of the enemy army, but by the fearful spectacle of the civilian dead."[1] Thus, siege warfare has the quality of actually inverting the principle of discrimination. Siege operates by restricting the economy of the entire community, creating shortages of food, water, and fuel. Those who are least able to survive the ensuing hunger, illness, and cold are the very young, the elderly, and those who are sick or injured. Thus the direct consequence of siege is that harm is done to those who are least able to defend themselves, who present the least military threat, who have the least input into policy or military decisions, and who are most vulnerable to hunger, cold, and illness. The harm done by the enemy's deprivation is exacerbated by domestic policy, which typically shifts whatever resources there are to the military and to the political leadership. This is sometimes done for security reasons, in the belief that defending against military attack is the highest priority, and is more immediately urgent than the slower damage of hunger and illness to which the civilian population is subjected. It may also happen because the leadership is corrupt, or because the desperation creates conditions for black marketeering. Both of these consequences—the suffering of the innocent and helpless, and the shifting of resources to the military and to the privileged—are as old as siege itself. . . .

[T]he argument can be made that siege has the character of being a form of warfare which itself constitutes a war crime. By its very nature, it is easily foreseeable or calculated to cause *direct* harm to those who are, in Just War Doctrine, supposed to be exempt from warfare—the apolitical and the unarmed—in order to influence *indirectly* those who are armed and those who are responsible for military and political decisions. Let us place siege in the context of war crimes and Just War Doctrine: in Just War Doctrine, we could demand a justification for a military strategy in terms of the obligation to minimize harm to civilians—the ammunition factory was a legitimate target, and there was no way to bomb it without collateral damage to nearby residential areas. But siege is peculiar in that it resists such an analysis—the immediate goal is *precisely* to cause suffering to civilians. In the case of the ammunitions factory, we can answer the question: How is this act consistent with the moral requirement to discriminate? In the case of siege, we cannot.

It may be argued that military necessity sometimes justifies the use of siege warfare, and that in this case, military necessity overrides the principle of discrimination. "Military necessity" is sometimes defined as consisting of acts "which are indispensable for securing the complete submission of the enemy as soon as possible," according to a version of the U.S. Army Field Manual. Alternatively, military necessity is sometimes understood to include, by definition, whatever limitations are required by international law, including humanitarian principles and the principle of discrimination. If military necessity legitimizes any act of war, then the principle of discrimination becomes a luxury rather than a limitation of military conduct; it would hold only that one may not target civilians gratuitously. On the other hand, if military necessity is constrained by the principle of discrimination, then one may not target civilians, even where it would be of great value to the war effort. . . .

It is sometimes said that military necessity is the exception that swallows Just War Doctrine altogether, since virtually anything can be justified—by the party doing it—as having a military purpose. An argument can be made, at least by the acting party, that there are circumstances in which it would be militarily necessary to demoralize the civilian population by conducting carpet bombing as a method of psychological warfare, or as a means of undermining the entire industrial base and labor force upon which military production depends. If military necessity can legitimate harm directly and intentionally done to civilians, then it is true that siege can invoke this justification; but if so, then the principle of discrimination has been lost altogether. If the principle of discrimination is to have any meaning at all, then directly harming children, the sick, and the elderly, in order to indirectly influence military and political leaders, must be ethically precluded, and this preclusion must not be overridden by a claim of military necessity. The alternative—to hold that military necessity can legitimate direct and intentional harm to civilians—is effectively to take a realist or nihilist position that ethical restraint has no place in war. But while that position would be available to those engaged in warfare, it would seem to be unavailable to those seeking to impose or justify sanctions on such grounds as international law or human rights, since these claims themselves invoke a legal and ethical framework.

In certain respects, sanctions are obviously the modern version of siege warfare—each involves the systematic deprivation of a whole city or nation of economic resources. Although in siege warfare this is accomplished by surrounding the city with an army, the same effect can be achieved by using international institutions and international pressure to prevent the sale or purchase of goods, and to prevent migration. It is sometimes argued that an embargoed nation can still engage in some marginal trade, despite sanctions; but similarly in a siege there may be marginal ways of getting goods through gaps in the blockade. In both cases, however, the unit under embargo or siege is a mixed population rather than a military installation, or is entirely civilian. In both cases, the net effect is the same, which is the disruption or strangulation of the economy as a whole.

Christiansen and Powers argue that the Just War Doctrine, which holds that civilians and noncombatants should be immune from direct attack, does not apply to peacetime sanctions in the same way that this doctrine applies to sieges and blockades imposed as part of a war effort. Scholars in the Just War tradition, they note, "often treat economic sanctions as analogous with acts of war . . . along with blockades and sieges."[2] However, Christiansen and Powers argue that sanctions without war have a different moral status, for three reasons: first, unlike wartime blockades, economic sanctions are not imposed as a form of war, but as an alternative to warfare; second, some kinds of harms may in fact be justified, either because the population has consented to the state's policies or because it shares responsibility for them in some fashion; and third, with appropriate humanitarian measures built in, the harm inflicted by sanctions is not as extreme as the harm done by war. The fundamental difference, they hold, is that the use of economic sanctions is rooted in the intention to avoid the use of armed force, as opposed to the intent to multiply the effects of war; and that as a lower-level exercise of coercion, it raises the threshold for the use of actual force, thereby lowering the likelihood of actual warfare. . . .

Like many other commentators, Christiansen and Powers are partly basing their claim on two sets of empirical assumptions regarding the speed and degree of damage done by sanctions: "Whereas war's impact is speedy and frequently lethal, the impact of sanctions grows over time and allows more easily for mitigation of these harmful effects and for a negotiated solution than acts of war."[3] Christiansen and Powers suggest that the way to conceptualize sanctions is that warfare is akin to the death penalty, whereas sanctions are more like attaching someone's assets in a civil proceeding. In this analogy, the economic domain is seen as fully separate, and of a different nature altogether, than the domain of power and of violence. But economic harm, while it is not directly physical, can also be a form of violence. The sanctions-as-mere-seizure-of-assets theory, whether on the level of the individual or an entire economy, implicitly assumes a starting point of relative abundance. Whether the seizure of someone's assets is inconvenient or devastating depends entirely on what their assets are, and how much is left after the seizure. For an upper-middle-class person with, say, $50,000 in stocks and an annual income of $80,000, seizing $1000 from a checking account would at most cause inconvenience, annoyance, perhaps some slight reduction in luxuries or indulgences. For someone living at poverty level, seizing $1000 may mean that a family has lost irreplaceably the ability to pay for fuel oil for a winter's heating season, or lost their car in a rural area with no other transportation, or lost the security deposit and first month's rent on an apartment that would have given them a way out of a homeless shelter. Living in a home with a temperature of 40 degrees in the winter does not kill quickly, in the way that a bullet does, and may not kill at all. It may only make someone sick, or over some time, worsen an illness until death occurs. Living in a shelter or on the street for a night or for a week or for a month doesn't kill in the way that a bullet does, but it exposes someone to a risk of considerable random violence, including killings. To conceptualize economic deprivation in terms of mild punishment whose effects are reversible with no permanent damage—inconvenience, embarrassment, living on a budget—is to misunderstand the nature of the economic. "Economic deprivation" is not a uniform phenomenon; the loss of conveniences constitutes a different experience than the loss of the means to meet basic needs. There is a reason that infant mortality rates and life expectancy rates are used as measures of economic development: poverty manifests itself in malnutrition, sickness, exposure to the elements, exhaustion, dirty drinking water, the lack of means to leave a violent country or neighborhood—the shortening of one's life. It is for this reason that liberation theologians and others have argued that poverty is indeed a form of violence, although it doesn't kill in the way that a bullet does.

Christiansen and Powers argue that sanctions differ from siege partly on the grounds that the intent of sanctions is to prevent violence rather than exacerbate it. Under the doctrine of double effect, however, this does not seem to hold. The doctrine of double effect provides that

> the foreseen evil effect of a man's action is not morally imputable to him, provided that (1) the action in itself is directed immediately to some other result, (2) the evil effect is not willed either in itself or as a means to the other result, (3) the permitting of the evil effect is justified by reasons of proportionate weight.[4]

Although the doctrine of double effect would seem to justify "collateral damage," it does not offer a justification of sanctions. "Collateral damage" entails the unintended secondary harm to civilians. If a bombing raid is conducted against a military base, the collateral damage would be that the schoolhouse half a mile away was destroyed by a bomb that missed its intended target, which was the military base. In that case, the bombing raid would be equally successful if the base were hit, and the schoolhouse were undamaged. But the damage done by indirect sanctions is not in fact "collateral," in that the damage to the civilian population is necessary and instrumental. The *direct* damage to the economy is intended to *indirectly* influence the leadership, by triggering political pressure or uprisings of the civilians, or by generating moral guilt from the "fearful spectacle of the civilian dead." Sanctions directed against an economy would in fact be considered unsuccessful if no disruption of the economy took place. We often hear commentators objecting that "sanctions didn't work" in one situation or another because they weren't "tight" enough—they did not succeed in disrupting the economy. Thus, sanctions are not defensible under the doctrine of double effect. Although the end may indeed be legitimate, the intended intermediate means consists of the generalized damage to the economy, which violates both the first and second requirements of the doctrine. But there is a second reason why good intent [is] not available as a justification for sanctions: the intent cannot in good faith be reconciled with the history and the logic of sanctions, and with the likely outcome. We know from the history of siege warfare that, legitimately or not, in the face of economic strangulation, the military and political leadership will insulate themselves from its consequences, and place a disproportionate burden on the civilian population. We also know from history that economic strangulation will consolidate the state's power rather than undermine it; we know that sanctions are, for the most part, unlikely to prevent military aggression, or stop human rights violations, or achieve compliance with *any* political or military demand, even when sanctions drag on for decades. It is hard to reconcile the claimed "good intent" of sanctions with a history that makes it easy to foresee that those intentions are not likely to be realized. Thus, I would suggest that while sanctions may have very different goals than siege warfare—including goals such as international governance—they are nevertheless subject to many of the same moral objections: that they intentionally, or at least predictably, harm the most vulnerable and the least political; and that this is something which the party imposing sanctions either knows, or should know. To the extent that economic sanctions seek to undermine the economy of a society, and thereby prevent the production or importation of necessities, they are functioning as the modern equivalent of siege. To the extent that sanctions deprive the most vulnerable and least political sectors of society of the food, potable water, medical care, and fuel necessary for survival and basic human needs, sanctions should be subject to the same moral objections as siege warfare.

I do not deny that the contexts in which sanctions and sieges occur may be different, the intent of each may differ, the nature of the demands may be different, and the options of the besieged or sanctioned states may be different. But the moral objection to sanctions does not rest on the analogy; sanctions do not have to be identical to siege warfare in order to be subject to condemnation under Just War principles. Indeed, if the intent of sanctions is peaceful rather than belligerent, then the usual justifications in warfare are unavailable. I am morally permitted to kill where my survival is at stake; and in war, I am morally permitted to kill even innocents, in some circumstances. But if one's goal is to see that international law is enforced or that human rights are respected, then the stakes and the justificatory context are quite different. It is hard to make sense of the claim that "collateral damage" can be justified in the name of protecting human rights; or that international law might be enforced by means that stand in violation of international laws, including the Just War principle of discrimination. Thus, if sanctions are analogous to siege warfare, then they are problematic for the same reasons—both effectively violate the principle of discrimination. But if sanctions are not analogous to siege, then sanctions are even more problematic. If the goals of sanctions are the enforcement of humanitarian standards or compliance with legal and ethical norms, then extensive and predictable harm to civilians cannot even be justified by reference to survival or military advantage. Insofar as this is the case, sanctions are simply a device of cruelty garbed in self-righteousness.

To the extent that we see sanctions as a means of peacekeeping and international governance, sanctions effectively escape ethical analysis—we do not judge them by the same standards we judge other kinds of harm done to innocents. Yet, concretely, the hunger, sickness, and poverty which are ostensibly inflicted for benign purposes affect individuals no differently than hunger, sickness, and poverty inflicted out of malevolence. To describe sanctions as a means of "peacekeeping" or "enforcing human rights" is an ideological move, which, from the perspective of concrete personal experiences, is simply counterfactual. Sanctions are, at bottom, a bureaucratized, internationally organized form of siege warfare, and should be seen, and judged, as such.

◼ Notes

1. Michael Walzer, *Just and Unjust Wars: A Moral Argument with Historical Illustrations* (New York: Basic Books, 1977), p. 161.

2. Drew Christiansen, S. J., and Gerard F. Powers, "Economic Sanctions and the Just-War Doctrine," in *Economic Sanctions: Panacea or Peacebuilding in a Post–Cold War World,* ed. David Cortright and George A. Lopez (Boulder, Colo.: Westview, 1995), p. 102.

3. Ibid., p. 107.

4. John C. Ford, S. J., "The Morality of Obliteration Bombing," in *War and Morality,* ed. Richard A. Wasserstrom (Belmont, Calif.: Wadsworth, 1970), p. 26.

12 Technology and War

12.1

Introduction
The Editors

Major military powers have typically wasted very little time integrating technological advances into their warfighting capabilities. Indeed, the desire to stay at the forefront of military prowess, and if possible ahead of the state's main rivals, has provided an important impetus for the development of new technologies, even technologies with applications in the civilian sector. Sometimes military-technological advances can have profound effects both on the destructive capacity of the state's armed forces and on the military strategies and doctrines that direct their employment in the field. Defense analysts and military historians have called such periods of military-technological advance "revolutions in military affairs," or RMAs. The advent of nuclear weaponry and nuclear strategy after World War II is perhaps the clearest example in recent times, but many believe that the United States, in particular, is in the midst of a new RMA built upon advances in information technology.

It may be too much to expect that the traditional moral principles circumscribing warfare, like those found in just war theory, can adapt to military-technological revolutions and continue to offer practical guidance for the just resort to force and the conduct of battle. This position invites two possible responses. The first is that just war theory, in anything like its traditional form, is simply no longer relevant and should be correspondingly discarded. The second is that the type of warfare states engage in (or prepare to engage in), to the extent that the latest in destructive technologies are to be employed, simply cannot be fought justly and thus should not be fought under any circumstances. Both responses were heard during the Cold War in regard to the deployment of nuclear weapons and the development of strategies for fighting nuclear wars.

One moral question that arose with the dawning of the nuclear era was whether it was just for a state to make a threat that would be unjust to actually carry out. The earliest nuclear strategies adopted by the superpowers called for massive retaliation in response to a nuclear first strike by the other side. The expectation was that the result of such an exchange, dubbed "mutually assured destruction" (MAD), would be so horrible to contemplate that no rational leader would dare take that first step. Yet any plan for massive retaliation involves the targeting of the opponent's population centers on an exceptionally vast scale, a transgression of the discrimination principle at the core of *jus in bello*. Of course, nuclear strategists hoped (and most expected) that the MAD strategy would work and deterrence would not fail, but how could anyone threaten such an immoral act and really mean it? And of course, those states that availed themselves of the MAD strategy had to mean it, otherwise their threat would not be credible.

Paul Ramsey illustrates how this basic moral dilemma contained in the superpowers' respective postures of nuclear deterrence was made even more acute by the evolution of nuclear strategies and technologies designed to overcome the flaws of MAD. Ethical qualms aside, is the threat to retaliate massively to be believed if the threatener knows that the resulting annihilation will be mutual? If not, doesn't that give the other side an incentive to strike first? The strategic fix was to assure the opponent that a first strike could be absorbed and that a second, retaliatory strike would be forthcoming afterwards. The technological fix was to enhance the survivability of the state's retaliatory forces—for example, by placing them on submarines or underground railroads thereby making them hard to find, or by hardening the silos of those land-based weapons that the other side knew about. The moral problem did not disappear, however. In fact, it seemed worse, for now the state had to expend tremendous amounts of resources to protect its nuclear forces. Civilian populations were left at risk and, in the presence of only modest civil defense measures, continued to be held hostage to the threat of nuclear retaliation.

Nuclear deterrence nevertheless became a fact of Cold War life, even if the ethics of nuclear deterrence remained problematic from the perspective of just war theory. One response to the moral quandary troubling Ramsey and others is to accept, as a necessary evil, the need to make immoral threats. That is, a principled stance rejecting in advance the possibility of retaliating against an attacker's population centers is simply untenable in the nuclear age when so much is at stake if deterrence fails. As distasteful as it may be from a moral point of view, holding an opponent's population hostage to retaliation is necessary to avert a greater evil—becoming a victim to an opponent's first strike, brought on because the state was unable or unwilling to credibly threaten a devastating retaliation. And as a practical matter, it seems reasonable to ask if life in the shadow of a nuclear deterrence policy is really so bad. Though populations are forced to live under the specter of nuclear conflagration, individuals remain generally free to go about their business in much the same way as they would if nuclear weaponry didn't actually exist. Ramsey likens the hostage populations to babies strapped to the bumpers of automobiles, surely an effective but morally reprehensible means of deterring reckless driving on the highways. But the analogy is rather misleading, for nuclear deterrence places no comparable restraints on its hostages.

Another response to the moral dilemma posed by a deterrent strategy calling for massive retaliation is to shift from a counter-value deterrent posture, whereby retaliatory strikes are aimed at population centers, to a counter-force posture, in which only military assets are targeted. The US Catholic Bishops, for example, in their influential pastoral letter, "The Challenge of Peace," were reassured by official pronouncements that "it is not US strategic policy to target the Soviet civilian populations as such." They felt that such pronouncements "respond, in principle at least, to one moral criterion for assessing deterrence policy: the immunity of noncombatants from direct attack." Many others, however, were not convinced that the US government's official pronouncements told the whole story. With so many "military targets" located in and around population centers, the notion that US targeting plans intended to discriminate between military and civilian targets seemed implausible on its face. The bishops voiced their concern that such a deterrence posture runs afoul of the *jus in bello* principle of proportionality, and thus the doctrine of double effect. But in addition to this consequentialist objection, a principled objection might also be pressed. Even if a counter-force posture does not *target* civilians, isn't the collateral destruction visited upon the civilian population *intended?* The double effect doctrine requires not only that the bad effect of a military action be outweighed by the good effect, but also that the bad effect is unintended. Can any strategy of nuclear deterrence escape this moral objection?

It has been said that the nuclear revolution was unique in the history of military-technological advance in that nuclear weapons were designed for nonuse. If a nuclear exchange ever actually occurred, nuclear weapons and nuclear doctrine will have failed in their fundamental strategic purpose. That most certainly is not true in the case of the ongoing revolutionary advances in information technology and their integration in modern weaponry, most notably in the form of precision guided munitions (or "smart bombs"). The ability of these munitions to reach their intended targets with pinpoint accuracy is an impressive technological achievement. These weapons can be employed to destroy or otherwise neutralize their military targets with minimal collateral damage, even in urban settings. Whereas in the past concerns about civilian deaths and the destruction of civilian infrastructure may have restrained the use of aerial bombardment in urban areas except when states were engaged in total war, smart weapons now allow commanders to effectively discriminate between combatants and noncombatants and this would therefore seem to go some distance in removing a moral impediment to their use.

Of course, the availability of discriminating weapons does not mean that militaries will necessarily employ them in a discriminating fashion. Quite the contrary, argue Roger Normand and Chris af Jochnick, at least in the case of the Gulf War in 1992. They assert that despite being in a position to discriminate between military and civilian targets in Iraq—due not only to its possession of smart weapons, but also its total dominance of Iraqi airspace—the US military targeted Iraq's infrastructure to an extent far greater than what was required by military necessity. And especially galling to the authors is the self-congratulatory rhetoric that accompanied this morally questionable prosecution of the war. It was claimed, for instance, that this was "the most legalistic war ever fought."

Readers familiar with US tactics during the Gulf War may well come to a different conclusion than Normand and Jochnick, or perhaps a less harsh one, but their concluding observations regarding *jus in bello* provide food for thought. They claim, more generally, that "the laws of war legitimize almost any form of military conduct so long as it is arguably related to the defeat of enemy forces." We believe this indictment is better directed at states, when they attempt to legally justify morally questionable military acts, rather than the law of war itself or the just war tradition that has contributed to the shaping of that law. But there is another way in which international law, and the UN Charter in particular, may contribute to the prosecution of war beyond the traditional limits established by *jus in bello*. The UN Charter gives the Security Council the authority to identify and respond forcibly to threats to international peace and security (see Chapter 5). Normand and Jochnick contend that this authority, which reaches further than the right of individual or collective self-defense, may sanction military actions not necessarily required to defeat another state's armed forces. Military actions, including destruction of a state's social and economic infrastructure, may be intended to prevent the reemergence of a plausible threat to regional peace and security.

The United States and its allies regarded Security Council Resolution 678, passed in the aftermath of Iraq's invasion of Kuwait in 1990, as the source of the coalition's authority to invade Iraq in 2003, and this is also suggestive of the erosion of *jus ad bellum* limits. We may find something praiseworthy in military-technological developments that allow for a more discriminating use of armed force. But the availability of these technologies provides no assurance that smart weapons will in fact be employed in a manner upholding the distinction between combatants and noncombatants as legitimate objects of attack. We may be further concerned that the usability of this new generation of weaponry (in sharp contrast to nuclear weaponry), combined with a certain permissiveness contained in the UN Charter, will lead to the more frequent use of military force under the color of international law.

12.2

The Hatfields and the Coys

Paul Ramsey

The subtitle of this story might be phrased, "My, How Feuding Has Changed!" or "What's Wrong Won't Work." The theme is not that of a positive pragmatism, which holds that military conduct is right because it works. It is rather that of a negative pragmatism, which holds that inherently wrong actions cannot be made to work. Morally unshootable weapons or ways of using them cannot be made politically shootable by any kind of technical arrangement. Morally un-do-able *military* conduct can be shown to be politically unsuccessful in the present age.

In its shifting scenes, this tale summarizes the successive weapons policies on which this nation has relied in recent years. First we go to the 1950's.

Down in the mountains of Tennessee where for decades there has been fun and feuding, the Hatfields and the Coys suddenly one day found themselves in a most extraordinary posture toward one another. High up on one ridge, the eldest Hatfield discovered in the sights of his rifle the youngest Coy gurgling in a cradle, while at the very same moment the eldest Coy on the opposite ridge draws deadly aim at the youngest Hatfield lying on a quilt on the porch. Each knows, and knows that the other knows, that this is the case. For some weeks that seem a very long time indeed, each tries to improve his situation by calling on all the other Hatfields and Coys to come and station themselves at various places in the hills, each aiming at the last human life on the other side. The deterrence is truly "massive"; and if this system is ever used it will have failed completely. It looks as if effective feuding has been abolished. Such has long been the desire of the few sentimental ones born from time to time in both families; and now technology has achieved what religion never could. While the lion and the lamb have not exactly lain down together, the Hatfields and the Coys seem capable of forever standing there together, since each sustains the other and prevents his firing. This is in effect a condition, it is supposed, equivalent to mutual total disarmament. Since neither could fight if he wanted to, he cannot want to.

From *The Just War: Force and Political Responsibility* by Paul Ramsey. New York: Charles Scribner's Sons, 1968. Used by permission of the Estate of Paul Ramsey. Excerpt from chap. 8 ("The Hatfields and the Coys").

This seems so clear that strategists on both sides have declared that not so many guns are needed; that one has only to be able to deliver unacceptable damage; that "overkill" is not needed; and that a finite amount of deterrence is enough. War has been stopped. Only a few of these weapons seem to suffice to banish the use of force from human history, while the rest of society can devote itself to chewing sugar cane and making moonshine whiskey (the obvious ends of policy: consumer goods in an affluent society).

Then begins the second scene of the first act of this drama, without any alteration in the weapons systems or in the external military postures. There takes place a radical and subtle change simply because both gunners have second thoughts. Each began by saying in effect: "I'll not strike first unless you do." Then the next moment each realizes that the other must strike first before his enemy does. Both sides begin to quake with fear because each realizes that this system of deterrence, this way of banishing force from human history, is quite unstable. Each begins to suspect that the other may launch a surprise attack, indeed that he should launch a surprise attack, in order to pre-empt against the launching of his own surprise attack (which is equally necessary), and *that* preemption in turn would have to be pre-empted, etc., etc.

Mutual "anticipatory retaliation" is always about to take control of this system, consisting of only first-strike weapons, which was supposed to unarm both sides. This is not because both sides are in danger of *mis*calculating, but because they are in danger of calculating *correctly*. On second thought, these first-strike weapons are of no use except for striking first. This is the case because each side knows that he who does not strike first loses everything. He therefore expects the other to strike first, and he expects to be expected himself to strike first. Each does what he expects to be expected to do. He strikes first in order not to be the second who is struck. Each does this. Thus, wonderful to behold, we have on both sides a *defensive* war fought with unlimited aggression. Each side can justify its action by bringing it under the category of legitimate defense; yet each must strike first and all-out, in order to have any defense at all. Douglass Cater calls this "the theory of immaculate aggression."[1] If each calculates *correctly*, war will break out. The only reason it doesn't is that politics is never a rational enough human enterprise. The question has now become: When is a surprise or pre-emptive attack *not* justified—on both sides? At no moment is a defensively motivated first strike without justification! An almost automatic two-sided defensive war has been built into these massive first-strike weapons, as long as their bases are *vulnerable*. Thus, "*immaculate* aggression" or "anticipatory retaliation" has practically been read into the computers of both sides. Each will act as expected, because of how he expects the other side to act and himself expects to be expected to act. Therefore, both will strike first. Both must become limitlessly aggressive—all for the sake of defense, so long as no limitation has been placed on the weapons it is willing under any circumstances to use even in retaliation. On second thought, massive deterrence tends to produce the war it thought to prevent forever. Surprise attack is the only reasonable *use* to be made of these weapons. They do not deter or abolish war; rather, they tend always to produce it.

Meantime it has become apparent that ordinary feuding has not been deterred. Under the umbrella of deterrence, the grown Hatfield and Coy boys continue fighting whenever there seems an opportunity to increase their power-control of the valley in face of any weakness in conventional forces. Each time this occurs, Hatfield says firmly, "No one should doubt our resolution"; and Coy exclaims, "We will bury you." The side wins which acts as if it is the more capable of wholly irrational action, since each knows that the system exceeds any of the reasonable purposes feuding ever had. So far as the main threat, or "central war," is concerned, they work on each other's minds and not with physical force upon each other's bodies. But war has actually not been abolished; we have only attempted to exceed it. And the side most bemused by this possibility loses in every encounter of real power.

In the second act of this drama, we go to the 1960's. Technological changes take place which seem capable of abolishing surprise attack itself—without, however, removing the immobilization of politics and the confusion and partial immobilization of ordinary feuding and fighting as an extension of purposive policy, especially among the peace-loving Hatfields. The promise of invulnerable bases is that they will prevent surprise attack, and stabilize this system. We find a way to protect the guns and the gunners, if not the babies. Some of the Hatfields—the peace-loving ones—fall into wells, and begin to take aim through periscopes. These are Minuteman missiles. A way is found to harden and protect the guns. The gunners begin to move around, so that you don't know where they are. The bases are placed on mobile railroad cars, planes, barges, and submarines (Polaris). The retaliatory forces are made invulnerable to surprise attack.

This act of our drama also has two scenes. While still aimed at baby Hatfield and baby Coy, counter-*people* warfare seems miraculously to have been transformed into counter-*forces* warfare. Only counter-*forces* war seems now to be possible since it would be necessary for either side first to find a way of getting at the other side's guns before using his own in the way originally intended (or in the way it was originally intended that by them the other side would be deterred from using his in the way *he* originally intended). Plans for "cooperating with the enemy" in tacit agreements to maintain the mutual "invulnerability" of deterrence, and arms control schemes to "stabilize" the deterrent gain wide currency, especially among the Hatfields.

After this flight of fancy, our statesman may have some sober thoughts that will cut athwart basing national policy on any such expectation. While still daydreaming and before altogether returning to the real world, he might even reflect for one moment as a moralist. If so, he will conclude that it would be totally immoral to "stabilize" the deterrent and "prevent" war by such means without fundamentally altering war's present shape *even if this succeeded*. Still somewhat in the mood for myth-making, he might suppose that one Labor Day weekend no one was killed or maimed on the highways; and that the reason for the remarkable restraint placed on the recklessness of automobile drivers was that suddenly every one of them discovered he was driving with a baby tied to his front bumper! That would be no way to regulate traffic *even if it succeeds* in regulating it perfectly, since such a system makes innocent human lives the *direct object* of attack and uses them as a mere *means* for restraining the drivers of automobiles. It would even have to be assumed that the drivers will tacitly agree never to remove the baby from the bumper, since that would destabilize the entire system of controls! Against such a proposal it obviously should be said that restraints and penalties ought to be objectively brought to bear only upon the drivers of automobiles, even if this means the abandonment of the hope of saving the lives of every human being (guilty and innocent alike) who ventures upon the highways on any holiday weekend. The rational and only just thing to do, if we wish no longer to accept the necessity of the number of deaths that repeatedly take place in the face of vain moral injunctions to drive carefully, would be to introduce basic changes into the machines that are driven, by compulsory safety devices and built-in maximum speeds of forty miles an hour, and enforce with heavier penalties the laws defining the proper conduct of drivers.

But in the real world of political and military encounters, the question is: *can* any scheme hope to succeed which accepts retaliatory strategies directed against populations, and only tries to stabilize these deterrent forces and perfect the mutual invulnerability of counter-people weapons? It would have to be tacitly agreed that baby Hatfield and baby Coy will not be protected directly, and a piece of sheetmetal never be placed between them and the bullets. A successful civil defense program on either side of the valley would not be impossible so much as it would be undesirable, for to succeed in protecting the last possible survivors of such defense plans if they are ever used would be destabilizing to the very system calculated to prevent its having to be used (always without any basic alteration in the design itself of war and defense). Here, the morality of the matter insists on obtruding, for this defines what is politically wrong in all such products of man's artistic, technical reason in designing weapons, arms control, and deterrence systems. No government can effectively communicate to its people the fact that it is accepting the complete reversal of a proper relation between a nation and its armament. It cannot tell them, so that they feel it along their pulses, that old ladies and children are now the "fighters" to be maneuvered into position in the struggle for national advantage; that civil defense is a weapon that perhaps should not be used; that a "race" in shelter programs might be exceedingly dangerous and the Russians may even now be mounting this in a clandestine manner; that it is the arms alone that can be and are now sought to be protected, and not the nation, except as a hoped-for consequence of protecting the forces; and that it is essential to this precisely that the people generally be left with no protection.

Moreover, task forces of Hatfields and Coys are already at work out in the woodshed developing anti-gunnery gunnery (anti-submarine warfare and anti-missile missiles). Their barns are said to contain stores of bacteriological, chemical, and radiological weapons. These capabilities for total war cannot of themselves be miraculously transformed into counter-forces weapons. Nothing will automatically insure that germs will have first to be let loose on the forces of an enemy bearing these same weapons before one would dare use them in attacks upon civilians or in civilian reprisal. Not only in active defense but in offensive plans as well there may be an upsetting scientific breakthrough that will make vulnerable every supposed invulnerable system of deterrence and destabilize any system of supposedly stable arms control erected upon the preservation and use of counter-*people* warfare (or its use for deterrence). "We are having a complete technological revolution in the art of war approximately every five years. . . . Technological progress is so rapid that there are almost bound to be doctrinal lags,"[2] in any of the proposed schemes for subduing our galloping war-technology *only by means of that technology itself* without any decision to alter the weapons themselves.

Exposed to view is the fact that the Hatfields and the Coys cannot make war or *make defense* in any such fashion that accepts as its premise a fundamental reversal of the subordinate relation of arms to the fabric of a nation's life and its purposive policies. Faced with such manifold difficulties, it would seem that the eldest Hatfield (if he is a realist) would rather make some gesture in the direction of indicating to the chief Coy that he is willing to lower his rifle and direct his aim upon the *forces* opposing him and not upon the babies. Graduated steps to make just war possible would seem to contain as much or more promise than delicate schemes for attempting to stabilize the altogether extraordinary and fluid situation in which one now finds himself as head of a powerful feuding family.

Moreover, if Hatfield listens to the more sober among his advisors they will be heard making plans for what to do should deterrence fail and weapons have to be used. Making just war possible may then appear as feasible as making the fighting of a thermonuclear war feasible (and thereby making deterrence credible). Our statesman may have read . . . an apology for resting the whole defense of the nation at its core upon "the rationality of irrationality." This is defined as follows: "The Rationality of Irrationality war corresponds to a situation in which neither side really believes the issue is big enough to go to war but both sides are willing to use some partial or total committal strategy to force the other side to back down; as a result they may end up in a war that they would not have gone into if either side had realized ahead of time that the other side would not back down even under pressure."[3] A "committal strategy" to make *credible* a nation's resolve to go through with a "rationality of irrationality" policy may be compared to what might work to deter one's opponent in the case of two hot-rod drivers playing the game of "Chicken!" by racing their cars at break-neck speed toward one another, each with his left wheels on the wrong side of the white dividing-line in the middle of the road, to see which will give in first and pull over to avoid a collision: one or both drivers might *strap the steering wheel* in order to make it mechanically necessary for him to carry out this irrational action. Thus, Kahn asserts that in this uncertain world "it is just possible that the enemy, in spite of our best thought and preparation, may (either because he is clever, or because he or we have made a miscalculation) develop a technique which he believes will destroy more than 80 percent of our strategic forces on the first blow. We wish to assure him that *even if he thinks he can be this successful he is still in serious trouble.* To the extent that he could rely on our using our small remaining force 'sensibly,' this might not be true."[4] Thus, *stabilized* counter-people deterrence, or the supposed technological diversion of this into counter-forces warfare, not only may but, to be maintained, *must be planned* to break down into actual, irrational, purposeless counter-people retaliation. This whole effort to impose limits upon thermonuclear war depends upon the rationality of *committal* to irrational behavior, to which it inevitably returns. Kahn knows very well how alone this can be done: not by contemplating the beauties of the contrivance while it is working to deter surprise attack, but by thinking through and planning our *committal strategy* for when it may not work. "If there were some politically acceptable accident-proof way to make this kind of retaliation completely automatic," he writes, "it would be sensible to put it into immediate effect"; and he unflinchingly calls attention to the fact that the idea of using our forces finally with insensible sensibility against an enemy's society, rather than against his forces, is not credible "*unless we really intend to do it.* If we are only *pretending* that we would do it, the credibility and therefore the deterrent value of our force is almost certain to be lessened by the automatic and inevitable leaks. While we can probably keep the details of our war plans secret, it is most unlikely that we can keep the philosophy behind them secret."[5] In other words, to have "the courage of rashness" we must simply strap the wheel; and the stabilization of invulnerable deterrent forces depends on guaranteeing that this has been done, by some determination *equivalent* to the mechanization of the ultimate political-military decision.

Having learned about the rationality of irrational systems, our statesman can be instructed by another sober weapons analyst in what might realistically be called "the virtue of vice" or "the humanity of inhumanity" as
the foundation upon which to base this nation's policy, while providing also
for the eventuality that such a policy may not be able to be "virtuously" stabilized and therefore may not work. T. C. Schelling believes that it may be
virtuous and wise to keep people hostage and integrate the weapons directed at them into plans for preventing a war directed upon them. . . .
"Weapons," he writes, "may be more stabilizing and less aggressive if they
are more capable of civilian reprisal than of military engagement. A stand-
off between two retaliatory forces is in some ways equivalent to an
exchange of hostages; and 'inhumane' weapons, capable of inflicting damage but not able to go after the enemy's strategic forces, *acquire virtue*
because of their clearly deterrent function and the lack of temptation they
give either side to strike first."[6] This type of arms stabilization depends not
so much on formal agreement between the two powers as upon tacit agreement on the part of each to direct its policies to this end. It calls for "mutual
arms accommodation" to have and to hold hostages; for "reciprocated unilateral actions and abstentions."[7] Making *decisions,* even some *unilateral*
decisions, that this should be the shape of war, of defense and deterrence,
lies at the root of the matter. Yet in the end Schelling faces the eventuality
that the surface wisdom, virtue, humaneness, and rationality of this system
may break down and disclose that upon which it is based: purposeless war,
vice, inhumanity, and irrationality. He discusses not only the possibility and
actuality of an outbreak of thermonuclear war, but also *how on earth* either
side can then manage to *surrender,* even *unconditionally* surrender; and
what terms should be exacted of a surrendering enemy. "In the future, at the
close of a general war, one might have to allow the conditionally surrendering enemy to retain some retaliatory weapons, these being the only kind that
two major powers can use to enforce promises from each other. . . .
Certainly more drastic measures than any that have yet been considered [to
'safeguard against surprise attack'] might be the minimum requirement of a
conditionally surrendering enemy."[8]

Plainly this will not only have to be *allowed,* and allowed a *conditionally* surrendering enemy. This would also be a minimum *requirement,* and a
requirement also in the case of an *un*conditionally surrendering enemy, if
we are going to stabilize armaments after the war as was attempted before.
After deterrence "fails," the next war after that could then be "prevented"
only by basing deterrence again on the preservation of war and the deterrence of war in its present shape. This gruesome conclusion follows unless
we take hopefully reciprocated but yet persistent graduated unilateral steps
to make counter-forces warfare possible. No wonder Kenneth Boulding
writes: "The grotesque irony of national defense in the nuclear age is that,

after having had the inestimable privilege of losing half (or is it three quarters, or all?) our population, we are supposed to set up again the whole system that gave rise to this holocaust!"[9]

The fact is that contemporary weapons analysts are not simply using pure reason, in the form of technical reason wholly stripped of moral *scientia,* in producing their designs for invulnerable weapons systems and arms control. They are using pure reason interfused with moral themes and judgments furnished them by characteristics of the American ethos. They are persuaded by this that it is possible to banish the use of force from human history; and that, when force is actually used (because of the stupid, aggressive, and evil wills of some men) there then supervenes a state of war to which no norms or limits apply. There used to be an oscillation in successive periods of time between all-out peace and all-out (aggressor-defender) war. Contemporary proposals for arms controls based on the total deterrent represent the final product of this ethos. Their distinctiveness is only that they may claim to have banished force and provided in advance for the irrational use of violence in one timeless scheme. There is no hope for purposive political applications of power or for survival unless it is possible to break decisively with this modern doctrine of warfare; and, on both counts, in "peace" or in "war," make just war possible. This should become the regulative context of political decision and of the exercise of technical reason in designing weapons, war, and deterrence systems, in the present age. There is no other course of action, if, as President Eisenhower said, the great powers are not "doomed malevolently to eye each other indefinitely across a trembling world." We need fight-the-war plans that may be less "deterring," but whose consequences are less catastrophic *when* deterrence fails. . . .

▪ Notes

1. Douglass Cater, "Foreign Policy: Default of the Democrats," *The Reporter,* March 10, 1955, p. 23.

2. Herman Kahn, "The Arms Race and Some of Its Hazards," *Daedalus,* vol. 89, no. 4 (Fall 1960), pp. 765–778.

3. Herman Kahn, *On Thermonuclear War* (Princeton, N.J.: Princeton University Press, 1960), p. 293.

4. Ibid., p. 185.

5. Ibid.

6. Thomas C. Schelling, "Reciprocal Measures for Arms Stabilization," *Daedalus,* vol. 89, no. 4 (Fall 1960), p. 892 (italics added).

7. Ibid., p. 904.

8. Ibid., p. 914.

9. Kenneth Boulding, "The Domestic Implications of Arms Control," *Daedalus,* vol. 89, no. 4 (Fall 1960), p. 858.

12.3 ⎯⎯⎯⎯

War and Peace in the Modern World

US Catholic Bishops

Both the just-war teaching and nonviolence are confronted with a unique challenge by nuclear warfare. This must be the starting point of any further moral reflection: nuclear weapons particularly and nuclear warfare as it is planned today, raise new moral questions. No previously conceived moral position escapes the fundamental confrontation posed by contemporary nuclear strategy. Many have noted the similarity of the statements made by eminent scientists and Vatican II's observation that we are forced today "to undertake a completely fresh reappraisal of war." The task before us is not simply to repeat what we have said before; it is first to consider anew whether and how our religious-moral tradition can assess, direct, contain, and, we hope, help to eliminate the threat posed to the human family by the nuclear arsenals of the world. . . .

Precisely because of the destructive nature of nuclear weapons, strategies have been developed which previous generations would have found unintelligible. Today military preparations are undertaken on a vast and sophisticated scale, but the declared purpose is not to use the weapons produced. Threats are made which would be suicidal to implement. The key to security is no longer only military secrets, for in some instances security may best be served by informing one's adversary publicly what weapons one has and what plans exist for their use. The presumption of the nation-state system, that sovereignty implies an ability to protect a nation's territory and population, is precisely the presumption denied by the nuclear capacities of both superpowers. In a sense each is at the mercy of the other's perception of what strategy is "rational," what kind of damage is "unacceptable," how "convincing" one side's threat is to the other.

The political paradox of deterrence has also strained our moral conception. May a nation threaten what it may never do? May it possess what it may never use? Who is involved in the threat each superpower makes: gov-

From *The Challenge of Peace: God's Promise and Our Response,* United States Pastoral Letter on War and Peace. Washington, D.C.: United States Conference of Catholic Bishops © 1983. Used with permission of the United States Conference of Catholic Bishops. Excerpts from section II.

ernment officials? or military personnel? or the citizenry in whose defense the threat is made?

In brief, the danger of the situation is clear; but how to prevent the use of nuclear weapons, how to assess deterrence, and how to delineate moral responsibility in the nuclear age are less clearly seen or stated. Reflecting the complexity of the nuclear problem, our arguments in this Pastoral must be detailed and nuanced; but our "no" to nuclear war must, in the end, be definitive and decisive. . . .

■ Deterrence in Principle and Practice

The moral challenge posed by nuclear weapons is not exhausted by an analysis of their possible uses. Much of the political and moral debate of the nuclear age has concerned the strategy of deterrence. Deterrence is at the heart of the U.S.-Soviet relationship, currently the most dangerous dimension of the nuclear arms race.

The Concept and Development of Deterrence Policy

The concept of deterrence existed in military strategy long before the nuclear age, but it has taken on a new meaning and significance since 1945. . . . In the nuclear age, deterrence has become the centerpiece of both U.S. and Soviet policy. Both superpowers have for many years now been able to promise a retaliatory response which can inflict "unacceptable damage." A situation of stable deterrence depends on the ability of each side to deploy its retaliatory forces in ways that are not vulnerable to an attack (i.e., protected against a "first strike"); preserving stability requires a willingness by both sides to refrain from deploying weapons which appear to have a first strike capability. . . .

The evolution of deterrence strategy has passed through several stages of declaratory policy. Using the U.S. case as an example, there is a significant difference between "massive retaliation" and "flexible response," and between "mutual assured destruction" and "countervailing strategy." It is also possible to distinguish between "counterforce" and "countervalue" targeting policies; and to contrast a posture of "minimum deterrence" with "extended deterrence." These terms are well known in the technical debate on nuclear policy; they are less well known and sometimes loosely used in the wider public debate. It is important to recognize that there has been substantial continuity in U.S. action policy in spite of real changes in declaratory policy.[1]

The recognition of these different elements in the deterrent and the evolution of policy means that moral assessment of deterrence requires a series of distinct judgments. They include: an analysis of the *factual character* of the deterrent (e.g., what is involved in targeting doctrine); analysis of the *historical development* of the policy (e.g., whether changes have occurred which are significant for moral analysis of the policy); the relationship of deterrence policy and other aspects of *U.S.-Soviet affairs;* and determination of the key *moral questions* involved in deterrence policy.

The Moral Assessment of Deterrence
The distinctively new dimensions of nuclear deterrence were recognized by policymakers and strategists only after much reflection. Similarly, the moral challenge posed by nuclear deterrence was grasped only after careful deliberation. The moral and political paradox posed by deterrence was concisely stated by Vatican II:

> Undoubtedly, armaments are not amassed merely for use in wartime. Since the defensive strength of any nation is thought to depend on its capacity for immediate retaliation, the stockpiling of arms which grows from year to year serves, in a way hitherto unthought of, as a deterrent to potential attackers. Many people look upon this as the most effective way known at the present time for maintaining some sort of peace among nations. Whatever one may think of this form of deterrent, people are convinced that the arms race, which quite a few countries have entered, is no infallible way of maintaining real peace and that the resulting so-called balance of power is no sure genuine path to achieving it. Rather than eliminate the causes of war, the arms race serves only to aggravate the position. As long as extravagant sums of money are poured into the development of new weapons, it is impossible to devote adequate aid in tackling the misery which prevails at the present day in the world. Instead of eradicating international conflict once and for all, the contagion is spreading to other parts of the world. New approaches, based on reformed attitudes, will have to be chosen in order to remove this stumbling block, to free the earth from its pressing anxieties, and give back to the world a genuine peace. . . .[2]

In Pope John Paul II's assessment we perceive two dimensions of the contemporary dilemma of deterrence. One dimension is the danger of nuclear war, with its human and moral costs. The possession of nuclear weapons, the continuing quantitative growth of the arms race, and the danger of nuclear proliferation all point to the grave danger of basing "peace of a sort" on deterrence. The other dimension is the independence and freedom of nations and entire peoples, including the need to protect smaller nations from threats to their independence and integrity. Deterrence reflects the radical distrust which marks international politics, a condition identified as a major problem by Pope John XXIII in *Peace on Earth* and reaffirmed by Pope Paul VI and Pope John Paul II. Thus a balance of forces, preventing either side from achieving superiority, can be seen as a means of safeguarding both dimensions.

The moral duty today is to prevent nuclear war from ever occurring and to protect and preserve those key values of justice, freedom, and independence which are necessary for personal dignity and national integrity. In reference to these issues, Pope John Paul II judges that deterrence may still be judged morally acceptable, "certainly not as an end in itself but as a step on the way toward a progressive disarmament." . . .

Relating Pope John Paul's general statements to the specific policies of the U.S. deterrent requires both judgments of fact and an application of moral principles. In preparing this letter we have tried, through a number of sources, to determine as precisely as possible the factual character of U.S. deterrence strategy. Two questions have particularly concerned us: (1) the targeting doctrine and strategic plans for the use of the deterrent, particularly their impact on civilian casualties; and (2) the relationship of deterrence strategy and nuclear war-fighting capability to the likelihood that war will in fact be prevented.

■ Moral Principles and Policy Choices

Targeting doctrine raises significant moral questions because it is a significant determinant of what would occur if nuclear weapons were ever to be used. Although we acknowledge the need for deterrence, not all forms of deterrence are morally acceptable. There are moral limits to deterrence policy as well as to policy regarding use. Specifically, it is not morally acceptable to intend to kill the innocent as part of a strategy of deterring nuclear war. The question of whether U.S. policy involves an intention to strike civilian centers (directly targeting civilian populations) has been one of our factual concerns.

This complex question has always produced a variety of responses, official and unofficial in character. . . . Essentially these statements declare that it is not U.S. strategic policy to target the Soviet civilian population as such or to use nuclear weapons deliberately for the purpose of destroying population centers. These statements respond, in principle at least, to one moral criterion for assessing deterrence policy: the immunity of noncombatants from direct attack either by conventional or nuclear weapons.

These statements do not address or resolve another very troublesome moral problem, namely, that an attack on military targets or militarily significant industrial targets could involve "indirect" (i.e., unintended) but massive civilian casualties. We are advised, for example, that the United States strategic nuclear targeting plan (SIOP—Single Integrated Operational Plan) has identified 60 "military" targets within the city of Moscow alone, and that 40,000 "military" targets for nuclear weapons have been identified in the whole of the Soviet Union.[3] It is important to recognize that Soviet policy is subject to the same moral judgment; attacks on several "industrial targets" or politically significant targets in the United States could produce massive civilian casualties. . . . This problem is unavoidable because of the way modern military facilities and production centers are so thoroughly interspersed with civilian living and working areas. It is aggravated if one side deliberately positions military targets in the midst of a civilian population. In our consultations, administration officials readily admitted that, while they hoped any nuclear exchange could be kept limited, they were prepared to retaliate in a massive way if necessary. They also agreed that once any substantial numbers of weapons were used, the civilian casualty levels would quickly become truly catastrophic, and that even with attacks limited to "military" targets, the number of deaths in a substantial exchange would be almost indistinguishable from what might occur if civilian centers had been deliberately and directly struck. These possibilities pose a different moral question and are to be judged by a different moral criterion: the principle of proportionality.

While any judgment of proportionality is always open to differing evaluations, there are actions which can be decisively judged to be disproportionate. A narrow adherence exclusively to the principle of noncombatant immunity as a criterion for policy is an inadequate moral posture for it ignores some evil and unacceptable consequences. Hence, we cannot be satisfied that the assertion of an intention not to strike civilians directly, or even the most honest effort to implement that intention, by itself constitutes a "moral policy" for the use of nuclear weapons.

The location of industrial or militarily significant economic targets within heavily populated areas or in those areas affected by radioactive fallout could well involve such massive civilian casualties that, in our judgment, such a strike would be deemed morally disproportionate, even though not intentionally indiscriminate.

The problem is not simply one of producing highly accurate weapons that might minimize civilian casualties in any single explosion, but one of increasing the likelihood of escalation at a level where many, even "discriminating," weapons would cumulatively kill very large numbers of civilians. Those civilian deaths would occur both immediately and from the long-term effects of social and economic devastation.

A second issue of concern to us is the relationship of deterrence doctrine to war-fighting strategies. We are aware of the argument that war-fighting capabilities enhance the credibility of the deterrent, particularly the strategy of extended deterrence. But the development of such capabilities raises other strategic and moral questions. The relationship of war-fighting capabilities and targeting doctrine exemplifies the difficult choices in this area of policy. Targeting civilian populations would violate the principle of discrimination—one of the central moral principles of a Christian ethic of war. But "counterforce targeting," while preferable from the perspective of protecting civilians, is often joined with a declaratory policy which conveys the notion that nuclear war is subject to precise rational and moral limits. We have already expressed our severe doubts about such a concept. Furthermore, a purely counterforce strategy may seem to threaten the viability of other nations' retaliatory forces making deterrence unstable in a crisis and war more likely.

While we welcome any effort to protect civilian populations, we do not want to legitimize or encourage moves which extend deterrence beyond the specific objective of preventing the use of nuclear weapons or other actions which could lead directly to a nuclear exchange.

These considerations of concrete elements of nuclear deterrence policy, made in light of John Paul II's evaluation, but applying it through our own prudential judgments, lead us to a strictly conditioned moral acceptance of nuclear deterrence. We cannot consider it adequate as a long-term basis for peace.

This strictly conditioned judgment yields *criteria* for morally assessing the elements of deterrence strategy. Clearly, these criteria demonstrate that we cannot approve of every weapons system, strategic doctrine, or policy initiative advanced in the name of strengthening deterrence. On the contrary, these criteria require continual public scrutiny of what our government proposes to do with the deterrent.

On the basis of these criteria we wish now to make some specific evaluations:

(1) If nuclear deterrence exists only to prevent the *use* of nuclear weapons by others, then proposals to go beyond this to planning for prolonged periods of repeated nuclear strikes and counter-strikes, or "prevailing" in nuclear war, are not acceptable. They encourage notions that nuclear war can be engaged in with tolerable human and moral consequences. Rather, we must continually say "no" to the idea of nuclear war.

(2) If nuclear deterrence is our goal, "sufficiency" to deter is an adequate strategy; the quest for nuclear superiority must be rejected.

(3) Nuclear deterrence should be used as a step on the way toward progressive disarmament. Each proposed addition to our strategic system or change in strategic doctrine must be assessed precisely in light of whether it will render steps toward "progressive disarmament" more or less likely.

Moreover, these criteria provide us with the means to make some judgments and recommendations about the present direction of U.S. strategic policy. Progress toward a world freed of dependence on nuclear deterrence must be carefully carried out. But it must not be delayed. There is an urgent moral and political responsibility to use the "peace of a sort" we have as a framework to move toward authentic peace through nuclear arms control, reductions, and disarmament. Of primary importance in this process is the need to prevent the development and deployment of destabilizing weapons systems on either side; a second requirement is to insure that the more sophisticated command and control systems do not become mere hair triggers for automatic launch on warning; a third is the need to prevent the proliferation of nuclear weapons in the international system. . . .

These judgments are meant to exemplify how a lack of unequivocal condemnation of deterrence is meant only to be an attempt to acknowledge the role attributed to deterrence, but not to support its extension beyond the limited purpose discussed above. Some have urged us to condemn all aspects of nuclear deterrence. This urging has been based on a variety of reasons, but has emphasized particularly the high and terrible risks that either deliberate use or accidental detonation of nuclear weapons could quickly escalate to something utterly disproportionate to any acceptable moral purpose. That determination requires highly technical judgments about hypothetical events. Although reasons exist which move some to condemn reliance on nuclear weapons for deterrence, we have not reached this conclusion for the reasons outlined in this letter.

Nevertheless, there must be no misunderstanding of our profound skepticism about the moral acceptability of any use of nuclear weapons. It is obvious that the use of any weapons which violate the principle of discrimination merits unequivocal condemnation. We are told that some weapons are designed for purely "counterforce" use against military forces and targets. The moral issue, however, is not resolved by the design of weapons or the planned intention for use; there are also consequences which must be assessed. It would be a perverted political policy or moral casuistry which tried to justify using a weapon which "indirectly" or "unintentionally" killed a million innocent people because they happened to live near a "militarily significant target."

Even the "indirect effects" of initiating nuclear war are sufficient to make it an unjustifiable moral risk in any form. It is not sufficient, for example, to contend that "our" side has plans for "limited" or "discriminate" use. Modern warfare is not readily contained by good intentions or technological designs. The psychological climate of the world is such that mention of the term "nuclear" generates uneasiness. Many contend that the use of one tactical nuclear weapon could produce panic, with completely unpredictable consequences. It is precisely this mix of political, psychological, and technological uncertainty which has moved us in this letter to reinforce with moral prohibitions and prescriptions the prevailing political barrier against resort to nuclear weapons. Our support for enhanced command and control facilities, for major reductions in strategic and tactical nuclear forces, and for a "no first use" policy (as set forth in this letter) is meant to be seen as a complement to our desire to draw a moral line against nuclear war.

Any claim by any government that it is pursuing a morally acceptable policy of deterrence must be scrutinized with the greatest care. We are prepared and eager to participate in our country in the ongoing public debate on moral grounds.

The need to rethink the deterrence policy of our nation, to make the revisions necessary to reduce the possibility of nuclear war, and to move toward a more stable system of national and international security will demand a substantial intellectual, political, and moral effort. It also will require, we believe, the willingness to open ourselves to the providential care, power and Word of God, which call us to recognize our common humanity and the bonds of mutual responsibility which exist in the international community in spite of political differences and nuclear arsenals.

Indeed, we do acknowledge that there are many strong voices within our own episcopal ranks and within the wider Catholic community in the United States which challenge the strategy of deterrence as an adequate response to the arms race today. They highlight the historical evidence that deterrence has not, in fact, set in motion substantial processes of disarmament.

Moreover, these voices rightly raise the concern that even the conditional acceptance of nuclear deterrence as laid out in a letter such as this might be inappropriately used by some to reinforce the policy of arms buildup. In its stead, they call us to raise a prophetic challenge to the community of faith—a challenge which goes beyond nuclear deterrence, toward more resolute steps to actual bilateral disarmament and peacemaking. We recognize the intellectual ground on which the argument is built and the religious sensibility which gives it its strong force.

The dangers of the nuclear age and the enormous difficulties we face in moving toward a more adequate system of global security, stability and justice require steps beyond our present conceptions of security and defense policy. . . .

■ Notes

1. Desmond Ball, "U.S. Strategic Forces: How Would They Be Used?" *International Security,* vol. 7 (1982/83), pp. 31–60.
2. Vatican II, *The Pastoral Constitution on the Church in the Modern World,* para. 81.
3. Solly Zuckerman, *Nuclear Illusion and Reality* (New York: HarperCollins, 1982); Ball, "U.S. Strategic Forces," p. 36; Thomas Powers, "Choosing a Strategy for World War III," *The Atlantic Monthly,* November 1982, pp. 82–110.

12.4 ⎯⎯⎯⎯

The Legitimation of Violence
Roger Normand and Chris af Jochnick

▓ The Gulf War and the Laws of War

Military Force in the Gulf War

The Coalition's war against Iraq constituted one of the most unbalanced applications of military force in history. Employing the latest technology, the United States and its allies decimated the Iraqi armed forces, driving them from Kuwait and southern Iraq after thirty-nine days of aerial bombardment followed by four days of ground war. . . .

Many of the Coalition's claims of military success turned out to have been exaggerated. For example, the size and danger of the Iraqi army, the effectiveness of the Patriot missile, the accuracy of the bombing, and the amount of precision-guided munitions used were overstated. Nonetheless, the Coalition inflicted a devastating military blow on an overmatched adversary. The combination of air supremacy, precision guided munitions, and open terrain enabled the Coalition to bypass the army entrenched in Kuwait and southern Iraq and strike at Iraq's modern infrastructure, which was vitally linked to both the army and civilian life support systems. One commentator illustrated the unique nature of this new military technology by noting that in World War II, the German command was still able to direct the army from Berlin after five years of intensive bombing. In comparison, "Iraq's leader and his military commands were already blind, deaf, and mute in their paralyzed capital city"[1] forty-eight hours after the start of the Coalition air offensive.

Coalition forces enjoyed the unprecedented ability to locate and destroy targets of military significance without fear of retaliation. The importance of this dominance, in legal terms, is that the Coalition's obligation to spare Iraqi civilians and civilian property rose accordingly. As a prominent lawyer for the United States Air Force explained, "[t]he belligerent who faces no opposition in his bombing operations has a heavy burden of proof to show that civilian casualties were necessary, unavoidable, and proportionate to the military advantage gained."[2] Thus, in evaluating the Gulf War, Coalition forces must be held to a higher standard of conduct, given their military superiority.

Legal Rhetoric in the Gulf War

This unique ability to respect the laws of war dovetailed neatly with the public rhetoric of Coalition leaders, who touted respect for law as a prime justification for the Gulf War. Most politicians and commentators welcomed what they saw as a new paradigm in war and in law, conjuring visions of a global army using the latest military technology in the service of international law and justice.

The extraordinary legal measures taken by the Coalition against Iraq seemed to justify this faith in the power of law even in time of war. President Bush received congressional approval to commit United States military forces, and the Coalition prosecuted its war under the legal authority of United Nations Security Council resolutions. More significantly, Coalition political and military leaders repeatedly referred to the laws of war to justify their actions and to condemn Iraq's conduct, both leading up to and during actual combat. It was often stressed that by respecting the law, Coalition forces were sparing Iraqi civilians from the hardships of war to the greatest extent possible. The small number of direct civilian casualties relative to the intense firepower employed, along with the televised barrage of "surgical strikes" from laser-guided weapons, seemed to support this claim. The use of Security Council resolutions to authorize first sanctions and then military force added to this impression of a war constrained by law. . . .

The Coalition's legal rhetoric was intended to defend specific actions as well as to justify the war as a whole by making it more acceptable to the American public. Coalition leaders used the law to protect specific attacks and military policies from criticism. As General Norman Schwarzkopf, commander of the Coalition forces, put it:

> I think that the very actions [of] the Iraqis themselves demonstrate that they know damn well that we're not attacking civilian targets . . . since right now they've dispersed their airplanes into residential areas, they've moved their headquarters into schools . . . they've put guns and things like that on top of high-rise apartment buildings. Under the Geneva Convention, that gives us a perfect right to go after those things if we want to. . . .[3]

On a broader level, the Coalition justified the overall war effort by stressing compliance with the fundamental legal principle that belligerents must distinguish between soldiers and civilians and between military objectives and civilian objects and accordingly attack only the former. Combined with overemphasis of its reliance on precision guided munitions, the Coalition's legal rhetoric had the effect of promoting a vision of a clean, morally acceptable war in which, except for a few unavoidable accidents, innocents were being spared the horrors common to wars. Coalition rhetoric even insisted that its forces were going beyond the law's requirements by foregoing military targets and risking pilots' lives in order to minimize civilian casualties. President Bush expressed these themes in the following remarks:

> I'd like to emphasize that we are going to extraordinary—and I would venture to say unprecedented—lengths to avoid damage to civilians and holy places. We do not seek Iraq's destruction, nor do we seek to punish the Iraqi people for the decisions and policies of their leaders. In addition, we are doing everything possible and with great success to minimize collateral damage, despite the fact that [Iraqi President] Saddam [Hussein] is now relocating some military functions, such as command and control headquarters, in civilian areas such as schools.[4]

It is almost impossible to measure the impact of such legal legitimization on public attitudes towards the Gulf War. Coalition leaders, however, clearly felt it was critical to preempt the concerns of their citizens through reassurances that the war was clean and legal. The press magnified the public impact of the Coalition's legal rhetoric, particularly in the United States where the constantly televised images of mastery and precision in the war's conduct contrasted with the total absence of coverage devoted to the war's impact on Iraqi civilians. . . .

Civilian Impact of the Gulf War

Although the United States media never truly challenged the Pentagon's version of events in the Gulf War, independent investigations conducted in post-war Iraq flatly contradicted the image of a clean, surgical war with minimal civilian casualties. The investigations revealed that the Coalition's systematic destruction of Iraq's infrastructure, particularly its electric power grid, resulted in catastrophic damage to civilian lives and property. In marked contrast to the Pentagon's claims that it attacked only military targets and "left most of the basic economic infrastructure intact,"[5] the first United Nations observer team described a country whose entire industrial base had been deliberately decimated: "most means of modern life support have been destroyed or rendered tenuous. Iraq has, for some time to come, been relegated to a pre-industrial age, but with all the disabilities of post-industrial dependency on an intensive use of energy and technology."[6]

The massive attacks on Iraq's electric power, civilian industry, transportation, telecommunication, and oil sectors paralyzed the country and deprived its urbanized population of essential life support systems. In particular, the destruction of electric power impacted the full range of basic services available to Iraqi civilians. Water and sewage purification plants stopped functioning, the public health system was disrupted, irrigation and food production ground to a halt, drinking water became contaminated with pathogenic fecal coliforms, and epidemic levels of waterborne disease spread throughout Iraq. A survey of 16,000 Iraqi children published in the New England Journal of Medicine concluded that a post-war surge in disease and malnutrition caused child mortality to triple, resulting in 47,000 excess deaths among children under five in the first eight months following the Gulf War. Increased mortality for the overall civilian population was much higher: demographic surveys place the total civilian deaths one year after the war at a minimum of 100,000. The continuation of sanctions has not only exacerbated these problems by preventing effective infrastructure repair, but has also driven up the food price index by 1,500–2,000 percent, thereby contributing to malnutrition and disease.

Unnecessary Destruction

Although the high number of civilian casualties suggests hypocrisy in Coalition rhetoric, it does not necessarily indicate illegal conduct. The law of proportionality states that attacks against legitimate military targets may "legally" cause collateral civilian casualties. Nevertheless, the manner in which the air campaign was conducted suggests that the Coalition attacked many other targets to achieve economic or political objectives, rather than simply attacking military targets to defeat the Iraqi Army.

Attacks on the electrical system. The Coalition targeted eleven of Iraq's eighteen main electrical power stations on the first day of the war, many by sea-launched cruise missiles. During the war, the Coalition damaged sixteen power stations to varying degrees, destroying generators, converters, switchyards, sub-stations, administration buildings, and even spare parts warehouses. Most stations were bombed on several different occasions, despite having already been disabled by previous attacks. The largest station in southern Iraq was attacked thirteen times. The last raid occurred minutes before the cease-fire.

Coalition war planners were well aware that the health and welfare of the civilian population depended on its access to electricity. A comprehensive Pentagon survey of the effects of United States bombing during World War II suggested that bombing public utilities had a "demoralizing effect" on the civilian population due to "the dread of disease."[7] At a briefing on January 30, 1991, General Schwarzkopf specifically expressed concern for the civilian impact of bombing electrical power stations, reporting that only twenty-five percent of Iraq's electrical generating facilities had been rendered "completely inoperative" and fifty percent "degraded":

I think I should point out right here that we never had any intention of destroying all of Iraqi electrical power. Because of our interest in making sure that civilians did not suffer unduly, we felt that we had to leave some of the electrical power in effect, and we've done that.[8]

Despite these stated concerns, by the end of the war, systematic bombing had reduced Iraq's electrical output to less than four percent of pre-war capacity, creating conditions for a public health catastrophe.

The repeated bombing of previously disabled electrical facilities served no military purpose. Evidence suggests that the Coalition's overall campaign against Iraq's electrical system provided negligible military gains relative to the amount of civilian suffering that it caused. After gaining early air superiority, the Coalition directly targeted command-and-control centers, communications facilities, weapons plants, troop concentrations, and other military targets, thereby vastly decreasing the utility of attacking power sources. Furthermore, General Powell acknowledged that Iraq possessed sophisticated alternative power and communications systems for military use, including mobile stand-by generators and a buried fiber-optics network. Most damning from the perspective of military necessity, however, was the fact that the Coalition did not attack the Kuwaiti electrical system, which supplied the Iraqi Army entrenched in the militarily crucial Kuwaiti theater of operations, until several hours before the ground war started on February 24, if at all.

Attacks on the oil sector. Much of the bombing campaign followed this pattern of excessive and unnecessary destruction. To deny supplies of oil to the Iraqi Army, it would have been sufficient to destroy just one element of the oil production chain, which consists of extracting, refining, piping, degassing, storage, and distribution. Nonetheless, the Coalition repeatedly attacked each element of production in oil fields, from Rumailah in the south to Kirkuk in the north, well after production and distribution had been halted by initial attacks. It also destroyed water injection systems that maintain pressure on underground reserves for purposes of long-term exploitation and have no value as military targets. Most of the destruction of Iraq's oil industry, which resulted in billions of dollars of damage on the most important sector of Iraq's economy, was unnecessary from a strictly military perspective. As one military analyst has noted, Coalition strategists were aware that Iraq's army had stockpiled enough oil to last well over one month, the Pentagon's estimate of how long the war was expected to last. To pump, refine, and distribute new oil to Iraqi forces, however, would have taken well over one month. As a result, the repeated bombings of all Iraq's major refineries, while dealing a significant blow to Iraq's ability to achieve post-war economic recovery, did not result in any military advantage to the Coalition's war effort.

Attacks on other nonmilitary objects. Although the destruction of central microwave and television transmission facilities had already rendered subordinate facilities inoperable, the Coalition continued to destroy such local facilities throughout the war. The Coalition also destroyed bridges in north and central Iraq long after traffic to the Kuwaiti theater of operations had been interdicted. Finally, the Coalition attacked factories producing textiles, foodstuffs, cement, household goods, and other civilian products, particularly in central and southern Iraq, right up to the cease-fire.

Economic objectives of the attacks. In light of the Coalition's sophisticated intelligence equipment and ability to destroy selected targets at will, the deliberate and systematic destruction of Iraq's industrial infrastructure strongly indicates that the air campaign had economic goals in addition to military ones. Public statements by Coalition leaders support this hypothesis. Air Force General Buster Glosson, who was responsible for compiling the target lists, explained that the Coalition expected to rebuild the system after the war, under a new Iraqi government. Colonel John Warden, another architect of the air campaign, fleshed out the political considerations behind the destruction of the electrical system and consequent civilian suffering, stating that "Saddam Hussein cannot restore his own electricity. He needs help. If there are political objectives that the U.N. Coalition has, it can say, 'Saddam, when you agree to do these things, we will allow people to come in and fix your electricity.'"[9]

Based on post-war interviews with Coalition target planners, the Washington Post observed that:

> [a]mid mounting evidence of Iraq's ruined infrastructure and the painful consequences for ordinary Iraqis, Pentagon officials more readily acknowledge the severe impact of the 43-day air bombardment on Iraq's economic future and civilian population. . . . [The Pentagon's] explanations these days of the bombing's goals and methods suggest that the allies, relying on traditional concepts of strategic warfare, sought to achieve some of their military objectives in the Persian Gulf War by disabling Iraqi society at large.[10]

The article also noted that many of the targets in Iraq "were chosen only secondarily to contribute to the military defeat of Baghdad's occupation army in Kuwait." Thus, the Coalition's actual war objectives, as evidenced by both the choice of targets and the public justifications for the air campaign, apparently differed from the official United States objectives, which targeted only the Iraqi military.

■ Legal Reaction to the Gulf War

It is not surprising that the popular media and general public, dazzled by smart bombs and blinded by patriotism, did not challenge the Coalition's claim to have waged a strictly legal war. More significant was the acquiescence of the academic community, particularly that of international legal scholars, to this claim of the moral achievement of compliance with the laws of war. Reports by human rights and humanitarian organizations traditionally critical of United States policy concluded that the Coalition bombing campaign was legally justified. Even a comprehensive Middle East Watch report on the Gulf War, which analyzed hundreds of separate attacks in light of the laws of war and devoted sections to the devastating consequences of the attacks on Iraq's electrical power system and suspected economic objectives of the bombing campaign, concluded that, on the whole, the Coalition had exhibited commendable restraint in general accord with the law:

> [I]n noting these discrepancies between duty and conduct, we do not suggest that the allies in general violated the requirements of the laws of war. To the contrary, in many if not most respects the allies' conduct was consistent with their stated intent to take all feasible precautions to avoid civilian casualties.[11]

In similar fashion, a Greenpeace report on military strategy and civilian casualties of the Gulf War, while asserting that many Coalition attacks against Iraq's infrastructure seemed intended to "demoralize" the civilian population rather than weaken the military, nevertheless concluded that "[t]hrough the repudiation of civilian attacks . . . the U.S. and its allies tacitly behaved in accordance with provisions of the Geneva Protocols."[12]

In noting this widespread consensus on the legality of Coalition conduct, we do not contend that international lawyers and human rights organizations consciously subverted the intent of the laws of war. The coincidence of apparent adherence to the laws of war and terrible civilian suffering is not unique to the Gulf War. It is merely the most recent example of a consistent historical pattern. This pattern follows from the fact that the laws of war, despite their noble rhetoric, were deliberately structured to disregard humanitarian considerations. In wars throughout history, belligerents have used law to legitimize conduct that might otherwise have received closer scrutiny. The legal lesson of the Gulf War is in degree rather than kind: a belligerent with overwhelming military superiority and a publicly professed commitment to respect the laws of war, especially in relation to protection of civilians, nonetheless managed to kill an enormous number of civilians in attacks that had very little military significance. And for this, the Coalition has been praised for conducting "the most legalistic war ever fought."

■ A Final Blow to *Jus in Bello*?

In one respect, Coalition actions represent a departure from past wars. The laws of war legitimize almost any form of military conduct so long as it is arguably related to the defeat of enemy forces. As made explicit by the Nuremburg tribunal, military conduct violates the laws of war at the point that it causes gratuitous damage—damage unrelated to military victory. Thus, the bombings of the civilian populations of Berlin and Hiroshima were deemed legitimate insofar as they were aimed at inducing military surrender. Coalition forces, however, took this baseline one step further: Iraqi civilians were intentionally made to suffer for reasons unrelated to the defeat, surrender, or weakening of the Iraqi military. Coalition attacks on civilian infrastructure thus raise one of two possible legal conclusions: either (1) the Coalition flagrantly violated a legal regime (the laws of war) that has already been rendered so forgiving as to make violations almost impossible, or (2) the Coalition legitimately employed a United Nations resolution to undermine the fundamental proscription that wartime attacks must be directly or indirectly aimed at weakening an opponent's military forces.

The widespread approval for Coalition conduct in the Gulf War lends credence to the notion that under United Nations mandate a belligerent may legitimately employ military force to secure its war objectives, unrelated to the weakening or surrender of the enemy's military. Three basic assumptions underlie this legal possibility: first, that civilian suffering is a legitimate target when linked to a war's overall objectives; second, that the legitimacy of military attacks is measured cumulatively, with an eye towards the war's overall purposes, rather than on a case-by-case basis; and third, that a broad United Nations mandate covering a war's purposes removes the need to focus purely on the weakening or surrender of the enemy's military. In practice, the first and second steps are well-established; the third step has been broached by popular perceptions of resolution 678.

The laws of war have been moored to the principle that force should only be directed towards defeating the enemy's military. As the St. Petersburg Declaration of 1868 made clear: "[t]he only legitimate object which States should endeavor to accomplish during war is to weaken the military forces of the enemy."[13] *Jus ad bellum,* as codified in the United Nations Charter, limits resort to force to cases of self-defense (article 51) or collective security (chapter VII). While states have interpreted these principles broadly, the use of force is clearly bounded, and the principles have never been construed so permissively as to allow attacks unrelated to the defeat or weakening of a military. Thus, to the extent that attacks on civilian morale have been sanctioned, they have been linked to military surrender.

The use of resolution 678 to legitimize broad-based attacks on Iraqi infrastructure suggests a way around this final requirement. The United States and its allies treated resolution 678 as a separate source of authority for their military conduct. The resolution expanded the scope of military actions already available to them under article 51 from self-defense (reading the provision narrowly) to a broad license "to restore international peace and security" to the region. As one commentator observes, "the Security Council gave the [United Nations] members carte blanche vis-à-vis Iraq after January 15, including the waging of war on whatever terms and in whatever ways they might choose."[14] For the public at large, this would have been a natural understanding of the resolution's role. Indeed, military planners explicitly discussed wartime objectives unrelated to the defeat of the Iraqi military. As the Washington Post reported after interviewing Coalition officials, "[s]ome targets, especially late in the war, were bombed primarily to create postwar leverage over Iraq, not to influence the course of the conflict itself. Planners now say their intent was to destroy or damage valuable facilities that Baghdad could not repair without foreign assistance."[15]

These issues are raised in part to underscore the irony of the Gulf War's image as "the most legalistic war ever fought." Whatever upper limits the *jus in bello* regime placed on wartime conduct have been jeopardized by the legitimation of Coalition attacks on civilian infrastructure unrelated to military advantage. To rule this conduct legal would be the final blow to the laws of war.

■ Conclusion: The Need for Legal Reform

We have tried to dispel widely held myths about the humanitarian accomplishments of the present laws of war and their relationship to the Gulf War in order to demonstrate the need for new legal approaches toward war. But before proposing reform, it is necessary to reject two theories that hold that law can never restrain war. First is the "political realist" claim that law is irrelevant in war, a claim that reduces the complex, reciprocal relationship between law and politics to an absolute contradiction. The reality is that law does matter; that is both the problem and the promise. States will modify their behavior in response to the perceived benefits of complying with international law. To the extent that the international community considers a law legitimate and to the extent that the law's dictates are clearly defined, states will be deterred from violating the law and restrained from manipulating it.

Similarly misguided is the "deterministic" belief that all efforts to control war are doomed to failure. The present relationship between law and war is neither necessary nor natural; it has been constructed in response to a series of particular historical, social, and political conditions and decisions. The fact that nations have already adopted a legal framework that allows them to conduct wars relatively uninhibited by humanitarian constraints will not prevent them from adopting alternative legal frameworks that effectuate new values and lead to new results.

The Challenge of Legal Reform

Despite the potential for reform, the Gulf War and other wars of this century provide ample evidence that states can manipulate vague humanitarian principles of the laws of war to shield their conduct from closer scrutiny. This poses a significant challenge to humanitarian lawyers; effective humanitarian advocacy must not only recognize the shortcomings of the existing legal regime, but also appreciate the genesis of these failings. The process of demystification thus constitutes an essential first step in a program of constructive legal reform.

The contention that law applies public consciousness to reify existing power relations must modify the liberal optimism that law will act as a progressive force on states. While liberal jurists view law as a tool to influence belligerent conduct, the critical view adds the possibility that law may actually legitimize, and thereby encourage, the commission of atrocities. This understanding encourages a more comprehensive analysis of law's likely impact within its particular context.

At the same time, international law, as the primary mechanism by which states recognize and formalize the progressive development of normative values in custom and practice, can both embody normative standards and influence state behavior. Once a treaty is signed, a state will inevitably find that certain actions are limited by its normative standards. As a noted legal scholar points out:

> [t]he fact that nations feel obliged to justify their actions under international law, that justifications must have plausibility, that plausible justifications are often unavailable or limited, inevitably affects how nations will act.[16]

International law develops through a series of struggles about the distribution of power in the international system, and therefore remains open to challenge and change. While the current laws of war are fundamentally grounded in military practices, sovereign states may still be pressured to respect further humanitarian limits, which in turn may exert an influence on conduct. With this understanding, humanitarian lawyers must engage in a form of law-politics to develop humanitarian principles into a concrete, normative political agenda; mobilize support for such an agenda among allies in social and political movements; and make strategic decisions about whether the support is sufficient to induce states to inscribe the principles into law. The decision to codify a humanitarian principle into law also requires an assessment of whether the principle, once enacted, will likely serve its intended goals. This assessment, in turn, hinges on the continuing balance of force behind the competing alternatives.

Legal reform must also take into account the dominant trend in international relations—the increasing globalization of the traditional system of sovereign and independent states. Recent international relations scholarship has described this trend as a paradigm shift away from state-oriented international arrangements. The weakening of state sovereignty, evident throughout the field of international law, has resulted in a transfer of rights from nations to both international organizations on one hand and individuals and groups on the other. In the field of international economic law, for example, the global market has developed standardized norms of contract and exchange within a legal framework that vests rights in corporations and individuals independent of national power. Similarly, human rights and environmental laws grant entitlements to individuals and groups at the expense of sovereign prerogatives in such crucial areas as internal coercion and development policy.

National insistence that the right of survival implies a right to war will ensure that this paradigm shift proceeds more slowly in the laws of war than in other fields of international law. Nevertheless, it is clear that the trend towards weaker state sovereignty will present opportunities to promote, implement, and enforce a legal regime that limits the right of belligerents to massacre civilians under an overly broad definition of military necessity. Humanitarian lawyers must seize these opportunities to advocate reforms to expand the rights of individuals and groups in times of war. . . .

■ Notes

1. Edward N. Luttwak, "The Gulf War in Its Purely Military Dimension," in *War and Its Consequences: Lessons from the Persian Gulf Conflict*, ed. Thomas Mayer, John O'Loughlin, and Edward Greenberg (New York: HarperCollins, 1994), p. 33.

2. Burrus M. Carnahan, "The Law of Air Bombardment in Its Historical Context," *Air Force Law Review* 17 (1975), p. 60.

3. Dan Balz and Edward Cody, "U.S. Raises Estimate of Iraqi Armor Destroyed; Bodies Pulled from Rubble in Baghdad," *Washington Post*, 15 February 1991, p. A1.

4. Transcript of President Bush's News Conference, *Washington Post*, 6 February 1991, p. A21.

5. US Department of Defense, "Conduct of the Persian Gulf Conflict: An Interim Report to Congress," p. 6.

6. Report to the Secretary-General on Humanitarian Needs in Kuwait and Iraq in the Immediate Post-Crisis Environment by a Mission to the Area, UNSCOR, UN Doc. S/22366 (1991), p. 5.

7. United States Strategic Bombing Survey, "The Effect of Bombing on Health and Medical Care in Germany" (1947), p. 229.

8. Middle East Watch, "Needless Deaths in the Gulf War" (1991), pp. 10, 175.

9. Barton Gellman, "Allied Air War Struck Broadly in Iraq; Officials Acknowledge Strategy Went Beyond Purely Military Targets," *Washington Post*, 23 June 1991, p. A1.

10. Ibid.

11. Middle East Watch, "Needless Deaths in the Gulf War," p. 4.

12. Greenpeace, *On Impact: Modern Warfare and the Environment, A Case Study of the Gulf War,* ed. William M. Arkin (1991), p. 145.

13. St. Petersburg Declaration Renouncing the Use, in Time of War, of Explosive Projectiles Under 400 Grammes Weight, Dec. 11, 1868, preamble.

14. Burns H. Weston, "Security Council Resolution 678 and Persian Gulf Decision Making: Precarious Legitimacy," *American Journal of International Law,* vol. 85, no. 3 (1991), p. 526.

15. Gellman, "Allied Air War," p. A1.

16. Louis Henkin, *How Nations Behave: Law and Foreign Policy* (New York: Council on Foreign Relations, 1968), pp. 40–41.

Part 4

War Crimes and Judgment
(Jus post Bellum)

13 War and Crime

13.1

Introduction
The Editors

If the idea of crimes of war is to be anything but metaphorical, there must exist a system or code of law that places authoritative constraints upon the actions of those subject to it. And if such a system of law is to be the least bit functional, it must have some way to recognize the norms associated with it as lawful, and it must have an institutional structure to adjudicate disputes that arise under it and authoritatively determine findings of liability. Institutional mechanisms for the adjudication of disputes and the determination of criminal or civil liability are considered in the western legal tradition important components of the process of promoting and supporting the ends of justice. These mechanisms take the form of courts of law.

Courts of law have historically been used, of course, as instruments of what is commonly called political justice—the pursuit of political ends by the state under the color of the rule of law. In what is perhaps the most famous instance of political justice, Athens used the subterfuge of law to condemn Socrates for the crime of blasphemy. But the political leadership of Athens was just looking for an apparently legitimate way of ridding themselves of a political thorn in their side. To say that courts have been used for the ends of political justice, however, is not to say that they should be used this way. In the western liberal tradition, using the courts in this fashion is an abuse of justice, and in the United States, for example, courts of law are separated from the political process in order to avoid this sort of thing as much as possible.

These reflections invite readers to ponder whether war crimes trials qualify as anything more than victor's justice, a form of political justice. In the liberal political tradition that encases US and much western thinking about justice and legal process, there can be no legitimate punishment without law. But there can also be no punishment without an authoritative finding of criminal liability, and this necessarily follows a trial in which the standards of legal due process are observed. A finding of criminal liability, this is to say, follows a trial process governed by established rules that permit the accused to answer the charges brought against them and that detail the process by which the court is able to make an authoritative determination of criminal responsibility. If justice (understood in the terms of the western legal tradition) is to be done in the case of war crimes, the accused must deserve punishment for their legal transgressions as determined by an appropriately neutral and authoritative judicial body.

The notion of war crimes, by its nature, invites this kind of conceptualization; or rather, the notion itself is caught up in the legalistic conceptualizations at home in the western legal tradition. There are, however, other ways to deal with a defeated enemy. Rather than think that the agents of some conquered state are subject to legal punishment, as dictated by the standards of legal justice, they might instead be thought the proper targets of revenge or reprisal for their vicious actions. Or they might simply be considered the agents of a defeated state with whom the victors must still deal in the process of their international relations. It is not always easy to distinguish a desire for revenge from a commitment to justice. But if the idea of a viable international law that authoritatively implements the morality of war is to make much sense, this is the distinction that must be kept in mind.

But problems emerge when one confronts the historic lack of established and neutral tribunals that might adjudicate disputes that arise from warfare or from human rights violations more generally. While it is states that go to war with one another, international law sanctions the idea that individuals can be held (criminally) responsible for their actions in engaging in war *(jus ad bellum)* and in the process of fighting the war *(jus in bello)*. Traditionally, states have used their own domestic courts to try noncitizens that their prosecutors believe to have violated international law, limited only by the proviso that the state or its citizens have suffered some wrong as a result of the alleged legal transgression. Thus, for example, states settled disputes involving prize cases in warfare and piracy by using their own judicial mechanisms. In international law, proceeding in this way is a legitimate feature of state sovereignty.

In terms familiar to students of US law, this presumes first that disputes of this sort are legitimate legal disputes that courts of law are able to adjudicate and second that these courts are properly authorized to hear and resolve these disputes. The first condition introduces the question of justiciability; an issue is justiciable if it is the type of dispute that is amenable to judicial remedy. The second condition refers to the question of jurisdiction; a court has jurisdiction of a case if the dispute is legitimate and if it falls within the proper authoritative reach of the court. In US law, courts may not hear all cases that arise under their jurisdiction; they will decline to hear a case, for example, if it is nonjusticiable. Thus the United States Supreme Court refused to hear a case challenging the constitutionality of the war in Vietnam on the grounds that it was nonjusticiable; it raised a political question best left to another branch of government to settle. But courts in the United States will also refuse to hear a case if they lack proper jurisdiction. If a citizen of California kills another Californian on the streets of San Francisco, a prosecutor in Rhode Island cannot bring a charge of murder against the perpetrator in Providence. The crime was not committed there and consequently it is beyond the jurisdiction of Rhode Island courts.

Are crimes of war justiciable and can ad hoc tribunals, like the one established at Nuremberg following World War II, have legitimate jurisdiction over them? If the standards of due process associated with the western legal tradition are to be satisfied, and thus if alleged war criminals are to be legitimately prosecuted (and not merely persecuted) by international courts, these questions must be affirmatively answered.

The fact that violations of the international laws of war are now considered properly subject to criminal prosecution suggests that the question of justiciability is no longer pertinent. By conceptualizing the matter in terms of western standards of legal justice, the problem of justiciability is effectively begged. But not all critics of past war crimes trials are satisfied with this response. It has been objected that war crimes trials may intrude upon a larger political process that makes postwar relations among states worse rather than better. And in fact it seems difficult if not impossible to tease political considerations out of the equation of how best to deal with postwar legal proceedings. Following World War II, for example, the United States refused to allow the Japanese Emperor to stand trial for war crimes at the Tokyo international military tribunal in spite of objections from its allies. The US position, however, was that including the Emperor in the proceedings would make the reconstruction of Japan, and postwar relations with Japan, far more difficult. But if political considerations do in practice trump the concerns of international legal justice on occasion, why should one take them seriously on other occasions? Justice cannot be served if politics is allowed to intrude, but if it is considered important to let politics intrude, it might be best to concede that this is not an issue where justice can really be done.

The problem of jurisdiction is perhaps even more complicated. Quincy Wright makes a strong case for the legitimate jurisdiction of the international military tribunal at Nuremberg. Wright defends the tribunal's contention that its jurisdiction derived both from the fact that the prosecuting states were the legitimate legal authorities in Germany following the war and from the fact that the tribunal simply constituted a legitimate extension of the right of states to try war criminals in their domestic courts. The first condition is far more restrictive of jurisdiction than the second, however, and it is worth pondering whether the second condition alone would suffice to establish an international tribunal's jurisdiction over war crimes if the individuals charged were not the agents of a conquered state.

The problem of jurisdiction has taken a distinctive new shape, however, with the emergence of a treaty establishing an International Criminal Court. (See the Rome Statute of the International Criminal Court below.) As Michael Newton illustrates, the Rome Statute has done much to complicate the issue of jurisdiction in the name of simplifying it. Is the new ICC a limitation upon state sovereignty, or does it work in conjunction with state sovereignty as a supplement to the domestic legal systems of states that might be overly taxed if called upon to try war crimes and crimes against humanity? Newton argues that the notion of complementarity indicates that the ICC is formally intended as a complement to domestic legal jurisdictions and should not be viewed as a superior court with the authority to trump domestic legal jurisdictions. But the court is also designed to guarantee that war criminals do not go unpunished, and it is difficult to see how the ICC could effectively function to realize this objective without becoming in fact a superior court capable of preempting domestic legal jurisdiction.

Newton's most intriguing concern is that the ICC is empowered by the Rome Statute to determine its own jurisdiction under Articles 13(c) and 15 and is not answerable to any other international body. There is, in effect, a conflict with other jurisdictional conditions that seems to allow prosecutors and judges in practice to exercise a jurisdictional control that works against complementarity, without institutional oversight permitted by any other body. Given the disinclination of states to tolerate de facto limitations upon their sovereignty, by means of intrusions into the operation of their domestic legal systems, and corresponding concerns about the unchecked power of prosecutorial authority in the ICC, this issue is likely to detract from the future success of the court. Still, the establishment of the ICC is a promising response to the problem of victor's justice, but it remains far from clear that the court will meet with great success in an international environment where politics continues to obscure the requirements of justice.

13.2

Charter of the International Military Tribunal (Nuremberg)

Signed: August 8, 1945

■ **Section II: Jurisdiction and General Principles**

Article 6

The Tribunal established by the Agreement referred to in Article 1 hereof for the trial and punishment of the major war criminals of the European Axis countries shall have the power to try and punish persons who, acting in the interests of the European Axis countries, whether as individuals or as members of organizations, committed any of the following crimes.

The following acts, or any of them, are crimes coming within the jurisdiction of the Tribunal for which there shall be individual responsibility:

(a) *Crimes against peace:* namely, planning, preparation, initiation or waging of a war of aggression, or a war in violation of international treaties, agreements or assurances, or participation in a common plan or conspiracy for the accomplishment of any of the foregoing;

(b) *War crimes:* namely, violations of the laws or customs of war. Such violations shall include, but not be limited to, murder, ill-treatment or deportation to slave labor or for any other purpose of civilian population of or in occupied territory, murder or ill-treatment of prisoners of war or persons on the seas, killing of hostages, plunder of public or private property, wanton destruction of cities, towns or villages, or devastation not justified by military necessity;

(c) *Crimes against humanity:* namely, murder, extermination, enslavement, deportation, and other inhumane acts committed against any civilian population, before or during the war; or persecutions on political, racial or religious grounds in execution of or in connection with any crime within the jurisdiction of the Tribunal, whether or not in violation of the domestic law of the country where perpetrated.

Leaders, organizers, instigators and accomplices participating in the formulation or execution of a common plan or conspiracy to commit any of the foregoing crimes are responsible for all acts performed by any persons in execution of such plan.

Article 7

The official position of defendants, whether as Heads of State or responsible officials in Government Departments, shall not be considered as freeing them from responsibility or mitigating punishment.

Article 8

The fact that the Defendant acted pursuant to order of his Government or of a superior shall not free him from responsibility, but may be considered in mitigation of punishment if the Tribunal determines that justice so requires.

Article 9

At the trial of any individual member of any group or organization the Tribunal may declare (in connection with any act of which the individual may be convicted) that the group or organization of which the individual was a member was a criminal organization.

After the receipt of the Indictment the Tribunal shall give such notice as it thinks fit that the prosecution intends to ask the Tribunal to make such declaration and any member of the organization will be entitled to apply to the Tribunal for leave to be heard by the Tribunal upon the question of the criminal character of the organization. The Tribunal shall have power to allow or reject the application. If the application is allowed, the Tribunal may direct in what manner the applicants shall be represented and heard.

Article 10

In cases where a group or organization is declared criminal by the Tribunal, the competent national authority of any Signatory shall have the right to bring individual to trial for membership therein before national, military or occupation courts. In any such case the criminal nature of the group or organization is considered proved and shall not be questioned. . . .

■ Section IV: Fair Trial for Defendants

Article 16

In order to ensure fair trial for the Defendants, the following procedure shall be followed:

(a) The Indictment shall include full particulars specifying in detail the charges against the Defendants. A copy of the Indictment and of all the documents lodged with the Indictment, translated into a language which he understands, shall be furnished to the Defendant at reasonable time before the Trial.

(b) During any preliminary examination or trial of a Defendant he will have the right to give any explanation relevant to the charges made against him.

(c) A preliminary examination of a Defendant and his Trial shall be conducted in, or translated into, a language which the Defendant understands.

(d) A Defendant shall have the right to conduct his own defense before the Tribunal or to have the assistance of Counsel.

(e) A Defendant shall have the right through himself or through his Counsel to present evidence at the Trial in support of his defense, and to cross-examine any witness called by the Prosecution.

13.3

The Law of the Nuremberg Trials

Quincy Wright

On the afternoon of October 1, 1946, the International Military Tribunal at Nuremberg sentenced twelve of the twenty-two Nazi defendants to death by hanging and seven to imprisonment for terms ranging from ten years to life. Three were acquitted. Three of the six accused organizations were found to be criminal. The reading of these sentences was preceded by the reading, through the whole of September 30, of the general opinion of the Tribunal on the four counts of the indictment and, on the morning of October 1, of the opinion on the charges against each defendant.[1] The Control Council for Germany considered applications for clemency for most of those convicted but did not grant them and carried out the executions of those sentenced to death on October 16 with the exception of Martin Bormann who had not been found and Hermann Goering who had succeeded in committing suicide a few hours earlier. Thus came to an end what President Truman described as "the first international criminal assize in history."[2] . . .

The trial was begun on November 20, 1945, and continued until October 1, 1946. It was conducted in four languages facilitated by a simultaneous interpretation device. The case of the prosecution was opened by the Americans who dealt with the first count, conspiracy to commit war crimes, on which all defendants had been indicted. The British prosecution followed the second count, planning, preparing, initiating or waging aggressive war on which sixteen defendants had been indicted. The French prosecution then dealt with counts 3 and 4, as applied to the West, and the Soviet prosecution followed with the same counts in the East. Count 3 charged violation of the laws and customs of war, and count 4 crimes against humanity. Nineteen defendants were indicted under each of these counts. . . .

The trial has had both champions and critics. The former point out that it gave publicity to thousands of documents discovered by the prosecution and over 17,000 pages of oral evidence and argument of great historic and educational value in establishing the activities of the Nazis and the origins of the war. It manifested the practicability of a fair trial of war crimes in an international tribunal, and may encourage the establishment of a permanent tribunal with a wider jurisdiction for the trial of such crimes and other offenses against the law of nations not dealt with by national tribunals. It established important precedents for the development of international law concerning the definition of certain crimes, particularly that of aggressive war, and concerning the criminal liability of individuals acting in the name of a state, under official orders, or as members of criminal conspiracies or organizations. . . .

■ Criticisms of the Trial

Critics of the trial fall into two classes, those who object to the decisions and sentences and those who object to the law. Critics of the first class question the judgment of the Tribunal in weighing the evidence and appraising the magnitude of offenses. No attempt can be made here to examine the careful weighing of evidence applicable to each individual defendant and each accused organization in the judgment. The Tribunal's theory in sentencing may, however, be considered. The Charter [of the International Military Tribunal] authorized death sentences or less, thus confirming the usual practice of military commissions. Some critics, including the Soviet judge, have expressed dissatisfaction that some of those found guilty on counts 1 and 2 (conspiracy and aggressive war), like Hess, were not given death sentences. The Tribunal declared "to initiate a war of aggression is the supreme international crime, differing only from other war crimes in that it contains within itself the accumulated evil of the whole."[3] It gave no reason for deciding that this crime deserved a less severe punishment than crimes against humanity. The following explanation may be suggested. Though aggressive war may result in larger losses of life, property and social values than any other crime, yet the relationship of the acts constituting the crime to such losses is less close than in the case of crime against humanity. . . . Only those defendants in the Nuremberg trial who added brutality, manifested by other crimes, to aggression were sentenced to hang. The others were given life imprisonment or even less if there were special mitigating circumstances. . . .

Critics from a legal point of view have contended that the Tribunal had no jurisdiction in international law and that it applied *ex post facto* law. Related to these criticisms have been the contention that morally the trial was unfair because constituted by one side in a war or because some of the prosecuting states had been guilty of the same offenses for which they were trying their enemies; and that politically the trial was inexpedient because it may make conciliation between victor and vanquished more difficult, because it may make heroes and martyrs of the defendants, or because its principles if generally accepted may reduce the unity of the state, increase the difficulties of maintaining domestic order, and deter statesmen from pursuing vigorous foreign policies when necessary in the national interests. These moral and political arguments depend upon ethical, psychological, and sociological assumptions which are controversial. They should be distinguished from the legal arguments which alone are under consideration here.

Legally belligerent states have habitually assumed jurisdiction to try in their own military commissions captured enemy persons accused of war crimes and to try in their own prize courts captured enemy and neutral vessels. All states in time of peace have assumed jurisdiction to try captured pirates in their own criminal courts and some states have extended the jurisdiction of such courts to other offenses against the law of nations committed by aliens abroad. The Hague Conference of 1907 adopted a convention for an international prize court to which cases could be appealed from national prize courts, and a conference held at Geneva in 1937 adopted a convention for an international criminal court to try persons accused of "terrorism" in certain circumstances but these conventions never came into force. . . .

Sovereign states, it is true, cannot be subjected to a foreign jurisdiction without their consent but no such principle applies to individuals. The Nuremberg Tribunal did not exercise jurisdiction over Germany but over certain German individuals accused of crimes. . . .

The object of legal procedure is to segregate issues sufficiently narrowly to permit of a thorough examination of the factual evidence and the legal sources bearing upon those issues. Criminal courts have not considered it appropriate to inquire during a trial whether their jurisdiction ought to be wider, whether others ought to have been indicted, whether punishment for the crime charged or for any crime is expedient, but have concerned themselves only with the questions: Does the Court have jurisdiction? How should it proceed to assure a fair trial? Does the evidence support the charges? Do the charges if proved render the accused liable under the law? Whether some statesman of the United Nations should be accused of aggressive war or of crimes against humanity, whether some soldiers or sailors of the United Nations should be accused of war crimes, whether the court should have been differently constituted with a different jurisdiction, whether Goering and the other defendants will become heroes and martyrs, whether it is desirable that aggressive war be a crime or that national sovereignty be unable to throw a cloak of immunity around persons accused of crimes—all these are important questions, but not legal questions which the Tribunal could deal with. These were doubtless considered by the four powers that made the agreement and Charter of August 8, 1945, and criticisms based on these questions are criticisms of these powers or of international law not of the Tribunal.

Some of the critics who have emphasized these points appear to dislike the trend of international law recognized in the Charter. Opinion is coming to realize that international law cannot survive in the shrinking world, threatened by military instruments of increasing destructiveness, if sanctioned only by the good faith and self-help of governments. Sanctions to be effective must operate on individuals rather than on states. But regularly enforced world criminal law applicable to individuals necessarily makes inroads upon national sovereignty and tends to change the foundation of the international community from a balance of power among sovereign states to a universal federation directly controlling individuals in all countries on matters covered by international law. In such a regime of law, aggressive war is necessarily outlawed and with it the right of states to decide when forcible self-help is permissible. Many, doubtless, look upon this reduction of national sovereignty with apprehension. Some may even be concerned lest the free decision of their government to make a "preventive war" be impaired. The Charter of the Tribunal recognized principles generally believed to be essential for a law governed world under present conditions, and naturally those who are afraid of the restrictions of a law governed world upon the nation or who think world opinion has not developed to a point that would make such a world possible, view these principles with apprehension. . . .

▪ The Tribunal Jurisdiction

. . . International law does not permit states to administer criminal law over any defendant for any act. There are limits to the criminal jurisdiction of a state. Every state does, however, have authority to set up special courts to try any person within its custody who commits war crimes, at least if such offenses threaten its security. It is believed that this jurisdiction is broad enough to cover the jurisdiction given by the Charter. If each party to the Charter could exercise such jurisdiction individually, they can agree to set up an international tribunal to exercise the jurisdiction jointly. . . .

[S]tates have habitually authorized military commissions, prize courts and criminal courts to exercise jurisdiction over many offenses against international law committed by aliens abroad. While many states apply the universality principle of criminal jurisdiction only in the case of piracy, some states have applied it to all offenses against the law of nations especially if dangerous to their security. In principle international law imposes few limitations upon the competence of states to try individuals for such acts. In the case of the steamship *Lotus,* the Permanent Court of International Justice held that a state can extend its criminal jurisdiction to any case whatever unless a rule or principle of international law forbids.

There appears to be no rule or principle of international law which forbids the parties to the Charter from exercising jurisdiction over the defendants for the offenses alleged in the Charter, provided they threatened the security of those states, a condition which can hardly be doubted, and that they were crimes under international law, a matter to be considered later.

The derivation of the Tribunal's jurisdiction from the sovereignty of Germany also appears to be well grounded. The Nazi government of Germany disappeared with the unconditional surrender of Germany in May 1945, and on June 5, 1945, the four Allied powers, then in complete control of Germany by public declaration at Berlin, assumed "supreme authority with respect to Germany, including all the powers possessed by the German Government, the High Command, and any state, municipal, or local government or authority" in order "to make provision for the cessation of any further hostilities on the part of the German armed forces for the maintenance of order in Germany, and for the administration of the country," but without intention to "effect the annexation of Germany."[4] Under international law a state may acquire sovereignty of territory by declaration of annexation after subjugation of the territory if that declaration is generally recognized by the other states of the world. The Declaration of Berlin was generally recognized, not only by the United Nations but also by neutral states. This Declaration, however, differed from the usual declaration of annexation in that it was by several states, its purposes were stated, and it was declared not to effect the annexation of Germany.

There is no doubt but that sovereignty may be held jointly by several states as has been the case in a number of *condominia*. There also have been instances of temporary exercise of sovereignty for purposes more limited than permanent annexation. The American position in Cuba from 1899 to 1903 was of this type and so also are Mandates under the League of Nations and Trusteeships under the United Nations. In principle it would appear that if a state or states are in a position to annex a territory they have the right to declare the lesser policy of exercising sovereignty temporarily for specified purposes with the intention of eventually transferring the sovereignty to someone else. This appears to be the proper construction of the Declaration of Berlin. The four Allied powers assumed the sovereignty of Germany in order, among other purposes, to administer the country until such time as they thought fit to recognize an independent German government. Their exercise of powers of legislation, adjudication, and administration in Germany during this period is permissible under international law, limited only by the rules of international law applicable to sovereign states in territory they have subjugated. Their powers go beyond those of a military occupant. It would appear, therefore, that the four states who proclaimed the Charter of August 8, 1945, had the power to enact that Charter as a legislative act for Germany provided they did not transgress fundamental principles of justice which even a conqueror ought to observe toward the inhabitants of annexed territory. . . .

■ The Law Applied

The law, defining the crimes and the conditions of liability to be applied in the trial, was set forth in the Charter and the Tribunal recognized that the law "is decisive and binding upon the Tribunal."[5] Was this law declaratory of preexisting international law binding the defendants at the time they committed the acts charged? The issue has been discussed particularly in regard to the crime of "aggressive war."

The Tribunal listened to argument on the question and concluded that a rule of international law, resting upon "general principles of justice," affirmed in this respect by several recent international declarations that aggressive war is an international crime, had been formally accepted by all the states concerned when they ratified the Pact of Paris which condemned . . . recourse to war for the solution of international controversies and renounced it as an instrument of national policy. . . .

The Tribunal therefore considered that the well-known legal maxim *nullum crimen sine lege* had been duly observed in the case.

It quoted the text of the Pact of Paris of August 27, 1928, binding sixty-three nations, including Germany, Italy, and Japan at the outbreak of the war in 1939, referred to the analogous situation of the Hague Convention, violation of which created individual criminal liability, and held that the result was to make the waging of aggressive war illegal and those committing the act criminally liable.[6] . . .

After referring to the United States Supreme Court decision in *Ex parte Quirin* and the practice cited in that case, the Tribunal said that individuals could be held responsible for criminal acts even if committed on behalf of their states "if the state in authorizing action moves outside its competence under international law." Furthermore they could not shelter themselves behind the plea of superior orders if "moral choice was in fact possible."[7] . . .

■ Offenses Against the Law of Nations

The concept of offenses against the law of nations was recognized by the classical text writers on international law and has been employed in national constitutions and statues. It was regarded as sufficiently tangible in the eighteenth century so that United States Federal Courts sustained indictments charging acts as an offense against the law of nations, even if there were no statutes defining the offense. Early in the nineteenth century it was held that the criminal jurisdiction of federal courts rested only on statutes as though the definition of crimes denounced by statutes might be left largely to international law. . . .

In the nineteenth century the development of the positivist doctrine that only states are subject to international law and that individuals are bound only by the municipal law of states with jurisdiction over them led to a decline in the application of the concept of offenses against the law of nations. This idea, however, has acquired renewed vigor in the twentieth century. . . . There is, however, still disagreement as to the scope of the concept. An analysis of general principles of international law and of criminal law suggests the following definition: A crime against international law is an act committed with intent to violate a fundamental interest protected by international law or with knowledge that the act will probably violate such an interest, and which may not be adequately punished by the exercise of the normal criminal jurisdiction of any state. States ordinarily punish crime in the interest of their own peace and security and those interests are often parallel to the general interests of the community of nations, defined by international law. Consequently the latter interests are in considerable measure protected by the normal exercise of criminal jurisdiction by states. There are, however, circumstances when this exercise of normal criminal jurisdiction is not adequate. To protect itself in such circumstances international law has recognized four methods of supplementing the normal criminal jurisdiction of states.

International law has imposed obligations on states to punish certain acts committed in their territory, punishment of which is primarily an interest of other states or the community of nations and which therefore might be neglected in the absence of such a rule. Offenses against foreign diplomatic officers, against foreign currencies, or against the security of foreign states fall in this category.

International law has permitted a state to exercise jurisdiction over acts committed by aliens abroad either on the ground that such acts endanger states or their nationals. The jurisdiction of military commissions over offenses against the law of war, of prize courts against contraband carriers, and blockade runners, of admiralty courts against pirates, and of criminal courts against offenses defined in general international conventions or customary international law are of this character.

International law has recognized the competence of states to establish international law tribunals for the trial of grave offenses not dealt with by national tribunals such as terrorism and aggression.

International law has favored or, in the opinion of some writers, required, the cooperation of states in the apprehension and punishment of fugitive criminals through extradition or other treaties. This cooperation concerns particularly persons accused of universally recognized crimes such as murder, rape, mayhem, arson, piracy, robbery, burglary, forgery, counterfeiting, embezzlement, and theft. Political and military offenses are normally excluded. . . .

From a consideration of the obligation arising from these principles of international law, of the fundamental interests of states and of the community of nations protected by international law, of the acts which violate these obligations and threaten these interests, and of the circumstances which are likely to prevent punishment of such acts by the exercise of the normal jurisdiction of states, it is possible to determine whether a given act is a crime against the law of nations.

■ War Crimes and Crimes Against Humanity

No one has questioned this conclusion as regards the "war crimes" in the narrow sense. Military commissions in wars of the past have habitually tried and punished enemy persons captured and found to have been guilty of acts in violation of the customary and conventional law of war. . . .

The "crimes against humanity" were considered with the "war crimes" from which they differed only in being directed against German nationals rather than against enemies. The Tribunal had no doubt that the acts in pursuance of policies of "genocide" and clearing land by extermination of its population, if carried on in occupied territories or against enemy persons, constituted "war crimes." . . . The idea that the individual is entitled to respect for fundamental rights, accepted by the earlier writers on international law, has come under extensive consideration recently and has been accepted in the United Nations Charter, one of whose purposes is "to achieve international cooperation in promoting and encouraging respect for human rights and for fundamental freedoms for all without distinction as to race, sex, language, or religion."

It is also to be noted that the acts which constitute "crimes against humanity" have habitually been the subject of extradition treaties. States have recognized the duty of cooperating in bringing persons guilty of such crimes to justice. . . .

The Tribunal had no difficulty in assuming that war crimes and crimes against humanity in the narrow sense of the Charter were crimes under customary international law at the time the acts were committed and felt it unnecessary to give to this question the elaborate discussion which it devoted to the "crimes against peace." It merely said:

> In so far as the inhumane acts charged in the Indictment, and committed after the beginning of the war, did not constitute war crimes, they were all committed in execution of, or in connection with, the aggressive war, and therefore constituted crimes against humanity. . . .[8]

The world shattered by two world wars needs to have its confidence in law restored. Such confidence can only develop if people believe that formal law embodies justice and that it will be enforced. The Nuremberg trial is likely to contribute to both of these ends. The general opinion that aggressive war and mass massacre are crimes has been recognized in formal international law and that law has been sanctioned by trial and punishment of many of the guilty. Much remains to be done but opinion will be reassured that international law is neither esoteric nor helpless. The time may be ripe for further development by the establishment of a permanent international criminal court as drafted in the Geneva Convention of 1937 and the codification of international criminal law as suggested by Judge Biddle with President Truman's approval, and recommended by the General Assembly of the United Nations on December 11, 1946.

■ Notes

1. The judgment was mimeographed on 293 pages of legal size paper with a table of contents and also appeared, followed by the sentences, on pp. 16794 to 17077 of the daily record of the trial. The former is here referred to as "Judgment" and the latter as "Record."

2. *Department of State Bulletin,* vol. 15, p. 776 (Oct. 27, 1946).

3. Judgment, p. 186.

4. Quincy Wright, *Mandates Under the League of Nations* (Chicago: University of Chicago Press, 1930), pp. 13, 306–309, 315–339, 530–537.

5. Judgment, p. 216.

6. Judgment, pp. 218–219.

7. Judgment, p. 221.

8. Judgment, p. 249.

13.4 ____

Rome Statute of the International Criminal Court

Signed: July 17, 1998
In Force: July 1, 2000

■ Part 1: Establishment of the Court

Article 1: The Court

An International Criminal Court ("the Court") is hereby established. It shall be a permanent institution and shall have the power to exercise its jurisdiction over persons for the most serious crimes of international concern, as referred to in this Statute, and shall be complementary to national criminal jurisdictions. The jurisdiction and functioning of the Court shall be governed by the provisions of this Statute. . . .

■ Part 2: Jurisdiction, Admissibility and Applicable Law

Article 5: Crimes Within the Jurisdiction of the Court

1. The jurisdiction of the Court shall be limited to the most serious crimes of concern to the international community as a whole. The Court has jurisdiction in accordance with this Statute with respect to the following crimes:
    (a) The crime of genocide;
    (b) Crimes against humanity;
    (c) War crimes;
    (d) The crime of aggression.
2. The Court shall exercise jurisdiction over the crime of aggression once a provision is adopted in accordance with articles 121 and 123 defining the crime and setting out the conditions under which the Court shall exercise jurisdiction with respect to this crime. Such a provision shall be consistent with the relevant provisions of the Charter of the United Nations.
. . .

Article 8: War Crimes

1. The Court shall have jurisdiction in respect of war crimes in particular when committed as part of a plan or policy or as part of a large-scale commission of such crimes.

2. For the purpose of this Statute, "war crimes" means:

(a) Grave breaches of the Geneva Conventions of 12 August 1949, namely, any of the following acts against persons or property protected under the provisions of the relevant Geneva Convention: (i) Willful killing; (ii) Torture or inhuman treatment, including biological experiments; (iii) Willfully causing great suffering, or serious injury to body or health; (iv) Extensive destruction and appropriation of property, not justified by military necessity and carried out unlawfully and wantonly; (v) Compelling a prisoner of war or other protected person to serve in the forces of a hostile Power; (vi) Willfully depriving a prisoner of war or other protected person of the rights of fair and regular trial; (vii) Unlawful deportation or transfer or unlawful confinement; (viii) Taking of hostages.

(b) Other serious violations of the laws and customs applicable in international armed conflict, within the established framework of international law, namely, any of the following acts: (i) Intentionally directing attacks against the civilian population as such or against individual civilians not taking direct part in hostilities; (ii) Intentionally directing attacks against civilian objects, that is, objects which are not military objectives; (iii) Intentionally directing attacks against personnel, installations, material, units or vehicles involved in a humanitarian assistance or peacekeeping mission in accordance with the Charter of the United Nations, as long as they are entitled to the protection given to civilians or civilian objects under the international law of armed conflict; (iv) Intentionally launching an attack in the knowledge that such attack will cause incidental loss of life or injury to civilians or damage to civilian objects or widespread, long-term and severe damage to the natural environment which would be clearly excessive in relation to the concrete and direct overall military advantage anticipated; (v) Attacking or bombarding, by whatever means, towns, villages, dwellings or buildings which are undefended and which are not military objectives; (vi) Killing or wounding a combatant who, having laid down his arms or having no longer means of defence, has surrendered at discretion; (vii) Making improper use of a flag of truce, of the flag or of the military insignia and uniform of the enemy or of the United Nations, as well as of the distinctive emblems of the Geneva Conventions, resulting in death or serious personal injury; (viii) The transfer, directly or indirectly, by the Occupying Power of parts of its own civilian population into the territory it occupies, or the deportation or transfer of all or parts of the population of the occupied territory within or outside this territory; (ix)

Intentionally directing attacks against buildings dedicated to religion, education, art, science or charitable purposes, historic monuments, hospitals and places where the sick and wounded are collected, provided they are not military objectives; (x) Subjecting persons who are in the power of an adverse party to physical mutilation or to medical or scientific experiments of any kind which are neither justified by the medical, dental or hospital treatment of the person concerned nor carried out in his or her interest, and which cause death to or seriously endanger the health of such person or persons; (xi) Killing or wounding treacherously individuals belonging to the hostile nation or army; (xii) Declaring that no quarter will be given; (xiii) Destroying or seizing the enemy's property unless such destruction or seizure be imperatively demanded by the necessities of war; (xiv) Declaring abolished, suspended or inadmissible in a court of law the rights and actions of the nationals of the hostile party; (xv) Compelling the nationals of the hostile party to take part in the operations of war directed against their own country, even if they were in the belligerent's service before the commencement of the war; (xvi) Pillaging a town or place, even when taken by assault; (xvii) Employing poison or poisoned weapons; (xviii) Employing asphyxiating, poisonous or other gases, and all analogous liquids, materials or devices; (xix) Employing bullets which expand or flatten easily in the human body, such as bullets with a hard envelope which does not entirely cover the core or is pierced with incisions; (xx) Employing weapons, projectiles and material and methods of warfare which are of a nature to cause superfluous injury or unnecessary suffering or which are inherently indiscriminate in violation of the international law of armed conflict, provided that such weapons, projectiles and material and methods of warfare are the subject of a comprehensive prohibition and are included in an annex to this Statute, by an amendment in accordance with the relevant provisions set forth in articles 121 and 123; (xxi) Committing outrages upon personal dignity, in particular humiliating and degrading treatment; (xxii) Committing rape, sexual slavery, enforced prostitution, forced pregnancy, as defined in article 7, paragraph 2 (f), enforced sterilization, or any other form of sexual violence also constituting a grave breach of the Geneva Conventions; (xxiii) Utilizing the presence of a civilian or other protected person to render certain points, areas or military forces immune from military operations; (xxiv) Intentionally directing attacks against buildings, material, medical units and transport, and personnel using the distinctive emblems of the Geneva Conventions in conformity with international law; (xxv) Intentionally using starvation of civilians as a method of warfare by depriving them of objects indispensable to their survival, including willfully impeding relief supplies as provided for under the Geneva Conventions; (xxvi) Conscripting or enlisting children under the age of fifteen years into the national armed forces or using them to participate actively in hostilities.

(c) In the case of an armed conflict not of an international character, serious violations of article 3 common to the four Geneva Conventions of 12 August 1949, namely, any of the following acts committed against persons taking no active part in the hostilities, including members of armed forces who have laid down their arms and those placed hors de combat by sickness, wounds, detention or any other cause: (i) Violence to life and person, in particular murder of all kinds, mutilation, cruel treatment and torture; (ii) Committing outrages upon personal dignity, in particular humiliating and degrading treatment; (iii) Taking of hostages; (iv) The passing of sentences and the carrying out of executions without previous judgment pronounced by a regularly constituted court, affording all judicial guarantees which are generally recognized as indispensable.

(d) Paragraph 2 (c) applies to armed conflicts not of an international character and thus does not apply to situations of internal disturbances and tensions, such as riots, isolated and sporadic acts of violence or other acts of a similar nature.

(e) Other serious violations of the laws and customs applicable in armed conflicts not of an international character, within the established framework of international law, namely, any of the following acts: (i) Intentionally directing attacks against the civilian population as such or against individual civilians not taking direct part in hostilities; (ii) Intentionally directing attacks against buildings, material, medical units and transport, and personnel using the distinctive emblems of the Geneva Conventions in conformity with international law; (iii) Intentionally directing attacks against personnel, installations, material, units or vehicles involved in a humanitarian assistance or peacekeeping mission in accordance with the Charter of the United Nations, as long as they are entitled to the protection given to civilians or civilian objects under the international law of armed conflict; (iv) Intentionally directing attacks against buildings dedicated to religion, education, art, science or charitable purposes, historic monuments, hospitals and places where the sick and wounded are collected, provided they are not military objectives; (v) Pillaging a town or place, even when taken by assault; (vi) Committing rape, sexual slavery, enforced prostitution, forced pregnancy, as defined in article 7, paragraph 2 (f), enforced sterilization, and any other form of sexual violence also constituting a serious violation of article 3 common to the four Geneva Conventions; (vii) Conscripting or enlisting children under the age of fifteen years into armed forces or groups or using them to participate actively in hostilities; (viii) Ordering the displacement of the civilian population for reasons related to the conflict, unless the security of the civilians involved or imperative military reasons so demand; (ix) Killing or wounding treacherously a combatant adversary; (x) Declaring that no quarter will be given; (xi) Subjecting persons who are in the power of another party to the conflict to physical mutilation or to medical or scientific experiments of any kind which are neither justified by the medical, dental or hospital treatment of the person concerned nor carried out in his or her interest, and which cause death to or seriously endanger the health of such person or persons; (xii) Destroying or seizing the property of an adversary unless such destruction or seizure be imperatively demanded by the necessities of the conflict.

(f) Paragraph 2 (e) applies to armed conflicts not of an international character and thus does not apply to situations of internal disturbances and tensions, such as riots, isolated and sporadic acts of violence or other acts of a similar nature. It applies to armed conflicts that take place in the territory of a State when there is protracted armed conflict between governmental authorities and organized armed groups or between such groups.

3. Nothing in paragraph 2 (c) and (e) shall affect the responsibility of a Government to maintain or re-establish law and order in the State or to defend the unity and territorial integrity of the State, by all legitimate means. . . .

■ Part 3: General Principles of Criminal Law

Article 27: Irrelevance of Official Capacity

1. This Statute shall apply equally to all persons without any distinction based on official capacity. In particular, official capacity as a Head of State or Government, a member of a Government or parliament, an elected representative or a government official shall in no case exempt a person from criminal responsibility under this Statute, nor shall it, in and of itself, constitute a ground for reduction of sentence.

2. Immunities or special procedural rules which may attach to the official capacity of a person, whether under national or international law, shall not bar the Court from exercising its jurisdiction over such a person.

Article 28: Responsibility of Commanders and Other Superiors

In addition to other grounds of criminal responsibility under this Statute for crimes within the jurisdiction of the Court:

(a) A military commander or person effectively acting as a military commander shall be criminally responsible for crimes within the jurisdiction of the Court committed by forces under his or her effective command and control, or effective authority and control as the case may be, as a result of his or her failure to exercise control properly over such forces, where: (i) That military commander or person either knew or, owing to the circumstances at the time, should have known that the forces were committing or about to commit such crimes; and (ii) That military commander or person failed to take all necessary and reasonable measures within his or her power to prevent or repress their commission or to submit the matter to the competent authorities for investigation and prosecution.

(b) With respect to superior and subordinate relationships not described in paragraph (a), a superior shall be criminally responsible for crimes within the jurisdiction of the Court committed by subordinates under his or her effective authority and control, as a result of his or her failure to exercise control properly over such subordinates, where: (i) The superior either knew, or consciously disregarded information which clearly indicated, that the subordinates were committing or about to commit such crimes; (ii) The crimes concerned activities that were within the effective responsibility and control of the superior; and (iii) The superior failed to take all necessary and reasonable measures within his or her power to prevent or repress their commission or to submit the matter to the competent authorities for investigation and prosecution. . . .

Article 31: Grounds for Excluding Criminal Responsibility

1. In addition to other grounds for excluding criminal responsibility provided for in this Statute, a person shall not be criminally responsible if, at the time of that person's conduct: . . .

(d) The conduct which is alleged to constitute a crime within the jurisdiction of the Court has been caused by duress resulting from a threat of imminent death or of continuing or imminent serious bodily harm against that person or another person, and the person acts necessarily and reasonably to avoid this threat, provided that the person does not intend to cause a greater harm than the one sought to be avoided. Such a threat may either be: (i) Made by other persons; or (ii) Constituted by other circumstances beyond that person's control. . . .

Article 33: Superior Orders and Prescription of Law

1. The fact that a crime within the jurisdiction of the Court has been committed by a person pursuant to an order of a Government or of a superior, whether military or civilian, shall not relieve that person of criminal responsibility unless:

(a) The person was under a legal obligation to obey orders of the Government or the superior in question;

(b) The person did not know that the order was unlawful; and

(c) The order was not manifestly unlawful.

2. For the purposes of this article, orders to commit genocide or crimes against humanity are manifestly unlawful.

13.5 _____

Comparative Complementarity

Michael A. Newton

■ Introduction

The ongoing diplomatic and political efforts to create the International Criminal Court (ICC) are forever altering the landscape of the international community and the face of international law. The Chairman of the Drafting Committee working on the negotiations towards the Rome Statute of the International Criminal Court (Rome Statute) proclaimed that "[t]he world will never be the same after the establishment of an international criminal court."[1] Indeed, as the Rome Conference began, formal adoption of a foundational document was widely considered to be impossible. After five weeks of intense debate, the final text emerged as a take-it-or-leave-it "package" that had been cobbled together behind closed doors during the middle of the night. The leaders of the Rome Conference completed the final text at two o'clock in the morning of the last day of the conference, Friday, 17 July 1998. Far from achieving consensus, the final text postulated solutions to some drafting questions that delegates had been unable to resolve, and went so far as to include a number of provisions that the conference Bureau selected and presented to the floor without open debate on either the text itself or its substantive merits. . . .

For the proponents of the Rome Statute, the reality that it was adopted only by abandoning the historic diplomatic practice of consensus is immaterial. Many ardent treaty supporters and the non-governmental organizations (NGOs) that pushed for the Rome Statute ignore its structural flaws and view it as a triumph of international aspiration over the political and pragmatic realities of the international system that have prevented the evolution of an effective and permanent international criminal court since the end of

---

World War I. Seen in the best possible light, the Rome Statute represents the hope of governments from all around the world that the force of international law can restrain the evil impulses that have stained history with the blood of millions of innocent victims. . . .

Logically, an effective supranational court should function as a fallback forum to prosecute individuals who commit crimes while in the service of authoritarian regimes that ignore the binding norms of international law. Those regimes are the most prone to commit the crimes within the jurisdiction of the ICC, and yet those same states could previously invoke principles of sovereignty to protect their nationals from prosecution in their domestic judicial forums. At the conclusion of the Rome Conference, treaty supporters concluded that an effective ICC could not rest the full extent of its judicial power on the consent of a state because regimes that ignore the rule of law would be virtually certain not to submit their nationals to the jurisdiction of the court. Hence, the final "package" that became the Rome Statute bypassed the traditional rule of international law that a treaty "does not create obligations or rights for a third [s]tate without its consent."[2]

To attain the goal of international justice, Article 1 of the Rome Statute promulgates in simple language that the court will "be a permanent institution and shall have the power to exercise its jurisdiction over persons for the most serious crimes of international concern . . . and shall be *complementary* to national criminal jurisdictions."[3] The Rome Statute nowhere defines the term "complementarity," but the plain text of Article 1 compels the conclusion that the International Criminal Court is intended to supplement the foundation of domestic punishment of international violations, rather than supplant domestic enforcement of international norms. . . .

The complementarity principle is the fulcrum that prioritizes the authority of domestic forums to prosecute the crimes defined in Article 5 of the Rome Statute. Phrased another way, the complementarity principle is intended to preserve the power of the ICC over irresponsible states that refuse to prosecute nationals who commit heinous international crimes, but balances that supranational power against the sovereign right of states to prosecute their own nationals without external interference. . . .

The monumental and controversial development in the Rome Statute is that the proponents of international justice established a framework for a supranational court that enshrines the principle that state sovereignty can on occasion be subordinated to the goal of achieving accountability for violations of international humanitarian law. . . . The complex blend of civil law, common law, customary international law, and *sui generis* that combine in the Rome Statute is held together by the notion that the sovereign nations of the world are joined, not as competitors in the pursuit of sovereign self interest, but as interdependent components of a larger global civil society. . . .

As noted above, the Rome Conference concluded with a rush of momentum towards an international court empowered to impose international law on individual citizens of sovereign nations, even when that state does not consent to the exercise of supranational power over its nationals. The term "complementarity" is a newly minted phrase that builds on the well-established practice of nations enforcing international law. . . .

The International Criminal Court is intended to be an autonomous supranational institution that possesses international legal personality. As such, it will be required to work alongside sovereign states in a wide array of investigative, prosecutorial, and administrative activities. . . .

▇ Jurisprudential Roots of Complementarity

The discipline of international criminal law springs from the intersection of two legal traditions that are separate yet interrelated. The criminal aspects of international law are historically and juridically intertwined with the international aspects of national criminal law. The criminal aspects of international law can be traced to a variety of sources in which the nations of the world united to criminalize certain conduct under established international norms. . . .

Since discussions concerning a permanent International Criminal Court began, the challenge to the international community has been to distill a practical formula for reconciling or prioritizing the jurisdictional claims between an emerging supranational institution and the domestic forums that would otherwise have jurisdiction. Paradoxically, the substantive norms of international criminal law did not develop as a coexistent component of the early efforts to develop the framework for an international criminal court. The articulation of a defined set of international offenses proceeded in separate negotiations for different reasons than the discussions over the development of an international criminal institution. This lack of synchronization helps explain why the crimes proscribed in the Rome Statute do not replicate every act that is prohibited as a matter of international law. Nevertheless, the judicial authority of domestic forums to impose criminal responsibility for serious violations of international law is an essential underpinning of the jurisprudential framework of the complementarity principle. . . .

Legal Foundations
The ICC is intended to reinforce rather than overturn the well-established right of sovereign states to enforce international humanitarian law; the principle of complementarity embodies this linkage. The legal authority of domestic states to proscribe and adjudicate cases involving violations of humanitarian law is so firmly rooted in the international legal regime that

the Rome Statute makes no distinction between states party and non-states party with respect to complementarity. Put simply, for every single act by every single accused that could theoretically be subject to the jurisdiction of the ICC, there would be one or more sovereign states that have legal authority to investigate and prosecute the case. . . .

[A]s a mirror image of the fact that the complementarity principle applies to all states in the international community and all crimes within the jurisdiction of the ICC, international law today justifies universal jurisdiction for any state to adjudicate the crimes of genocide, crimes against humanity, and serious war crimes. This facet of international law developed despite the practice of some states that used the pretext of war crimes prosecutions for the purpose of political repression or psychological manipulation. Today, every state possesses the juridical ability to proscribe and prosecute the crimes detailed in the Rome Statute. . . .

As a logical corollary, domestic prosecutions form the basis for deducing that international law permits individual criminal responsibility for those who commit heinous crimes under the color of state authority. The field of international humanitarian law developed around the notion that the legal norms were not just theoretical matters between states, but actual restraints to guide the conduct of individuals. There can be no remaining doubt that the Rome Statute does not stretch the bounds of established legal principle with the sweeping declaration that a "person who commits a crime within the jurisdiction of the Court shall be individually responsible and liable for punishment."[4] As Justice Jackson observed in his oft-quoted opening statement to the International Military Tribunal (IMT) seated in the ruins of Nuremberg, Germany: "[T]he idea that a State, any more than a corporation, commits crimes, is a fiction."[5] Based on the finding that "international law imposes duties and liabilities on individuals as well as upon States has long been recognized,"[6] the IMT rejected defense arguments that international law governs only states, as well as the contention that the doctrine of state sovereignty shields perpetrators from personal responsibility for their actions. . . .

Crimes Beneath the ICC Threshold

Against this backdrop of international law and practice, the Rome Statute implicitly concedes that states will remain responsible for prosecuting the vast majority of offenses even in a mature ICC regime. History shows that the overwhelming number of prosecutions for violations of international humanitarian law have come in domestic forums as opposed to international tribunals. . . .

As a fundamental check on its power, the substantive jurisdiction of the ICC is restricted to only "the most serious crimes of concern to the international community as a whole."[7] Article 5(1) requires that the jurisdiction of the ICC "shall be limited" by the "most serious crimes of concern" threshold. This textual limit on the scope of ICC jurisdiction has both a descriptive and subjective component. Indeed, the myriad of offenses detailed in Articles 6, 7, and 8 are tragic and inherently serious from a humanitarian perspective. In order to fall within the jurisdiction of the ICC, however, the offense must be on the high end of a scale of relative severity, and must have some quality that warrants the subjective assessment that the crime is of "concern to the international community as a whole." . . .

While representing a substantive check on the court's jurisdiction, the "most serious crimes" threshold also establishes the ICC as a supranational institution working within a system of sovereign states. This precludes the misconception that the Rome Statute enacts some new regime of international federalism where sovereign states are deemed to be subordinate to the authority of the ICC. . . .

■ Textual Implementation of Complementarity in the Rome Statute

Complementarity at the Rome Conference

The balance of penal prerogative between sovereign states in the international community and a permanent supranational criminal court has been a prominent issue of concern since the beginning of serious diplomatic efforts towards creating such an institution. The detailed progression of diplomatic negotiations towards the text that eventually became the Rome Statute documents a complex, contentious, and incremental process, which ultimately produced a treaty adopted by an emotional vote rather than by international consensus. . . .

[T]he principle of complementarity represents one golden thread of consensus that runs through every documentary step along the road towards the supranational criminal court. This axiom, that the ICC is "neither designed nor intended" to supplant independent and effective domestic judicial systems, served as a guiding principle found throughout the long series of diplomatic interchanges culminating in the Rome Statute. . . .

[T]he most controversial issues associated with jurisdiction—state consent as a requirement for ICC jurisdiction over its nationals and the allocation of power between the Security Council and the ICC—were not resolved until the last day of the Rome Conference. These issues were so intertwined that compromises in one area would impact other ongoing debates. Hence, states were reluctant to compromise on each critical point in succession without "having a clear sense of how the total picture would appear."[8] Complementarity, on the other hand, enjoyed a unique role in the negotiating history of the Rome Statute because debate centered not on its merits or appropriateness, but on perfecting the most agreeable textual approach that would gain state consensus. All delegations understood the meaning of complementarity as an organizing principle, but the articulation of its substantive and descriptive parameters required sustained negotiations.

Rather than serving as the point of initial consensus in one isolated text, the complementarity principle became the cornerstone for many other debates, much like the first domino in a series, to begin the process of negotiation and agreement. As a result, the Rome Statute emerged with a complex, layered procedural structure, but one in which the complementarity principle was preserved. To illustrate, once a particular offense rises above the "most serious crimes of concern" threshold, the case must meet the preconditions for jurisdiction outlined in Articles 12 through 16. . . . The complementarity principle is further embedded as an additional procedural requirement found in Article 17, which requires the ICC to "determine that a case is inadmissible" where certain criteria are met. . . .

In order to implement the complementarity principle implemented by the Rome Statute, the ICC prosecutor and judicial chambers must respect and adhere to the Statute's admissibility criteria. Article 17 represents the most direct mechanism for allocating responsibility for a certain prosecution between the ICC and one or more domestic sovereigns that may have jurisdictional authority. Where the textual criteria of Article 17 are satisfied such that a case is "inadmissible," the Rome Statute constrains the authority of the ICC prosecutor and judicial chambers. . . .

Relevant Treaty Provisions

Articles 12–16, Jurisdictional Competence. The jurisdictional patchwork of the ICC represents its most central and controversial component. This series of provisions did not emerge until the final day of the Rome Conference. The concept of ICC jurisdiction involves much more than a simple assessment of whether a particular act fits the definition of a substantive crime within the meaning of the Statute. . . . The Rome Statute is unique in the field of international law because it commingles the jurisdiction to prescribe, the jurisdiction to adjudicate, and the jurisdiction to enforce international norms into one quasi-legislative treaty. . . . The Trial Chamber is accordingly required to "satisfy itself that it has jurisdiction in any case brought before it."[9]

The final package that became the Rome Statute is structured around a dual track system of jurisdiction. Article 13 implicitly rejects a simple assertion of universal ICC jurisdiction by limiting the court's jurisdictional authority to cases referred either by the United Nations Security Council or to those referred using carefully described jurisdictional competence. . . .

As a check on the power of states, and hence a limit to complementarity, Article 13(b) is particularly relevant. Article 13(b) allows the Security Council to refer a case to the ICC prosecutor acting under its [UN Charter] Chapter VII authority. . . . The Security Council has absolute authority to define the territorial, temporal, or normative scope of the prosecutor's license to proceed based on its plenary power with regard to actions designed to maintain or restore international peace and security.

With regard to the complementarity principle, a Chapter VII referral would override a state's inherent national authority to insist on using its own judicial processes. Even though jurisdiction under Article 13 is a legal inquiry distinct from admissibility under Article 17. . . . a Security Council referral would supersede the state's right to use its own courts as the forum of first resort. While the text of the Rome Statute ostensibly preserves a state's authority to implement complementarity following a Security Council referral, the obligation of all states to "accept and carry out the decisions of the Security Council" effectively nullifies this right of complementarity. Furthermore, all members of the United Nations are obligated to comply with orders of the Security Council, even if the Rome Statute or any other international agreement would impose conflicting obligations. . . .

In contrast, the second jurisdictional track under Article 13 invokes the very principles of state consent and territorial jurisdiction that the complementarity principle was intended to protect. Article 13 allows either a state party or the prosecutor proceeding *proprio motu* [by one's own motion] to refer a case to the ICC. The *proprio motu* power of the prosecutor was adopted over the opposition of the United States. . . . For cases referred by either a state party or the prosecutor (that is, cases not dependent on Security Council referral under Chapter VII authority), Article 12 implements a consent regime based on the territory on which the crime was committed *or* the nationality of the perpetrator. Thus, a case is subject to ICC jurisdiction if the crime was committed on territory that belongs to a state party or another state that consents to the jurisdiction of the court. Similarly, a case may be referred to the ICC if the accused is the national of a state party or of a state that consents to the jurisdiction of the court.

The consent regime embodied in Article 12 marks the fault line between the rights of states under the Rome Statute and the residual right of sovereign states to use domestic forums to prosecute violations of international humanitarian law committed by their nationals. The consent regime makes no reference whatsoever to the sovereign prosecutorial rights of nonstate parties. . . . Article 12 on its face permits the anomaly in which a nonstate party commits heinous crimes on its own territory, but consents to the exercise of ICC jurisdiction only over the members of other nations, such as a United Nations coalition, that enter its territory to prevent further violations. Despite the right of the non-state party to consent to crimes committed by some but not all persons on its soil, the non-state party retains the primary presumption of jurisdiction under the complementarity principle.

In light of the complementarity principle, the provisions for nationality and territoriality jurisdiction can be considered as a set of "conflicts of jurisdiction rules."[10] For example, in the case of a crime committed by the national of a non-state party on the territory of another non-state party that consents to the jurisdiction of the court, both states would have jurisdiction under the established norms of international law. Although the case could meet the Article 12 preconditions for jurisdiction by the ICC, the complementarity principle operates to delay an assertion of ICC jurisdiction. . . .

◼ Obstacles to Implementing Complementarity

The Proprio Motu *Problem*

. . . [T]he Rome Statute includes a comprehensive set of provisions and procedures that are designed to insulate sovereign authority to prosecute from unreasonable extension of ICC authority over sovereign judicial systems. Some treaty proponents argue that the web of protections inspired by the complementarity principle gives "ample assurance" that the ICC will minimally curtail sovereign authority only by displacing domestic trials in "exceptional circumstances."[11] At the same time, the Rome Statute contains absolutely no institutional constraints on the power and discretion of the ICC and prosecutor. In fact, a key reason that the complementarity regime is so thorough and detailed in the Rome Statute lies in the recognition by treaty proponents that the "interpretation and application" of those provisions and standards is left solely to the ICC.

Since complementarity is built on the premise that the ICC is not inherently superior to sovereign states, the supranational court is not supreme in theory. The very autonomy that proponents sought for the ICC and its prosecutor, however, prevents external review or resolution of disputes over the court's implementation of the Rome Statute. Arguably, the lack of any external checks and balances limiting the discretion of the ICC manifests a structural flaw creating de facto ICC superiority over sovereign states. From this perspective, the mandatory phrasing of the complementary provisions and their binding nature fail to guarantee realization of the complementarity principle. . . .

One of the hallmarks of the complementarity regime is that it protects the prosecutorial and investigative prerogatives of all states without distinction based on membership in the ICC club. While the Rome Statute provides that an unresolved dispute between two or more parties to the Rome Statute will be referred to the Assembly of States Parties, the Rome Statute is strikingly silent regarding any similar right of non-state parties. This discrepancy could be viewed as an incentive to become a party to the Rome Statute. It could also create a strong incentive for the ICC to avoid disputes with states that are represented in the Assembly of States Parties, thus creating the potential for a tiered system of complementarity in which non-state parties are not accorded the same degree of deference. . . .

The provisions implementing complementarity are complex and often call for difficult subjective assessments by the court and prosecutor. For instance, in reviewing a state's unwillingness, the prosecutor bears the burden of showing sufficient circumstantial evidence to warrant a finding that a delayed movement towards domestic prosecution "in the circumstances is inconsistent with an intent to bring the person to justice."[12] The Rome Statute is silent on the need for any direct evidence of unwillingness in this case, and there is no provision for review of the court's decisions outside the ICC itself.

Article 17(2)(a) further requires the prosecutor to show that the domestic disposition of the case "was made for the purpose of shielding the person concerned from criminal responsibility for crimes within the jurisdiction of the Court." In this endeavor, the Rome Statute is structured to allow the ICC prosecutor a wide margin of error. If circumstantial evidence fails to establish the improper domestic purpose, a further provision allows admissibility if the ICC prosecutor persuades the ICC chamber to find a lack of independence or impartiality in the domestic court coupled with a manner of conducting the proceedings that was "inconsistent with an intent to bring the person concerned to justice." . . .

The very criteria that establish the prosecutorial burden of proof and specify the requisite evidentiary standards designed to implement complementarity may hold the seeds of its unchecked erosion. The ICC prosecutor and court always bear the burden of showing that the standards have been met, but there is no external check to monitor adherence to the standards. The ICC prosecutor must assess the admissibility criteria in light of undefined "principles of due process recognized by international law." These standards are themselves defined by the ICC, which allows wide latitude for the ICC prosecutor to meet the "objective" admissibility criteria. Moreover, if an ICC investigation is originally deferred to national jurisdiction, the ICC prosecutor is not restricted from taking later actions, subject to the requirement that "he or she shall notify the State to which deferral of the proceedings has taken place."[13]

Finally, the *propio motu* power of the prosecutor allows abuse of the complementarity principle because the admissibility criteria invite ICC intrusion into the domestic processes of sovereign states. Because the ICC and its prosecutor can reasonably be expected to develop some guidelines and standards for evaluating domestic systems, the Rome Statute sets up an essentially circular paradox. If a state does not meet the standards that the ICC announces through its internal procedures and court decisions, the domestic state may be deemed "genuinely unwilling" to handle the case by the ICC. Furthermore, states with scarce resources may be unable to reshape their entire domestic judicial systems in response to subjective ICC standards, thereby warranting an ICC finding that any trial that the ICC prosecutor wants to take over is admissible because the state is unable "genuinely to prosecute."

Properly Describing Jurisdiction

Aside from the dispositive power of an unconstrained supranational court and prosecutor, the complementarity principle could be corroded by the very jurisdictional mindset of the ICC. The concept of complementarity does not logically lead to a scheme of national and supranational concurrent jurisdiction. Properly understood and implemented in accordance with the Rome Statute, the jurisdictional allocation of power between the ICC and states is best thought of as a tiered allocation of authority to adjudicate. The ICC does not have authority to take a case or initiate an investigation until the issues associated with domestic jurisdictional criteria and admissibility standards are resolved.

The complementarity principle was the motivating force behind a court built around a limited and defined authority to take jurisdiction that operates when needed to supplement domestic court systems. From the prosecutor's point of view, jurisdiction under the provisions of Article 13 and admissibility under Article 17 are both mandatory prerequisites for ICC authority. This scheme is a significant evolution from earlier drafts that allowed an "inherent" ICC jurisdiction over some crimes. . . .

A system built on a straight assertion of supranational primacy was not a "politically viable alternative for a permanent ICC."[14] A scheme of concurrent jurisdiction would have almost certainly resulted in jurisdictional clashes between the ICC and one or more states with valid claims based on established principles such as nationality, territoriality, or passive personality. Rather than a flawed system of inherent or explicit concurrent jurisdiction, the Rome Statute's jurisdictional scheme requires the progressive factual inquiries and judicial findings that implement complementarity. Over time, the complementarity provisions may chafe an ICC prosecutor that sees them as an overly restrictive manifestation of arcane sovereignty principles. The ICC prosecutor may begin to think of jurisdiction as concurrent rather than tiered, and thereby minimize the complementarity requirements. Because the ICC does not have any external checks and balances, there is no institutional mechanism for controlling a court and prosecutor that seeks to expand supranational power over domestic forums in order to vindicate considerations of international justice.

If the ICC prosecutor begins to view supranational jurisdiction as concurrent with sovereign state jurisdiction, the importance of the complementarity provisions as the trigger mechanism for ICC jurisdiction would obviously begin to erode. This would produce more than just the technical undermining of abstract treaty provisions; it would minimize the ability of states to exercise their courts as proper forums for prosecuting violations of international humanitarian law. Additionally, the ICC prosecutor might begin to assert jurisdiction in cases where one state with a jurisdictional claim consented to ICC adjudication of a particular case, but other states with equally valid claims were either not consulted or mooted based upon the prosecutor's unilateral assessment of inadmissibility. . . .

■ Conclusion

"Complementarity" is an intellectually simple concept that masks the deep philosophical and political difficulties that the International Criminal Court must overcome if it is ever to become a functioning institution. The drafters of the Rome Statute and the delegates who negotiated the Rules of Evidence and Procedure clearly understood that the ICC should not be the court of first resort. . . .

If it can function effectively as an apolitical supranational institution with autonomous legal personality, the ICC can fulfill an important function in buttressing domestic justice by serving as an additional forum for dispensing justice when domestic forums are inadequate. Despite the well-intentioned goals of the Rome Statute, the ICC will survive and thrive only if it manages to balance the reality of sovereign political and legal competition between states with the aspiration for international justice. The complementarity provisions are the designated mechanism for balancing enforcement of international norms against protection of state sovereignty.

Complementarity is in theory an impartial, reliable, and de-politicized process for identifying the cases of international concern, and hence international jurisdiction. However, the thicket of subjective provisions designed to implement complementarity allows treaty opponents to argue that national justice systems are threatened with displacement at the hands of an unrestrained international prosecutor.

■ Notes

1. M. Cherif Bassiouni, Address to the Ceremony for the Opening of Signature of the Treaty on the Establishment of an International Criminal Court, at Il Campidoglio, Rome (18 July 1988).

2. Vienna Convention on the Law of Treaties, 23 May 1969, UN Doc. A/CONF. 39/27, art. 34.

3. Rome Statute of the International Criminal Court, UN Doc. A/CONF. 183/9 (1998) (United Nations Diplomatic Conference of Plenipotentiaries on the Establishment of an International Criminal Court, 17 July 1998), art. 1 (emphasis added).

4. Ibid., art. 25(2).

5. Opening Statement of Justice Robert Jackson to the International Military Tribunal (21 November 1945), in *International Military Tribunal, Trial of German Major War Criminals* 83 (1946), pp. 1–3.

6. *Trial of the Major War Criminals Before the International Military Tribunal* (1947) (Judgment), p. 223.

7. Rome Statute, preamble, para. 9.

8. John T. Holmes, "The Principle of Complementarity," in *The International Criminal Court: The Making of the Rome Statute,* ed. Roy S. Lee (New York: Springer, 1999), p. 43.

9. Rome Statute, art. 19(1).

10. Leila Nadya Sadat and S. Richard Carden, "The New International Criminal Court: An Uneasy Revolution," *Georgetown Law Journal,* no. 88 (2000), p. 413.

11. Human Rights Watch, *Justice in the Balance: Recommendations for an Independent and Effective International Criminal Court* (New York: Human Rights Watch, 1998), p. 71.

12. Rome Statute, art. 17(2)(b).

13. Ibid., art. 19(11).

14. Bartram S. Brown, "Primacy or Complementarity: Reconciling the Jurisdiction of National Courts and International Tribunals," *Yale Journal of International Law,* vol. 23 (1998), p. 431.

14 Judgment and Enforcement

14.1 _____

Introduction
The Editors

It is relatively easy for victors in war to take an element of vengeance against their vanquished adversaries by means of the subterfuge of law and hold putatively legal trials in which the leaders and soldiers of defeated enemies are charged and condemned for their actions during war. In the absence of a clear and acknowledged criminal code governing the prosecution of war, however, this looks like little more than victor's justice. If the notion of war crime is to make sense, and if the prosecution of the leaders and soldiers of defeated states is to be anything more than a legal chimera, there must be a code of conduct in place that controls the standards of permissible and impermissible conduct during war. Additionally, the institutional and procedural mechanisms must exist for the prosecution and punishment of those individuals charged with war crimes.

With these requirements in mind, it might seem reasonable to be rather suspicious of the legal standing of war crimes. The morality of conduct in warfare *(jus in bello)* introduces the substance of a criminal code that might govern warfare. In fact, under the old natural law tradition, from which the notion of *jus in bello* derives, the moral norms associated with the morality of warfighting would actually constitute a criminal code of warfare, although questions would remain about who could prosecute war criminals and enforce the norms of *jus in bello*. But legal positivists have raised a number of legitimate and powerful arguments against thinking that the moral norms that might regulate human behavior automatically qualify as legal norms also. Consider an analogy with domestic legal systems. Some elements of a state's criminal code prohibit certain actions because they are morally wrong *(mala in se)*, but other elements of these codes prohibit actions that are otherwise morally innocent *(mala prohibita)*. Moreover, not all moral wrongs qualify as legal wrongs; lying and cheating, for example, are generally considered morally wrong, but not all forms of lying and cheating are, or ought to be, legally prohibited. For a moral norm to also qualify as a criminal act, then, something must be added to the equation. The wrong in question must be established as a legal wrong—a criminal act—by a duly constituted and recognized legal authority.

Many states, including the United States, have addressed the problem of war crimes by stipulating and adopting standards of warfare that are intended to govern the behavior of their own soldiers in times of war. But these codes of military conduct belong to the domestic legal jurisdiction of the states that promulgate them, and claims about the putative violation of these standards are correspondingly adjudicated by the appropriate legal authorities within these states, and according to the procedural and evidentiary standards that belong to these domestic legal systems. Such codes of military conduct, however, have little standing in international law and are not subject to international adjudication of the sort illustrated by the Nuremberg trials, in the European theater, following World War II.

It is advisable, then, to separate the adjudication of violations of a state's military code of conduct under a state's domestic jurisdiction from the adjudication of war crimes brought against defeated states by their victorious opponents. If there are international laws governing the way states are to fight wars, that is, if there are war crimes with the status of law in international law, they must have come into being in the way that other forms of international law have come into being—either as a result of customary practice or of treaty formation. There are, in this regard, a number of treaties that outline permissible and impermissible conduct in warfare, like the Hague and Geneva conventions. But not all states have signed and ratified these treaties, and under international law, states that are not signatories to these treaties may not be bound to follow them, although it could be argued that the treaty regulations are so generally accepted as to constitute customary law.

The identification of an international code of warfighting conduct, that is, war crimes, raises additional legal problems, however, for if such a legal code is to have practical effect, there must also be mechanisms and procedures in place for the adjudication of disputes that arise under it as well as for implementing punishment upon a finding of criminal liability. To again avoid the specter of victor's justice, the adjudication of these disputes must proceed according to reasonable and just standards of due process. Here again it is important to consider international standards of criminal prosecution in relation to standards of domestic criminal justice. In the United States, for example, a finding of criminal liability typically depends upon the establishment of criminal responsibility. Someone accused of a crime is subject to punishment only if the person is found to have committed a criminal act, according to the standards of due process of law, and to have acted in a manner that they could, and should, have understood to be wrong. Correspondingly, someone who has not participated in a criminal act— someone who is innocent of criminal wrongdoing—cannot be held criminally liable for the legal transgressions of others.

The link between criminal responsibility and criminal liability typical of the US legal system introduces some difficulties when it comes to prosecuting war crimes. In the event a war crime is committed, who should be prosecuted, those soldiers who might have actually committed the crime, or commanders who might or might not have ordered these soldiers to behave as they did? It is certainly reasonable to hold commanders responsible for the actions of their troops if they have given explicit orders to their troops to perform criminal acts. But as Justice Murphy's famous dissent in the *Yamashita* case aptly illustrates, this clear chain of responsibility is not always in evidence. Troops in time of war, fighting under the fog of war, are likely to do horrible things and to have little time for the rules of proper warfare. When one's life is on the line, little else but survival will matter much. It is the law of the jungle, and not the law of war, that will likely matter under these circumstances. Is it reasonable, then, to hold commanders legally responsible for the illegal actions of those under their authority?

A failure to do so, of course, will necessarily weaken the force of war crimes. Soldiers fighting for their lives will act first and worry about prosecution for war crimes later. Holding commanders criminally liable for the actions of their subordinates may have the salutary effect of encouraging commanders to develop a more disciplined command and thus to make soldiers more sensitive to the crimes of war even during the stress of combat. It may also deter the possible inclination of commanders to disregard the behavior of those under their authority and quietly condone criminal behavior. These are reasons to introduce a standard of strict criminal liability into the adjudication of war crimes. But this still strains at the common standards of justice. Commanders are not always able to control the behavior of their troops, and the further up the chain of command the commanders are from the soldiers who actually perform war crimes, the more tenuous a commitment to strict criminal liability becomes.

The adjudication and prosecution of war criminals has undoubtedly been colored by the Nuremberg experience following World War II. Thanks to the scrupulous records kept by German authorities, it was a relatively simple matter to construct a nexus of criminal wrongdoing between German authorities and the activities of the soldiers who put this wrongdoing into effect. While the actions of individual soldiers, who typically performed the illegal actions, are hardly excusable, it is both reasonable and natural to suppose that these actions were both inspired and demanded by commanders holding positions of responsibility in the German government. True responsibility, it may legitimately be supposed, must lie with the authorities that were the instigators of the war crimes. But the German example is perhaps more anomalous than it is typical. To hold commanders responsible for the conduct of their troops, particularly when and if commanders are powerless to exercise precise battlefield control over their troops, simply stretches to the breaking point the traditional link between criminal liability and criminal responsibility.

The difficulty on display here may simply be an inevitable feature of the effort to regulate in a law-like manner an activity that seems to defy regulation. At a rather high level of generality, it makes perfect sense to say that even warfare should be conducted according to rules that inject an element of decency and humanity into the procedure. But on the field of battle it becomes apparent that war is simply indecent and inhuman to the core. Brutality and insensitivity are the ways of war, and it asks a great deal of warriors to have them restrain their conduct within the confines of what others, not on the field of battle, consider morally obligatory. The tensions this generates come into clear view when we turn to the details of adjudicating war crimes and sanctioning those found guilty, for it is just here, as in any system of law, that the ideals of lawfulness must take practical effect.

14.2 ——

Dissent from the US Supreme Court's Ruling in *Yamashita v. Styer*

Justice Frank Murphy

Original proceeding in the matter of the application of General Tomoyuki Yamashita for leave to file petition for writ of habeas corpus and writ of prohibition and on petition for writ of habeas corpus and for writ of prohibition, consolidated for hearing with the petition of General Tomoyuki Yamashita for certiorari to review an order of the Supreme Court of the Commonwealth of the Philippines in the matter of General Tomoyuki Yamashita against Lieutenant General Wilhelm D. Styer, Commanding General, United States Army Forces, Western Pacific, denying petitioner's application to that court for writs of habeas corpus and prohibition. Denied. . . .

■ Mr. Justice Murphy, Dissenting

The significance of the issue facing the Court today cannot be overemphasized. An American military commission has been established to try a fallen military commander of a conquered nation for an alleged war crime. The authority for such action grows out of the exercise of the power conferred upon Congress by Article I . . . of the Constitution to "define and punish . . . Offenses against the Law of Nations. . . ." The grave issue raised by this case is whether a military commission so established and so authorized may disregard the procedural rights of an accused person as guaranteed by the Constitution, especially by the due process clause of the Fifth Amendment.

The answer is plain. The Fifth Amendment guarantee of due process of law applies to "any person" who is accused of a crime by the Federal Government or any of its agencies. No exception is made as to those who are accused of war crimes or as to those who possess the status of an enemy belligerent. Indeed, such an exception would be contrary to the whole philosophy of human rights which makes the Constitution the great living document that it is. The immutable rights of the individual, including those

From *Yamashita v. Styer*, 327 U.S. 1 (1946).

secured by the due process clause of the Fifth Amendment, belong not alone to the members of those nations that excel on the battlefield or that subscribe to the democratic ideology. They belong to every person in the world, victor or vanquished, whatever may be his race, color or beliefs. They rise above any status of belligerency or outlawry. They survive any popular passion or frenzy of the moment. No court or legislature or executive, not even the mightiest army in the world, can ever destroy them. Such is the universal and indestructible nature of the rights which the due process clause of the Fifth Amendment recognizes and protects when life or liberty is threatened by virtue of the authority of the United States.

The existence of these rights, unfortunately, is not always respected. They are often trampled under by those who are motivated by hatred, aggression or fear. But in this nation individual rights are recognized and protected, at least in regard to governmental action. They cannot be ignored by any branch of the Government, even the military, except under the most extreme and urgent circumstances.

The failure of the military commission to obey the dictates of the due process requirements of the Fifth Amendment is apparent in this case. The petitioner was the commander of an army totally destroyed by the superior power of this nation. While under heavy and destructive attack by our forces, his troops committed many brutal atrocities and other high crimes. Hostilities ceased and he voluntarily surrendered. At that point he was entitled, as an individual protected by the due process clause of the Fifth Amendment, to be treated fairly and justly according to the accepted rules of law and procedure. He was also entitled to a fair trial as to any alleged crimes and to be free from charges of legally unrecognized crimes that would serve only to permit his accusers to satisfy their desires for revenge.

A military commission was appointed to try the petitioner for an alleged war crime. The trial was ordered to be held in territory over which the United States has complete sovereignty. No military necessity or other emergency demanded the suspension of the safeguards of due process. Yet petitioner was rushed to trial under an improper charge, given insufficient time to prepare an adequate defense, deprived of the benefits of some of the most elementary rules of evidence and summarily sentenced to be hanged. In all this needless and unseemly haste there was no serious attempt to charge or to prove that he committed a recognized violation of the laws of war. . . . It was simply alleged that he unlawfully disregarded and failed to discharge his duty as commander to control the operations of the members of his command, permitting them to commit the acts of atrocity. The recorded annals of warfare and the established principles of international law afford not the slightest precedent for such a charge. This indictment in effect permitted the military commission to make the crime whatever it willed, dependent upon its biased view as to petitioner's duties and his disregard thereof, a practice reminiscent of that pursued in certain less respect-ed nations in recent years.

In my opinion, such a procedure is unworthy of the traditions of our people or of the immense sacrifices that they have made to advance the common ideals of mankind. The high feelings of the moment doubtless will be satisfied. But in the sober afterglow will come the realization of the boundless and dangerous implications of the procedure sanctioned today. No one in a position of command in an army, from sergeant to general, can escape those future implications. Indeed, the fate of some future President of the United States and his chiefs of staff and military advisers may well have been sealed by this decision. But even more significant will be the hatred and ill-will growing out of the application of this unprecedented pro-cedure. That has been the inevitable effect of every method of punishment disregarding the element of personal culpability. The effect in this instance, unfortunately, will be magnified infinitely for here we are dealing with the rights of man on an international level. To subject an enemy belligerent to an unfair trial, to charge him with an unrecognized crime, or to vent on him our retributive emotions only antagonizes the enemy nation and hinders the reconciliation necessary to a peaceful world.

That there were brutal atrocities inflicted upon the helpless Filipino people, to whom tyranny is no stranger, by Japanese armed forces under the petitioner's command is undeniable. Starvation, execution or massacre without trial, torture, rape, murder and wanton destruction of property were foremost among the outright violations of the laws of war and of the con-science of a civilized world. That just punishment should be meted out to all those responsible for criminal acts of this nature is also beyond dispute. But these factors do not answer the problem in this case. They do not justify the abandonment of our devotion to justice in dealing with a fallen enemy com-mander. To conclude otherwise is to admit that the enemy has lost the battle but has destroyed our ideals.

War breeds atrocities. From the earliest conflicts of recorded history to the global struggles of modern times inhumanities, lust and pillage have been the inevitable by-products of man's resort to force and arms. Unfortunately, such despicable acts have a dangerous tendency to call forth primitive impulses of vengeance and retaliation among the victimized peo-ples. The satisfaction of such impulses in turn breeds resentment and fresh tension. Thus does the spiral of cruelty and hatred grow.

If we are ever to develop an orderly international community based upon a recognition of human dignity it is of the utmost importance that the necessary punishment of those guilty of atrocities be as free as possible from the ugly stigma of revenge and vindictiveness. Justice must be tem-pered by compassion rather than by vengeance. In this, the first case involv-ing this momentous problem ever to reach this Court, our responsibility is both lofty and difficult. We must insist, within the confines of our proper jurisdiction, that the highest standards of justice be applied in this trial of an enemy commander conducted under the authority of the United States. Otherwise stark retribution will be free to masquerade in a cloak of false legalism. And the hatred and cynicism engendered by that retribution will supplant the great ideals to which this nation is dedicated.

This Court fortunately has taken the first and most important step toward insuring the supremacy of law and justice in the treatment of an enemy belligerent accused of violating the laws of war. Jurisdiction properly has been asserted to inquire "into the cause of restraint of liberty" of such a person. Thus the obnoxious doctrine asserted by the Government in this case, to the effect that restraints of liberty resulting from military trials of war criminals are political matters completely outside the arena of judicial review, has been rejected fully and unquestionably. This does not mean, of course, that the foreign affairs and policies of the nation are proper subjects of judicial inquiry. But when the liberty of any person is restrained by reason of the authority of the United States the writ of habeas corpus is available to test the legality of that restraint, even though direct court review of the restraint is prohibited. The conclusive presumption must be made, in this country at least, that illegal restraints are unauthorized and unjustified by any foreign policy of the Government and that commonly accepted juridical standards are to be recognized and enforced. On that basis judicial inquiry into these matters may proceed within its proper sphere. . . .

As I understand it, the following issues in connection with war criminal trials are reviewable through the use of the writ of habeas corpus: (1) Whether the military commission was lawfully created and had authority to try and to convict the accused of a war crime; (2) whether the charge against the accused stated a violation of the laws of war; (3) whether the commission, in admitting certain evidence, violated any law or military command defining the commission's authority in that respect; and (4) whether the commission lacked jurisdiction because of a failure to give advance notice to the protecting power as required by treaty or convention.

The Court, in my judgment, demonstrates conclusively that the military commission was lawfully created in this instance and that petitioner could not object to its power to try him for a recognized war crime. Without pausing here to discuss the third and fourth issues, however, I find it impossible to agree that the charge against the petitioner stated a recognized violation of the laws of war. . . .

The petitioner was accused of having "unlawfully disregarded and failed to discharge his duty as commander to control the operations of the members of his command, permitting them to commit brutal atrocities and other high crimes." The bills of particular further alleged that specific acts of atrocity were committed by "members of the armed forces of Japan under the command of the accused." Nowhere was it alleged that the petitioner personally committed any of the atrocities, or that he ordered their commission, or that he had any knowledge of the commission thereof by members of his command.

The findings of the military commission bear out this absence of any direct personal charge against the petitioner. The commission merely found that atrocities and other high crimes "have been committed by members of the Japanese armed forces under your command . . . that they were not sporadic in nature but in many cases were methodically supervised by Japanese officers and noncommissioned officers . . . that during the period in question you failed to provide effective control of your troops as was required by the circumstances."

In other words, read against the background of military events in the Philippines subsequent to October 9, 1944, these charges amount to this: "We, the victorious American forces, have done everything possible to destroy and disorganize your lines of communication, your effective control of your personnel, your ability to wage war. In those respects we have succeeded. We have defeated and crushed your forces. And now we charge and condemn you for having been inefficient in maintaining control of your troops during the period when we were so effectively besieging and eliminating your forces and blocking your ability to maintain effective control. Many terrible atrocities were committed by your disorganized troops. Because these atrocities were so widespread we will not bother to charge or prove that you committed, ordered or condoned any of them. We will assume that they must have resulted from your inefficiency and negligence as a commander. In short, we charge you with the crime of inefficiency in controlling your troops. We will judge the discharge of your duties by the disorganization which we ourselves created in large part. Our standards of judgment are whatever we wish to make them."

Nothing in all history or in international law, at least as far as I am aware, justifies such a charge against a fallen commander of a defeated force. To use the very inefficiency and disorganization created by the victorious forces as the primary basis for condemning officers of the defeated armies bears no resemblance to justice or to military reality.

International law makes no attempt to define the duties of a commander of an army under constant and overwhelming assault; nor does it impose liability under such circumstances for failure to meet the ordinary responsibilities of command. The omission is understandable. Duties, as well as ability to control troops, vary according to the nature and intensity of the particular battle. To find an unlawful deviation from duty under battle conditions requires difficult and speculative calculations. Such calculations become highly untrustworthy when they are made by the victor in relation to the actions of a vanquished commander. Objective and realistic norms of conduct are then extremely unlikely to be used in forming a judgment as to deviations from duty. The probability that vengeance will form the major part of the victor's judgment is an unfortunate but inescapable fact. So great is that probability that international law refuses to recognize such a judgment as a basis for a war crime, however fair the judgment may be in a particular instance. It is this consideration that undermines the charge against the petitioner in this case. The indictment permits, indeed compels, the military commission of a victorious nation to sit in judgment upon the military strategy and actions of the defeated enemy and to use its conclusions to determine the criminal liability of an enemy commander. Life and liberty are made to depend upon the biased will of the victor rather than upon objective standards of conduct. . . .

The Government claims that the principle that commanders in the field are bound to control their troops has been applied so as to impose liability on the United States in international arbitrations. The difference between arbitrating property rights and charging an individual with a crime against the laws of war is too obvious to require elaboration. But even more significant is the fact that even these arbitration cases fail to establish any principle of liability where troops are under constant assault and demoralizing influences by attacking forces. The same observation applies to the common law and statutory doctrine, referred to by the Government, that one who is under a legal duty to take protective or preventive action is guilty of criminal homicide if he willfully or negligently omits to act and death is proximately caused. No one denies that inaction or negligence may give rise to liability, civil or criminal. But it is quite another thing to say that the inability to control troops under highly competitive and disastrous battle conditions renders one guilty of a war crime in the absence of personal culpability. Had there been some element of knowledge or direct connection with the atrocities the problem would be entirely different. Moreover, it must be remembered that we are not dealing here with an ordinary tort or criminal action; precedents in those fields are of little if any value. Rather we are concerned with a proceeding involving an international crime, the treatment of which may have untold effects upon the future peace of the world. That fact must be kept uppermost in our search for precedent.

The only conclusion I can draw is that the charge made against the petitioner is clearly without precedent in international law or in the annals of recorded military history. This is not to say that enemy commanders may escape punishment for clear and unlawful failures to prevent atrocities. But that punishment should be based upon charges fairly drawn in light of established rules of international law and recognized concepts of justice.

But the charge in this case, as previously noted, was speedily drawn and filed but three weeks after the petitioner surrendered. The trial proceeded with great dispatch without allowing the defense time to prepare an adequate case. Petitioner's rights under the due process clause of the Fifth Amendment were grossly and openly violated without any justification. All of this was done without any thorough investigation and prosecution of those immediately responsible for the atrocities, out of which might have come some proof or indication of personal culpability on petitioner's part. Instead the loose charge was made that great numbers of atrocities had been committed and that petitioner was the commanding officer; hence he must have been guilty of disregard of duty. Under that charge the commission was free to establish whatever standard of duty on petitioner's part that it desired. By this flexible method a victorious nation may convict and execute any or all leaders of a vanquished foe, depending upon the prevailing degree of vengeance and the absence of any objective judicial review.

At a time like this when emotions are understandably high it is difficult to adopt a dispassionate attitude toward a case of this nature. Yet now is precisely the time when that attitude is most essential. While peoples in other lands may not share our beliefs as to due process and the dignity of the individual, we are not free to give effect to our emotions in reckless disregard of the rights of others. We live under the Constitution, which is the embodiment of all the high hopes and aspirations of the new world. And it is applicable in both war and peace. We must act accordingly. Indeed, an uncurbed spirit of revenge and retribution, masked in formal legal procedure for purposes of dealing with a fallen enemy commander, can do more lasting harm than all of the atrocities giving rise to that spirit. The people's faith in the fairness and objectiveness of the law can be seriously undercut by that spirit. The fires of nationalism can be further kindled. And the hearts of all mankind can be embittered and filled with hatred, leaving forlorn and impoverished the noble ideal of malice toward none and charity to all. These are the reasons that lead me to dissent in these terms.

14.3 _____

Responsibility for Crimes of War

Sanford Levinson

. . . Great difficulties emerge when one considers the question of criminal responsibility for actions occurring within an organizational context. If we wish to engage in communal condemnation of such acts, against whom should the opprobrium be directed? It is no answer, of course, to say only the organization itself, for this simply begs the question, as I shall show below, of whether or not it is just to punish everyone connected with it. No sanction can be directed at an organization—whether the method chosen is a fine or dissolution—without also affecting at least some of the individuals with ties to the entity. . . .

The problem of "war crimes," of course, raises these problems in an especially vivid way. Following World War II there was obvious interest in punishing those who were responsible for the acts of the Nazi state, and the subsequent trials of alleged war criminals raised very sharply the problems involved in trying to assess the responsibility of a given individual relative to a very complex scheme of organizational behavior. What follows are a description and analysis of the notions of responsibility that were put forth at four of the war crimes trials and an examination of their implications regarding the actions of American officials concerning the Vietnam War. . . .

Collective criminal punishment is in principle open to the charge that it violates fundamental standards of fairness by being "overinclusive": the category of individuals actually stigmatized or otherwise treated as criminal would include some who could successfully defend themselves, if given the chance to do so. This objection to collective responsibility is, obviously, independent of the fact that it may be more practical or efficient to label everyone connected with a group "responsible." . . .

To say that every German or every American is "guilty" for every act committed by persons acting under the authority of their respective States rests on a host of begged questions. And even if one accepts, for the sake of argument, the notion of collective guilt, we can still distinguish among degrees of responsibility. It would be unjust for everyone to have to pay the *same* fine for war crimes unless we assume equal guilt or assume that guilt varied directly by income, so that the progressive income tax would be an adequate collection device. . . .

We are thus impaled on the horns of a dilemma: to adopt collective responsibility is either to commit an injustice or to undermine the community condemnation on which the criminal law rests and which especially should be the basis for the punishment of war crimes. If one wants to preserve the force of the notion of war *criminality*, he must find discrete criminals or else argue that in fact everyone *is* guilty and deserving of punishment.

I shall be considering the judgments of four trials held at Nuernberg following World War II. Those four are the Trial of the Major War Criminals, held before the International Military Tribunal (IMT), which consisted of judges appointed by the four major Allied powers, in addition to three trials held under the aegis of Allied Control Council Law No. 10, by which the individual powers were given authority to prosecute "lesser" alleged war criminals. These three trials, held before American tribunals, are usually called "The Ministries Case," "The High Command Case," and "The Hostage Case." All four of the cases featured multiple defendants; all four included defendants who were acquitted as well as more numerous ones who were found guilty. . . .

The trial before the IMT is, of course, the most famous of the war trials, largely because of the inherent drama provided by the celebrity of the defendants. Here were Goering, Rosenberg, von Ribbentrop, Speer, and eighteen others, most of whom were "household words" to the communities involved in fighting the war. Precisely because of the rank of the defendants, however, the judgment is relatively unilluminating from the point of view of this paper, for there was, in fact, little difficulty in proving the criminal behavior of most of them, save only for the three who were acquitted—Schacht, von Papen, and Fritzsche.

The IMT judgment is most helpful in considering the problem of responsibility not for traditionally recognized war crimes but rather for the more controversial category of "crimes against peace" and conspiracy to commit such crimes. These were two of the four counts upon which most of the defendants were tried. . . .

Upon count one, conspiracy to wage crimes against peace through planning and waging aggressive war, only eight of the twenty-two were convicted: Goering, Hess, von Ribbentrop, Keitel, Rosenberg, Raeder, Jodl, and von Neurath. A similar charge was leveled at the various officials involved in the Ministries and High Command Cases, but it was ordered dropped by the tribunals. The reason for this chariness to convict was the restriction of liability under this charge to those members of the German regime who were within "Hitler's inner circle of advisors" or otherwise "closely connected with the formulation of the policies which led to war."[1] . . .

Two things should be noted. First, as mentioned above, responsibility for crimes against peace is restricted to a relatively few senior officials. For better or worse, the notion that adoption of a theory of crimes against peace or of aggressive warfare threatens to make every citizen a war criminal is incorrect. This leads to the second point, that the resolution of the key questions under counts one and two involves complex empirical judgments about the structures of power within the society in question. . . . It is undoubtedly true that the circle of responsibility would be widened as the circle of "inner advisors" or otherwise influential associates broadened, but severe limits would still be imposed in terms of the absolute numbers of officials who could ever be held responsible for aggressive wars. . . .

If the tribunals were hesitant to find guilt under the innovative and controversial charges of aggression and conspiracy to commit same, they were much less reluctant in regard to the much more traditional counts of war crimes and crimes against humanity. Thus, of the eighteen Germans accused of war crimes before the IMT, only two, Rudolph Hess, who was in a British prison throughout the war, and Fritzsche, a propagandist, were acquitted. These two were also the only two of a slightly different eighteen to escape conviction as criminals against humanity. . . .

What were "war crimes"? Article 6(b) establishing the IMT defined them as

> violations of the laws or customs of war. Such violations shall include, but not be limited to, murder, ill-treatment or deportation to slave labor or for any other purpose of civilian population of or in occupied territory, murder or ill-treatment of prisoners of war or persons on the seas, killing of hostages, plunder of public or private property, wanton destruction of cities, towns, or villages, or devastation not justified by military necessity.[2]

Article 6(c) in turn defined "crimes against humanity":

> namely, murder, extermination, enslavement, deportation, and other inhumane acts committed against any civilian population, before or during the war; or persecutions on political, racial, or religious grounds in execution of or in connection with any crime within the jurisdiction of the Tribunal, whether or not in violation of the domestic law of the country where perpetrated.[3]

As pointed out above, the IMT is relatively unilluminating as to the actual standards by which guilt is to be determined. The only real clue comes from its acquittal of the propagandist Fritzsche. Although speeches he delivered indicated anti-Semitism, they "did not urge persecution or extermination of Jews."[4] . . .

The war trials therefore stand for two linked principles: (1) Officials of governments *will* be judged on their behavior and will not be allowed to claim either obedience to superior orders or the act-of-state doctrine in justification. But (2), mere participation in even the Nazi regime is not enough to label one a "war criminal." Direct evidence of participation in the criminal acts themselves is necessary. To be found guilty of war crimes and crimes against humanity, "there must be a breach of some moral obligation fixed by international law, a personal act voluntarily done with knowledge of its inherent criminality under international law."[5] There is no strict liability for war crimes; *mens rea* in addition to an *actus reus* is necessary. The necessity to find both of these elements, indeed, raises the principal problem of this essay, for the acts themselves were most often performed by those who were in fact never tried by any major tribunal—the ordinary soldier. To find a governmental official guilty demanded the linkage of his activity to that of the final actors themselves, a most complex task. . . .

Both knowledge and actual responsibility are, of course, difficult to establish for members of complex organizations. Indeed, there is some reason to think that the convictions under the enunciated standards were the result of a fluke—that is, "the German proclivity for systematic records and the unexpectedly swift final victory, which placed files of documents in Allied hands."[6] Without such records, convictions might have been impossible. . . .

On occasion the office held by an official could itself be probative as to whether or not certain knowledge was in fact possessed. Given that all the documentation in the world, unless personally initialed, cannot actually "prove" that an official in question actually read the documents, it was stipulated that "an army commander will not ordinarily be permitted to deny knowledge of reports received at his headquarters, they being sent there for his special benefit."[7] Moreover, there is an affirmative duty to become cognizant of the actions of one's subordinates. . . .

The problem of allocating responsibility becomes even more complex when we consider the distinction between line and staff officials, whether in a civilian or military context. Line officials are those who have the authority within a given structure to command others to behave in certain ways. Staff officials, on the other hand, usually have no direct authority over anyone. Their function is simply to advise, secure information, draft documents, etc. The question then arises, can staff officers be "responsible" for acts they neither directly (i.e., physically) committed nor "ordered" others to commit? The answer is affirmative. The basic rationale is eloquently spelled out by the Tribunal in the Ministries Case:

> If the commanders of the death camps who blindly followed orders to
> murder the unfortunate inmates, if those who implemented or carried out

the orders for the deportation of Jews to the East are properly tried, convicted, and punished; and of that we have no question whatsoever; then
those who in the comparative quiet and peace of ministerial departments,
aided the campaign by drafting the necessary decrees, regulations, and
directives for its execution are likewise guilty.[8]

. . . It is time now to turn from Nuernberg to Vietnam. What inferences can
we draw from the preceding material? What would be necessary were we to
decide to try individual high officials of the American government, past or
present, for war crimes which have undoubtedly taken place as part of the
Vietnam War?

At least two distinct questions are raised by suggestions for holding
war crimes trials. The first is deceptively simple: taking the Nuernberg principles sketched above as given, what kinds of evidence would be needed in
order to convict officials of war crimes? The second question is more obviously complex: given the extreme unlikelihood that trials for war crimes
will in fact be held under official auspices, either domestically or internationally, what alternatives are open to the lay citizenry who remain convinced not only that crimes have occurred, but also that there may be criminals to whom can be allocated responsibility? The first question can be
answered from within the accepted legal tradition. The second, however,
involves what would frankly be an exercise of extralegal judgment, an
attempt to make at least quasi-legal findings . . . without legal authority to
do so. The second question is not logically entailed by the principal topic of
this essay—theories of responsibility. It is, however, linked to any affirmative response to the question of whether viable standards of responsibility
exist, for we are then faced with the dilemma of a positive legal system
which refuses to apply "the law." What response is then open to the citizen
who sees a conflict not between law and morality, but rather between law
and a particular legal structure which refuses enforcement?

As to the first question it is clear from the discussion above how
dependent the Nuernberg trials were on captured documents. The judgments
were careful to document the connections between given officials and the
acts for which they were accused of responsibility; there was a minimum of
reliance on purely formal analysis of responsibility within governmental
organizations. Such documents were available for two separate reasons. The
first was, of course, the fortuitous capture of the papers of the regime by the
victorious Allies. But the second reason is perhaps of greater relevance
insofar as application of the Nuernberg precedents to American officials is
concerned, and that is simply that the most essential fact about the Nazi
regime was that it consciously articulated and executed such policies as the
Holocaust or the brutal murders of prisoners of war and hostages. Having
consciously adopted the policies, the regime took great care to measure
their enforcement through the preparation of copious reports, memoranda,

etc. Individuals in turn proved their fidelity to the regime by documenting their own acquiescence in its orders.

Not even the most bitter critic of American policy would suggest that it has been the result of clearly articulated, clearly ordered, and clearly executed desires to flaunt international law and morality in the same way as was true of Germany. Thus, even if American documents were capable of being subpoenaed or captured, it is doubtful that evidence similar to that introduced at Nuernberg would be found. . . .

It is also important to distinguish clearly problems attendant on trying civilian officials from those present regarding military officers. Thus, concerning the latter, it is quite possible . . . that the very failure to investigate charges of war crimes that have been leveled is itself criminal under the standards articulated in the High Command Case. Without accepting the scope of *Yamashita,* one can still argue that military commanders are obliged to organize the armed forces so as to maximize the likelihood of exercising meaningful discipline over the troops and preventing the commission of criminal acts. Insofar as evidence does exist that the American command in Vietnam breached his duty, there would seem to be few purely legal problems involved in trying officers for at least some of the crimes committed there. . . .

In summary, then, although it might be disputed whether or not the lack of copious documentary evidence raises a "well-nigh insuperable" obstacle to the holding of American war crimes trials, it can scarcely be disputed that severe problems are raised if we wish to adhere to the standards set at Nuernberg. It is arguable, though, that the problems are of differential severity in regard to the specific kinds of war crimes under discussion. Thus convictions for waging aggressive war do depend on specific information relating to both knowledge and actual power in a way that does not seem to be the case for more traditional war crimes. Critics of the war who focus more on the means with which it has been fought rather than its allegedly aggressive character would seem to have a slightly easier task in terms of proving culpability. . . .

Moreover, it is worth mentioning that information, even if less reliable than the captured German documents, *is* available about the policy-making apparatus in charge of the war. There are not only the Pentagon Papers, but also such studies as David Halberstam's *The Best and the Brightest;* it is possible, as well, that more officials of the relevant administrations will feel it wise or necessary to publish accounts of how *they,* at least, were never so foolish as Walt Rostow, and thus illuminate further, even if self-servingly, the parameters of power.

But, of course, official trials are not going to be held, and discussion about procedures that might be used at such trials is academic. If law is indeed only that which courts are prepared to enforce, then the status of the law of war is weak. Yet, as noted above, it is possible to argue that law has an existence independent of the willingness of the state to enforce it, and that it is fruitful to discuss what alternatives to official trials might exist for establishing who, if anyone, bears blame for illegalities attached to the Vietnam War. Two general alternatives suggest themselves. One is the establishment by inevitably self-appointed groups or individuals of a citizens' tribunal which would consider the guilt of named officials and publish its assessments. A second alternative would be the preparation by individual scholars of articles, to be published perhaps in law reviews, as to the guilt or innocence of named individuals under the applicable precedents. . . .

The problems with both alternatives, of course, are obvious. They raise spectres of at best a "left-wing McCarthyism" and at worst a peculiarly academic version of lynch law. It is one thing to have such extralegal tribunals or individuals consider the question of whether or not the United States, as a reified entity, committed crimes. The affirmative answer which would be forthcoming could be used to support the idea that this country has an obligation, in spite of the problems noted . . . to provide reparations to the North and South Vietnamese victimized by its criminal activities. But it is entirely different to discuss the responsibility of named individuals—or so the argument would run. . . .

And, it must be stressed, recourse to extralegal determination of "guilt" is entirely separate, analytically, from recourse to similar determinations of "punishment." One can oppose, that is, the actions of a lynch mob, without necessarily denying the accuracy of their perception that the individual in question is "in fact" guilty of the crime for which he is accused, even though the formal system, for given reasons, is incapable of declaring him guilty.

The most appalling aspect of America's participation in the Vietnam War, aside from the slaughter itself, has been the refusal to take seriously the allegations of war criminality which have been put forth. The obvious reason for this reluctance is that to take the Nuernberg principles seriously is to admit the reality of criminal responsibility on the part of high officials. At the same time even some critics who would accept the notion that criminal activities have occurred would still attribute these activities (outcomes) to the mechanisms of impersonal institutions. . . .

■ Notes

1. *Trials of the Major War Criminals Before the International Military Tribunal* 22 (1948), p. 547 (acquittal of Julius Stretcher on charge of crimes against peace).

2. Ibid., p. 471.

3. Ibid., p. 496.

4. Ibid., pp. 584–585.

5. *Trials of the War Criminals Before the Nuernberg Military Tribunals Under Control Council Law No. 10, 11,* p. 510.

6. Harold Leventhal, et al., "The Nuernberg Verdict," *Harvard Law Review* 60, no. 6 (July 1947), p. 904.

7. *Trials of the Major War Criminals* 11, p. 1260.

8. *Trials of the Major War Criminals* 14, pp. 645–646 (conviction of Stuckart).

14.4 _____

The Politics of War Crimes Tribunals

Gary Jonathan Bass

What makes governments support international war crimes tribunals? And, conversely: What makes governments abandon them? . . . The answers, such as they are, are in patterns of politics from historical events that have largely been forgotten. The dominant—and incorrect—view of war crimes tribunals centers on Nuremberg as an almost unique moment. In fact, war crimes trials are a fairly regular part of international politics, with Nuremberg as only the most successful example. International war crimes tribunals are a recurring modern phenomenon, with discernible patterns. Today's debates about war criminals in Rwanda, Bosnia, and Kosovo are partial echoes of political disputes from 1815, 1918, and 1944.

There are at least seven major comparable times when states confronted issues of international justice: abortive treason trials of Bonapartists in 1815 after the Hundred Days War; botched trials of German war criminals after World War I; an abortive prosecution of some of the Young Turk perpetrators of the Armenian genocide; the great trials of top German war criminals at Nuremberg after World War II; a parallel but less successful process for major Japanese war criminals at the Tokyo international military tribunal; the current ex-Yugoslavia tribunal; and a twin tribunal for Rwanda. . . .

Why support a war crimes tribunal? The treatment of humbled or defeated enemy leaders and war criminals can make the difference between war and peace. If the job is done well, as after World War II, it may lay the foundation for a durable peacetime order; if botched, as when Napoleon was exiled to Elba, it may spark a new outbreak of war.

Still, if one wants to get rid of undesirables, using the trappings of a domestic courtroom is a distinctly awkward way to do it. Sustaining a tribunal means surrendering control of the outcome to a set of unwieldy rules designed for other occasions, and to a group of rule-obsessed lawyers. . . . There are easier ways to punish vanquished enemies.

_____

Victorious leaders have come up with an impressive array of nonlegalist fates for their defeated foes. One could shoot them on sight. One could round them up and shoot them en masse later. One could have a perfunctory show trial and then shoot them. One could put them in concentration camps. One could (as both Winston Churchill and Franklin Roosevelt suggested) castrate them. One could deport them to a neutral country, or perhaps a quiet island somewhere. Or one could simply ignore their sordid past and do business with them. Of all things, why bother to go to the trouble of a bona fide trial, with the possibility of acquittals, of cases being thrown out on technicalities, of embarrassing evidence and irritating delays, of uncooperative judges, of a vigorous defense? After World War I, one of the reasons why efforts to punish German and Ottoman war criminals failed was that the Allies found they could not get convictions in the respective courts. Why give up direct state control to independent lawyers? . . .

[S]ome leaders do so because they, and their countries, are in the grip of a principled idea. There is nothing structural that necessitates the adoption of this idea. A tribunal is not necessarily part of a punitive peace, nor of a generous one. Nevertheless, some decision makers believe that it is right for war criminals to be put on trial—a belief that I will call, for brevity's sake, legalism.

There are strict limits to the influence of legalism. Above all, legalism is a concept that seems only to spring from a particular kind of liberal domestic polity. After all, a war crimes tribunal is an extension of the rule of law from the domestic sphere to the international sphere. Although illiberal or totalitarian states accustomed to running domestic show trials might try to do the same at the international level, the serious pursuit of international justice rests on principled legalist beliefs held by only a few liberal governments. Liberal governments sometimes pursue war crimes trials; illiberal ones never have.

Still, the power of legalist ideas alone is not wholly sufficient as an explanation, because nonrhetorical calls for international justice are fitful. Why is it right at some times for some states, and not at other times for other states? If principled ideas are so important to foreign policy, why do states so often fail to live up to those ideas? These questions lead to two other major arguments. . . . First, even liberal states almost never put their own soldiers at risk in order to bring war criminals to book. Second, even liberal states are more likely to seek justice for war crimes committed against their own citizens, not against innocent foreigners. These two arguments are flip sides of a common coin: the selfishness of states, even of liberal ones. We put our own citizens first—by an amazing degree. The war crimes policy of liberal states is a push-and-pull of idealism and selfishness.

■ Idealism in International Relations

Victors' Justice

Tojo Hideki had few doubts about the true character of the Allies' international military tribunal at Tokyo. In December 1948, he said, "In the last analysis, this trial was a political trial. It was only victors' justice."[1] . . . Wilhelm II, hiding in Holland after World War I, scorned Allied efforts to bring him to book: "[A] tribunal where the enemy would be judge and party would not be an organ of the law but an instrument of political tyranny aiming only at justifying my condemnation."[2] . . . Even the victors sometimes make this argument. "I suppose if I had lost the war, I would have been tried as a war criminal," said Curtis LeMay, who targeted some sixty-three Japanese cities for annihilation by American bombing in World War II. "Fortunately, we were on the winning side."[3]

It is perhaps not surprising that these men felt this way. What is striking is the extent to which their skepticism is reflected in typical good-faith beliefs about war crimes tribunals today. . . . The frequently expressed argument that war crimes tribunals are simply victors' justice has deep roots. As Thrasymachus says in Plato's *Republic*, "[E]verywhere justice is the same thing, the advantage of the stronger."[4]

The Thrasymachus tradition in the study of international relations is usually called realism. Realists—the dominant thinkers in America and Britain since at least 1945—argue that international relations differ from domestic politics in the lack of a common ruler among self-interested states. To survive in such conditions of anarchy, states must rely on self-help for their own security. . . . In the dangerous brawl of international anarchy, realists argue, idealistic and legalistic policies are a luxury that states can ill afford. . . . Thus to realists, international moralizing in general—and punishing war criminals in particular—is mystifying. . . .

Realists often fear that war crimes tribunals will interfere with the establishment of international order. Carrying the hatreds and moral passions of war over into a peace settlement is dangerous. Kissinger admired the Congress of Vienna's generous treatment of France after the Napoleonic Wars: "A war without an enemy is inconceivable; a peace built on the myth of an enemy is an armistice. It is the temptation of war to punish; it is the task of policy to construct. Power can sit in judgment, but statesmanship must look to the future." Overheated moral judgments and particularly "personal retribution," Kissinger implied, risk undermining a peace.[5] . . .

These realists take a dim view of international legalism. International norms and institutions are epiphenomenal, mere veils over state power. . . . To realists, a war crimes tribunal is simply something that the countries that decisively win a war inflict on the helpless country that loses it. It is punishment, revenge, spectacle—anything but justice.

It is hard not to be impressed with the force of much of the realist line of argument. . . . When the Ottoman Empire was defeated, it faced war crimes trials; when Ataturk drove Britain and Greece back, the new peace treaty dropped those demands. Criminals such as Stalin, Mao, and Pol Pot never faced justice from Western states appalled at their atrocities because they had not been militarily defeated first. . . .

The Liberal Approach

Realists argue that the exigencies of anarchy force states to similar behavior—an amoral struggle for security—regardless of their domestic ideals. So democracies and dictatorships alike do what they need to do to survive. This runs contrary to a long tradition of seeing domestic politics as crucially important for foreign policy. Plato accused tyrants of stirring up wars to distract their subjects from their misery at home. . . .

So the foreign policy of liberal states might reflect liberal principles, at least up to a point. This opens the door to idealism in foreign policy. The reintroduction of domestic norms even in the extremities of wartime shows that states have options, and that their choices can therefore be morally judged. . . .

What does this mean for war crimes tribunals? If a war crimes tribunal is victors' justice, it makes a difference who the victors are. Victorious legalist liberal states tend to operate abroad by some of the same rules they observe at home. "A trial, the supreme legalistic act," wrote liberal political theorist Judith Shklar, "like all political acts, does not take place in a vacuum. It is part of a whole complex of other institutions, habits, and beliefs. A trial within a constitutional government is not like a trial in a state of near-anarchy, or in a totalitarian order."6 . . .

Liberal diplomats can be startlingly explicit about their exportation of domestic norms. In 1918, as the Imperial War Cabinet decided to seek Wilhelm II's trial, Frederick Smith, the British attorney general, said, "Grave judges should be appointed, but we should . . . take the risk of saying that in this quarrel we, the Allies, taking our stand upon the universally admitted principles of the moral law, *take our own standards of right and commit the trial of them to our own tribunals*."7 As Woodrow Wilson put it in his address to Congress on declaring war in 1917, "We are at the beginning of an age in which it will be insisted that the same standards of conduct and of responsibility for wrong shall be observed among nations and their governments that are observed among the individual citizens of civilized states."8 . . . Even those who do not welcome such statements agree on the underlying dynamic. [George] Kennan wrote that such international legalism "undoubtedly represents in part an attempt to transpose the Anglo-Saxon concept of individual law into the international field and to make it applicable to governments as it is applicable here at home to individuals."9 Idealism begins at home.

There are two strong pieces of evidence to support the liberal view of international relations. First, *every* international war crimes tribunal that I am aware of—Leipzig, Constantinople, Nuremberg, Tokyo, The Hague, and Arusha—has rested on the support of liberal states. Second, conversely, when illiberal states have fought each other, they have *never* established a bona fide war crimes tribunal. They may trade accusations of atrocities as propaganda, but nothing more legalistic. . . .

■ War Crimes Legalism

Due Process Across Borders

. . . [L]egalism mostly manifests itself as a fixation on process, a sense that international trials must be conducted roughly according to well-established domestic practice—not just rule-following, but rule-following when it comes to war criminals. . . . Liberal states are legalist: they put war criminals on trial in rough accordance with their domestic norms.

Liberal states believe, with varying degrees of intensity and seriousness, in universal rights. Such states also have well-established judicial systems and domestic norms of nonviolent contestation in politics. From such peaceful ways of politics and tribunals, liberal leaders learn a respect for due process. And because of their belief in the universal applicability of their liberal principles, liberal leaders are tempted to use those methods of fair trial even outside their own borders.

The Universal Application of Domestic Norms

Liberal states—that is, states that respect civil and political rights—almost never commit atrocities at home. Liberal politicians do not profess radical violence or revolution, do not rise to power by killing, and do not stay there by repression. The quietude of liberal polities is enhanced by a strong, well-respected judicial system. Whatever the domestic imperfections and ethnic hatreds in liberal states, in their domestic nonviolence and well-established judicial systems they are still qualitatively different from illiberal states. Accustomed to such norms, liberal leaders can be genuinely shocked by overseas atrocities. . . . Liberal elites think: we do not do such things here. Even in the darkest days of World War II, when he wanted to execute the top Nazis, Churchill did not trust his country to tolerate such killings, "for I am certain that the British nation at any rate would be incapable of carrying out mass executions for any length of time, especially as we have not suffered like the subjugated countries."[10]

There is more underlying liberal states' legalism than just the rule of law. After all, some authoritarian states also respect the rule of law, albeit often harsh laws. But the liberal acceptance of the rule of law comes in the context of rights, often protected by the courts. Political trials cut deeply against the liberal grain. . . .

The Importance of Due Process

What exactly does it mean to be legalist? From World War I to Kosovo, liberal states have consistently seen attacks on civilians and cruelty to prisoners of war as criminal acts. Even with foggier and less easily justifiable charges, like aggression, legalists remain devoted to the idea that a *trial* is the proper way of dispensing justice. This is only one rule among many that could guide the legalistic mind, but it is a crucial one. . . . Legalism is above all about due process. Thus, Jackson, in his report on the London Conference, wrote of the importance of

> provisions which assured to the defendants the fundamentals of procedural "due process of law." Although this famous phrase of the American Constitution bears an occasionally unfamiliar implication abroad, the Continental countries joined us in enacting its essence—guaranties securing the defendants every reasonable opportunity to make a full and free defense. Thus the charter gives the defendant the right to counsel, to present evidence, and to cross-examine prosecution witnesses.[11]

America might have been willing to fudge a bit by creating new categories of crimes, but it was conservative about the essential modalities for a trial: jurists steeped in Western domestic legal traditions, the possibility of acquittal, standards of evidence, proportionate punishment, and so on. . . .

The accusation may be murder, rape, or theft—or genocide, or aggression—but the case will wind up in a court. Cruelty to prisoners of war, or mass killing of civilians, have been criminal throughout this century—and well before. . . . To be sure, there is a distinct danger that politicized charges . . . may make a mockery of the method of a trial. There are charges so unfair that they undo any notions of due process. But such excesses are usually checked by the judges who will eventually hear such cases. Liberal states have not been willing to seriously compromise their domestic standards of a fair trial when putting foreign leaders on trial. Nuremberg was a stripped-down version of domestic British or American trials, but not so much that it could fairly be called a naked exercise of state power. State power was exercised before Nuremberg, to put the Nazis in the dock; but once they were there, they faced full-blown Western legalism as it had developed in its domestic context. . . .

Once a president or prime minister has turned the judgment of defeated enemies over to the judges, the outcome is in the hands of laws that developed from domestic traditions. . . . America sent some of its finest jurists to

Nuremberg; Jackson, a Supreme Court justice, was in the habit of ignoring
executive wishes. . . . The leaders of the executive branch understand perfectly well what risks—acquittals, technicalities, tedium—they are taking.
But a liberal executive still sometimes leaves the fate of war criminals up to
the courts. . . .

■ The Politics of War Crimes Tribunals

Liberals need to ask why liberal states so often fail to pursue war crimes tribunals, and realists need to ask why war crimes trials happen at all. Moving
from theory to practicalities, there are at least five important recurring
themes in the politics of war crimes tribunals. . . .

First Proposition: The Legalism of Liberal States

Only liberal states have legalist domestic norms that have a clear impact on
foreign policy. Illiberal states can do things the easy way: summary executions, show trials, or ignoring the issue of war crimes altogether. Liberal
states find it much tougher to do so. No doubt, there will be decision makers
in liberal governments who scoff at the idea of war crimes trials. But liberal
governments, even if they might otherwise prefer to either ignore war criminals or summarily execute them, tend to be bound by their own liberalism.

Ironically, this legalism can interfere with war crimes prosecutions. The
recourse to law brings in a series of standards that can make it difficult to
prosecute. Robert Lansing had legal objections to putting Wilhelm II on
trial; some American officials were reluctant to include Nazi atrocities
against German Jews in the Nuremberg charges; and it has been difficult to
find adequate evidence to convict Arkan or Milosevic. Liberal diplomats
often find themselves squirming at the challenge of exporting their domestic
standards.

Second Proposition: Protecting Soldiers

For want of a better term, call this the Scott O'Grady phenomenon. In June
1995, O'Grady, an American F-16 pilot, was shot down by the Bosnian Serb
Army. While the White House still refused to send American troops to save
Bosnian civilians, America went to extraordinary lengths to bring O'Grady
home safe, sending Marine commandos into hostile Serb territory. O'Grady
got a hero's welcome back in America, and his name is still fairly well
known. What is striking is not just that even liberal states value the lives of
their own more than those of foreigners, but how *radically* the lives of foreigners are discounted. There is no doubt that O'Grady's life is precious;
the puzzle is why Bosnian lives were seen as so cheap.

To realists, this makes a kind of sense. Security is paramount, and if there is a trade-off between protecting soldiers and protecting the innocent, the innocent are liable to get the worst of it. Hans Morgenthau wrote, "[T]he principle of the defense of human rights cannot be consistently applied in foreign policy because it can and it must come in conflict with other interests that may be more important than the defense of human rights in a particular instance."[12] Here, the protection of soldiers stands as a kind of rough proxy for some of these other interests. Liberal universalism only goes so far. . . .

This proposition is also perhaps a way of explaining the absence of a call for a war crimes tribunal in the aftermath of the horrors committed by Mao, Stalin, or (until very recently) Pol Pot. Western complicity aside, what country was going to risk its soldiers to bring them to trial? This also explains why war crimes tribunals are almost invariably linked to a peace settlement. In war, the soldiers are already at risk. If a proposed tribunal puts them at greater risk, the tribunal idea is in serious trouble; if the proposal calls for putting them in harm's way in the first place, it has even slimmer chances. . . .

Third Proposition: Putting Citizens Before Foreigners

When will states be outraged at war crimes? Countries are first and foremost outraged by wars waged against them. . . . There is no doubting the sincerity of British outrage during the Blitz, or the depth of Russian feeling during Hitler's invasion—or, for that matter, German outrage during the fire-bombing of Dresden, or Japanese outrage at the atomic bombings of Hiroshima and Nagasaki. The fact that the names of O'Grady and Nurse Edith Cavell (a Briton executed by Germans in World War I) are widely known shows a great concern for even a handful of one's own citizens. Any state, liberal or otherwise, may be solicitous of its own citizens. . . .

A liberal state that has suffered in a war will be more likely to seek international justice than one that has not. And a liberal state will probably be more concerned with prosecuting war crimes against its own citizens than those against foreigners, even when the suffering of the foreigners far outweighs that of the citizens of that liberal state. [But l]iberal states do make universalistic arguments for the protection of those who are *not* their citizens. Liberal states are more apt to pursue prosecution for war crimes committed against their own citizens; . . . [however,] because they are universalists, liberal states may also be outraged by crimes against humanity committed against noncitizens. Selfishness predominates, but not totally.

Fourth Proposition: Outrage, Mass and Elite

Legalism alone is not enough; one also needs outrage. Any country, liberal or not, can be outraged by an enemy's war crimes. Such fury is a necessary but not sufficient condition for supporting a war crimes tribunal. Outrage alone could result in summary executions, as proposed by Prussia in 1815 and, on a vast scale, by the Soviet Union in 1943. Conversely, legalism without outrage could result in a dreary series of futile legal briefs. . . .

Polls from World War II show that the British and American publics were bitterly punitive toward the Axis, and policymakers responded to that. . . . The dynamic can work in reverse, too: elite outrage can stoke mass outrage, through speeches and propaganda. The British election of 1918, in which Lloyd George's government rode and stoked public anger at Wilhelm II, is a fine example of both. One could equally well explain British enthusiasm for war crimes trials for Wilhelm II and other Germans by pointing to the British public's anger, or to that of Lloyd George and Curzon.

This is not to say that liberal diplomats will not sometimes try to stand against their public's wishes. In France in 1815, Castlereagh, Britain's foreign secretary, did not mind doing business with Bonapartists whom the English public could not stomach. In such situations, one would expect the elites to win out in the short term. Elites are simply closer to policy decisions; mass opinion may not influence them fast enough. A determined leader can act now and worry about public opinion later. . . .

Fifth Proposition: Nonstate Actors

Since the 1960s, international human rights groups have grown stronger. In the debates over ex-Yugoslavia and Rwanda, nongovernmental organizations (NGOs) have been a noticeable voice—although states are still by far the most powerful international actors. The Hague tribunal has taken advantage of NGO resources: forensic experts from Physicians for Human Rights, documentation from Human Rights Watch, funding for the commission of experts by the Soros Foundation, and so on. But in the end, these NGOs can claim credit, or bear responsibility, for the establishment of the tribunal mostly insofar as they were able to persuade the liberal members of the Security Council. The pleas of Human Rights Watch presumably had little impact in Beijing, but they were a source of embarrassment in Washington. . . .

*   *   *

. . . [T]he pursuit of war criminals can only be explained with reference to domestic political norms in liberal states. Authoritarian and totalitarian powers may seek to punish defeated foes, or they may choose to do business with them. When they have chosen punishment, they did not use legal methods; rather, they took arbitrary steps like shooting their enemies, or at best putting on an obviously rigged show trial. And in one respect, liberal and illiberal states are similar: they have tended not to put their own soldiers at risk for international justice.

But unlike illiberal states, liberal states are often constrained by their domestic norms. Liberal states commonly see their enemies not as mere foes, but as war criminals deserving legal punishment. Liberal states are unlikely to shoot war criminals, although they can be tempted by that prospect. Rather, even when liberal decision makers are painfully aware of the risks of acquittal, delay, and embarrassment posed by a war crimes tribunal, domestic norms push them to apply due process beyond their own borders. Liberal states are most likely to seek such legalistic punishment when it is their own citizens who have suffered war crimes, but they also sometimes pursue war criminals for atrocities against foreigners. So in the crucial question of how to treat a defeated foe, liberal states are profoundly different from illiberal ones.

■ Notes

1. Richard H. Minear, *Victors' Justice: The Tokyo War Crimes Trial* (Princeton, N.J.: Princeton University Press, 1971), p. 3.

2. Serie Europe 1918–1929, sous-serie Allemagne, vol. 28, Wilhelm II to Hindenburg, 5 April 1921.

3. Richard Rhodes, "The General and World War III," *New Yorker,* 19 June 1995, p. 48.

4. Plato, *Republic* (New York: Basic Books, 1968), trans. Alan Bloom, book 1, 339a, p. 16.

5. Henry A. Kissinger, *A World Restored: Metternich, Castlereagh, and the Problems of Peace 1812–1822* (Boston: Houghton Mifflin, 1973), pp. 138, 140.

6. Judith N. Shklar, *Law, Morals, and Political Trials* (Cambridge, Mass.: Harvard University Press, 1986), p. 144.

7. CAB 23/43, Imperial War Cabinet 39, 28 November 1918, 11:45 A.M., p. 4, italics added.

8. *Public Papers of Woodrow Wilson: War and Peace: Presidential Messages, Addresses, and Public Papers 1917–1924,* ed. Ray Stannard Baker and William E. Dodd (NewYork: Harper, 1925), vol. 5, p. 11.

9. George F. Kennan, *American Diplomacy* (Chicago: University of Chicago Press, 1984), p. 95.

10. CAB 66/42, Churchill war criminals note, War Cabinet, W.P. (43) 496, 9 November 1943.

11. *Report of Robert H. Jackson, United States Representative to the International Conference on Military Trials: London, 1945* (Washington, D.C.: US Department of State, 1947), p. xi.

12. Hans Morgenthau, "Human Rights and Foreign Policy," in *Moral Dimensions of American Foreign Policy,* ed. Kenneth W. Thompson (New Brunswick, N.J.: Transaction, 1984), p. 344.

Index

About the Book

When and why is war justified? How, morally speaking, should wars be fought? *The Morality of War* confronts these challenging questions, surveying the fundamental principles and themes of the just war tradition through the words of the philosophers, jurists, and warriors who have shaped it.

The collection begins with the foundational works of just war theory, as well as those of two competing perspectives, realism and pacifism. Subsequent selections focus on issues related to the resort to war, the conduct of war, and the judgment of war crimes. Both traditional just war concerns and those that have emerged in response to contemporary developments—such as the US "war on terror"—are thoroughly covered.

With articles that are crucially relevant to today's world paired with contextual introductions to each section, the reader is ideally constructed to inform and guide students as they consider the morality of past and current military actions.

David Kinsella is associate professor of political science at the Hatfield School of Government, Portland State University. He is editor of *International Studies Perspectives* and coauthor of *World Politics: The Menu for Choice*. **Craig L. Carr** is professor of political science at the Hatfield School of Government. He is author of *The Liberal Polity* and *On Fairness,* and editor of *The Political Writings of Samuel Pufendorf.*